Twelve Who Ruled

Twelve Who Ruled

The Year of the Terror in the French Revolution

By R. R. PALMER

PRINCETON

PRINCETON UNIVERSITY PRESS

Copyright, 1941, © 1969 by Princeton University Press
L. C. Card. A63-3
ISBN 0-691-00761-6 (paperback edn.)
ISBN 0-691-05119-4 (hardcover edn.)

First Princeton Paperback Printing, 1970

Third Printing, 1973

Printed in the United States of America
by Princeton University Press, Princeton, New Jersey

To Raymond J. Sontag

MY VALUED FRIEND

PREFACE

THIS is not a new book; indeed, in its narrative and biographical treatment it is positively old-fashioned. Even when it was written, now thirty years ago, it was far from being a work of technical scholarship, though I hasten to add that it was a product of serious research and that all the numerous quotations are drawn word-for-word from authentic sources. The book has aged less than its author. I hope that it will continue to give its readers a lifelike feeling for the French Revolution, which cannot be understood unless it is also felt.

The text is unchanged from the first edition. Much new work has been done in the past dozen years on the Revolution, and especially on the climactic year II, or 1793-94, with which the present volume is concerned. The labors of Albert Soboul in France, and of R. C. Cobb and George Rudé in England, not to mention others, have in common one feature which is subordinate in this book though not absent. These writers look at the Revolution "from below." They explore the popular militancy and mass action of the anonymous (but in 1793 hardly inarticulate) common people. The present book, by design, sees the Revolution "from above." It deals with the twelve strangely assorted men who were set up as a committee of the National Convention—the Committee of Public Safety—and who attempted to govern France in the turmoil of revolution, war, civil war, and invasion.

The new school argues that the Committee of Public Safety, the Convention, and the Jacobins in general were middle-class revolutionaries pursuing a middle-class revolution, but that they cannot be understood without reference to the tremendous popular pressures upon them, and that without this popular or lower-class movement their own middle-class revolution would have been overwhelmed by the conservative forces of France and Europe. It is noted, too, that the first successful action against popular revolutionism was taken by Robespierre and the Committee of Public Safety, who thus appear, as precursors to a later social democracy, in a more ambiguous light than they did for Albert Mathiez and the earlier Robespierrist historians. Albert Soboul, in particular, sees in all this the elements of genuine tragedy: the popular revolutionaries or sansculottes called the Revolutionary Government of the Year II into being, not seeing that this government would have to destroy their independence in the course of organizing the country for war. Robespierre offered a program of representative democracy in place of the direct democracy demanded by popular activists. The regime of the Committee of Public Safety arose in alliance with the sansculottes, and it fell when it lost their support. Without claiming to have anticipated any of these ideas, I see no conflict between them and what is said in the present book.

The year of the Terror was the year of the guillotine, but it was also the year in which many democratic ideas, if not realized, were at least defined and launched into the world. Those who prefer to look back to the American Revolution in this connection should reflect that it was the French Revolutionaries who first introduced a universal male suffrage on a national scale, projected a national system of public schools, and decreed the abolition of slavery. In fact, if this book were being written today, more would be said on the movement for racial equality which reached its height in February, 1794. For other ways in which my ideas have changed, anyone interested may turn to the second volume of my *Age of the Democratic Revolution*, published in 1964. It is not possible to bring up to date the Notes and References at the end of the present book, but for two of the twelve men who are its subject mention should be made of Marcel Reinhard's great work in French on Lazare Carnot, and the biography of Bertrand Barère published in 1962 by Leo Gershoy.

I am mindful of the acknowledgments made in earlier prefaces, but some of those concerned are no longer in need of thanks; and in any case I wish to thank the Princeton University Press and its director, Mr. Herbert S. Bailey, Jr., who have already given this book a far wider diffusion than it ever received in its first edition.

R. R. Palmer

Yale University
New Haven, 1970

CONTENTS

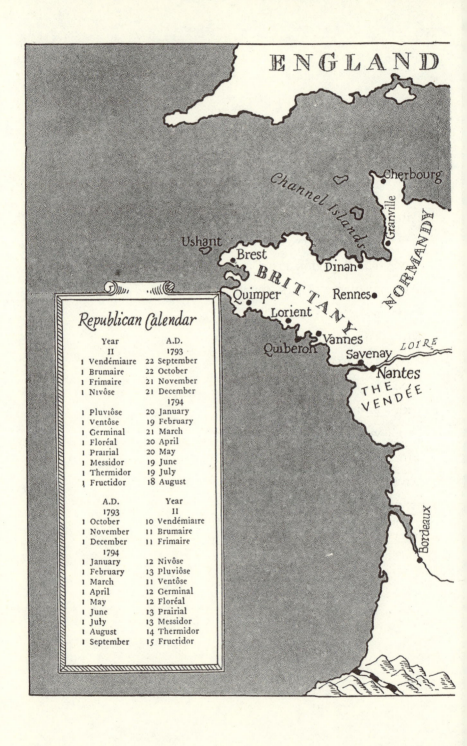

ENGLAND

Channel Islands

Cherbourg

Granville

NORMANDY

Ushant

Brest

Dinan

BRITTANY

Quimper

Rennes

Lorient

Vannes

LOIRE

Quiberon

Savenay

Nantes

THE
VENDÉE

Bordeaux

Republican Calendar

Year II		A.D. 1793	
1	Vendémiaire	22	September
1	Brumaire	22	October
1	Frimaire	21	November
1	Nivôse	21	December
			1794
1	Pluviôse	20	January
1	Ventôse	19	February
1	Germinal	21	March
1	Floréal	20	April
1	Prairial	20	May
1	Messidor	19	June
1	Thermidor	19	July
1	Fructidor	18	August

A.D. 1793		Year II	
1	October	10	Vendémiaire
1	November	11	Brumaire
1	December	11	Frimaire
	1794		
1	January	12	Nivôse
1	February	13	Pluviôse
1	March	11	Ventôse
1	April	12	Germinal
1	May	12	Floréal
1	June	13	Prairial
1	July	13	Messidor
1	August	14	Thermidor
1	September	15	Fructidor

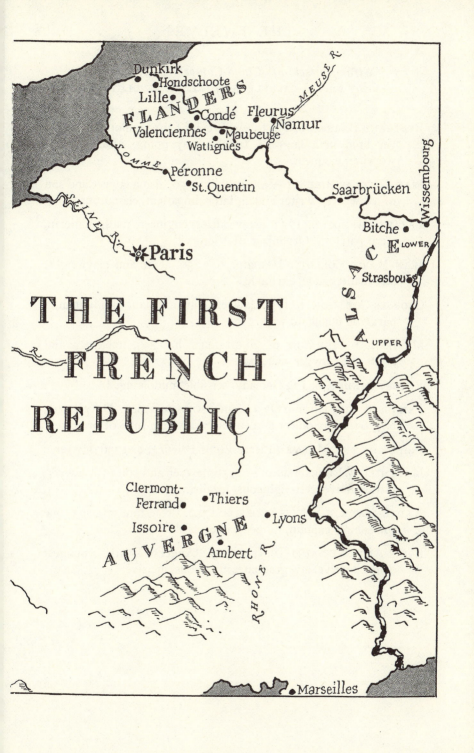

THE TWELVE

BERTRAND BARÈRE, b. 1755, "Anacreon of the Guillotine," a lawyer bred in a lawyer's family, easy going, affable, hardworking, eloquent.

JEAN-NICOLAS BILLAUD-VARENNE, b. 1756, also a lawyer and son of a lawyer, a writer and agitator, impatient, clamorous.

LAZARE CARNOT, b. 1753, army officer, engineer, mathematician, stern patriot, "Organizer of Victory."

JEAN-MARIE COLLOT D'HERBOIS, b. 1750, actor and playwright, self-made, crude, excitable.

GEORGES COUTHON, b. 1756, lawyer, humanitarian, family man, a paralytic unable to walk.

MARIE-JEAN HÉRAULT DE SÉCHELLES, b. 1759, nobleman and aristocrat, lawyer, wit, poseur.

ROBERT LINDET, b. 1743, steady, sensible, middle aged.

PRIEUR OF THE CÔTE-D'OR (Claude-Antoine Prieur-Duvernois), b. 1763, army officer and engineer, a young man of promise.

PRIEUR OF THE MARNE (Pierre-Louis Prieur), b. 1756, lawyer.

MAXIMILIEN ROBESPIERRE, b. 1758, lawyer and son of a lawyer, introspective, self-righteous, idealistic.

ANDRÉ JEANBON SAINT-ANDRÉ, b. 1749, Protestant minister, one time ship's captain, diligent, masterful.

LOUIS-ANTOINE SAINT-JUST, b. 1767, "Angel of Death," youngest of the Twelve, law graduate, imperious, incisive.

CHAPTER I

Twelve Terrorists to Be

ANYONE who had business with the government of the Reign of Terror directed his steps to the Tuileries, an old palace of the kings of France on the right bank of the Seine between the Louvre and the Tuileries Gardens, in which then as now children played and chestnut trees blossomed in April. Entering the courtyard on the opposite side of the building from the garden, the visitor saw signs of a government not very sure of itself, for two cannon and a file of soldiers guarded the door. Passing these sentries and climbing what had lately been called the Queen's Staircase, he came into a series of communicating chambers crowded with all manner of people, busy little functionaries of one kind and another, clerks carrying papers to be signed by the great men within, army officers, politicians and contractors waiting for interviews, errand boys, porters, secretaries and factotums, and couriers with the mud of distant provinces still spattered on their boots. If the visitor's business was urgent, or if he was a person of exceptional consequence, he eventually reached the last in the series of chambers, a room which Louis XVI had used as a private office, and which in a few years was to serve Napoleon Bonaparte for the same purpose.

Here if left for a moment alone the caller might reflect on past and present. Outside the window he saw the garden or public park, knowing that beyond the trees, half a mile away, it opened upon the superb Place Louis XV, the finest square in Europe, a triumph of city planning in the last days of the monarchy. He would remind himself to call it the Place de la Révolution—appropriately enough, for at the center of the new square (which we call the Place de la Concorde), in full view of the new Champs-Elysées and the new Madeleine, stood a new invention of late monarchical times, now symbolizing a new order—the guillotine.

Turning from the window he saw more traces of the last Louis, whom this same guillotine had put to death a few months before. The clock bore the inscription, "clockmaker to the King." The rich carpet, the polished mirrors, the glistening chandeliers still kept alive the elegance of royalty. But the main object in the room was severely utilitarian, a large oval table covered with green cloth, matching the green paper on the walls. Inkwells and piles of papers littered the table, marking the places for a number of men to work. It was the council table of the Committee of Public Safety, one of whose members would soon appear to receive the visitor, of whom therefore we can now take leave.

The Committee of Public Safety governed France during the Terror, the chaotic France of the year-old First Republic. Twelve men made up the Committee, always the same twelve from September 1793 to the following July 27, or 9 Thermidor of the Year Two in revolutionary parlance. The twelve never once sat at the green table at the same time. One presently ceased to sit at all, for he was put to death by the others. Some were habitually away, stationed in Brittany or Alsace or Flanders. But their presence was felt; their dispatches came in regularly, along with the vast streams of correspondence with which those remaining in Paris had to deal. Of those who sat in the green room, though they had no chairman and recognized no one of themselves as chief, the best known outside its walls was Robespierre.

The Committee transacted its affairs at all hours, but its real sessions took place secretly, behind closed doors, at night. No one knows exactly what happened at these conclaves. Anyone interested today can read, in large clear print, thousands of documents emanating from the Committee, ordinances, proclamations, letters of command, advice and instruction. No one can say what passed over the green table before the decisions were reached. No evidence for these matters exists except a few contemporary innuendos made for political purposes, a few indiscretions, a great many rumors, and a few recollections written down years later by two or three of the survivors. But the debates were undoubtedly lively, and the Twelve had many secrets. They fought and disputed with each other, sometimes differing widely in policy, their nerves on edge from sheer fatigue, their minds inflamed by revolutionary passions. As individuals they were almost all autocratic, jealous and short-tempered. But they managed until near the end to act as a single body, keeping their private differences to themselves.

They ruled a country convulsed in its fifth year of revolution. The National Convention claimed sovereign authority, but in half of France its authority was denied. The west and south fell apart in civil war. The plans made in the earlier and supposedly wiser phase of the Revolution had broken down. Local and outlying authorities could not be controlled and were now centers of independent agitation. Initiative had fallen into the hands of political clubs and revolutionary committees. Paris was in turmoil. Street orators and demagogues, secret agents both of the government and of its enemies, radicals and counter-revolutionaries of every description roamed the streets. Deserters from the army, disguised priests and strange foreigners jostled with half-crazed patriots and self-appointed saviors of the nation. On the frontiers the armies of England, Holland, Spain, Prussia and Austria were thrusting themselves into France. The ports were practically closed by the British navy. Beyond the battlelines lay a Europe unanimously hostile, stirred up by French émigrés, by conservatives of all nationalities almost hysterical with fear, by the pope and the Catholic hierarchy, and by Catherine the Great of Russia, an old woman near death who urged on the Allies while declining to join them.

Anarchy within, invasion from without. A country cracking from outside pressure, disintegrating from internal strain. Revolution at its height. War. Inflation. Hunger. Fear. Hate. Sabotage. Fantastic hopes. Boundless idealism. And the horrible knowledge, for the men in power, that if they failed they would die as criminals, murderers of their king. And the dread that all the gains of the Revolution would be lost. And the faith that if they won they would bring Liberty, Equality and Fraternity into the world.

This was the situation in which the twelve men who came to the green room acted. Who were the twelve?

They were on the whole not very unusual people—only twelve rather typical men of the old régime, brought into prominence by an upheaval which no one could control. Glowering at each other across the green table, they must sometimes have pondered on the circumstances that had brought them together. Their position was a curious one. No human wisdom could have foretold it. They had been strangers to each other not long before, scattered through France, with small prospect of any political career and with no political experience, each apparently destined for the humdrum life of his own occupation, all of them loyal to the "good king Louis" whose headless body now rotted in its grave.

Aristocratic Europe was appalled to see France governed by "nobodies." Who then, or what, were they in the peaceful years that preceded their great adventure?

At Arras, near the Straits of Dover, shortly before the Revolution lived a lawyer about thirty years old, named Maximilien Robespierre. He was a competent lawyer, a man of integrity, respected. He won most of his cases, partly because he preferred to defend victims of obvious injustice. He was a great believer in progress and the march of reason, which he vindicated by winning the case of a client who had been sued for putting up so ungodly an instrument as a lightning rod. Robespierre had been to Paris, where for many years he enjoyed a scholarship at the University, receiving the best education that the country had to give. Like many others, he was dissatisfied with conditions, though he himself had not been deprived of opportunity.

Robespierre's home life had been upset since his middle childhood, but he was well brought up by two aunts, and able to go away to school. He turned out to be a very serious and rather lonely man. His expression, his sister tells us, was often smiling, but he was hardly capable of a hearty laugh. He scarcely touched wine; he was unmarried, chaste, and a trifle puritanical. Constant rumination made him extremely absent-minded. His failure to recognize people in the street gained him the reputation of being proud. In company, his attention would wander if the conversation turned to small talk. He was preoccupied with an inner vision, the thought of ills which it seemed to him could easily be corrected, the picture of a world in which there should be no cruelty or discrimination. He was humane to the point of disapproving capital punishment; his sympathies were always with the underdog; he believed in equality seriously and profoundly.

Robespierre had the fault of a self-righteous and introverted man. Disagreement with himself he regarded simply as error, and in the face of it he would either withdraw into his own thoughts, or cast doubt on the motives behind the other man's opinion. He was quick to charge others with the selfish interests of which he felt himself to be free. A concerted action in which he did not share seemed to him to be an intrigue. He had the virtues and the faults of an inquisitor. A lover of mankind, he could not enter with sympathy into the minds of his own neighbors.

At Arras there was a literary society, where the members, besides reading each other orations and odes, often discussed public questions. Their discussions were likely to be bookish and abstract, for few of them, under the bureaucratic monarchy, had ever had any experience in affairs. These societies were numerous in France. They gave future revolutionists practice in expounding their sentiments and ideal ends, but none in parliamentary methods. Robespierre was an active member at Arras. In the club rooms he met an army officer, a captain of engineers stationed in the locality. The acquaintance was only casual at the time, but the two were to be colleagues, years later, on the Committee of Public Safety.

This man was Lazare Carnot, one day to be called the "organizer of victory." He came from Burgundy, but had been living for years in one army post after another. He was not unlike Robespierre. He, too, was austere in manner, rather chilly except to his own friends, inattentive in company, absorbed in his own problems. His private world was a mathematical one, in which he was just short of being a genius. He was the author of abstruse books. The famous Lagrange once admitted that Carnot had anticipated one of his discoveries. The captain, however, was not a mere thinking machine. He could unbend on occasion. His verses were a delight to the local literati. Kind-hearted, he once made use of Robespierre's professional services in a case of the sort that they both enjoyed. A poor woman servant of Carnot's had fallen heir to an unexpected legacy; and Robespierre, acting for Carnot, saw the case through the courts.

Carnot in these years was no politician. In normal times he might have left a name simply as a scholar, as his two sons did when the hurricane was over. But in the 1780's there were a number of matters which even the most unpolitical army officer could not ignore.

The army was almost monopolized by persons of noble blood. Hardly any of the officers were commoners, except in the engineers where technical knowledge was indispensable. And the tendency was toward more discrimination.

If Carnot looked to the future he saw his career blocked. As captain, he had already risen as far as the laws allowed a commoner to go. If he looked to the past he could remember restrictions that were absurd in the light of social realities. To be admitted to military school he had had to prove that his family for several generations had "lived nobly," that is, had refrained from degrading commercial occupations. Or he might remember his teacher Monge, now his friend, only a few years older than himself. Monge had been refused admission to the school for want of pedigree. He had then been hired, being very able, to teach the boys with whom he was deemed too low-born to associate as an equal.

The long leisure of garrison life gave Carnot plenty of time for reflection. He drew up plans for making the army more national by opening its ranks to merit. These seem to have been about the only definite reforming ideas that he had. He was too much wrapped up in his own business to be radical. In this respect the Revolution was to change him greatly. It was a different man who became master of the fourteen armies of the Republic.

Robespierre and Carnot were northerners, sober to the point of grimness. Far in the south, at the foot of the Pyrenees, lived a typical son of the Midi, Bertrand Barère. Like Robespierre he was a lawyer and the son of a lawyer, but in personality he was everything that Robespierre was not. He was sociable, popular, a good liver and a man of the world. Urbane and pliant, but a little reserved, he was at ease even in the drawing rooms of Paris, where his smoothness was noted as unusual in a provincial. He liked people too well to believe that those who differed with him were evil men.

Barère became known as one of the most shifty politicians of the Revolution. He was, in truth, not a fanatical party man.

Barère called himself Barère de Vieuzac when such cognomens were still in fashion. His mother had noble blood. The family possessed certain forms of property which the Revolution was to abolish, among them the manor of Vieuzac, where the peasants paid feudal dues. There were other privileges from which young Barère profited. A special dispensation admitted him to the law school at Toulouse at the age of fifteen, years before the age required. He could expect to inherit, as another piece of family property, a seat as judge in the court at Tarbes.

His abilities, however, were equal to his opportunities. He was soon a practising lawyer. He had an extraordinary memory, a strong grip on facts, and an interesting way of presenting them to others. Like almost everyone else he took pains to acquire fluency and eloquence—qualities that were to be the making of Barère, but almost the ruin of the Revolution. He won the coveted honor of admission to the Academy of the Floral Games at Toulouse, one of the oldest and most famous of all the literary societies.

"Too bad," said the president of the Floral Games when Barère delivered his entering address, "that he has already sucked in the impure milk of modern philosophy. Be sure of it, this lawyer is a dangerous man."

Barère dangerous? He could be so only in a society that was too rigid for its own good. He was willing enough to compromise and maneuver. He had no dream of a fantastically ideal world. He was no leader; it was his weakness to agree with whichever group was successful. He was a liberal, even in his vacillation. He surrendered his rights as overlord of Vieuzac before they were legally abolished. What he wanted was public participation in government, the rights of citizenship, a curb put upon the position of the nobility and the church. Such demands were enough to make a man dangerous in the circumstances. But the real danger to France, and to the world as it turned out, was rather in the men of inflexible convictions, the conservatives who would accept no change, and the more heated patriots who would accept nothing short of their idea of perfection.

Meanwhile, as Barère and Robespierre were arguing the law and Carnot considering his mathematics, a young man in a small town in Picardy was beginning to experiment with life. Louis-Antoine de Saint-Just became the *enfant terrible* of the Revolution. Before the Revolution he was hardly more than a bad boy. Undisciplined, impudent and self-willed, he lived with his widowed mother and his sisters. He was handsome, fiery, conceited. He was apparently an unruly child at school. At the age of nineteen he ran away to Paris, taking with him some of his mother's silver. He sold most of it, and spent the proceeds so fast that within a few days he was appealing for help. His mother thereupon had him arrested, and kept him in protective custody under a *lettre de cachet.* She soon let him out to allow him to study the law. He took his degree at Reims, but showed little inclination to practise. He stayed idly at home engaging in sundry amours and composing a long narrative poem. Then just as political events in France were moving toward their climax he went off to Paris to look for a publisher. He was not yet quite twenty-two years old.

His poem appeared on the bookstands in May 1789, the month in which the Revolution may be said to have begun. Neither the author's nor the publisher's name was given. The work, called *Organt, poem in twenty cantos,* was an odd compound of platitude and pornography. Few people read it, but those who did found their attention drawn to interminable love affairs, the raping of nuns, and discourses on the right to pleasure. The author made no secret of his views. He inveighed against kings, courtiers, generals and priests. There was a broad and impertinent satire on the queen of France. Sympathetic biographers have tried to find a budding political philosophy in *Organt,* but even if there were one the man who would present it in such form would hardly show much promise as a statesman.

A statesman he nevertheless became, or at least a leader, for no one was changed more by the Revolution than Saint-Just. The stubborn child became a man of principle and determination. The self-indulgent youth had a stronger character than his own mother probably imagined.

It is interesting to conjecture how the young Saint-Just, scribbler and playboy, would have impressed one of his future colleagues who was then a Protestant minister. Jeanbon Saint-André was not a man to encourage frivolity. Yet in one respect he resembled Saint-Just. There was something dogmatic and absolute in his manner, an air of positiveness that was sometimes annoying. This we hear from certain Protestants who once considered him for their pastor.

The French Protestants, who formed about five per cent of the population, lived mostly in the south. Jeanbon Saint-André came from Montauban not far from Toulouse. To be a Protestant before 1787 was to be technically a kind of outlaw. That was why Jeanbon, like other Huguenot pastors, changed his name, adding the Saint-André. The Protestants despite all laws had not been much molested for some time. They flourished openly, shut out of government and the honorific professions, but distinguishing themselves in commerce and manufacturing. The Jeanbons were an old and conservative family. Jeanbon Saint-André, already nearly forty in 1789, was a man of wide experience. He had studied with the Jesuits, been a merchant and sea captain, gone to a Protestant theological school in Switzerland, and followed his present occupation for several years.

Saint-André had the utmost respect for the government of the king. He looked to it to protect the Protestants from the Catholic hierarchy and from Catholic mobs. He was by temperament a government's man, always seeing the administrator's point of view, though excluded by law from taking part in public affairs. He quarreled with his congregation because, on a local issue, he did not wish to embarrass the royal authorities. Admitting that in earlier times the Huguenots had caused disorder in France, he now, as a step toward winning toleration, tried to restrain the religious zeal of his fellows, who, he said, must "avoid the merest shadow of argument with Catholic priests or others on articles of religion." For Saint-André religious doctrine had become something not worth disputing over. Calvinism in him was diluted into a generalized morality. He disliked religious excitement because it interfered with public order, and he demanded toleration for Protestants, not as a right, but as a means of making Frenchmen cooperate in worldly and national concerns.

Like most French liberals of the day, Saint-André did not believe that the church should be independent of the state. Religion, it seemed to him as to others, would benefit from supervision by an enlightened government. He recommended that the Bourbon monarchy, in granting toleration, should introduce a system of regulating and licensing the Protestant clergy. This idea was an outrage to old-fashioned Calvinists. But Saint-André was not an old-fashioned Calvinist, suspicious of secular government, preaching the wickedness of kings and the damnation of the ungodly. Had he been so he would have gone into the camp of the counter-revolution, as all the more devout clergy, Catholic and Protestant, eventually did. His real interests were in practical affairs, and though he had a long and amazingly varied career, he was always the same in one respect—he always believed in firm government, and he always stood for order.

Billaud-Varenne was an opposite to Saint-André, who became revolutionary in the course of the Revolution. Billaud was a radical from the start. Before the Revolution, Billaud was an ineffectual drifter. Educated to be a lawyer (calling himself "de Varennes" to distinguish himself from his father, who was a lawyer also), the young Billaud could find no practice in his home town, La Rochelle. He wrote a comedy, which failed. He took up teaching, diverting himself by composing more comedies, which no players could be persuaded to accept. The head of his school observed that he knew little Latin, but that his personal habits were above reproach. At the age of twenty-eight he went to Paris on his father's money, and was admitted to the Paris bar. Few clients sought him out. Three years later, in 1787, we find him writing a philosophical tract, *The Last Blow Against Prejudice and Superstition,* aimed at the church. An attack on the government soon followed. In substance neither book was original. It is the tone and manner that are to be noted, for the *Last Blow,* which was not published until 1789, shows the mind of a revolutionist in some ways fully formed. More than any other of the Twelve, Billaud gave intimations of the terrorist that he was to become.

"However painful an amputation may be," he wrote in his discussion of the church, "when a member is gangrened it must be sacrificed if we wish to save the body." This fatal metaphor of the gangrened limb spread like a contagion through French politics for five years. It was a commonplace in the Jacobin clubs, and it was the justification for the guillotine.

Billaud's ideas on religion were no less radical in 1787 than in 1793. Believing that the Catholic church was a fraud pure and simple, he outlined what he thought should be done to reform it. He went far beyond Saint-André's ideas of government supervision. All property of the church was to be confiscated. The clergy were to be controlled by the state; the office of bishop should if possible be abolished. The borders of dioceses and parishes should be redrawn. Dogmas should be reduced to one, the "useful" doctrine of the immortality of the soul. Ritual should be simplified to the point where the most ignorant observer could understand it, so that the clergy might no longer impose on the people. Vows should be forbidden. The clergy should be allowed to marry. Priests should be no different from "citizens." Everything in Christianity that did not arise from nature and a few simple words of Jesus was to be rejected as mystification invented by cunning priests to entrench their power.

We are not now considering Billaud as a philosopher but as a future political leader dealing with a nation of Catholics. Observe his conclusion:

"It is possible, no doubt, that a vile interest, seconded by a stupid ignorance, may still dare to rise up against so advantageous a reform; but its motives will be too contemptible for anyone to give ear to its clamor. The only cry to be listened to is that which takes for device Conscience and Truth." When a man in his ordinary moments takes this attitude toward those who oppose his opinions, it is not surprising if he puts them to death a few years later, in a time of crisis and excitement.

Georges Couthon was a provincial lawyer in the mountains of Auvergne. He was a mild-mannered humanitarian, known for his courteous and gentle ways, generally liked and trusted. He got a little political experience in the short-lived Provincial Assembly of 1787. As a member both of the Masonic lodge and the literary society of Clermont-Ferrand, he mingled freely with the people among whom ideas were stirring, men who were proud of the intellectual advance of the eighteenth century, and optimistic about political reform. At the literary society Couthon won applause by a discourse on "Patience." Of this quality the revolutionary leaders usually had little. Couthon was not patient in politics, but there was a benevolence in his character that did not quite desert him even during the Terror, and an endurance in personal affliction which perhaps entitled him to be called a patient man.

As the Revolution approached, Couthon was fast becoming a cripple, so that by 1793 he was unable to walk. Doctors in 1792 gave a diagnosis of meningitis, in which modern consultants, reexamining the evidence, have concurred. Couthon told his doctors that from an early age he had freely indulged his sexual proclivities. He thought his paralysis might be due to such excesses. He lost the use of one leg shortly after an amorous adventure in which, surprised by the girl's father, he caught a severe chill while hiding outside her window. He took mineral baths and electric treatments, but the trouble grew worse, spreading into the other leg. In 1793 he was happily married, but so helpless that he had to be carried from place to place in a chair.

Three of the Twelve we need but name, for little is known of their lives before the Revolution. Robert Lindet and Pierre-Louis Prieur were lawyers; Claude-Antoine Prieur-Duvernois was like Carnot a military engineer. The two Prieurs, who were not related, came to be called, after their home districts, Prieur of the Marne and Prieur of the Côte-d'Or. Lindet, born in 1743, was the oldest man of the twelve; C.-A. Prieur the youngest, except Saint-Just. All three in the 1780's were leading busy and undistinguished lives, typical of the anonymous world that lies behind all revolutions.

The eleventh character in our dramatis personae was the only one who had made himself at all conspicuous under the old order. He was also the only nobleman of the Twelve. It was nothing extraordinary to be a noble, for the French nobility, numbering perhaps 400,000, counting men, women and children, included most of the class that in England was called the gentry. The family of Hérault was unusual, however, in boasting of noble blood since the year 1390.

Marie-Jean Hérault de Séchelles, born after his father's death, possessed the ancestral fortunes from the cradle. He was rich, he grew up among women, and he was spoiled. Good-looking and precocious, he became a much admired young man about town. At eighteen he was king's attorney in the Paris courts—by special privilege, since the age required by law was twenty-five. All doors opened before him. Everything he undertook seemed to prosper.

Having no worries or reverses, enjoying the freedom given by wealth and station, he had little to do except cultivate himself. He was a good-hearted, agreeable and completely unmoral person, who saw other people chiefly as beings on whom it was advantageous to make a favorable impression. To this end he studied elocution with great care. He was very conscious of his voice. He practised his gestures at home before large mirrors. His interest in church was to observe the eloquence of the sermon. He wrote a book called *Reflections on Declamation*. In another, the *Theory of Ambition,* he reveals himself as a smiling egotist, not deceived by his own antics, coining maxims for achieving fame without deserving it, complacent, cheerful and entirely self-centered.

It is as a connoisseur, even as a connoisseur of his own personality, that Hérault is best to be understood. He would indulge himself in anything that satisfied his acute sense of discrimination. He knew wines, clothes, women, tones of voice, books, ideas—and he was fastidious about them all. He travelled to Bordeaux to finger the original manuscripts of Montesquieu, and looked far and wide for the autograph of Rousseau's *Nouvelle Héloïse,* which he bought in Holland for 24,000 livres. A man can scarcely be imagined more different from Rousseau than this assured and pampered worldling, this "triumph of artifice" as an understanding biographer calls him, who expected to prevail upon men by the way in which he moved his hands.

New ideas attracted the young king's attorney. He was a serious believer in "physiognomy," the science then in vogue of reading character in the face. He sent his portrait to Lavater, chief expert in the supposed science, beseeching him for a reading, eager to hear something favorable to himself. Lavater replied with copious flattery, but predicted vaguely (and accurately) that he would have "much to suffer." Again, Hérault sought out the most eminent real scientist in France, the aged naturalist Buffon, and in a moment of persiflage told him of his plan for a book to review "all the rights of men, all their laws, to compare and judge them, and then to erect the new edifice."

The new edifice he did in time erect, on paper; for he became the chief author of the republican constitution of 1793, which never went into effect.

Except for Billaud, whom it would be flattering to call a lawyer, a teacher, a dramatist or a publicist, and except for Saint-Just, who was hardly out of his adolescence, the eleven men we have surveyed were all established, in 1789, in one of the more respected professions. The same is not true of the twelfth, Jean-Marie Collot, who, although he called himself Collot d'Herbois, was the nearest of all to being a plain man of the people.

Collot was a native of Paris. Playing his first rôle at seventeen, he became a professional actor. He toured the provinces for years. Actors at the time were social outcasts. Law, custom and religion discriminated against them. Collot was a successful actor, but a discontented man. He was admitted to bourgeois homes, but was patronized and regarded lightly as an entertainer. Experience made him rather sullen, unsocial and uneven in disposition. He craved recognition, yet was afraid of exposing himself. He wanted to be accepted, yet feared that he might seem too eager. He became impatient and contemptuous of the bourgeoisie on whose favor his standing depended.

He turned to writing, for authors were more highly esteemed, but his plays were only moderately successful. Finally the chance opened up for him to become a theater manager, a position which he filled first at Geneva and later at Lyons. Here he ran into bad luck. He was reasonably capable, but both ventures failed through no fault of his own, unless a rather difficult personality is to be blamed.

From all accounts, he was an excitable person, quick to take offense, resentful and inclined to feel himself persecuted, irritable from being so often snubbed, given to violent gestures and imprudent speech, enjoying dramatic effects, climaxes and tirades, a hearty man of the people whom the more refined would think definitely vulgar. He loved admiration and disdained it at the same time. He had a grievance against the world. His political ideas were of the vaguest, but more than any of his eleven future colleagues, he entered the Revolution with an acute sense of personal frustration.

The lives of these twelve give a glimpse into the old prerevolutionary France. It is a very partial glimpse. Little appears of the Church, hardly anything of the nobility—for Hérault de Séchelles, a Paris lawyer and boulevardier, was not typical of the thousands of noble families. There is above all not an inkling of the peasantry, who constituted four-fifths of the population. Saint-Just's grandfather had indeed been a farmer, but his father had settled in town, and he himself wished to be a man of letters.

Not one of the twelve had ever labored with his hands. Not one of them, except Collot d'Herbois, had ever experienced any economic insecurity. Not one of them in 1789 lived in fear of poverty, for even Collot had worked to the top of the actor's profession. Hérault was wealthy; Barère well off; Lindet, Carnot and Prieur of the Côte-d'Or had fortunes approaching 50,000 livres before the Revolution. Robespierre in 1781 possessed, jointly with his sister, a small capital of 3,000 livres. The purchasing power of a livre (so far as any comparison is possible) roughly resembled that of a dollar in 1940. Investment was chiefly in land, and generally brought an income of five per cent.

All except Hérault were of the middle class. None, however, except Saint-André for a short while, had ever engaged in trade. They had no personal knowledge of industry. They had no experience with wage-earning people, except in hiring a few clerks or domestic servants or occasional craftsmen. What could they know of the proletariat of Paris, the silk weavers of Lyons, or the iron workers of Le Creusot? Paris then had over 600,000 inhabitants, Lyons over 100,000; but except for Collot, who was born in Paris, and Hérault, who lived there, these future rulers of France were all provincials, used to small town life.

All except Collot had received a good deal of formal schooling. Even Collot had acquired enough learning to become a writer. The others had been exposed to rhetoric and philosophy in the schools, and had in addition graduated from professional studies. Eight of them were lawyers by education. Two were engineers. Saint-André had studied theology at Lausanne. They were certainly not ignorant men.

They were not suffering from want, or from political oppression. They were not deprived of the elements of a comfortable and satisfying life. They were probably better off, most of them, than their fathers had been. They were not maddened by the drive of material need, as many of the peasants and city workers were. Why, then, did they become radical revolutionists?

To answer this question would require more knowledge both of psychology and of the causes of the French Revolution than anyone can be certain of having.

The group was relatively young. Only Robert Lindet was over forty when the Revolution began. Four of them were under thirty. All of them might feel that they still had a career to make. Yet Carnot and C.-A. Prieur were shut out from promotion. Saint-André as a Protestant would remain a mere spectator of events. Collot had had bad luck. Billaud had succeeded at nothing. And eight of them were lawyers! Lawyers were often leaders in their communities, men of opinions, convincing talkers, likely to see the seamy side of the government, eager to enter public affairs themselves, perhaps even concerned about the improvement of justice.

All twelve were intellectuals. They were steeped in the philosophy of the eighteenth century, a body of ideas so pervasive that even a Protestant minister and an actor-playwright could hardly escape it. They were acutely aware of change. Business had been expanding for a century; new inventions were appearing on every side. Thinkers set forth elaborate theories of progress. Change seemed to be easy; the most ingrained customs were to be refashioned by the enlightened reason. Society was artificial; it needed only to be made more natural. It was confused, a mere hand-me-down from the past; it should be given a new and purposeful "constitution." Never had there been an age with such faith in social planning.

Thousands of people in France, educated, materially well off, conscious of their powers, were irritated at the paternalism of government, resentful at the bars of law and etiquette that stood in their way. The middle classes detested the privileges of the nobles. Liberty and equality had been freely talked of for years. The country surged already with a sense of being a nation. Barère and Robespierre were both French. Why then should they not practise the same uniform national law, in the shadow of the Pyrenees and by the Straits of Dover? Saint-André was as loyal as the Archbishop of Paris. Why then should the Protestants be treated with suspicion? Carnot knew more than the Count de Rochambeau. Why should the Rochambeaus reap all the glory? Lindet and Hérault were both lawyers. Then why should Hérault get the better job, and Lindet have to defer to him as a noble? Hérault himself did not know. Many of the aristocracy had lost faith in the social system.

At the same time, thanks to the philosophy of the eighteenth century, large elements of the educated classes were estranged from the Catholic church. Billaud's *Last Blow Against Prejudice* was only one of many books of its kind. The church had lost the intellectual and moral leadership that it had once enjoyed. Many people thought that it was too powerful as an organized force in politics. It was widely supposed to possess more landed wealth than it actually did. It was thought of as a public corporation which had ceased to perform its functions efficiently, and which an enlightened government might reorganize and direct. Philosophy was a catchword of the day, and those who took a philosophical view, besides thinking that the state should be supreme, were very dubious of revelation, impatient of the claims of any established clergy, scornful of solemn religious processions, pompous vestments, the consecration of wafers and the clanging of bells. They preferred a more natural religion, some pure and simple form of belief which would make people socially conscious, teach them their civic duties, and still preserve the "consoling doctrines" of the existence of God and of survival in a somewhat hazy afterlife.

These religious ideas were to bring the revolutionary intelligentsia into conflict with the majority of the people of France, the peasants and others who still respected their priests.

Intellectuals were not only out of sympathy with the world in which they lived; many of them were attached emotionally to a world of their imagination. They looked to America, and saw thirteen small republics of simple manners and exemplary virtues. They remembered their ancient history, or moral episodes which they took to be history, and they saw more idealized republics, the polished citizenry of Athens, the stern patriots of Sparta, the incorruptible heroes of early Rome. They did not expect to duplicate any such society in France. They did not even have much practical belief in a republic. But their conception of statesmanship was patterned on their dream. Their ideal statesman was no tactician, no compromiser, no skilful organizer who could keep various factions and pressure groups together. He was a man of elevated character, who knew himself to be in the right, a towering monument in a world of calumny and misunderstanding, a man who would have no dealings with the partisans of error, and who, like Brutus, would sacrifice his own children that a principle might prevail.

Nor were the ideas to be gleaned from Rousseau more suited to encourage conciliation. In the philosophy of the *Social Contract* the "people" or "nation" is a moral abstraction. It is by nature good; its will is law. It is a solid indivisible thing. That the people might differ among themselves was a thought that Rousseau passed over rather hurriedly. Believers in the *Social Contract* thus viewed political circumstances in a highly simplified way.

All struggles were between the people and something not the people, between the nation and something antinational and alien. On the one hand was the public interest, self-evident, beyond questioning by an upright man; on the other hand were private interests, selfish, sinister and illegitimate. The followers of Rousseau were in no doubt which side they were on. It is not surprising that they would not only not compromise with conservative interests, but would not even tolerate free discussion among themselves, or have any confidence, when they disagreed, in each others' motives. Robespierre in the first weeks of the Revolution was already, in his own words, "unmasking the enemies of the country."

But all the ideas, hopes and ambitions that we may impute to our twelve men, and to others like them, would perhaps never in themselves have been enough to make them revolutionists. None of our twelve was consciously revolutionary before 1789. There was no such thing as a professional revolutionist before the nineteenth century—before the French Revolution set the example. The old régime drifted to its Niagara without knowing it. Its most restless spirits reconstructed society mentally, but they had no planned and organized movement to destroy the existing order. People expected change. But they expected the fortress of the old order to collapse before the horn of reason.

The breakdown of the government and the attendant confusion allowed these optimists to take a hand at revolution. Groaning under its load of debt (acquired largely in the fight for American independence), creaking in every part of its outmoded machinery of taxation, unable to borrow from the bankers, the monarchy of the Bourbons simply failed. So a general election was held; the old Estates-General met for the first time in one hundred and seventy-five years. Among the delegates to Versailles were three of the Twelve: Robespierre, Barère, and Prieur of the Marne.

Events moved rapidly. A constitutional monarchy was instituted. It would not work—because it set up somewhat impractical institutions, because France went to war, because prices soared, because neither the king, nor the royalists, nor the churchmen nor the working classes were satisfied with their new position. On August 10, 1792, a tremendous uprising occurred in Paris. The government yielded, wrote its own death warrant, and summoned a convention to draw up another constitution. It was called a convention from the precedent of constitutional conventions in the United States.

The elections were held in the next few weeks. Our twelve men, who by this time if not active in Paris were at least prominent local politicians, were all chosen as deputies, along with more than seven hundred others.

The great Convention met on September 20, 1792. Two days later Collot d'Herbois moved the abolition of royalty. The Convention so ordered. Billaud-Varenne proposed and the Convention decreed that September 22, 1792, should be the first day of the French Republic, which was affirmed to be One and Indivisible in defiance of all powers that might tear it to pieces. With the execution of Louis XVI in the following January the men of the Convention made their irrevocable commitment, challenging the monarchies of Europe, horrifying public opinion in France itself, consciously appealing from the world in which they formed a revolutionary minority to the world of the future which they hoped to create. We are of that world. We are the posterity on whose judgment they relied. Whether or not we can give them a perfectly fair judgment, we can at least try to give them understanding.

CHAPTER II
The Fifth Summer of the Revolution

IMAGINE an old house built at various dates, of different materials, and in conflicting styles. The inhabitants decide to remodel; workmen come and erect scaffolds. The scene soon swarms with activity, but the workmen do not work together. Some lay axes to ancient timbers and pull down old chimneys with shouts of joy. Others rush forward with new lumber, fresh mortar, bricks scarcely dry. Foremen stand by giving directions from blueprints, but the blueprints do not correspond. A few eccentrics will labor only at little corners of their own. A great many struggle to keep standing what others would tear down. Some are doing nothing constructive; workmen who have turned against their work, or inhabitants who dislike the way the alterations are turning out, they run about tripping the hod carriers, knocking the tools from the carpenters' hands, scribbling over and defacing the plans. The puzzled workmen wrangle and argue; they accuse each other of sympathy with the trouble makers. The foremen implore cooperation, but themselves fall to quarreling. Meanwhile, in the distance, coming closer, may be seen a band of armed attackers, whether gangsters or policemen is not clear, but obviously bent on stopping the whole proceeding.

The house so beset is France in the fifth summer of the Revolution. The approaching band is the armed force of monarchical Europe. The distracted throng is a babel of revolutionists and counter-revolutionists, royalists and republicans, constitutionalists and insurrectionists, civilly sworn clergy, refractory clergy, renegade clergy, aristocrats and plebeians, Jacobins, Girondists, Mountaineers, Vendéans, Muscadins, federalists, moderatists and Enragés.

Louis XVI died on the scaffold on January 21, 1793. On February 1 the National Convention declared war on the British Empire and the Dutch Republic. Already fighting the two powers, Austria and Prussia, which after France had the mightiest of eighteenth century armies, the Convention now added to its enemies, in challenging England and Holland, the two powers that led the world in shipping, finance and credit. The Convention had no choice; war with the Dutch and British became unavoidable late in 1792, when the French not only invaded Belgium but proclaimed assistance to revolutionists of all countries. The Dutch and British governments, already on the point of decision, received in the execution of Louis XVI a moral issue on which to rally support in their countries. A wave of horror (not very lasting) united European opinion against the regicides in France.

In France the king's death caused new divisions. "The state is myself," Louis XIV had said, and in a sense he was right. For centuries the unity of France existed by the Crown. Brittany and Languedoc, noblemen and non-noble, the people of Paris and of a hundred thousand villages, possessed nothing in common except what centered in the king. Monarchy was then what nationality became—it subordinated class and regional differences. Nowhere in the world did 25,000,000 people live together without such a personal allegiance. Thinkers in the eighteenth century doubted the very possibility; they all held that republics must be small. With Louis XVI dead, and monarchy abolished, would not France dissolve into the elements of which it was composed?

It did so dissolve, almost, in 1793. In the west the Vendéan war broke out. The peasants there objected to the taxation, the conscription, the legislation of a central government no longer clothed with the majesty of hereditary right. Stirred up by priests and gentry they crusaded for the Bourbon monarchy and the Catholic church. In the south also and in Normandy dissension brewed. Here the middle classes took the lead. The bourgeois of the great provincial cities objected to the influence of Paris and its mobs. Their disaffection was called federalism, a word meaning the opposite of what it meant in the United States at the same time. It signified the decentralization and scattering of power. The federalists in France were neither royalist nor counter-revolutionary by original intention. Federalism was a heresy within republicanism, but it was the supreme heresy against the Republic One and Indivisible.

The army suffered also. The bulk of the French troops were still professional soldiers from the old régime. Military tradition, martial virtue, was nourished upon service to the throne. The officers especially, and most particularly those in high command, still royalist at heart, might think Louis XVI unfit to rule and yet see in his execution an unholy murder. Many refused to wear the republican uniform, or would wear it only in the field, and appear in camp in the white coats and gilt epaulettes of the Bourbons. Officers could not keep discipline. They objected to the political agitation among their men encouraged by revolutionists in Paris. The generals distrusted the government, and were distrusted by it. Desertions were frequent. Dumouriez, the commanding general in Belgium, like Lafayette before him, disowned the Revolution and decamped to the Allies. This same Dumouriez ten years later was to help organize the defense of England against invasion by Napoleon.

The French advance in the Low Countries came to a standstill. The "miracle of Valmy" lost its force. The Allies began a steady, gradual, seemingly irresistible progress toward the French frontiers. Within those frontiers thousands awaited them as liberators. And if the Republic fell? The late king's brothers, the counts of Artois and Provence, would return flaunting the divine right of the house of Bourbon. The imprisoned queen would be exalted above her captors. The clergy would preach retribution upon the godless, and a hundred thousand émigrés, streaming back into every corner of France, would re-entrench themselves in the privileges of their class. It would be worse than if the Revolution had never been, for the old régime would be restored with a fury of persecution and revenge that the old régime had not known.

All hope for the Revolution now rested with the Convention. No other body stood for the unity of the Republic. No other body, since the suspending of the constitution of 1791, could claim authority from the whole nation. Yet the Convention too was divided. The execution of Louis XVI had here also its fateful consequences. Almost half the Convention had refused to approve it. Should monarchy be restored, some members would undoubtedly be hanged, others deny all responsibility for the sentence. Some were committed as regicides, some were not; some were gambling for their own lives, some were not. Mutual suspicion killed the feeling of partnership, and the distrust deepened with every new issue that had to be decided. Two groups took form, the Gironde and the Mountain, not created by the king's death (since the differences had appeared before January 21), nor absolutely distinguished by that event (since a few Girondists had voted for death, and a few Mountaineers for mitigation), and yet in general set against each other by the irretrievable and fatal roll-call, in which each man in the Convention had publicly declared his verdict on the "tyrant."

The Gironde fell far short of being a compact party. It lacked even a name; "Girondists" is a word used later to denote a mixture of Rolandists, Brissotins, federalists and moderatists. Nor were the Girondists really moderates. We should not think of the Gironde as the right wing of the Convention, the Mountain as the left, and the mass of milder deputies (called the Plain) as the center. The Plain occupied the middle only in the sense that its votes determined which group of revolutionary leaders should enjoy the sanctions of relative legality.

The Girondists were the men who, having taken a strong initiative the year before, were now compromised by the resulting adversities. They were reluctant to adopt emergency measures in an emergency which they had themselves in large part brought about. They had been the most vociferous war party, yet they opposed the growth of wartime regulation. They had done much to make constitutional government difficult before August 1792, yet now they demanded constitutional methods. They had been among the first to cry tyranny and make monarchy unworkable, yet they had evaded the responsibility for disposing of the king. They had used the violence of Paris while it served their purpose; now they denounced it as dangerous radicalism. They had lauded the patriotism of their appointee Dumouriez; Dumouriez was now with the Austrians.

The Mountain was no more a unified party than the Gironde. Its leaders were Robespierre, Danton and Marat. It now dominated the Jacobin club, to which the Girondists no longer came. The Jacobins met in the rue Saint-Honoré, a few steps from the Tuileries where the Convention assembled. Their nightly sessions served as a kind of party caucus for the Mountain. Of our twelve, Robespierre, Couthon, Saint-André, Collot d'Herbois and Billaud-Varenne were most diligent in the club business. The Paris club had thousands of affiliates throughout the country, known as popular societies or local clubs, a huge organization with some half a million members, who exchanged literature, sent deputations to each other, watched over public officials, advised on appointment to office, denounced suspicious activity and informed themselves of the opinions of all persons in their locality.

Both Mountaineers and Girondists were overwhelmingly of the middle class, but the chief Mountaineers in the Convention represented Paris constituencies, while the strength of the Gironde lay in the provinces. The Girondists kept their middle-class outlook, having a philosophic faith in the "people" but no liking for the ignorant workingman, and frightened with good reason by an aroused populace which they could not lead. The Mountaineers responded to stimulus from the city. They were willing to work with the smaller fry of revolutionary politicians in Paris, to make concessions demanded by working-class organizers, and to enforce national unity by claiming primacy for the capital. This brings us to the famous Commune of Paris.

There were about forty thousand communes in France. They were the municipal units in both town and country. Together with the eighty-three "departments" into which the old provinces had been reshaped, most of the communes counted as "constituted authorities," so named because created by the constitution of 1791, whose provisions for local government were still in force. The constituted authorities, with their thousands of public offices, were like an enormous tree with many branches on which birds of every plumage perched. Officials of the departments had strong leanings toward federalism. Those of the communes, as one went from manufacturing centers to the quiet byways, might be anything from the wildest hotheads to pious followers of church and king.

The Commune of Paris was not exactly a constituted authority, though called so in the language of the day. It owed its origin to the insurrection of the preceding August. This revolutionary commune had forced the deposition of the king, the discarding of the constitution, and the election of the National Convention.

The Paris Commune comprised forty-eight sections, or what we should call wards. These sections were the very springs of revolution. Here met the true "sans-culottes," the men who did not wear the knee-breeches of the upper classes. Direct popular government was the rule. Each section had an assembly in which its citizens (males over twenty-one) were supposed to deliberate and vote. Some three thousand citizens lived in each section on the average, but only a fraction ever attended the meetings. When the mayor of Paris was elected he received only 14,137 votes in a city of over six hundred thousand—somewhat less than an average of three hundred in each section assembly. Some members of the city council had been elected by as few as twenty votes. Hébert, assistant procurator of the Commune and the man whose name came to stand for the proletarian movement, held office by virtue of fifty-six votes in his section. Chaumette, the procurator and Hébert's follower, received fifty-three.

Even in Paris not one Frenchman in five cared anything about the vote, and many of those who did would not put themselves to the trouble of attending a section assembly, in which, if they found themselves in a minority, they might be jeered and hooted, yelled down as aristocrats, and henceforth regarded as persons under suspicion. Laboring men who worked all day had little time for politics. Shopkeepers had to stay in their shops and middle-class people at their business, even in 1793. To have any influence, any political friends or even any knowledge of the rapidly changing issues, a man had to spend more than a few leisure hours at his section assembly. Section affairs were therefore controlled by a small minority who made the Revolution their business.

The sections exercised their power through committees. At first each section had only a "civil committee" which, under direction of the Commune, did general administrative work. In March 1793 "committees of surveillance" were formed under a law of the Convention. The law assigned them only the surveillance of foreigners, but they soon took upon themselves more extended duties. As their functions widened they came to be called revolutionary committees or committees of public safety. They kept watch over everybody, hunted out priests and aristocrats, searched private houses and questioned the occupants, denounced to the police the persons whom they held in suspicion, or shut them up without further ceremony in jail. They supervised recruiting, collected unauthorized taxes, distributed food, and spread republican propaganda. Sometimes the forty-eight revolutionary committees met to take counsel together, forming a power in rivalry with the Commune and the Convention.

The sections were extremely unruly, and their most acute grievances were economic. Paris suffered from hunger, and still more

from the fear of hunger. Prices rose, the currency fell, employment was sporadic under revolutionary conditions, agriculture
declined in the disorders that racked the country, and imports of
food, on which France had long relied, became uncertain with the
war. Common men asked themselves whether liberty and equality
should not apply to the urgent questions of their daily lives. Obscure leaders preached in the sections. Their doctrine was not put
into books. It hardly reached the level of the writing and reading
classes, and so it is not easy for historians to recover. It was the
eternal cry of the have-nots against the haves, made menacing
by the turbulence of the day. Frightened middle-class revolutionists called these people Enragés.

The Commune, which had in a sense brought the Convention
into being, kept up a steady pressure, pushing the higher body
constantly to the left. Middle-of-the-road deputies, or those who
could not make up their minds, followed easily in the lead of those
who called for drastic measures—especially when frantic onlookers
shrieked in the galleries, and rough-looking men, organized by the
Commune or the Jacobins, defiled through the hall, haranguing
the chairman and calling themselves the people. To threats of
violence were added the arguments of reason, or of a strange
compound of reason, desperation and fear. Somehow France had
to be ruled as a single nation; only thus could the foreigner be
repelled. Crowds kept crying for measures that would serve this
end. And many deputies, when they yielded to threats of force,
could say with truth that they were forced to be of their own
opinion. Thus the Plain came to the Mountain.

Step by step the Convention built its house, not at all the house
of philosophic dreams. It appointed a Committee of General Security as a supreme police. It set up the Revolutionary Tribunal
to try enemies of the new order. It authorized local revolutionists
to form surveillance committees. It dispatched its members as
"representatives on mission" with unlimited powers over the lukewarm army commands and the stubborn department officials. And
on April 6, 1793, it created the Committee of Public Safety.

Someone proposed to call the new body an executive commission. But the Convention had a philosophical belief in the separation of executive and legislative powers, and could not bring itself
to grant the title of executive to a group of its own members. The

BARÈRE

new committee was simply to "watch over and speed up" the Executive Council of six ministers, a somewhat ineffectual body inherited from the preceding August. The Committee remained legally dependent on the Convention, which could change its membership at will, and had to reconfirm its powers once a month.

Barère, the lawyer from the Pyrenees, was the first man elected to the Committee of Public Safety. Robert Lindet was chosen the next day to replace another who would not serve. Danton also was elected, and six others who belonged to the Dantonist wing of the Mountain. This Dantonist group held office until July 10. Of its original members only Barère and Lindet were to remain in power among the Twelve.

Lindet, little known to the public, at first worked chiefly in the field, sent on mission to Lyons and to Normandy to deal with the federalist rebellion, but it was as an administrator that he eventually excelled, installed in Paris among sheaves of reports and squadrons of assistants.

Barère shone on the floor of the Convention. His was the eloquence that audiences then loved. At great crisis other speakers came forward, but Barère could throw a spell of words over any usual topic—a battle, a conspiracy, a guillotining, a statistical report, a democratic idea—always fluent, always forceful, always attuned to his hearers, sometimes soberly expository, sometimes passionately excited. His views were pretty much those of the Plain. More concerned for the Revolution than for party triumphs, he was willing to join a group coming into power or to abandon one headed for destruction. He could be in turn something of a Girondist, a Dantonist and a Robespierrist—and easily cease to be. Not accepting the factions at their own valuation he incurred the displeasure of them all. Fiercer spirits considered him a mere flabby politician. But the Convention approved of him, choosing him for the Committee with more votes than any other member ever received, 360 in the balloting of April 6, when because of mounting absences 150 were sufficient to elect. Barère was unique among the Twelve in obtaining a virtual majority from the whole Convention.

The Committee under Danton, its powers not yet made very extensive, failed to get control of either the domestic or the military situation. The Girondists and the Commune continued to lash at each other, the Commune winning a victory on May 4, when the first "law of the maximum" fixed a legal price for bread. Danton interested himself mainly in foreign affairs, exploring the possibilities of a negotiated peace. Mountaineers hoped to quiet the agitation by producing a constitution. To draft the document five new members were added to the Committee of Public Safety on May 30. They included Saint-Just, Couthon and Hérault-Séchelles.

Revolt burst upon the city the next day, May 31. Thirty-three of the most radical sections captured the city hall, subjugated the Commune officials, and put their candidate Hanriot in command of the national guard, the only armed force in Paris or its environs. Two days of confusion followed. On June 2 guardsmen besieged the Convention with loaded cannon and fixed bayonets. Eighty thousand people milled about the Tuileries. Insurrectionists marched into the hall demanding the arrest of twenty-two Girondist members. The Mountaineers welcomed their arrival, but wished, in dropping the Girondists, to observe parliamentary forms.

Hérault-Séchelles, onetime noble, presided. He could hardly keep order. The assembly voted to submit the demands of the Commune to the Committee of Public Safety. Barère presented the hurried decision of the Committee a few minutes later, recommending that the twenty-two voluntarily resign. When some of them refused, declaring that they would not yield to armed force, Barère suggested that the Convention march from the hall in a body to demonstrate that it was free. The deputies did march out, led by Hérault-Séchelles. The bayonets did not budge. The frustrated Convention reassembled.

Then Georges Couthon rose to speak, physically a broken man, paralytic and ailing, who propelled himself through noisy crowds in a wheelchair, and had to be bodily carried where his wheelchair would not go. But his mind raced as furiously as ever, and he was determined to save the face of the Convention, which three days before had named him to the Committee of Public Safety.

"Citizens," he said, "all members of the Convention should now be assured of their liberty. You have marched out to the people; you have found it everywhere good, generous and incapable of threatening the security of its mandataries, but indignant against conspirators who wish to enslave it. Now therefore that you recognize that you are free in your deliberations, I move . . . a decree of accusation against the twenty-two denounced members. . . ."

The twenty-two were placed under arrest. The theory that the Convention was free, and the people good, had been maintained.

So began the fatal process of purging the Convention that was to continue for more than a year. Indeed the same process, the periodic ousting of representatives of the people, went on spasmodically until 1799, when General Bonaparte, again with the connivance of politicians and the cooperation of soldiers, put an end to representative government.

The immediate consequence of the mutilation of the Convention was to spread more widely the federalist civil war. Lyons had thrown off Jacobin rule on May 29. Marseilles did the same on hearing the news from Paris. Girondists fleeing from the capital scattered through France after June 2, proclaiming their piteous story, telling how the Convention, elected from all France, was now dominated by the mobs of Paris. Within two weeks more than sixty departments were in rebellion. Department officials, disgruntled politicians, comfortable bourgeois fearful of more violence, and passive peasants suspicious of city trickery inclined to sympathize with the movement. The thousands of popular societies generally stood by the Convention, repeating far and wide the latest dogma from on high—that the Convention had acted in perfect freedom and registered the will of the people.

"The people is sublime," said Robespierre on June 14, "but individuals are weak. Nevertheless in a political torment, a revolutionary tempest, a rallying point is needed. The people in mass cannot govern itself. This rallying point must be in Paris. . . ."

"The people," he declared a little later, "is everywhere good; hence at Bordeaux, at Lyons, at Marseilles we must blame only the constituted authorities for the misfortunes that have arisen. . . ." It was true that the constituted authorities, i.e. officeholders brought to power by an earlier phase of the Revolution, were largely responsible for the federalist revolts; but Robespierre reached this truth independently of factual observation, deducing it from the axiom that the people could not do wrong.

It was a cardinal principle of the Mountaineers (and of the Girondists, too, who in their time had been Jacobins and were still Rousseauists) that the people, the real people, could not be divided in its will. The struggle, in their eyes, was between patriots and enemies of the public weal; between the people and various weak individuals, private interests and purveyors of false doctrine. But where Mountaineers saw the people, Girondists saw merely a faction; and the people whose goodness was touted by the Gironde seemed to the Mountain only a vast network of private schemers

To conciliate the frightened provinces the Mountaineers made haste with their constitution. The five appointed on May 30 set to work after the disturbance of June 2. Couthon contributed little but advice. Saint-Just, now twenty-six, turned by events from a scatterbrained adolescent into an energetic and domineering man, had more effect on the discussions. Hérault-Séchelles did the most; it was his pen that framed the words. He finished in eight days, realizing the dreams he had once confided to Buffon. The Committee of Public Safety, accepting the work of its five members, reported to the Convention on June 10, and the Convention, making no important changes, adopted a final draft on June 24. "In a few days," Barère told the deputies, "we have reaped the enlightenment of all the ages." To those who thought the work somewhat hurried, it was replied that evident truths needed no lengthy discussion. In any case sporadic debates on constitutional questions had been going on for months in the Convention.

The new document expressed very democratic ideals. It confirmed universal manhood suffrage, and enlarged the list of man's natural rights, qualifying the right to property by considerations of public interest, and adding the rights to subsistence and to revolt against oppression. The Jacobins meant to appeal to the masses, but at the same time, hoping to win back the insurgent federalists by persuasion, they took pains not to appear too radical. No one henceforth, Couthon wrote from Paris, will be able to call us atheistical, irreligious or communistic, because the constitution recognizes the Supreme Being, grants freedom of worship and the right to property under law, declares morality to be the basis of society, and guarantees the public debt.

But the Enragés and working class leaders held aloof. The Mountaineer constitution in fact strongly resembled the one proposed by the disgraced Girondists. Robespierre, it is true, about this time, wrote in his private notebook that the chief remaining menace to the Revolution was the bourgeoisie. But he kept apart from the proletarian spokesmen, many of whom, like the prominent Jacobin Chabot, were demagogues less concerned to cure poverty than to exploit it. These men, pointing to the increasing scarcity and rising prices, complained that the new constitution offered no protection to the sans-culottes. They blamed the food scarcity on profiteers, hoarders and monopolists. Robespierre blamed it on political agitators, among whom he included both bourgeois moderates and proletarian extremists.

It is impossible to sense the atmosphere of the time without listening to some of the speeches.

On June 10, at the Jacobins, Robespierre announced the completion of the constitution.

"When the destinies of the French people floated in uncertainty," he said, "intriguing men sought to control the wreckage of the government, and called upon despots for aid in their criminal projects. All good citizens demanded a constitution, and feared that they might demand in vain. It has been decreed this morning, and it fulfils the wishes of the people." Actually, the constitution had been simply submitted to the Convention that morning.

"We can now present to the universe a constitutional code, infinitely superior to all moral and political institutions, a work doubtless capable of improvement, but which presents the essential basis of public happiness, offering a sublime and majestic picture of French regeneration. Today calumny may launch its poisoned darts. The Constitution will be the reply of patriotic deputies, for it is the work of the Mountain (*Applause*). . . .

"In the Convention have been found pure men who have proved that good institutions are not founded on the subtle spirit of intriguers, but on the wisdom of the people. This Constitution has emerged in eight days from the midst of storms, and becomes the center where the people can rally without giving itself new chains."

The speech went on at some length, elaborating these same characteristic ideas of Robespierre, who concluded by proposing that the Jacobins circularize the provinces on the blessings of the new constitution. A member pointed out that most of those present had not read it. Chabot then took the floor.

"The project presented to you today," he declared, "no doubt deserves your highest praises, because it surpasses anything given to us until now; but does it follow that the Mountain should extol this same project with enthusiasm, without examining it to find whether the happiness of the people is assured? Not enough attention has been given to the lot of the people, and that is what is lacking in the constitutional act submitted to us. It fails to assure bread to those who have none. It fails to banish beggary from the Republic." (*Applause*)

Robespierre answered vaguely, expressing a willingness to hear discussion. Jeanbon Saint-André came to his support, noting that it was "not the intention of the Mountain that any laborious and unhappy being should exist." All could agree that the people were to be made happy.

Not much more was said on the matter at the Jacobins for several days. Too many other issues distracted their attention. The Convention, as has been said, proceeded to adopt the constitution on June 24. On the next day Jacques Roux, an ex-priest and noted Enragé, delivered a petition of protest to the Convention. Roux then went to the Cordeliers, a rival political club to which some Jacobins belonged, and there denounced a number of prominent Jacobins as enemies of the people. The Jacobins were thrown into an uproar. They took up the matter on the evening of June 28.

"The Jacobins, the Mountaineers, the Cordeliers," cried Robespierre, "the old athletes of liberty, are calumniated! A man covered with the mantle of patriotism, but whose intentions may well be suspected, insults the Majesty of the National Convention. On the pretext that the Constitution contains no laws against monopolists, he concludes that it is not suited to the people for whom it is made

"Men who love the people without saying so, who work tirelessly for its good without boasting, will hear with amazement that their work is called anti-popular and an aristocracy in disguise."

He went on to tell how Roux had gone to the Cordeliers, there repeating "the so-called patriotic insults that he had already vomited against the Constitution."

"Not one of you who sit here in this room was not denounced as a furious enemy of the people to whom you sacrifice your whole existence."

After outcries, Robespierre resumed:

"Do you think that this priest, who in concert with the Austrians denounces the best patriots, can have pure views or legitimate intentions?" (Roux was not in concert with the Austrians. Robespierre easily identified with foreign conspirators anyone who deviated from the program of the Mountain.) If Jacques Roux, he added, had been in the advance guard of patriotism for four years he would never have stood firm. He was a mere upstart, a beginner in revolutions.

Collot d'Herbois, a violent man himself, launched a tirade against Roux for wanting "to provoke disorder and bring back anarchy."

It is clear that the old leaders of the Mountain, having established themselves in power on June 2, were already beginning to use oddly conservative language, vaunt the merits of order, and look with suspicion and a pained surprise upon those who still were not contented.

The worst of the Roux affair was that Roussillon, a Jacobin who was also a Cordelier, had presided over the Cordeliers at the time when Roux let loose his charges, and had actually, as chairman, given the villain the fraternal kiss. Others of the Jacobins had been present. And now that the greater society, under Robespierre's lead, was formally disowning Roux, the compromised Jacobins scurried frantically for cover, straining every nerve to maintain their reputation for orthodoxy.

Roussillon admitted that he erred in embracing Roux. ". . . I lacked for the moment the energy for which I am known. The cause is in the mortification that I experienced a few days ago in this assembly. I was annihilated. The efforts of aristocrats are vain against me, but the lightest reproach from a patriot throws me into despair.

"I was forced to embrace Jacques Roux, but never did I find a kiss so bitter." With this recantation the session ended. The party line had been temporarily laid down.

Meanwhile the federalist revolt rapidly ebbed, the Committee of Public Safety wisely allowing offenders to recant, but it left in Paris a nightmarish horror, a sense of provinces slipping away on every side. Federalists who remained obstinate, despairing of their original cause, combined with royalists against the Convention. Lindet failed in his mission to Lyons, which went to war with the central government, as did Marseilles and Bordeaux. The Republic was losing ground in the Vendée. Paris was full of plotters, and was thought to be more full of them than it probably was. Federalists were supposed to know each other by their shoelaces. The ex-duke of Créquy walked the boulevards clothed in rags with an entourage of dubious followers, and the basement cafés of the Garden of Equality (the Palais-Royal) teemed with deserters from the army and flunkeys of emigrated noblemen. The Allied armies pushed relentlessly nearer, Danton's efforts to find peace terms proving fruitless. Patriots denounced him as a defeatist and an appeaser. The economic crisis grew worse; Chabot complained that the Committee of Public Safety, when he went to consult it, dismissed him as too radical.

So, when the monthly question of renewing the Committee arose on July 10, the Dantonist government fell, which is to say that Danton and some others failed of reelection, although party lines were so vague that some friends of Danton remained.

The group chosen on July 10 included seven of the twelve who were to rule. Barère, still in the lead, obtained 192 votes—the Convention had visibly diminished since April 6. Jeanbon Saint-André, former Protestant minister, also received 192 votes; he was considered to be both a sound Jacobin and a man of common sense. Next came, in order of choice, Gasparin, Couthon, Hérault-Séchelles, Thuriot, Prieur of the Marne, Saint-Just and Lindet. Gasparin resigned a few days later. Thuriot was definitely a Dantonist, as less definitely were some of the others, but Dantonists and Robespierrists did not yet exist as antagonistic personal followings.

Scarcely was the new Committee assembled when Charlotte Corday, a young Norman girl abetted by Girondists, stabbed Marat to death as he sat in a medicinal bath. The Mountain won a new martyr, and so did the Gironde, since the comely Charlotte soon paid for her audacity. Jacobins feared, as one of them said, that Paris was full of Charlotte Cordays, "monsters foaming with rage, who are only waiting for the favorable moment to fall on patriots and cut their throats." Pictures of the assassination were soon put on sale. Patriots looked with horror on the image of their blood-stained hero. Royalists and Muscadins bought up the same pictures, took them home and feasted their eyes upon their angel of mercy.

The Committee as composed on July 10 possessed no one of national eminence, no one who could guide and sway revolutionary opinion. Danton was out of favor. Marat was dead; he would not in any case have received office from the Convention. The turn of Robespierre was at hand. In four years of revolutionary activity he had never held official power.

Robespierre had no detailed or specific program at this time. His economic ideas were unformed. He gave expression to the feelings that patriots most widely shared, glorifying the people, calling for vengeance upon aristocrats and traitors, urging that government bodies be purified, branding as counter-revolutionary both middle-class moderates and proletarian malcontents. Eagerly heard at the Jacobins, respected as a democrat by the Commune, he was an idol, not a master, for the unruly cohorts from which he drew his strength.

He had a sense of the responsibility of government. Time and again he defended the Committee, even before he became a member. He resisted the proposals of some excited contemporaries, when they suggested that the constituted authorities be cashiered wholesale, or that the Jacobins keep running to the Committee with petitions and advice, or that the Committee deliberate in public where all citizens could hear its plans. He was aware, when he saw it in others, of one of the most unsettling of Jacobin proclivities, the habit of loose and unfounded denunciation, which undermined all feeling of confidence and security. He noted, in others, the extravagances of oratory, the use of "wild hyperbole and ridiculous and meaningless metaphors." He believed that "new men, patriots of a day, want to discredit in the people's eyes its oldest friends." Calling for order, authority, confidence, unity and efficiency, Robespierre was ceasing to be revolutionary in the old sense of the word. The term "revolutionary" had itself undergone a change. When men asked for revolutionary measures in 1793 they meant speedy and effective measures, not sweeping innovations. "Revolutionary" referred to the stabilizing of an accomplished fact, the Revolution.

Robespierre joined the Committee on July 27, selected to strengthen it by his hold over Jacobins and sans-culottes. The men on the Committee took different views of their new colleague. Saint-André, who appeared regularly at the Jacobin meetings, approved of him highly. Saint-Just had long worshiped him from afar. Couthon was not greatly impressed; in a voluminous political correspondence in these and the next twelve months, Couthon mentioned Robespierre only three or four times in the most incidental connections. Hérault-Séchelles, esthete and epicure, almost unique among the revolutionists in possessing an ironic mind, was amused, when he was not frightened, by the strait-laced little man who now sat beside him. Barère had never been an admirer; he had once cautioned against "raising pedestals to pygmies," meaning Robespierre; and had called him a "petty tradesman in revolutions." Robespierre, for his part, publicly declared Barère to be a good patriot but a weakling. It is to the credit of both that they could cooperate at all.

Two others, Billaud-Varenne and Collot d'Herbois, not yet of the Committee, agitated for action against the economic troubles. Collot, frustrated actor, had long hated the comfortable bourgeoisie. Billaud, for years a writer of radical tracts, now produced in his *Elements of Republicanism* one of the most advanced documents of the Revolution, arguing for a division of wealth and the right of every man to employment. These two, like everyone else, watched the misery grow worse through the midsummer. They knew that wagons were plundered at night in the Paris streets, and that housewives arose at dawn to stand before bakers' doors, waiting hours often for nothing. They knew that the law fixing the price of bread functioned poorly; Billaud, extremist though he was, pointed out that farmers would only conceal their produce if forced to sell at a price too low to suit them. They believed in the economics of the free market. The great evil, in their opinion, was that the market was not free, that selfish peasants, selfish provincial officials, selfish speculators, profiteers, hoarders and monopolists were withholding the necessities of life from sale.

Billaud and Collot therefore forced through the Convention, on July 26, a law against hoarding in the most general sense. It was the chief economic legislation of the summer of 1793. The law defined hoarding as withholding goods from circulation or allowing them to perish. It directed all communes and sections to appoint commissioners with powers of search and confiscation.

The law raised as many difficulties as it settled. Commissioners, locally appointed, were often illiterate and unfair. Private persons denouncing hoarders received a third of the goods confiscated in the event of conviction; hence enforcement passed into greed and petty vindictiveness. On the other hand, convictions were hard to obtain from the juries since the sole penalty was death. Worst of all, the rule against withholding stocks from immediate sale greatly handicapped the wholesale dealers on whom the government depended. According to one secret agent of the Ministry of the Interior, unless the law was modified in favor of wholesale grocers the scarcity would soon be worse than before the law was passed. "We shall be menaced," he reported, "within a few months by the danger of absolute want."

Failure on the home front was matched on the war front by catastrophe. The French fell back in the Rhineland; Custine, who had led the ephemeral conquest, was suspected by Jacobins and arrested on July 22. From Belgium the armies withdrew to points within France. Valenciennes surrendered on July 26 to the Austrians, who thus threatened, after a little mopping up, to descend the valley of the Oise toward Paris. The garrison at Valenciennes, allowed by the terms of surrender to go free, was so full of royalist sympathizers as to be useless to the republican government. Shudders of insecurity ran through the capital. Orators declared that the northern towns were inadequately defended; they were regarded as counter-revolutionaries for having said so. Other orators, or the same ones, urged the citizens of Paris to rush to the frontiers. They too were considered to be plotters, wanting the patriots to go to butchery unarmed.

The Committee of Public Safety included no one of military experience. Only members of the Convention could sit in its counsels, and few members of the Convention were soldiers by profession. Two there were, both absent on mission, both captains in the engineers, both determined republicans—Lazare Carnot, years before known to Robespierre (who by one report objected now to his appointment on political grounds), and young Prieur from the Côte d'Or, scarcely out of the prison where Norman federalists had confined him.

The Committee demanded the services of Carnot and Prieur; the Convention appointed them; the two captains entered the green room in the Tuileries toward the middle of August. Captains they remained, nor did they expect military promotion. The Republic was still profoundly civilian, and members of the Committee, in the warmth of political faith, recognized no rank above that of Representative of the People.

Paris early in August filled up with delegates from all parts of the country, and in their presence the new constitution was to be solemnly proclaimed. The popular vote had been accumulating during the summer, with results officially given out as 1,801,918 to 11,610, totals which represented about a quarter of the qualified electorate. The Mountaineers had no intention of soon calling their newly devised government into being. Their constitution was hardly more than a political prospectus, a picture of a future world held up to mollify public opinion. It was duly proclaimed before the assembled provincials, in vast patriotic ceremonies presided over by the grand-mannered Hérault-Séchelles. When it should go into operation remained unsettled.

How, indeed, was it possible to bring the constitution down from the skies into the real government of the country? How could the Mountaineers allow a new election? How could the existing Convention be disbanded? Since June 2 the Convention had been a purified body, from which the enemies of the Republic had presumably been expelled. A new election would be risky for regicides. A free election would represent the country only too accurately, represent it in all its appalling dissension, bring into the center of government the yawning fissures and irreconcilable estrangements left by five years of revolutionary change. There was not in France in 1793 a true majority in favor of anything, except to drive out the foreigners, and no majority to agree on precisely how that could be done.

Exalted by celebration of the constitution with its promise of justice and freedom, thrilled by fraternizing with delegates from all France, maddened by soaring prices and by empty shelves in the bakeshops, enraged at the elusive machinations of plotters, feverishly apprehensive at the lowering shadow of invasion, the revolutionary Parisians fell a prey to hysteria, losing faith in such government as they had, denouncing even the Committee of Public Safety, seeing no recourse but a tremendous upsurge of the people itself. "All France must be regarded as a general committee!" shouted one patriot. "Let us keep the people perpetually awakened," cried another. "Let us terrify it on the dangers it runs!" And he recommended that the perils be represented as more horrible than they were, on the ground that safety lay in exaggeration—also, of course, to keep the Mountain in power.

"Let us abandon those principles of philanthropy that have misled us until now! Let us remember that it is true humanity to sacrifice traitors for the security of good men!" The brigands of the Vendée should be hunted like wild boars. Aristocrats should be chained in sixes and thrust into the front ranks of the army. Or they should be deported, but first branded on the forehead with hot irons. The conspirators responsible for the sloppy printing of the Jacobin newspapers should be hunted out. Those other plotters who taught royalist songs to children in the streets must also be discovered.

So it went. Panic fear held the revolutionists in its grip, fear made more frenzied by the approaching destruction of great hope.

"We must forget that unfortunate love of mankind that is our ruin. . . . We have murdered our country on the altars of the human race!" From humanity men appealed to the nation.

This atmosphere produced, on August 23, the Levy in Mass, to which we will soon return. It produced also another of those great popular "days," an insurrection like that of June 2, designed to bring pressure upon the Convention. The impulse again came from the Paris sections, led and exploited by Hébert and Chaumette of the Commune, by Billaud-Varenne and Collot d'Herbois, and by the Jacobin club, which, though divided, gave its support. Robespierre and the Committee of Public Safety fought vainly to resist. The Jacobins pronounced "terror the order of the day." At dawn on September 4 Hébertist organizers made the rounds of the workshops, forcing workmen to quit, gathering the forces of rebellion. And later that day the Committee disclosed what was already wildly rumored: Toulon, with all the Mediterranean fleet, thanks to disaffected Frenchmen was in the hands of the British.

CHAPTER III

Organizing the Terror

TOWARD noon on September 5, 1793, as the crowds were gathering in the square before the city hall, preparing to march upon the Convention, a great darkness settled down upon Paris and all northern Europe. It was due to an eclipse of the sun, three-quarters of whose disc, as seen from Paris, was blackened at thirteen minutes before twelve. Further north the eclipse was total. In the capital of France men prepared for insurrection in an eerie atmosphere of twilight. They laughed and joked at this odd derangement to their plans.

In more than one way the eclipse was symbolic. It is significant that the Parisians laughed. The grandfathers of these same men would probably have been struck with fear. They would perhaps have seen in the darkness a sign of God's disapproval, abandoned their purpose, and either crept back into their homes or rushed headlong into the churches. The men of 1793 simply stared, exchanged a few witticisms and proceeded with their business. After fifty years of the Age of Enlightenment even men in the street, uneducated though they might be, saw in the eclipse a mere phenomenon of nature. Old superstitions had lost their force—a fact of importance in producing the French Revolution.

And yet an omniscient mind, peering down upon the Europe of 1793, might have interpreted the eclipse as a portent. This same day, September 5, was, in the judgment of most historians, the first day of the Reign of Terror. A shadow, more horrible and longer lasting than the passing shadow of the moon, fell over the minds of the people of France, eclipsing the sentiments of sympathy and humanity, obscuring the principles of liberty and justice. A shadow fell, too, over the rest of Europe, the shadow of interminable war, for during the Terror the French armies retrieved their losses, the Republican government consolidated its position, and the Allies, hopeful in 1793 of forcing peace, found themselves in 1794 on the defensive. After the Terror the French Republic could not be defeated, but neither could it impose on

Europe a peace of its own making. War followed, almost without interruption, for twenty years.

The all-seeing mind, to pursue the symbolism further, might reasonably conclude that the light of heaven was eclipsed, but he would also note, looking down through the gloom, that the flickers of man-made light were not extinct. Through all the terrible winter of the Year Two the street lamps in Paris burned. Efficient lighting of streets was then a novelty enjoyed in few cities in Europe. It had long been demanded by the citizens of Paris. In September, 1793, the Commune attacked the problem, and though its methods were somewhat arbitrary it succeeded in its purpose. The Reign of Terror was by no means the Reign of Darkness. Quite the contrary, it was, among other things, an attempt to force a new enlightenment upon the country.

All such thoughts, however, were far from the minds of those who milled before the building called, in aristocratic times, the Hôtel de Ville, now known as the Common House—the seat of the Commune, in short the city hall. It had been agreed the day before that they should meet now, a group sent by the Jacobin society against the wishes of Robespierre, and a miscellany of citizens brought together by municipal leaders, and including only a minority of genuine workingmen. The motley assemblage was soon gladdened by the sight of Pache, the mayor, and Chaumette, the procurator, who emerged from the building and moved off toward the Tuileries a mile away. A procession formed behind them, a band of shouting and excited men carrying placards that threatened "War on tyrants, hoarders and aristocrats."

At the Convention the chairman was none other than Robespierre himself, for whom the invasion by an unruly populace meant a political defeat. The authority of the Committee of Public Safety was at stake. Four members of the Committee were in the room that afternoon: Robespierre, Saint-André, Thuriot, and eventually Barère. Others may have been there and left no record of their presence; more probably they were elsewhere on the business of the Committee. In opposition, ready to back the insurrectionists, was a formidable battery of revolutionary orators, including Danton, anxious to revive a dying popularity, and above all Billaud-Varenne, who more than anyone else was to profit from the disorders of the day.

The proceedings were stormy even before the arrival of the demonstrators. It was enacted that the Revolutionary Tribunal should be divided into four sections, all to work simultaneously at the growing business of judging traitors. The issuance of bread cards by bakers was debated. A decree was passed for the more efficient control by the War Office of troops levied in the departments.

At this point the visitors from the Commune arrived. They streamed into the hall, bearing their banners. Some came and sat alongside the members, appropriating the many seats left empty by departed Girondists and by deputies on mission. Others poured into the galleries or stood up in the rear. Citizens and lawmakers chatted familiarly together. The Convention took on the appearance of a mass meeting. When the bustle had subsided a little and the cries of greeting were over, Chaumette, spokesman for the newcomers, read a petition.

"Citizen legislators," he began, "the citizens of Paris, tired of seeing their destinies too long floating in uncertainty, wish at last to fix them invariably. The tyrants of Europe and the domestic enemies of the State atrociously persist in their frightful system of starving the French people, to conquer it by forcing it to shamefully exchange its liberty and sovereignty for a morsel of bread. That will never happen."

"No! No!" came the shout from hundreds of throats.

"New lords no less cruel, no less greedy, no less insolent than the old have risen upon the ruins of feudalism. They have bought or leased the property of the old masters, and continue to walk in the paths beaten by crime, to speculate on the public misery, to dry up the sources of plenty and to tyrannize over the destroyers of tyranny."

In these words Chaumette portrayed the class struggle, anticipating the view of the Revolution later taken by Socialists. "This is the open war of the rich against the poor!" he had said the day before at the Commune; and he now developed the idea more fully before the Convention. But the philosophy of the petition was far from being proletarian. It was the familiar philosophy of the eighteenth century.

"It is time, legislators," Chaumette read on, "to end the wicked struggle between the children of nature and those who have

abandoned it." Or perhaps Chaumette said, "children of the nation," for the two equally authoritative records of his speech differ
in their rendering of this one word. "Nature" or "nation," he
might have said either one. The revolutionists in Paris, even the
Hébertists whom Chaumette represented, thought of themselves,
not as an economic class, but as the people, more national and
more natural than their misguided adversaries.

"No more quarter, no more mercy to traitors!"

"No! No!" answered the hearers.

"If we do not beat them, they will beat us. Let us throw between
us and them the barrier of eternity!" More applause. The people
of Paris, the petition continued, wanted only one thing: "Food—
and to have it, force for the law." Chaumette then reached the
main point of the petition; he demanded the immediate organization of a Revolutionary Army, a vast concourse of sans-culottes
to be equipped and led in a semi-military fashion, and to march
out into the country, forcing the farmers to yield their produce,
and guillotining the recalcitrant on the spot. The petition concluded with assurances that such a host would be no menace to
liberty. Wild and repeated cheers burst out from every part of the
room. It would have been a bold man who refrained from joining in.

Nothing could drive France further into anarchy than the proposed Revolutionary Army, a roving horde of undisciplined bullies
led by inquisitors and demagogues, turned loose with guns and
guillotines upon the wretched peasants, and free from any effectual
control by the authorities in Paris. Members of the Convention
were aware of the danger, and therefore, though they had voted
months ago, under pressure, that such an army should exist, they
had done nothing whatever to bring it into being. Robespierre
now, as presiding officer, answered Chaumette with meaningless
generalities, which in the circumstances were perhaps the best
thing that anyone could have said.

Even if united, the Convention could hardly have resisted
the demands of its invaders. And, as usual, the Convention was
not united. Some of its members were in league with the insurgents,
as Robespierre had been three months before. They had little
sense of the solidarity of a parliamentary body, little respect for
the elections of a year ago by which members held their seats; they

saw, or professed to see, the sovereign people present in the flesh beside them, and so, in allying with a mob against their colleagues in the Convention, they represented themselves as the true up-holders of the people's will. More than once during the past five years this little drama had been played. The characters changed, but the script remained almost unaltered.

Today it was Billaud-Varenne who played the rôle of Couthon on June 2.

"In profiting from the energy of the people," he declared, "we shall at last exterminate the enemies of the Revolution. . . . It is time, more than time, to fix the destiny of the Revolution; and surely we should congratulate ourselves, for the very misfortunes of the people arouse its energy, and put us in a position to extermi-nate our enemies. . . ."

Do we see the cat here squirming from the bag? Has Billaud incautiously revealed his real intentions? Is it possible that these men are using the misery in Paris as a means of overthrowing their political opponents?

"I heard it said yesterday," Billaud went on, "that there are only three thousand exalted heads [i.e. ardent revolutionists] in Paris. So! Let us show these men that the whole people is as exalted as we are, that it is ready to march against its enemies, and that from this day liberty is assured."

He proposed that the Ministry of War be directed to submit a plan for the Revolutionary Army within the next few hours, be-fore the day's session of the Convention ended. He urged that the Convention send out "an electric commotion of patriotism" to all the departments. And finally he demanded that a new committee be created to watch over the machinery of government and the public spirit of the country. This was a direct assault on the Com-mittee of Public Safety.

Jeanbon Saint-André took up the challenge. With the hall full of insurrectionists, he had to be circumspect.

"I speak as a member of the Committee of Public Safety. The Committee has not seen without the greatest solicitude the cruel situation into which a crowd of conspirators and counter-revolu-tionists have thrown the French people. . . . The Committee of Public Safety is preparing the report which it owes you in the cir-cumstances. It will propose measures. Some of those proposed to

BILLAUD-VARENNE

you today are included in its plans. At this very moment we are considering and maturing them."

The room filled with murmurs of disapproval.

"I say that we must begin by considering and maturing them. . . . The reporter of the Committee will be here in an hour. It is not a long time, and it is important that the measures we take should coincide and be coordinated—"

"A fine thing for us to amuse ourselves here in deliberating! We must act!" cried Billaud. Loud cheers followed his remark.

"But observe that I think as you do. . . ." In this manner Saint-André played for time, hoping to calm the agitation, hoping at least to forestall action until Barère could arrive and state the program of the Committee.

Presently Danton stepped into the tribune. For several minutes he could hardly speak, so prolonged was the ovation. His words combined demagogy and compromise.

"I agree," he said, "with several members, notably Billaud-Varenne (*applause*), that we must know how to take advantage of the sublime impulse of the people. I know that when the people presents its needs, when it offers to march against its enemies, no other measures should be taken but those which it presents itself; for the national genius has dictated them. I think it well for the Committee to make its report, to arrange and propose methods of execution; but I see no disadvantage in decreeing instantly a Revolutionary Army."

Danton had another and equally significant proposal. To prevent the section assemblies of Paris from falling under the control of aristocrats, and to encourage true sans-culottes to attend the meetings, he demanded that these meetings be limited to two a week, to take place on Thursdays and Sundays, and that those citizens who needed the money be reimbursed for each meeting by a payment of forty sous. Poor workingmen were thus to be subsidized in the exercise of their citizenship. A few political puritans objected but were overridden. Danton proposed a third motion to grant 100,000,000 livres to the Ministry of War for the manufacture of arms, and, concluding with a peroration addressed to "the sublime people," descended.

Cheers, whistles and cries of "Vive la République!" burst forth on every side. The whole assemblage rose to its feet. People waved their arms, threw their hats into the air, embraced each other. "The enthusiasm seemed universal," according to the newspaper account in the *Moniteur*. It need not be said that Danton's three motions were carried.

The discussion, turning to the subject of conspirators and suspects, was interrupted in a half-hour or so by the arrival of a new delegation, sent by the Jacobin society sitting conjointly with the forty-eight section committees of Paris. The message that they communicated was an ominous one. The foreign foes, it said, ferocious though they were, were less a danger to the French people than the enemies within. Brave sans-culottes languished in federalist dungeons, while the friends of Brissot, the arrested Girondists, lolled unharmed in Parisian palaces! These scoundrels must be brought to trial. "It is time, in short, for all Frenchmen to enjoy that sacred equality that the Constitution assures them; it is time to impose this equality, by signal acts of justice, upon traitors and conspirators. Make terror the order of the day!"

Robespierre promised in reply that all the guilty should perish, and the deputation then paraded through the aisles amid tumultuous applause.

A member became uncontrollably excited. Too long, he said, we have been humane. "Are you not called rascals, brigands, murderers? Well! Since our virtue, our moderation, our philosophic ideas have been useless, let us be brigands for the good of the people—let us be brigands!" There were cries of protest, and demands that the speaker be called to order. But he went on, urging that all pity be forgotten. His voice was almost drowned by loud expressions of dissent.

Thuriot rushed frantically to the tribune, and in dead silence said:

"Citizens, it is not for crime that revolutions are made, but for the triumph of virtue." Vigorous and prolonged handclapping made the speaker pause. "Let us not say that it is for France that we work; it is for humanity. In achieving our task we shall cover ourselves in an eternal glory. Far from us be the idea that France thirsts for blood, she thirsts only for justice!" Terrific shouts of approval punctuated every word. Thuriot undoubtedly expressed the feelings of the vast majority in the Convention. He wound up by urging that, in the repression of traitors, nothing be done to destroy the brotherhood and unity of patriots.

Thuriot, though still a member of the Committee of Public Safety, could not really speak for his colleagues, for his affiliations with Danton made other members of the Committee distrust him. All would agree with him that France thirsted only for justice. But they had a somewhat different idea of justice, and thought it must be enforced by hands less compromised than his.

While the Convention excited itself in the hearing and applauding of speeches, the Committee of Public Safety, in a more quiet section of the Tuileries, deliberated on the crisis of popular insurrection. Fortunately Billaud's proposal for a new executive committee went for the time unheeded in the assembly. The Committee at least did not have to defend its existence that afternoon. It fixed its attention on the proposed Revolutionary Army, the one specific demand in the petition read by Chaumette. This much, the Committee decided, would have to be conceded to the Commune and the Jacobin club. The problem was to keep control over an armed throng whose existence could no longer be prevented.

Barère was the usual spokesman of the Committee before the Convention, and toward the end of the afternoon he finally appeared, no doubt to the relief of both Robespierre and Saint-André, prepared to address a turbulent crowd that was already almost drunk with oratory.

He gave out the official view that aristocrats and foreign spies had long been plotting an uprising in Paris. He praised the Commune for coining the ringing phrase, "Make terror the order of the day." He promised the blood of Brissot and Marie-Antoinette. He blamed the food shortage on conspirators. Explaining that the Committee was working incessantly, he offered only two measures for the Convention to enact. The purpose of one was to rid Paris of the great number of military men who, leaving their duty at the front, had flocked into the city to keep a hand in politics. The other was for the levying and organizing of a Revolutionary Army of 6,000 infantrymen and 1,200 cannoneers, under the supervision of the Committee. Barère, the accomplished speaker, concluded by disclosing a choice piece of news: the nephew of William Pitt— of Pitt, the hobgoblin of patriots and moving spirit in the foreign coalition—had been caught hiding in a French chateau. This revelation provoked "transports of joy."

As if to show the strange association of ideas in the minds of the revolutionists, the Convention then had to listen to an afterthought of Saint-André's. Certain women, Saint-André said, do great harm to the Republic. "They corrupt your young men, and instead of making them vigorous and worthy of ancient Sparta, they turn them into Sybarites incapable of serving liberty—I mean those immodest women who make a shameless traffic of their charms." The exhausted Convention again applauded. The matter was turned over to the Committee of Public Safety.

That evening, at a special session, Billaud-Varenne was elected president of the Convention for the ensuing two-week period. His election, though the office carried no power, was, like the creation of the Revolutionary Army, a sign that the national government had again succumbed to organized pressure from the city. It was clear, from the events of the day, that the National Convention was not the real government, that its most important committee could not guide its counsels in a crisis, that the policies of the Republic were still shaped, as they long had been, by the Jacobin club, the Commune, and a few members of the Convention who were out of office.

What happened that night in the green room we do not know. We can imagine the Committee in heated discussion, Robespierre and Saint-André reviewing for the others the scene in the Convention, someone perhaps reading the reports of government spies on the state of opinion in Paris, all trying to weigh the political significance of the forces that had shown their power that afternoon. It was decided that the Committee must be enlarged. A coalition government was to be formed, if we may speak of a coalition of elements so indistinct as the Hébertist and Dantonist parties. The Committee would silence trouble-makers by inviting some of them to share its responsibilities.

Barère requested the Convention on the next day to add three men to the Committee: Billaud-Varenne, Collot d'Herbois and Granet. The Convention not only named these three, but, outreaching the Committee, and reversing its own judgment of July 10, appointed Danton also, because, as a member observed, he had a "revolutionary head." But Danton refused to serve, probably knowing that he could not get along with Robespierre, knowing also from experience that the problems of the day were all but insoluble, and preferring the boudoir of his new wife to the grim burdens carried night after night in the green room of the Committee. Since Granet, a friend of Danton's, resigned immediately on the plea of sickly health, only two men were really added, Billaud and Collot, who were both of the Hébertist wing of the Mountain.

Collot at the time was absent on mission in the north. It was almost two weeks before he took up his new duties in Paris. Billaud, though obliged at this period to preside over the Convention in the daytime, immediately became one of the most active participants in the Committee's nightly sessions. Both men were volatile, headstrong and rash, more inclined to love action for its own sake than to speculate on consequences. They were the authors of the law of July against monopoly and hoarding. Their audacity had been evident from the first days of the Convention; for in those early meetings, now almost a year ago, when the assembly hesitated before the fateful step, it was Billaud and Collot who moved the resolutions by which France became a republic.

Once taken into the government these two breathers of fire and destruction, neither of whom had succeeded in his private affairs before the Revolution, showed a surprising capacity for steady and assiduous labor. They soon made themselves useful, the more so because Couthon was absent on mission in Auvergne, and Lindet in Normandy. They were put in charge of correspondence with authorities in the provinces, a congenial task which enabled them to spread the revolutionary gospel throughout the country. They toiled unremittingly, through September and October, weekdays and Sundays, at all hours, more constantly present and more attentive to routine than any of their colleagues except Carnot and Barère.

The Hébertists, through Chaumette, demanded "force for the law." In this demand the whole Mountain could concur. Force for the law, in the circumstances, was a euphemism for terror.

Terror was not a new thing in September. Violence and insecurity were endemic. Section committees had made arbitrary arrests for months. Over four hundred persons had already been put to death by revolutionary courts. Federalists and Jacobins,

Vendéan royalists and blue-coated republicans killed each other with little scruple. Prieur of the Côte-d'Or, before joining the Committee in August, spent two months in a federalist jail at Caen. Assassination and suicide had taken their toll. The preceding September had seen the horrible massacres in the prisons, where two thousand helpless men and women were butchered in cold blood. Before that, back to the bright dawn of the Revolution, bodies had been hung on lamp posts and heads stuck on the ends of pikes. The peasants had not yet altogether recovered from the Great Fear of 1789, an uncanny panic that swept much of the old order into ruin. And before the Revolution many parts of the country were far from calm; riots were not unknown in the cities; and the peasants in some regions were a prey to bandits, extortionists, beggars, outlaws and sundry other racketeers whom the royal government had been unable to suppress.

The new thing after September 1793 was that terror was organized, and became for the first time a deliberate policy of government. Perhaps some kind of terror was inescapable in a country so habituated to violence, so demoralized by suspicion and torn by irreconcilable parties. The Terror was born of fear, from the terror in which men already lived, from the appalling disorder produced by five years of Revolution and the lawless habits of the old régime. It was anarchy that stood in the way of the stabilization of the Republic, and it was anarchy that was causing France to lose the war.

In the fall of 1793 the war was the most urgent problem. Aulard, patriotic Frenchman and eminent authority on the Revolution, thought that the war was the main cause of the Terror, and the Terror a legitimate defense of a nation in danger. Sorel, equally patriotic and far more profound, believed that the Terror was a shocking distraction, irrelevant to the successful campaign against the Allies. Sorel did less than justice to the revolutionary government; Aulard failed to explain why the French, if as patriotic as he thought them, had to be terrorized into defending their country. The truth is that there was very little patriotism in France in 1793, if by patriotism we mean a willingness to suspend party conflict in wholehearted support of the government against foreign foes. To many Frenchmen the government seemed to be the worst enemy. In supporting it they would only encourage a body of men whose principles they detested, men who had outraged their monarchist sentiments, persecuted their religion, disrupted their business and made their property insecure.

The Terror was not simply an outburst of the fury of radicals, as Sorel would have it, nor was it a mere defense against perils for which the revolutionists were not responsible, as Aulard appears to have believed. It was made necessary by circumstances, but the chief of these circumstances was the internal chaos which the Revolution had produced. It began as a means of defense against the menace of invasion, but invasion was a menace because of the disunity in France.

Surely the Allies were not formidable by their own strength. They were quarreling over Poland, where the second partition took place in 1793. Austria received nothing in this second partition, and wished to compensate itself by fulfilling an old dream of its diplomats, the exchange of its Belgian province for Bavaria, whose annexation would make the Hapsburg dominions more compact. The Prussian government viewed this proposed strengthening of Austria with extreme distaste. The Prussian troops were under orders not to push the war against France, for the crushing of France would advance the Hapsburg schemes for Germany. The Austrians, for their part, were unwilling to exert their full military power in the west, fearing that Prussia and Russia, with Austria thus engaged, would further enlarge themselves at the expense of Poland. The Allied offensive against France therefore languished in the summer of 1793.

The Allies thought that they could wait, for they imagined that France, remaining in revolutionary disorder, could easily be defeated at some convenient moment in the future. The chancelleries were gratified at the fall of the Bourbon colossus, and looked upon the new France as they did upon Poland, seeing in it a country made helpless by anarchy, in which useful territorial acquisitions might easily be made. Plans circulated among them for the dismemberment of the lands of the late Louis XVI, whose sad end they professed unutterably to deplore. It was suggested that Austria take Alsace, Lorraine and northern France as far as the river Somme. Sardinia and Spain were invited to occupy parts of the south. The British were to have colonies. All these territories might then either be kept, or used as counters in intricate exchanges among the powers. What the process might mean for Frenchmen was revealed in the department of the Nord, where the Austrians, having won a few victories, were busy at restoring the tithes, feudal dues and other burdens which the Revolution had abolished.

Confident of success, the Allies rejected the overtures for peace made by Danton in June and July. The Allies, during this summer, would not make peace, but neither would they unite effectively for war. They contented themselves with joyful anticipations. But France was not Poland, and the Committee of Public Safety that took form between July and September was not the group of futile patriots who voiced their agony in Warsaw.

The sentiments of Robespierre toward the war were mixed. He had opposed the opening of hostilities, and had repeatedly said that the war was the chief menace to the Republic, that peace was prerequisite to the establishment of republican institutions. Yet when Danton sought to make peace, Robespierre did nothing to support him. It is doubtful whether Robespierre had such superior insight as to perceive that, in any event, peace probably could not be made. Robespierre saw in Danton, his fellow Jacobin and Mountaineer, a danger to the true republican ideal, a devotee of pleasure, a mere tactician and compromiser, a man without steady principles or real faith in liberty and equality, whom therefore it would be fatal to let win the prestige of a peacemaker and to emerge as the unquestioned leader of the Republic. Robespierre wanted peace, but still more he wanted a France that should be pure, and a world in which aristocrats and tyrants should be thwarted. He did not exactly believe in an expansionist war; he had predicted the consequences of attempts by France to conquer Belgium and the Rhineland; but he saw the peoples of other countries as groaning masses and their rulers as wicked men, and so could easily be brought, with a little impulsion, to favor a general ideological crusade.

This impulsion came from the Hébertists, who were partisans of the *guerre à outrance,* war to the knife upon the enemies of the human race. The Hébertists, or at least certain ones in the vague group so named, were the party of unmitigated violence, of war upon tyrants, war upon Christianity, war upon the starvers of the people. Historians of many shades of thought have agreed in calling them demagogues. Like Billaud-Varenne, who was one of them, they rejoiced that the misfortunes of the people helped them to exterminate their enemies.

Billaud and Collot brought this wild frenzy into the counsels of the Committee. Beside them Robespierre and Couthon were men of prudence, and the others, except Saint-Just, were by contrast almost guilty of moderatism. Yet it is difficult to estimate the influence of the two Hébertists on the policies of the Committee, because, after all, Billaud and Collot were not fundamentally different from their colleagues. Hébertism was a form of extremism, but was only an extreme version of the Jacobin orthodoxy of 1793. Followers of Hébert and of Robespierre might easily fuse together. They used the same phrases and had the same enemies. It was easy for Robespierre to appropriate Hébert's program, and it was not inconceivable that Hébert might one day oust Robespierre in turn. Therein lay a great danger to the Committee.

Whether from Hébertist influence or from voluntary decision, and probably from both, the Committee after September 5 took the Hébertist view of the war. Negotiation with the enemy was abandoned. Even diplomatic relations virtually ceased. Ministers and ambassadors were recalled from their posts, except those in Switzerland and the United States, the Committee henceforth dealing formally only with supposedly democratic republics. In other countries it left only chargés d'affaires to handle unavoidable details, and secret agents to maintain contact with the underground revolutionary societies of Europe. The war became a vast conflict without definite aims avowed by either side, the French proclaiming it as a struggle of liberty against tyrants, and the Allies as a defense of order against universal ruin.

The *levée en masse,* decreed by the Convention on August 23, was to be the means by which the Republic fought the war. The word *levée* means either a "levy" or a "rising." All France was to rise spontaneously in a wave of patriotic enthusiasm. Young and unmarried men were to join the armies, others to work at the manufacture of munitions; women were to act as nurses or to make tents and clothing; children also were to labor, and men past their active years were to deliver patriotic speeches, stirring up hatred of kings and arousing loyalty to the Republic. The idea of this national rising came from the Hébertists. Many others including Robespierre at first doubted its value, fearing that it represented only the desperation of anarchy. And indeed, it would have produced little more than a mad convulsion, had the country remained in what Robespierre called the wreckage of government.

It was the Committee of Public Safety that turned the *levée en masse* into a true national levy, an organized mobilization of the human and material resources of the country. Carnot and the others made the idea their own; they framed the decree and saw it through the Convention; and their chief concern in the next few months was to execute its manifold provisions.

For the first time the world saw a nation in arms. War became the struggle of a whole people—or at least was carried through on that principle, for in sober fact the whole people was hardly more eager to go to war in the France of 1793 than in the Europe of 1914 or 1939. Henceforth the old-fashioned idea of war was doomed. Before the Revolution wars had been clashes between governments or ruling families, fought by relatively small armies of professional soldiers. Many people suffered, but the people as such was not vitally concerned. The French Republic introduced a new system. When governments become the people's governments, their wars become the people's wars, and their armies the armies of the nation.

The recruiting of troops and management of the armies we shall consider in the next chapter. Before the Committee could raise a citizen army it had to provide equipment, uniforms and food. Its most immediate worries were therefore economic, especially since, at the same time, it faced the menace of famine in Paris.

The government entered itself into the business of producing munitions. The 100,000,000 livres granted by the motion of Danton on September 5 were used partly in the building of workshops, the hiring of workmen and purchase of raw materials. The industry was centralized in Paris, for the good reason that many outlying regions were politically untrustworthy, and with the additional advantage of giving employment to the restless sansculottes. Great shops were erected in the gardens of the Tuileries and the Luxembourg. The services of all workmen in the city were requisitioned for the manufacture of muskets, of which the Committee proposed to turn out a thousand a day. Pikes also were manufactured, and the Committee even gave thought to a suggestion, submitted by an unknown citizen, that Frenchmen if necessary should fight with bows and arrows. Perhaps at this idea even Robespierre smiled.

The provinces were not and could not be forgotten. Within a few days, early in September, each department council received 500,000 livres for the purchase of armaments. Inspectors made the rounds of France, sent out by the Committee, surveying supplies of wood and coal, ascertaining the capacities of iron foundries, gathering statistics on costs and prices, visiting the cities known for cutlery, where sword-blades and bayonets could be made. Other inspectors went from town to town and from village to village trying to enforce the laws against church bells; for bells, it had been decreed, must be melted down into material for cannon. On September 13 all objects of lead, copper, tin, iron and bronze, found in the churches or in houses belonging to the émigrés, were put at the disposal of the Ministry of War.

For most of its needs the government could not itself engage in production, and did not wish to. Government ownership was remote from Jacobin ideas. It was indeed scarcely conceivable at the time, since most of the processes of manufacturing were scattered among small craftsmen in both town and country. The Republican authorities had to deal extensively with middlemen, contractors and wholesalers, or send out their own agents to make purchases almost from door to door. In either case they needed money. Money was not easy for the Republic to get by the usual channels. Taxes came in poorly; the rich were disaffected; and the government, having only a problematical future, had virtually no credit. In this respect it was no different from the American Republic of 1776.

In France as in the young United States the use of paper money provided one solution. The French Republic, however, unlike the Continental Congress, was in reality very wealthy. It possessed lands and buildings valued at more than five billion livres, confiscated from the church and from the émigrés. Bills could of course not be paid in real estate; since 1789, therefore, long before the Republic, the Revolutionary governments had issued paper notes, called assignats. By 1793 these had become full legal tender, used in ordinary private transactions and in the payment of taxes. A holder of assignats could redeem them, if he wished, by exchanging them for confiscated lands; and the assignats which thus returned to the Treasury were supposed to be burned, in proportion as the landed wealth on which they were based passed into private hands.

The system had not worked badly. It had the advantage of distributing real property among those peasants or townspeople who could afford to buy it. Thus a large number of people were attached to the Revolution. The sale of real estate meant income for the government, which was thus able to meet its expenses and even to pay off a considerable fraction of the national debt. It is significant that the Revolutionary leaders, though they denounced the Bourbons as tyrants, had no desire to repudiate their debts. The Jacobins of the Terror, despite certain refunding operations, in effect staggered under a burden swollen by the wastefulness of the monarchy which they abhorred. This procedure may be contrasted with that of later revolutionists, not to mention more conservative governments of the twentieth century, and is enough to show that Jacobinism was not exactly communism.

The assignats, however, by the summer of 1793, had depreciated by about fifty per cent in comparison with gold. Prices in terms of assignats had risen. The cause was not primarily inflation, for many assignats had been destroyed as the law required, and the quantity in circulation was more than covered by the value of unsold lands. The cause of depreciation was rather in the enormous public indebtedness and in the mounting expenses of the war, in the difficulties in collecting taxes, and in the fact that no one knew whether the Republic would still exist in a year or even in a month.

In any case the government, obliged to meet its expenses with assignats, had to pay increasing prices to the contractors with whom it dealt, and increasing wages to the laborers and others whom it hired. Two paths were open: to print assignats without limit, or to regulate prices. The Committee of Public Safety chose the second course. From the midsummer, discussions of price fixing were in progress in the green room.

Control of prices had long been demanded by the Commune, the Enragés, the Hébertists and the working people of Paris, for the prices of household necessities had risen beyond the advances in wages. The distress of the summer continued unabated into September. The Revolutionary Army, organized under the supervision of Carnot in the week after the Hébertist rising, was more effectual in spreading fear than in bringing in provisions. Rumor had it that this Army was about to disarm all citizens, march to the prisons and repeat the massacres of a year ago. The story gained such credence that the Committee had Saint-André formally deny it in the Convention.

It was the women who suffered the most from scarcity and disorder. They sometimes plundered the nightly caravans which brought supplies into the city; on the night of September 9 a riot broke out when twenty women attacked a wagonload of coal. Housewives predominated in the lines which formed every morning before the bakers' doors. Some were seen in tears when, after waiting for hours, they found nothing left to take home to their families. Women in these circumstances were bitter against the government. Some joined the *Femmes Révolutionnaires,* a radical organization which embarrassed the Jacobin politicians. A larger number were sick of the whole business of political confusion. A government agent overheard one woman remark that if the husbands had made the Revolution the wives would have enough sense to bring about counter-revolution if it was needed.

The wrath of women with families to feed was exploited by more politically minded males. Agitators of all parties were at work. Some preached feminism, argued that women should have rights to vote and to hold office on equal terms with men. The authorities regarded these propagandists as malignants and counter-revolutionists. Perhaps they were; perhaps they were only sans-culottes a trifle too advanced. Gangs of men, organized by no one knew whom, at one time went about the streets, whipping women who refused to wear the republican cockade. Women at the Halles, the provisions market, were stabbed for not wearing this insignia; at the Porte Saint-Denis they were beaten if they did. There was an alarming belief in the feminine world that the tricolor was worn only by *putains*—an expression equivalent to "whores."

Men who whipped women in the streets may have been fanatical revolutionists; they may have been hired by royalists to throw odium on the Republic; or they may have been simply ruffians who, in the collapse of all restraints, found a chance to gratify an impulse to brutality. But who were the true plotters, the higher-ups, the master minds? No one knew. There were melodramatic explanations. One morning, just at dawn, a fine carriage of English make was seen rolling through the city. Three gentlemen sat in it, one of whom, wearing a black patch over his left eye, peered out curiously, with an evil one-eyed stare, at every bakery to see the people waiting for bread.

It was perfectly true that schemers like the one-eyed man were active, and that some of them were agents of foreign powers. It was probably true also that the Jacobins could assure their position only if they put a stop to such machinations. Where the Jacobins went astray was in believing that such plotters were the real cause of the disorders. This belief led to a fatal delusion —the idea that the country would be pacified if certain individuals, perhaps a few hundred or a few thousand, were put to death.

Hungry Parisians, when they saw bread disappear from the bakers' shelves, did not picture thousands of unknown farmers, each of whom, living his own life, was afraid in such uncertain times to part with his food supply, or eager to sell it at the highest possible price, in order, perhaps, to buy himself a piece of the confiscated lands. Ardent patriots, when they found many young men reluctant to join the army, did not call to mind an average youth of eighteen or twenty-five, concerned with his own affairs, attached to his home or his work or his flirtations, and none too eager to be forced to become a hero.

It was easier for revolutionary leaders to think that enemies of the Revolution, who undoubtedly did exist, were the true cause of this low state of public spirit. It was easier for them to blame, not themselves for demanding the impossible, nor unfavorable conditions which they had done much to bring about, nor human nature with its tendencies toward selfishness or indolence, but certain obstinate individuals—one-eyed men, malignants, hidden priests, profiteers, agents of Pitt and Coburg, sinister intelligences which somewhere, out of reach, were directing a baffling campaign against the defenders of the Republic.

The state of affairs in the middle of September was concisely summed up by Soulet, one of the confidential agents of the Minister of the Interior. The following was his whole report for one day:

"An endless number of people cry out against the levy of the young men.

"There is still difficulty in procuring bread.

"The aristocrats are meeting in the cafés and seem to be maneuvering more than ever.

"The section of the Tuileries began yesterday to arrest suspicious persons."

Young men who objected to military service of course fell under suspicion; those who rushed eagerly to the front were also suspected, at least by some super-patriots, who saw in such alacrity a hypocritical design of treachery. The professors at the Collège d'Égalité (formerly Louis-le-Grand), the one part of the University of Paris that continued to function, were also known to be unsympathetic to the government; dark charges were heard that they encouraged perversion among their students. Gambling houses and brothels flourished too openly to satisfy republicans, who regarded them, not erroneously, as resorts of aristocrats and plotters. Even the Convention could not quite be trusted; some Mountaineers observed that, with many good Jacobin members absent on mission, the right wing was gaining power and would perhaps have to be purged.

The Committee of General Security was responsible for the suppressing of counter-revolution. Its success had not been conspicuous, and a few days after the Hébertist uprising one of its members, Drouet, denounced it to the Jacobin club, urging in particular that certain of his colleagues were too susceptible to the blandishments of invitations to dinner. Another citizen denounced the Committee on Markets, which, he said, was in corrupt alliance with the army contractors.

The next day, September 9, Drouet moved in the Convention that the Committee of General Security be re-formed. The Convention acceded, and on the 11th elected a new committee of nine members. Meanwhile, at the Jacobins, Hébert led an attack on all the governing and administrative committees. The question was therefore reopened in the Convention on the 13th. A member denounced the Committee on Markets. Danton then took up the charge, demanding, like Hébert at the Jacobins, that all the committees be renewed. He proposed, however, that the Committee of Public Safety, left intact itself, should have the power of naming the members of all the others. The Convention so ordained. On September 14 Jeanbon Saint-André submitted a list of twelve men to form a new Committee of General Security. Only three on this list were among the nine named by the Convention three days before. Among those dropped was Chabot, who had shown proletarian inclinations in June, and been told by the committee in July that he was too radical. Saint-André's list was nevertheless adopted.

What had happened? It was clear that the Convention had lost control over the nomination of its own committees. Denunciation by the Jacobin club and the Hébertists threw into uncertainty the holding of important offices. Power passed, however, not to the Jacobins and Hébertists as such, but to the Committee of Public Safety, which was entirely Jacobin and partly Hébertist, but was at the same time an organized agency of government. Through the intervention of Danton, who would himself serve on no committee, the importance of one committee had been enormously enlarged.

The Committee of Public Safety henceforth appointed the members of the others. Another step toward dictatorship had been taken. A power which the Convention was too weak to wield, and which might have fallen to the Jacobin club, where it would have been a mere incitement to mutual denunciation, passed into the hands of the one body which might yet save France from chaos.

Meanwhile plans were being matured for a systematic treatment of persons suspected of counter-revolution. Many laws had been passed against refractory priests, émigrés, hoarders and monopolists. Section committees, representatives on mission and others had often arrested and detained persons of whose activities they disapproved. But there had never been any legal definition of "suspects," nor any organized or supervised manner of dealing with them.

The Law of Suspects of September 17 was an attempt to supply these deficiencies, and was novel chiefly in systematizing and legalizing a situation which already existed in fact.

The law defined suspects vaguely, reflecting the wild apprehensiveness of its authors. Suspects were of six kinds: "those who, by their conduct, relations or language spoken or written, have shown themselves partisans of tyranny or federalism and enemies of liberty"; those who could not give a satisfactory account of their means of support or their discharge of civic duties since the preceding March 21; those to whom had been denied the certificates of good citizenship issued by sections and communes; government employes discharged from office; ex-nobles and their families and retainers who had not shown a constant fidelity to the Revolution; and émigrés, even those who, by earlier laws, had legally returned to France. The first of these categories, and to a lesser extent the second, were so general that almost anyone might find himself compromised.

The spontaneous efforts of the local committees of surveillance, known also as revolutionary committees, were finally legalized. An attempt was made also to control them. Each committee was to draw up a list of the suspects in its district, secure their papers, and put them in a house of detention—or, that failing, guard them in their homes. No committee, however, was to act unless seven of its members were present (thus were petty personal rancors to be avoided), and each committee was to furnish the Committee of General Security with a list of persons arrested, a statement of the reasons for arrest, and the documents seized on the suspected premises. Thus the local committees became branches of the central government.

Concentration camps were unknown to the French Revolution; their equivalents were the "national buildings," improvised central prisons maintained by the departments, to which suspects were to be transferred within a week after arrest. Inmates of these national buildings had the right to use their own furniture. They also paid their own expenses and the wages of their guards, the more well-to-do prisoners contributing to the upkeep of the poorer ones. Favoritism under these circumstances was easily possible, and the guards, being dependent on their prisoners, might be tempted to soften the hardships of those who had money. The political prisoners of the French Revolution probably had less to suffer than those of the twentieth century upheavals.

Deserted convents, vacated chateaux, abandoned schools, hastily refurbished warehouses, buildings of any kind big enough for the purpose, served as living quarters for incarcerated suspects. In them took place many of the scenes described by the picturesque school of historians: fair ladies and fine gentlemen reduced to poverty, lost to their friends, tormented by sans-culottes, awaiting trial in the grim revolutionary courts, and soon thereafter marching out to the guillotine. As a matter of fact, with most of the suspects the purpose of the authorities was simply to detain them. Many were never tried, and only a small fraction were put to death. This low proportion was a reflection of the high number of persons confined, who in time numbered 100,000. In Paris, during the month of September, the population of the prisons rose from 1,607 to 2,365.

There would have been more deaths if Collot d'Herbois had had his way. He advised, about this time, that suspects be herded into mined houses, and that the mines then be exploded. It was rumored that the prisons in truth were mined, and news of Collot's opinion got abroad. Collot himself later admitted having held it.

Collot was emerging as the most insanely violent of the Twelve. The day after the enactment of the Law of Suspects he made a speech in the Convention. He raged against purveyors of false news. Many of the counter-revolutionists now in prison, he said, had committed no crime except to circulate wrong information. Were they therefore to be considered innocent and set at liberty? Obviously not; the law, therefore, must declare their offense to be a crime. Some grounds must be found for the conviction of all enemies.

"I add," he went on, "that it is time for you to deliver a last blow against the aristocracy of merchants. It is this aristocracy that has checked the progress of the Revolution and prevented us thus far from enjoying the fruit of our sacrifices. I demand that you add to the number of suspects the merchants who sell necessities at an exorbitant price."

A lively discussion followed. Some thought the proposal arbitrary, and the word "exorbitant" too vague. Robespierre spoke ambiguously, but with sense, urging that they must not let their indignation override their judgment. He succeeded in having Collot's two motions shelved. Sharp words passed between the two, showing that the Committee of Public Safety did not always present a united program to the Convention.

Collot's attack on the merchants was a sign of his ungovernable impatience, for a commission was already at work on the problem of regulating prices. Regulation, we have seen, had been decided upon by the Committee as an alternative to the endless printing of assignats. The Commune, moreover, had not yet received any very material gain from the insurrection of September 5. "Food and force to the law" had been the burden of Chaumette's petition. New means of applying force had been developed. The food problem remained.

It is to be observed that the needs of the middle-class Jacobins and the demands of wage-earning families ran together. Price control would be for the Jacobins both a financial convenience, enabling them to maintain the purchasing power of their paper money, and a political advantage, winning for them the support of the poorer classes, or at least drawing those classes away from the more radical Hébert and his followers. In addition, Robespierre, and probably Couthon, who was not then in Paris, felt a real compassion toward the victims of poverty.

The result of this mixture of interests, humane sentiments and patriotic detestation of the rich was the General Maximum, enacted by the Convention on September 29. It was one of the fundamental laws of the Terrorist régime. Like the Law of Suspects, it systematized and extended a body of practices that already existed haphazardly. The price of bread had been regulated since May; other prices had sometimes been fixed by local authorities or representatives on mission. The law of September 29 laid down a national rule.

Maximum prices were set for a number of articles considered to be of prime necessity: fresh and salted meat, salted fish, butter and oil; wine, brandy, vinegar, cider and beer; coal, charcoal, candles and soap; salt, soda, sugar and honey; leather, iron, steel, lead and copper; paper, wool, and various cloths; shoes and tobacco. For most of these items the highest lawful price was fixed at a figure one-third higher than the current local price in 1790

The level of wages was also determined—the maximum wage to be one-half more than the corresponding wage in 1790. An advantage was thus offered to wage earners, who might earn a half more than in 1790 while paying only a third more for commodities. It is to be noted, however, that the wage set was a maximum, not a minimum; and moreover workmen who refused to work were to spend three days in jail.

Price regulation was so repugnant to the social philosophy of the Jacobins that they could understand its necessity only by imagining some kind of conspiracy against themselves. The Subsistence Commission, which, under the Committee of Public Safety, drew up the law of September 29, believed firmly in laissez-faire. "In normal times," said its spokesman, "prices are formed naturally by the reciprocal interests of buyers and sellers. This balance is infallible. It is useless for even the best government to interfere."

"But," he continued, "when a general conspiracy of malignancy, perfidy and unparalleled fury joins together to break this natural equilibrium, to famish and despoil us, the welfare of the people becomes the highest rule." The law, therefore, provided that anyone who sold goods above the maximum price was to be treated as a suspect. The effect of the Maximum was immensely to broaden the scope of the Draconian law of September 17.

The month of September was the turning point in the transition from anarchy to dictatorship. The Levy in Mass, the enlargement of the Revolutionary Tribunal, the Law of Suspects and the General Maximum were means toward controlling the resources of the country in the interests of the Revolution. They would have been useless, however, without a relatively stable body of leaders to integrate and apply them. What the revolutionists needed, for their own salvation, was above all else an authoritative government. The Committee of Public Safety had begun to supply this need; but Jacobins, Mountaineers, Hébertists, Dantonists, etc. were not men to be easily governed. Not in five years had France possessed a government which enjoyed any effective authority. It remained to be seen whether men who were habituated to opposition, who regarded authority as repression and thought that to subordinate themselves would be a betrayal of the nation, and indeed the human race, could now be brought to acknowledge any power placed over them, even a power supposed to represent themselves.

In short, the strictly political question, the question of government, had not been settled.

The uncertainty became apparent on September 20, with the resignation of Thuriot from the Committee, and it lasted until October 10. Thuriot's departure left in office the Twelve. How permanent they were to be the next days were to determine.

Voices were heard in the Convention complaining of the Committee. Some said its policy was too extreme in purging the army officers; others objected that it was accomplishing nothing. On the 25th the Convention censured the Committee, accused it of suppressing news, and added, as a thirteenth member, a certain Briez to its counsels. Billaud-Varenne came to the defense of his absent colleagues. Twenty days ago he had led the opposition; he demanded unity now—"far be from us all spirit of party!" The Convention officially summoned the Committee to appear.

Robespierre, Barère, Saint-André and Prieur of the Marne made haste to arrive. Barère, who understood facts, explained the reasons for the policies adopted. Prieur added a few words to Barère's statement. Robespierre delivered the great political speech of the day.

"Whoever seeks to debase, divide or paralyze the Convention," he said, "is an enemy of our country, whether he sits in this hall or is a foreigner. Whether he acts from stupidity or from perversity, he is of the party of tyrants who make war upon us. This project of debasement does exist. . . .

"We are accused of doing nothing, but has our position been realized? Eleven armies to direct, the weight of all Europe to carry, everywhere traitors to unmask, agents paid by gold of foreign powers to confound, faithless officials to watch over, everywhere obstacles and difficulties in the execution of wise measures to smoothe away, all tyrants to combat, all conspirators to intimidate, almost all of them of that caste once so powerful by its riches, and still strong in its intrigues—these are our functions!"

He declared that the Committee could not face its gigantic tasks without the confidence of the Convention. If no such confidence was felt, then the existing group should be replaced by another.

In short, Robespierre, Barère and Saint-André offered their resignations, both for themselves and their colleagues. They met the threat of opposition by developing a common front, a collective unity in what may be called a cabinet. This maneuver won the day. Poor Briez, discovering in himself "insufficient talents to be a member of the Committee of Public Safety," declined the honor so recently bestowed on him. At Robespierre's continued insistence, the Convention solemnly affirmed its confidence in the Committee.

So the Twelve remained. Once a month, for ten months, the Convention reelected the same men to govern France.

The dictatorship of the Twelve was greatly advanced by their parliamentary victory of September 25. It became clear from Robespierre's speech that serious criticism of the government would henceforth be dangerous in the Convention. Opposition became a "project for debasement," dissent a treasonous connivance with foreign powers. The Committee, as Barère said, was an "extract," a résumé, a small image of the Convention, as the Convention was of the sovereign people; to raise difficulties for the Committee was therefore identical with counter-revolution. The will of the country was supposed to be embodied in twelve men, not as individuals, not by a principle of personal leadership, but because they were members, first, of the Convention, and, second, of that miniature of the Convention which was its governing body.

But the Committee was not yet a dictatorship, nor the Convention a mere aggregation of puppets. The Committee, as any organized government in its place would have done, looked with strong dislike upon the prevailing administrative chaos. On October 4 it sent Billaud with a draft decree before the Convention, where the Mountain now easily predominated, for more than a hundred members had been expelled as Girondists the day before. Billaud urged that the functions of the thousands of constituted authorities be delimited and clarified, that these authorities be forbidden to arrogate new powers, to correspond officially with each other or to league together; and he complained also against the swarm of representatives on mission, travelling members of the Convention, each of whom, virtually sovereign in the place to which he was sent, interfered as he chose in local affairs and enforced the laws at his personal discretion.

To doubt the value of the work of representatives on mission was an insult to the Convention, for it implied that a parliamentary body could not itself govern the country. Members therefore demurred, and the Convention showed its independence by sending back Billaud's proposals to the Committee to be reconsidered.

The Committee thus suffered a setback. Its project was premature; it was not really to gain control of the deputies on mission until December.

But the Twelve (or rather the seven remaining, for Couthon and Lindet were still away, Carnot had just gone to the armies, and Saint-André and Prieur of the Marne left on October 1 for Brittany) were determined to have some kind of political showdown, to systematize the powers which they had in fact acquired in the last few weeks, and to legalize their relation to the Convention. They therefore drew up a new decree. To present it and argue for it before the assembly, they chose Saint-Just.

This young man is one of the mysteries of the Revolution. He shot briefly across it, his time of prominence lasting less than two years, a flaming personality whose youth had been anything but promising, but whose mature years, had he lived to attain them, might conceivably have rocked the world. He was rather ashamed now of his youthful poem, *Organt,* which he had followed with a political study, *The Spirit of the Revolution,* written in 1791, when the Revolution was generally supposed to be over. The book showed a good deal of political insight and no trace of republican intentions. But its author, caught up in the disasters of 1792, his own ambitions stirring as the country became progressively more excited, was no longer, in 1793, the calm observer of two years before.

In the decisive events between the Levy in Mass and the General Maximum Saint-Just played little part. During these formative weeks in the construction of the new government, Saint-Just attended the meetings of the Committee infrequently and signed only a fraction of its decrees. Nor was he active, though he was in Paris, either at the Convention or at the Jacobin club. Little is known, in fact, of this period in his life except that, when a scandal arose over his alleged relations with a certain Mme. Thorin, he denied the charges and in doing so asserted that he was very busy.

He was nevertheless a marked man. Every other member of the Convention was older than he was, yet he dominated most of them easily. Tense, alert, seemingly unruffled; cold and superior in manner, sometimes purposely enigmatic; affecting to be unmoved by the feelings that governed others, he behaved like one who thought himself above humanity, and made his admirers feel the presence of a demigod. He resembled Robespierre, whom he had once worshiped as a hero and came rather to patronize as a colleague. Robespierre was vain, Saint-Just was overweening. Robespierre was rather stiff, Saint-Just was inflexible. Saint-Just was a Robespierre drawn in sharper lines, more full-blooded, more impetuous despite his impassive airs, a Robespierre without the wordiness, the indecision, the introversion and the soul-searching, but also without the saving elements of kindness and sincerity.

Saint-Just was an idea energized by a passion. All that was abstract, absolute and ideological in the Revolution was embodied in his slender figure and written upon his youthful face, and was made terrible by the unceasing drive of his almost demonic energy. He was a Rousseauist, but what he shared with Rousseau was the Spartan rigor of the *Social Contract,* not the soft day-dreaming of the *Nouvelle Héloïse,* still less the self-pity of the *Confessions.* He was no lover of blood, as Collot d'Herbois seems to have become. Blood to him simply did not matter. The individual was irrelevant to his picture of the world. The hot temperament that had disturbed his adolescence now blazed beneath the calm exterior of the political fanatic.

Members of the Convention, on October 10, found this alarming personage in the tribune before them. His proposal was a compromise in that it made no mention of the representatives on mission. But it provided that the Committee should supervise the Revolutionary Army, the generals in the real armies, the ministers of state and the constituted authorities; and it empowered the Committee to requisition and distribute food supplies and other necessities on a national scale. Politically the most significant article in the draft which Saint-Just submitted, and which the Convention enacted, was the first:

The provisional government of France is revolutionary until the peace.

In this proposition the developments of the preceding months were summarized. For the first time the great Committee, with its auxiliaries, was described officially as a government. It became the recognized executive of the country, still in theory subordinate to the Convention, which reconfirmed its powers that very day, as on the tenth of every month, but able in its new capacity to assert its priority and systematically to enforce its will. The new government was called revolutionary because it was not "constituted" in the manner demanded by contemporary ideas of law. The constitution, drawn up four months before, was now definitely put aside. The Convention (which was primarily a constitutional convention in the American sense), instead of dissolving upon completion of its task, gave notice that it intended to remain, and to govern by "revolutionary," i.e. exceptional and expeditious, methods. There is a deep truth in the observation of Hippolyte Carnot, son of Lazare Carnot, that the men who ruled France during the Terror had too great a respect for law to attribute to the law the course of action which they took.

The Revolutionary Government, as the régime set up on October 10, 1793, is specifically called, was not and was not supposed to be a model of lawfulness; but neither was it a mere creature of circumstance or expediency. It rested on a higher law, a law above law, a political dogma. Saint-Just stated the dogma clearly, in the speech in which he introduced the new decree to the Convention.

"Since the French people has manifested its will," he said, "everything opposed to it is outside the sovereign. Whatever is outside the sovereign is an enemy."

Here is the mystery of the "general will" as laid down in the *Social Contract*. What does it mean?

It means that in any country organized as a political unit there is something that may be called the people, which has an ascertainable will. This people is sovereign. Its will is not the will of any class or individual, nor of any combination of classes or individuals. Persons or parties who have different wills do not really belong to the people. They are "outside the sovereign," not true citizens, mere metics, stateless, virtually social outcasts. They have ostracized themselves by their stubbornness, and can claim no protection from laws which they have refused to accept.

There is something in this philosophy which is workable, and even necessary, in a settled political order. Members of a community must in truth agree on something. They must feel that their common ties are stronger than the interests that divide them; they must all, while differing over policy, respect the legal machinery by which policy is determined; they must accept, and be committed by, the decisions of lawful authority even when those decisions contradict their private wishes. Only by such a general will does a population become one people. To refuse such a minimum of agreement is to repudiate the rule of law.

But in France in 1793, where unity was absent, where parties were unwilling to tolerate each other and there was no agreement on the form of state, the philosophy expressed by Saint-Just, and shared by the others, could be exceedingly dangerous. The Mountaineers were not a majority in France. Sometimes they thought they were; more often they conceived of themselves as a small band of the righteous. It followed, in any case, especially since Saint-Just proposed to punish the lukewarm along with the openly treacherous, that most Frenchmen might be excluded from what Mountaineers recognized as the people. They were outside the sovereign—and, as Saint-Just said, with an indelicacy that suggests the eras of Machiavelli or of Hitler, what was outside the sovereign was an enemy.

Saint-Just himself had once seen the danger in the philosophy of sovereign will. As lately as April 1793, arguing against the Girondists, he had said that "this idea of the general will," meaning the Girondist use of the idea, "if it makes its fortune in the world, will banish liberty." Before that, in his book of 1791, he had accused Rousseau of a serious omission. Rousseau argued that the general will, whatever it willed, was always in the right; he made reason and right depend on political authority, and so became the ancestor to what is now called totalitarianism. Saint-Just amended the doctrine. Any will, said Saint-Just, even a sovereign will, if inclined to evil, is null and void. To be sovereign a will must be "just and reasonable." Saint-Just retained reason and right as higher standards beyond the reach of sovereignty to change.

Saint-Just did not believe in 1791, still less in 1793, that the majority of Frenchmen endorsed the revolutionary régime. He would agree, however, with Rousseau, who said: "What generalizes the will is not so much the number of voices as the common interest that unites them." He would add that only a virtuous will could be sovereign. And he believed absolutely in his own virtue. So did Robespierre and others, for in no trait were the French revolutionaries so much alike as in their moral self-approval. The doctrine of the *Social Contract,* with these moral overtones, became the theory of the Terror. A group of the consciously right-minded, regarding their enemies as "outside the sovereign," took to themselves, in the name of justice and reason, that majestic sovereign will which Rousseau had called indestructible, indivisible, imprescriptible, constant, unalterable and pure.

CHAPTER IV
The Beginning of Victory

AS IF the Hébertist uprising of September 5 were not enough to occupy the Committee, it was on that same day that a depressing message came from Houchard, general in command of the Army of the North. Writing on the 3rd, Houchard knew that he was on the eve of a decisive battle. His letter was a tale of woe. He shuddered, he said, to learn that the troops sent to reinforce him were 10,000 fewer than he had been promised. Those who arrived from the neighboring Army of the Moselle had brought no cannon. The artillery was in poor condition, and could not be moved without six hundred more horses; yet whether more horses would help was doubtful, for those already with the army had had no oats for fifteen days, and in any case the cavalry and field guns could probably not maneuver in a country cut to pieces by hedges and canals. The army was using up its food reserves, for the local political authorities would not cooperate in furnishing supplies. Worst of all, the quartermaster-general had just been denounced and arrested; his successor was a man without experience; and though ten million livres had just arrived from Paris, Houchard was not at all sure how his army was going to eat.

To this pessimistic communication Carnot had to draft some kind of reply, distracted though he was by the news from the Convention, which sent word that he must submit a plan, instantly, for a Revolutionary Army of Parisian sans-culottes. He contented himself with writing a few words on general strategy to Houchard, who, for all his gloom, had no intention of not fighting.

That afternoon, at four o'clock, while insurrection raged in Paris, Houchard sat at his new headquarters (for he had somehow managed to move) penning another note for his superiors. Contact with the enemy had been established; the outposts had already exchanged shots. But Houchard was still dejected. His generals were afraid to assume responsibility. They sometimes declared themselves unfit for their work; they declined important assignments, or raised petty difficulties and objections. Houchard said that he wished he could point out, among his subordinates,

three good divisional commanders and half a dozen good brigadiers.

Such were conditions, as described by the commander, in the
army which during the next three days fought and won the battle
of Hondschoote. This battle was a turning point. It checked the
progress of the Allies that had gone on since the preceding winter,
and it led to a succession of triumphs which by 1794 put the French
forces clearly on the offensive.

Victory began before the Terror was organized, before the Levy
in Mass could become effective, before the Committee of Public
Safety achieved a position of dictatorship. But of course no one
knew in September 1793 that Hondschoote was a turning point;
and it is extremely improbable, in view of the domestic situation
in France, that without dictatorial government victory would have
continued.

The Republic had about 500,000 men under arms at the end of
the summer. They were grouped in eleven armies, each named
after the scene of its proposed operations. Four of the largest were
stationed on the northern border, those of the Rhine, the Moselle,
the Ardennes, and the North. Over these eleven armies there was
no centralized military command, not even a general staff, but only
the Ministry of War and the Committee of Public Safety. The
revolutionists were afraid to make one general too strong.

The troops were in want, and to all appearances were undisciplined and demoralized. Few people, either in the ranks or in
Paris, had much confidence in the higher officers; for the experienced ones were not republicans, and those who were politically
suitable were seldom trained for responsible positions. The officers
reciprocated by having little trust in their men. A core of the old
professional army remained; but there were thousands of volunteers who, having enlisted in the excitement of revolutionary
patriotism, often had aggressive political ideas; and thousands of
conscripts, unwilling to serve and hard to train in the prevailing
atmosphere of liberty; and, as time passed, thousands of recruits
raised by the Levy in Mass, a mixed throng of young men under
twenty-five, of all shades of political opinion.

Generals complained—and it was not only aristocratic generals
who did so—that their men were impossible to control. Soldiers
broke hours, sat idly in cafés, joined the local Jacobin societies,

formed political cells of their own, read the radical newspapers from Paris, quarreled with each other over politics, corresponded with the Paris Commune, reported their superiors to the travelling representatives on mission. Careless of their equipment, they would abandon valuable cannon without making an effort to save them, thus wasting the substance of the Republic. If an engagement were lost, there was always danger of panic, led by the newer men, who were not brigaded with veterans but formed units of their own. Should there be a small success, the troops were inclined to relax prematurely, think unnecessary the further efforts that their officers called for, refuse to deliver a finishing blow, and sometimes, in the shortage of provisions, break up into marauding bands. One French village, redeemed from the "satellites of despots," saw its food, beds, assignats and all other valuables vanish before the onslaughts of its liberators. Lawlessness prevailed especially in the Army of the North, after Custine, an ex-nobleman, was relieved of the command.

If the troops were undisciplined it was in part because they thought themselves free men. The hordes of the Republic were very different from the hosts drawn up against them. The armies of Austria, Prussia, England, Holland, Spain and Sardinia were alike in one respect: they were all composed of two classes that could not mix, a vast concourse of rustics and of unfortunates lifted from the streets of towns (even of serfs, in some of the German regiments), and a small film of hereditary aristocrats, gently bred people who gave the orders. In the French armies every man from drummer-boy to commander-in-chief took care to address everyone else as "citizen." The familiarity that thus ensued was not altogether a military advantage; but it made the Frenchman feel that a gulf divided him from his abject opponents.

The French army was a nursery of patriotism. Not all were patriots when they joined it; but the bewildered or sullen recruit could not resist forever the influence of the more emphatic personalities, nor could he, if a normal man, long belittle a cause for which he was obliged to risk his life. He heard everywhere the great words Liberty and Equality, the Republic and the Nation, the rolling thunder of the "Marseillaise" and the lighter strains of the "Carmagnole." He saw the tricolor every day at his barracks, and again in the battlefield where it fused into his moments of most tense excitement and seemed to protect him in the hour of mortal danger. He would observe also, if a man of sense, his sergeants receiving commissions and his lieutenants rising to be generals; and while his attitude to officers thus created might not always be respectful, he could at least reflect that the men who led him were men of his own kind.

Unruly but patriotic, undisciplined but enthusiastic, discouraged by defeat and by the ineptitude and colorlessness of its generals, extremely political but inclined to take a low view of politicians, the army in August, like France itself, was a formless and fluctuating mass, a new and unknown quantity in eighteenth century calculations, potentially something that might revolutionize Europe, but as yet no one knew exactly what.

The Committee of Public Safety organized the army as it organized, or tried to organize, everything else. With respect to the army it acted chiefly through Carnot.

Carnot is the one man of the Twelve who today is a French national hero. He is also one of the figures about whom controversy rages. Modern conservatives, in admitting him to the national shrine, like to believe that he was not at heart a revolutionist. They represent him as a painstaking patriot who did his duty while the world tumbled about him, surrounded by ferocious Terrorists and suckers of human blood, obliged against his will to cooperate with radicals whom he despised. Carnot the republican disappears in Carnot the organizer of victory.

In truth, however, Carnot was a republican, a radical and a revolutionary, not as brutal as Collot to be sure, nor as doctrinaire as Saint-Just, but a man who believed that the glory of the Revolution lay more in the principles that it announced than in the battles that it might win. He never went to the Jacobin club, though he was a member; he rightly believed that the Jacobins often wasted their time in futile recrimination. He resembled Barère and Saint-André, and differed from Robespierre, Saint-Just, Collot and Billaud, in having a reasonably well adjusted personality. He was not subject to complexes, phobias or obsessions; he had no delusions of grandeur; he was as free from messianic ideas as any ardent revolutionist could be. He was not a party leader, and so, like Barère, he survived many changes of régime. He was indeed rather innocent in politics, a fact of which shrewder heads were in time to take advantage.

Carnot was ably assisted by the Minister of War, Bouchotte, who transacted much of the routine business. Bouchotte occupied a somewhat ambiguous position. He was repeatedly attacked for being insufficiently revolutionary, yet during his ministry the War Office became a hive of Hébertists and extremists. The Committee considered him indispensable and defended him publicly. Bouchotte had both administrative ability and constructive intelligence. He was a good judge of military talent. He could draw up and execute far-reaching plans. Under his orders the French army first used balloons; and it was he who built the first "telegraph" from Paris to Lille, a series of semaphores placed on hilltops which reduced to a few minutes the time needed for communication between the two cities. On this matter he had the full support of Carnot, who encouraged the inventor, and who, on August 25, transmitted 166,240 livres to Bouchotte to pay the costs.

The Committee kept watch over the armies either through Bouchotte's agents, who after September 11 were obliged to report directly to the Committee once a week, or for more important affairs through itinerant members of the Convention, who outranked all generals in the field. Sometimes the Twelve dispatched one or more of their own number. Prieur of the Marne and Saint-André made a rapid tour of the northern armies in August. Couthon left shortly after their return to carry through the reconquest of Lyons. Usually, however, the Committee worked through ordinary representatives on mission. The spirit of the relationship is shown in a conversation reported by René Levasseur, deputy from the Sarthe.

Levasseur tells how he was summoned by the Committee, and found Carnot alone. He was writing many years later, and perhaps exaggerates his own modesty.

"The Army of the North," said Carnot, "is in open revolt. We need a firm hand to put down this rebellion. You are the man we have chosen."

"I am honored, Carnot," said Levasseur, "but firmness is not enough. Experience and military ability are needed, and I lack these essentials."

"We know you, and we know how to value you. The sight of a man who is esteemed, a friend of liberty, will be enough to bring back those who have been led astray."

"But the truth is, Carnot, that I lack the physical powers. Look at my short stature, and tell me how I can inspire the respect of grenadiers with such an appearance."

"Alexander the Great was small in person," answered Carnot, quoting in Latin.

"Yes, but Alexander had spent his life in camps. He had been apprenticed to arms. He knew how to manage the minds of soldiers."

"Circumstances make men. Your strength of character and devotion to the Republic are our guarantee."

"Very well, I accept. In place of military knowledge I promise you zeal and courage. When must I go?"

"Tomorrow."

"I will be ready."

"Tomorrow you will receive the decree of the Convention, and the arms and uniform of a commissioner of the government."

"And my instructions?"

"They are in your heart and head; they will come out when needed. Go on, and succeed."

So Levasseur departed, exhilarated and eager, carrying with him in his luggage the odd costume of a representative commissioned to the armies. The costume was designed to make its wearer stand out, without seeming too military. It consisted of a blue coat with brass buttons, a flowing tricolor sash, and a soft hat adorned with tricolor feathers.

The main problem with the army, as Carnot saw it, was the problem of personnel. To this even the question of supply was secondary. Above all else, the government had to be sure that the armed forces were fighting on its side. It was necessary, therefore, to liquidate most of the older officers, and to carry on a vigorous propaganda among the troops, who, though generally revolutionary in their ideas, were not necessarily much attached to the Mountaineers who ruled in Paris.

According to Jacobin estimates, almost a thousand nobly born officers still remained, despite the waves of emigration of preceding years. These men were for the most part patriotic enough, in the sense of wanting to defend France against spoliation by foreigners. But they were rarely patriots in the Jacobin sense. The Revolution had long since gone beyond any program that they favored. They were prone, therefore, to engage in conspiracy or to lose interest in the war, not being eager to win victories for a government which they thought was ruining the country. They resented, moreover, being spied on by their enlisted men and ordered about by civilians in colored sashes. Custine, arrested on July 22, was put to death on August 27. The other generals were demoralized, fearing to assume responsibility when failure might mean the guillotine.

The purging of the army officers was one cry that could rally all the factions in Paris, the panacea from which all politicians promised a restoration of confidence. It was, however, not easy to carry out. Bouchotte went at it wholeheartedly, but with such caution as national urgency and Jacobin agitation would permit. He was aware that denunciation often sprang only from jealousy, petty irritation or personal vengefulness. He knew also that to dismiss officers wholesale, when successors were hard to find, might easily be suicidal. He therefore temporized; as late as September 7 he had only reached the point of removing officers who persisted in wearing the uniform of the Bourbons. Shortly after, as one of the many consequences of the Hébertist uprising, all officers of noble birth were suspended without more ado. On November 4 the Committee of Public Safety, feeling that the problem had become routine, turned over to the Committee of General Security the task of watching over the loyalty of the officers, and transmitted to that body its bulky records on the subject.

Houchard's complaints about his generals showed the difficulties in finding able men. Houchard was himself a proof of the same difficulty. He was not, and did not believe himself, qualified to be Custine's successor. He was timid from the fear of failure, slow from the want of experience. But no one had ever questioned the purity of his politics up to July 1793, and he was not a noble, though sufficiently well born to have been an acting captain before the Revolution. Fifty-five years old, he was a veteran of many campaigns, but had never commanded more than a company until the last few months, when, with some success, he passed through the ranks of colonel and brigadier.

He looked like a royalist's nightmare vision of a sans-culotte. He was six feet tall, crude and gruff in manner, and being of German background he spoke French incorrectly. His face was hideous with the scars of three saber cuts and a bullet wound, with a mouth twisted toward the left ear, an upper lip split in two, and a right cheek carved by long parallel gashes. A modest man, no more nor less than an old soldier, he leaned heavily and frankly upon the shoulders of his subordinates. He was naïve enough one day, shortly after taking command in the north, to wear an enormous cap of liberty as he reviewed the troops. The soldiers laughed, and poor Houchard was embarrassed.

No reasonable person to look at Houchard would take him for an aristocrat, but he had scarcely been appointed to the Army of the North, and had not yet joined it, when denunciations began to be heard, especially among the Jacobins of Strasbourg, who, as Saint-Just was later to find, were given to extremes. The day before he left his home in Sarrebourg, local vigilantes denounced him as a traitor, threatening to tear down his house and hang his wife and children. Prieur and Saint-André, during their mission in August, found that Houchard was no longer trusted by the more vehement patriots. Goaded into desperation he became ineffectual, failed to win respect, and viewed the future with apprehension.

He was the first and most unhappy of the commoners that the Committee of Public Safety called to high command.

With the enlisted men the management of personnel took the form of propaganda to build up loyalty to the government. Never before, except possibly in some religious wars, had a government gone to such lengths to assure its solidarity with the men who did its fighting. There was no such problem in the enemy armies, where common soldiers were seldom politically conscious and were indeed usually illiterate. The soldiers of the Republic— aroused by a new sense of freedom, feeling themselves to be citizens, aware of possessing rights (did not the Declaration say so?), half of them able to read, most of them until recently civilians, many of them volunteers—would not, like professionals, deliver their full powers merely at a word of command, but had also to have an idea of why they were fighting and to believe that the war was conducted for their own good.

Few allegations therefore are more doubtful than the theory of some modern French nationalists, who maintain that the Republican armies were not politically minded, and fought simply for the glory of France and the frustration of foreigners, while chatterers and cutthroats reigned in Paris. The armies were by no means likely to underrate the glory of France, but it was the new France, not the old, that aroused their emotions. They were nationalistic, but the "nation" in those days was a word of challenge to the old order.

Bouchotte and the War Office, under direction of the Committee, spent every effort to keep up revolutionary enthusiasm among the troops. Their agents were in every camp. The government took the side of enlisted men against officers, and of the volunteers against the decaying professional regiments. Between June and the following March, with funds assigned to him by the Committee, Bouchotte inundated the armies with 15,000 subscriptions to Paris newspapers. He virtually subsidized Hébert by buying up, and sending to the front, thousands of copies of Hébert's vitriolic paper, the *Père Duchesne*. He circulated 400,000 copies of the Constitution and its accompanying Declaration of Rights. Carnot himself eventually founded and edited a special journal to be read by soldiers.

The representatives on mission, men like Levasseur, had many tasks, but none was more important than their work as evangelists. They carried out the gospel from Paris. They preached hatred of tyrants, detestation of aristocrats, rigor toward suspects, dark threats for the lukewarm and the faint-hearted. They appealed to the soldier's attachment to the broad changes brought in by the Revolution, and from this vague feeling tried to create something more concrete and more impassioned—loyalty to the Republic. And they sought to identify, in the soldier's mind, the Republic with the Mountain, the purged Convention, and the Committee of Public Safety.

August 1793 saw the course of the war, for the Republic, at its nadir.

In the south the Spaniards and Sardinians threatened invasion. Toulon was occupied by the English on August 29. Lyons and

Bordeaux were unsubdued. Blood flowed freely in the Vendée. But the chief menace was in the north and east, along the borders that separated France from the Austrian Netherlands and the German Rhineland. The Prussians had taken Mainz and pushed the Army of the Rhine back into Alsace. The Austrians and British, led respectively by the Prince of Coburg and the Duke of York, had captured Condé and Valenciennes. The Army of the North stood by seemingly powerless to resist.

Condé and Valenciennes were fortified towns about five miles apart, on the upper waters of the Scheldt, just within the frontier, and little more than a hundred miles north of Paris. It was only a step from Valenciennes over low watersheds into the valleys that led southward. Austrian cavalry patrols rode through the northern departments, some ranging as far south as Saint-Quentin. The Allies, early in August, had over 160,000 men along the Netherlands border between the Moselle and the North Sea. The force opposed to them was neither so numerous nor so compact.

It seemed that York and Coburg, ignoring the other forts in the line which they had pierced, would drive on with overwhelming forces toward their main objective, Paris. Arriving there in a few days, they could disperse the Convention and annihilate the Committee of Public Safety; and since the country was already torn by anarchy and civil war, holding together only through the predominance of Paris, the Allies could then proceed to dictate such peace terms as they chose. The Revolution might be quashed, and the Bourbons restored to a weakened and partitioned France. In that case an era of relative peace might conceivably have followed; there might have been no Napoleon; and without Napoleon all history since 1800 would undoubtedly have been different, not only in France, but even more significantly in Germany and Central Europe.

As a matter of fact, to the amazement of the French, York and Coburg did nothing of the kind. The Duke of York was under orders from London to capture Dunkirk, which the English hoped to gain as a permanent base on the Continent. The Duke therefore strained at the leash, replied to all Coburg's remonstrances by citing his instructions, participated for a few days in minor actions near Valenciennes, and on August 12 marched his English, Hanoverian and Hessian regiments to the sea. The Austrians, turning in the opposite direction, threatened Le Quesnoy and Maubeuge. Thus the main Allied army broke in two, pursuing centrifugal lines, losing the strategic advantage of concentrated power,

This gigantic blunder, which can be traced to William Pitt and the necessities of English politics, saved the French Republic from extinction. The Allied armies, it became clear, suffered as much as the French from internal discord, military incompetence and political interference. The crowning irony is that, had York and Coburg combined in an attack on Paris, the English could probably have taken Dunkirk with the other spoils, whereas they lost it by being hasty and independent.

The French now had an opportunity for a counterattack. What form this should take was a question which, in the absence of a general staff in command of the eleven armies, had finally to be answered by the Committee of Public Safety and especially Carnot. Some authors have therefore attributed to Carnot's strategical ideas the victories of 1793.

Carnot, however, did not take the initiative in drawing up strategic plans. He was not even in accord with the advanced military thought of the time. Writers for a generation had been calling for a new system of warfare. They recommended the abandonment of the old strategy based on fortresses, each with a full garrison and store of provisions, commanding some geographically important position—town, valley, road or bridge. The new idea was to assemble large mobile masses, if necessary by depleting the garrisons and leaving some spots uncovered; to support these great armies by requisitions on the country; and to decide the issue less by intricate maneuvering of small units over a wide area than by gathering an overwhelming force in a single field. The French Revolution and the nationalizing of warfare made this new strategy feasible. The great Napoleonic victories embodied it.

Carnot was by training an engineer, and was partial to fortresses. While still a captain in the old army he had spoken out against the innovators. His arguments were both technical and humanitarian. The principle of fortification, he maintained, should be preserved because it was useful chiefly in defensive wars, which alone were just; because it put aggressors at a disadvantage, re-

CARNOT

duced slaughter to a minimum, and lightened the hardships of the defending troops by providing food reserves, living quarters and hospitals. As late as the spring of 1793, before joining the Committee of Public Safety, Carnot, sent on mission to help save Condé and Valenciennes, gave no evidence of wishing to employ the newer strategic ideas.

When York and Coburg parted, and a new French plan was called for, it came not from Carnot but from the professional officers on Houchard's staff. The plan was to enlarge the Army of the North into one of the overwhelming mobile masses that the new strategy favored. Troops were to be transferred from the Armies of the Rhine and the Moselle, which, filled in with recruits and volunteers, were temporarily to assume a purely defensive position. Carnot remonstrated; he thought the Army of the North large enough already. Others on the Committee, Barère, Couthon and Saint-André, were partisans of the new policy. Carnot yielded to the advice of colleagues, generals and representatives on mission; and the Committee of Public Safety sent the necessary orders to the Rhine and the Moselle.

To strengthen the Army of the North the garrisons were withdrawn from a number of towns. Lille and others protested; the inhabitants were not used to the new system; and local revolutionary leaders suspected some kind of snare. They had to be pacified by representatives on mission, of whom at this time there were no less than twelve attached to the Army of the North. Twelve such sovereign personages were likely to cause confusion, but in the prevailing chaos and atmosphere of suspicion there were difficulties which only a member of the Convention could overcome.

Carnot followed developments at the front rather passively, too sensible to interfere unduly with the men on the spot. Houchard's council of war decided first to strike at the Dutch at Menin, then to move north to Furnes, thus encircling the Duke of York and cutting off his retreat from Dunkirk. This move, if successful, would put both the Dutch and British forces out of commission, leaving the French then free to turn south against the Austrians. But Houchard at the last moment changed his mind. He was cautious and dispirited; the plan was risky, and failure might mean the guillotine; the troops, moreover, in preliminary engagements showed themselves hard to manage in orderly fashion, being likely to fall into confusion in executing difficult movements, or to be distracted by the chance to plunder. Houchard therefore decided to proceed directly against the English.

This change of plan was fatal to Houchard. He announced it in the letter which Carnot received on September 5. Carnot in reply expressed disappointment that the plan to surround the English had been given up, but gave Houchard a free hand, and reaffirmed his confidence in him. He instructed him to avoid dispersing his forces, and added somewhat ambiguously: "Try to deal the enemy a terrible blow, but without risking any decisive action if it be at all doubtful."

Houchard, in extenuation for what soon happened, could plead that Carnot had always set great emphasis on the relief of Dunkirk. Dunkirk had assumed in Carnot's eyes a place out of all proportion to its military value. For one thing, Dunkirk was a fortified town; but it had become also a political symbol. Carnot, like other ardent revolutionaries in 1793, greatly exaggerated the signs of unrest that he saw in England. He adjured Houchard to consider the campaign more in a political than in a military light. If the Duke of York should be foiled before Dunkirk, he wrote, the English people would inevitably rise up in revolution against George III.

The Army of the North joined battle on September 6. Its main attack was directed against York's "covering army," a force of Hanoverians that shielded the troops before Dunkirk. The French outnumbered these Hanoverians by more than two to one; yet the fighting was indecisive for two days. Military critics agree that Houchard lost his advantage by excessive scattering of his divisions. Finally on the third day, near the village of Hondschoote, in a sharp struggle in which the representatives Levasseur and Delbret rode in the front lines, and numerous acts of heroism were reported (as of a French soldier who, when one arm was cut off, rushed on waving the other, shouting "Vive la République!"), the Hanoverian force was routed and withdrew pell-mell with heavy losses across the frontier to Furnes.

Two courses were now open to Houchard. He could pursue the Hanoverians, take Furnes, and block the Duke of York, who prepared to retreat as soon as the covering army began to yield.

Or he could send men north to harry the retiring English, who were obliged to hug their way along the coast. Levasseur urged him to move on to Furnes. Houchard replied with unaccustomed tartness: "You are not an army man." Levasseur, accepting the rebuke, went about the less martial business of restoring order to the disorganized French battalions. Houchard, declaring that his men were fatigued, that the advance to Furnes would be risky, and that swollen marshes obstructed the routes to the sea, in the end did nothing. The Hanoverians were not pursued, and the Duke of York's force escaped intact.

Hondschoote was therefore a somewhat qualified victory, though Dunkirk was saved, and for the first time in months the Allies were worsted. Had Carnot been right, and had the English people now overthrown their government, the French gains at Hondschoote might have been sufficient. As it was, however, though York was seriously disabled, having abandoned most of his artillery and supplies before the walls of Dunkirk, and lost large numbers of his Hanoverian contingents, his army was nevertheless still in existence. The higher strategy of the campaign had miscarried. The Army of the North had not functioned as a mobile mass. Its achievement was small in view of the superiority of its numbers. Houchard had not unified its efforts, nor had he moved it when a rapid blow might have been decisive. He was not entirely at fault, considering the intractableness of his troops, the division of authority produced by the presence of twelve representatives on mission, and Carnot's explicit warning against embarking on dangerous enterprises. He was, indeed, pleased with the results because he had expected little.

The Committee of Public Safety congratulated Houchard on his "brilliant success." But Carnot, Bouchotte and the others were not satisfied. They believed, like Levasseur and other representatives on the spot, that the English force could have been captured or destroyed. Their discontent deepened when, in the next few days, Houchard involved himself in further bloody and inconclusive fighting. Nevertheless, for two weeks Hondschoote was celebrated in Paris as a victory. No adverse comment came from the representatives on mission—until September 20, when Hentz, who was one of them, arrived in the capital to accuse Houchard of treachery. The Committee issued the order for his removal two days later.

It was undoubtedly wise to remove Houchard. But more was to follow.

An established government, when it removes a general, can afford to admit that it made an error in appointing him. Revolutionary governments cannot so easily admit mistakes. Had the Committee simply given out that Houchard was unequal to his task it would have told the truth, but almost every Jacobin in France would then have denounced as incompetent the Committee which made such a selection. Had the Committee declared that one cause of the troubles in the north was the indiscipline of the troops it would again have stated a fact, for which it had ample evidence in its own files; but it was not politically expedient in September 1793 to cast public aspersions on common soldiers. Patriots were convinced that their armies were fierce with a holy rage against tyrants, that moral enthusiasm was the chief means by which victories were won, and that defeats were to be explained by the perfidy of commanders.

Houchard was charged, therefore, not only with failure but with treason. A few in the Convention remonstrated at his dismissal. They feared that the removal of army officers was reaching the point of endangering the country. Their protests raised the parliamentary crisis of September 25 which has been described. To Houchard's ruin, his case became part of the larger question of the stability of the Committee. Barère, Billaud, Robespierre and Saint-André, fearing that the Committee would lose the confidence of the Convention, were unanimous in asserting Houchard's guilt. Did they believe in it themselves? Perhaps they did —these were the days that produced the Law of Suspects. Perhaps not—even Collot for a moment doubted whether the evidence against Houchard offered anything but a presumption.

Houchard was accused of not having followed, in the Dunkirk campaign, the plan of the Committee of Public Safety, and of having failed, through this disobedience, to "hurl the English into the sea." The issues here were confused. The plan which Barere and the others claimed as their own had not originated with the Committee; it had been conceived by one of Houchard's aides, Berthelmy, who was now under arrest with his chief. The Committee had sanctioned the plan, which thus became the official program of the government. Houchard, apparently with the approval of at least one representative on mission, Duquesnoy, had then changed his strategy and decided to attack the Anglo-Hanoverian army directly. He notified Carnot of the change, and received Carnot's somewhat reluctant approval. But after the plan was changed in a council of war on August 30, he had waited until September 3 to send the news to Carnot. Carnot answered on the 5th, and before the reply could reach him Houchard was already engaged in the battle of Hondschoote. It seemed in retrospect that Houchard had wished to take from the Committee the power of independent decision. Carnot had approved, but his approval had nothing to do with the events that followed.

Barère and the others, in denouncing Houchard before the Convention, concealed the fact that their colleague Carnot, on the eve of Hondschoote, had endorsed Houchard's new plan and reaffirmed his confidence in Houchard's judgment. They concealed, too, the true origin of the first plan. They thus presented a false picture of the situation, a picture in which a wise government was frustrated by a disobedient general. The justification for this procedure, if any, is that it was better for the Republic to lose Houchard than to lose faith in the Committee of Public Safety. Houchard was to be sacrificed to the stability of the government.

To prove him treacherous as well as disobedient the Committee produced a packet of letters found at his headquarters. Some of these letters had been addressed to him by the Prince of Hohenlohe and other foreign commanders. They dealt with such matters as the exchange of prisoners; one, from a small German ruler, raised the problem of how French forces could purchase supplies in Germany when Germans would not accept their assignats and the French government prohibited the export of goods. But the letters were written with the ceremonious politeness of the old régime. Enraged sans-culottes found their citizen-general apparently the dear friend of foreign aristocrats. It is incredible that the educated men of the Convention and the Committee should have shared in this ridiculous idea.

But the cry went up, "He is the friend of our enemies!" He was the new Custine, the new Dumouriez, one more in the long line of hypocrites and seducers of the people. And the Committee—even if it knew, as Carnot must have known, that Houchard's fault was not his own, that the error lay rather with the men who, determined to have a non-noble general, had hurriedly raised him to a position for which he was unqualified—could not face the truth, still less make it public, without exposing itself to the wrath of patriots and perhaps itself incurring denunciations for treason.

So Houchard went to prison, where he found twenty-four other generals already confined. The bewildered old soldier protested his innocence, boasted of his plebeian birth, pointed to the scars that marred his face and body, declared that he had never wished to be more than a captain of dragoons. Nothing availed; on the 15th of November he appeared before the Revolutionary Tribunal, and on the next day went to the guillotine.

He had commanded in the north for only six weeks. The first brief experiment with a non-noble general had ended in tragedy and failure.

The Republic now faced a tremendous interrogation mark. In a world where generalship had been the business of aristocrats, could a régime that denounced aristocracy conduct a successful war? Was it possible to find commoners who could lead armies? Could the middle class, which had replaced the aristocracy in so many other ways, now replace it on the battlefield? If it could, then aristocracy, as known before the Revolution, would have lost still another reason for existence. If not, democratic ideas would remain a dream.

The right men were soon found. Representatives on mission sometimes commissioned promising young officers tentatively as generals, like medieval kings knighting the valiant on the field. It was thus that Bonaparte became a brigadier at the end of 1793. Sometimes the agents of Bouchotte, acting through local patriotic clubs, sent in glowing reports to the War Office. Bouchotte and Carnot digested and compared these reports, confirmed appointments, rectified mistakes. Somehow they discerned the men of ability amid the vapors of patronage, favoritism and suspicion. It may be doubted whether any other government, in an equal time, has matched their record, for before the end of 1793 they raised to the rank of general (among others) Bonaparte, Jourdan, Hoche, Pichegru, Masséna, Moreau, Davout, Lefèvre, Perignon,

Serrurier, Augereau and Brune. One of these became an emperor, eight others marshals of his empire; the remaining three (Hoche, Pichegru, Moreau) rose to be distinguished commanders under the Republic.

These twelve were all new men. Their average age in 1793 was thirty-three—four years less than that of the twelve who made up the Committee. A few were well enough born to have been officers in the Bourbon army. None, however, could have attained high rank under the old régime. They were among the first to profit from the removal of class barriers from their careers. In that respect they were successors to Houchard, and it seems fitting that Bonaparte, when he came to power, cleared Houchard's memory and granted his widow a pension.

Jourdan was Houchard's immediate successor in September 1793. Twenty-four years younger than Houchard, though possessed of as much experience in leading armies, he was a firm believer in the Revolution, which had snatched him from a humdrum life. His father, a surgeon, was of a profession then only coming into repute. The young Jourdan had worked for an uncle in the silk business, run away at sixteen to join the army, served six years as a common soldier, fought five campaigns in the War of American Independence, and then, seeing no military career before him, had retired to Limoges and set up a dry-goods shop. Revolutionists at Limoges made him a lieutenant in their national guard in 1790. Three years later he was a major general. He led a division at Hondschoote, and on September 24, aged thirty-one, accepted the command over the Army of the North, to which was soon added the Army of the Ardennes. Jourdan was confident in his own powers, full of zeal for the Revolution and of faith in the future. Otherwise he might excusably have been downcast, considering the fate of Custine and of Houchard in the office which he now took over.

He reached his new headquarters on the evening of the 25th. Carnot was already there, just arrived from Paris to meet face to face the man in whom the Committee now placed its hopes. He was won over to him at once. The young general was modest in manner, deferred to the judgment of the Committee, expressed appreciation for the services of the civilian representatives on mission. He declined, however, to arrange immediately with Carnot a plan of operations. He needed time, for, like Houchard before him, he found affairs in a high state of disorder. Carnot could not linger, and left for Paris within two days.

Jourdan had no means of knowing how many men he commanded, nor could he tell who his subordinate generals were. Most of Houchard's staff was under arrest. Some divisions had no brigadiers at all. The cavalry had no commander. At Maubeuge, a stronghold threatened by the Austrians, there were 17,000 men; but of the four generals in charge one was wounded, one arrested, and one sick; of the fourth, for some days, Jourdan did not know the existence. When Jourdan tried to send another from Dunkirk, the representatives there interfered to prevent him.

On September 29 the Austrians crossed the river Sambre and besieged Maubeuge. That day in the French army two hundred horses were reported dead of starvation; a plot was discovered at Lille to betray the city to the Allies; and at Maubeuge, according to the representatives there, conspirators were undermining the morale of the recruits.

It was vital for the Republic to save Maubeuge. Coburg occupied Valenciennes, Condé and Le Quesnoy. With Maubeuge he would have a compact group of fortresses, a base for an advance on Paris, or at the least a place to winter on French soil. In proportion as Coburg succeeded, the Committee of Public Safety would be accused of having failed. If Coburg took Maubeuge the Committee might be ruined; moderates would blame its policy of suspending army officers; radicals would cry out for the thousandth time, "We are betrayed!" The Jacobins and the Commune would again storm the Convention, demand more terror, more vigor and more purity—perhaps (who knows?) even Robespierre would find himself branded as the slave of despots. In short, politics, as well as the public safety, demanded that the Committee be triumphant.

Yet what was there to fight with? About 130,000 nondescripts —ragamuffins and heroes, veteran troops and boys just off the farm, strewn along a front from the Ardennes to the sea, and led by an ex-private and dry-goods dealer thirty-one years old.

Carnot rejoined this host at Péronne on October 7. He experienced for himself the difficulties that his generals faced. Food was hard to get. Buyers for the army, scouring the northern departments, competed with those of the Commune of Paris for the farmers' crops. The agents of the Commune usually won out; the Committee decreed, while Carnot was away, that requisitions for Paris must take precedence over those made for the army. By herculean effort a six-weeks supply of provisions was assembled for the soldiers on whom the existence of the government depended.

Horses were desperately needed. Without them there could be no cavalry, no usable cannon, and no movement of heavy loads. Jourdan, like Houchard, demanded eight hundred more. In time several hundred came in, but some meanwhile had died, and to add to the confusion a great many of the new ones arrived without harness. The Committee created twenty special commissioners to travel through the country with no other function than to requisition horses.

Munitions were scarce, and many soldiers were unarmed. Carnot sent for fifteen thousand bayonets. On his first day at Péronne he wrote to Paris asking for the muskets available there, and urging that men be sent to Lille to work in the repair shops. Artillery was immobilized by the lack of horses. There was an alarming shortage of cannon balls and cartridges. Carnot, on discovering it, arrested the general responsible, Merenveüe, charging him with a plot to paralyze the approaching campaign. Merenveüe soon cut his own throat in prison. Jourdan, in his memoirs written years later when he had become more conservative, declared that Merenveüe had been simply negligent, though it is hard to see how negligence in such circumstances could be excused.

Clothing was in worse condition than armaments. Many battalions were in rags. The worst shortage was in shoes. Some shoes were shoddy, palmed off through collusion of government agents with the contractors. Veterans had worn their footgear out; recruits sometimes arrived in their customary shoes of wood. Carnot reported to the Committee that three-quarters of the men were barefoot. Two days later the army received eight thousand pairs.

The Levy in Mass was beginning to swell the ranks, but the new men were not of much value. Undisciplined, untrained, at times unarmed, hardly knowing each other, ignorant of what to do in a battle, they could be employed only to relieve the better troops in places where there was no danger. Half of them deserted soon after reaching their encampments. The experienced troops, if they gave patriotic cheers, viewed them also with disgust. Tattered campaigners grumbled at the fine uniforms of the new arrivals. Regular soldiers resented the partiality shown by the government to the citizens in arms. The new recruits, Carnot wrote to the Committee, "are perfectly useless, for they do not so much as have sticks in their hands; they are fine looking, but they only consume provisions that are hard to procure."

One incident well shows the troubles of the time, the myriad fears, and the close watch kept by the Committee over details of every kind. Word reached the green room that some of the brandy lately dispatched to the north was poisoned. Robespierre, Barère and Hérault sent a circular letter to the representatives concerned, asking them to investigate quietly. Duquesnoy immediately shipped some of the suspected brandy from Péronne to Paris. The bottles were turned over to the chemist Berthollet and the mathematician Monge, Carnot's onetime teacher. These two, in the presence of Prieur of the Côte-d'Or acting for the Committee, submitted the brandy to laboratory tests, pronounced it free of poison, and drank some themselves to demonstrate their good faith. The Committee rushed a special messenger with the good news to Péronne.

Meanwhile Jourdan had been making his preparations for the battle. French columns were moving toward Maubeuge. Fifty thousand men (the rest of the 130,000 being either useless or stationed elsewhere) in ragged garments, with lean horses, led by novices, their artillery and their cavalry both generaled by hastily found substitutes, marched and countermarched for a week to find advantageous positions, and on October 13 prepared to fall, as Jourdan said, "upon that horde of slaves, whose courage comes from our weak resistance to their efforts and the perfidy of our chiefs." Coburg had about 65,000 including the Duke of York's force and some Dutch regiments under the Prince of Orange, who was not an obedient subordinate. The French were counting on their 17,000 compatriots shut up in Maubeuge, expecting them to attack the Allied rear as soon as operations were opened.

On the day before the battle Jourdan published a proclamation to the army just received from the Committee. It announced the fall of Lyons a few days before. It was an early specimen of modern war propaganda and was signed by all those of the Twelve who were then in Paris.

Paris, 20th of the 1st month, Year II
of the Republic [October 11, 1793]

Republicans,

The army of the Republic has entered in triumph into Lyons. Traitors and rebels have been cut to pieces. The standard of liberty floats upon and purifies the city's walls. See in it a presage of your victory.

Victory belongs to courage. It is yours. Strike, exterminate the satellites of tyrants. Cowards! They have never known how to conquer by force or by valor, but only by the treasons that they have bought. They are covered by your blood, and still more by that of your wives and children. Strike! Let none escape from your just vengeance. Your country watches you, the Convention supports your generous devotion. In a few days tyrants will be no more, and the Republic will owe to you its happiness and its glory. Vive la République!

HÉRAULT, COLLOT D'HERBOIS, BILLAUD-VARENNE,
B. BARÈRE, SAINT-JUST, ROBESPIERRE.

From this timely exhortation, from the feeling that the home front was solidly behind them and that rebels were being punished, from memories of success at Hondschoote, from faith in Jourdan, who was popular with his men, from the sight of Carnot, war lord of the Republic, toiling indefatigably in their midst, the French now faced their enemy with eagerness and determination, with a spirit better than at any time hitherto in the war, and a patriotic enthusiasm that seemed strange and fanatical to the old-fashioned Austrian commanders.

The skill of Jourdan and the fierce ardor of his men, plus Coburg's timidity and inability to profit by his enemy's mistakes, overcame the handicaps under which the French army labored, and won for it, on October 16, the famous battle of Wattignies. The fighting lasted for two days, until Coburg somewhat unnecessarily retreated in a heavy fog. His successful retirement meant that Wattignies, like Hondschoote, was not a decisive triumph. The republican army, though its patriotism was increasing and some of its new leaders giving promise of success, was not yet

a smoothly functioning organization. Miscarriages and misunderstandings made its victories incomplete.

Fromentin bungled with the left wing. He was a patriot, Jourdan boldly reported, who "believed firmly what was constantly
repeated in the tribunes of the Convention and the Jacobins, that
the whole talent of a general consists in charging headlong against
the enemy troops wherever found." Carnot added to the confusion
by causing Jourdan, against his better judgment, to attack prematurely in the center. Useless slaughter resulted, and the day
might have been lost had Coburg seized his advantage. More
trouble arose on the right wing, where Gratien, ordered to advance his brigade, retreated instead. For this flat disobedience he
was arrested by Carnot. He was tried later in a revolutionary
court, but was acquitted.

The worst misfortune for the French army was that the troops
in Maubeuge failed to come to its assistance. Had they done so,
the Allied force might have been divided and a large part of it
destroyed. That they did not was due to the decision of their
generals, who concluded, on hearing the sound of distant cannon,
that the Allies were trying to lure the garrison into a trap. The
man thought to be responsible for persuading the others to accept
this idea was soon guillotined in Paris. There is reason to believe
that he really intended to let Jourdan go unhelped.

But Maubeuge was saved, as Dunkirk had been before it, even
if the victory was somewhat unsatisfying, and the incompetence
of the enemy one of its main causes. Carnot wrote a glowing message to the Convention, praising the troops, eulogizing Jourdan.
"We have just entered Maubeuge," he said, "to the acclamations
of the people and of the large garrison that we have delivered."
He himself described this letter as "succinct." It was something
less than candid.

He sent a more confidential and more truthful dispatch to the
Committee on the same day. "Triumph of liberty, glory to the
arms of the Republic!" So he began, but his real news was dis-
quieting. The people of Maubeuge, it appeared, were not very
anxious to be saved. "The citizens of Maubeuge have not received
us with the transports which it seems they should manifest toward
their liberators." They were not very good Jacobins, not even
good republicans. "We must work to electrify these regions a little

and to rebuild the public spirit." This was a recommendation to bring the Terror to Maubeuge.

Carnot praised Jourdan highly to the Committee. Jourdan likewise extolled Carnot in his report to the War Office. Jourdan, said Carnot, was an exceptionally able man—also "a brave and honest sans-culotte." Nevertheless, Carnot went on, "success was necessary to him: he was lost if he failed; he was already being denounced as a traitor, and so was I, for withdrawing garrisons from the cities to join them to the main army." Even Carnot, to say nothing of Jourdan, looked upon the abyss into which Houchard had been swallowed. These men walked precariously upon a brink, living in mortal danger; but the most immediate danger was from their fellow revolutionists, not from the reactionaries and the foreign powers. The Jacobins had to win victories in order to protect themselves from each other. They had to check counter-revolution, or be denounced for supporting it themselves. Their fear of each other drove them relentlessly to more extremes; hence came the terrific crescendo of the Terror.

The Committee of Public Safety sat up the whole night of the 18th-19th, awaiting word from the north, in a state of helpless suspense, since the telegraph to Lille was not yet finished. Carnot's two letters arrived together at six o'clock. By the late twilight of an October morning the Committee learned that the Austrians were retreating. Reassured by this knowledge all except Billaud went home to bed. Carnot's confidential report was quietly filed away; the public announcement was read by Billaud to the assembled Convention a few hours later. The Convention, kept ignorant of details, purposely not even told how many troops had been engaged, applauded wildly what it took to be a colossal triumph, and decreed that the Army of the North had deserved well of its country.

Seen from the Tuileries, the campaign in the north, though of the utmost importance, was only one phase in an immensely complicated game. Every day the green table was piled with dispatches from all over France—from Toulon, Lyons, the Vendée, from commissioners charged with raising horses or recruiting men, from the Armies of the West, the Rhine, the Alps, the Eastern Pyrenees. Against this background the battle of Wattignies became hardly more than an incident. Like Hondschoote it settled nothing finally.

To save Dunkirk and Maubeuge men had been transferred from the Armies of the Rhine and the Moselle. The Prussians in those regions had then risen from their torpor. Almost simultaneously with the Allied retreat in Flanders an Austro-Prussian force broke through the French lines about Wissembourg. Alsace was threatened. Invasion checked in the north seemed now impending in the east. The French armies there, as elsewhere, were poorly organized, inadequately armed, irregularly fed, in part shoeless and in rags, commanded by perplexed beginners, and harassed by local politicians.

Various ways were open for meeting the new danger.

One was to strengthen the direct resistance. For this purpose the Committee decided to employ one of its own number. On October 17 Saint-Just was sent on mission to Alsace.

Another was to undermine the coalition by creating an alliance to oppose it. Reverting to old-fashioned diplomacy, the French Republic, which was ideologically so pure as to keep ambassadors only in Switzerland and the United States, entered into secret negotiations with the Turkish Empire. French officers went to Constantinople to instruct the sultan's sans-culottes. A sum of 4,000,000 livres was offered to the Turks to attack the Hapsburg dominions along the Danube.

A third method was to follow up the success at Wattignies by an offensive campaign against Coburg. Perhaps Condé and Valenciennes could be won back. At any rate the Austro-Anglo-Dutch-Hanoverian armies might thus be kept from reinforcing the Allied forces in the Rhineland. Orders were therefore sent to Jourdan a week after Wattignies, instructing him to pursue Coburg but not to do anything risky, to surround the enemy but not to divide his own force, to carry on a vigorous offensive but not to advance far into Belgium. Jourdan considered these orders impracticable; so did the representative Duquesnoy. Military historians have been of the same opinion.

Tension developed between the Committee and the victor of Wattignies. The Committee demanded action; it had reasons of general strategy which were more apparent in the Tuileries than in Flanders; and, being subject to agitation and clamor in Paris, it could not afford politically to assume a passive rôle. Jourdan insisted that the Army of the North must go into winter quarters. He rehearsed the long tale of its afflictions: desertion continued; dysentery broke out, attributed by the doctors to bad bread; the hospitals were overflowing; unshod soldiers, as the weather grew colder, were wrapping their feet with straw. Moreover, as usual, it was raining in Flanders; the stores were damp, and the roads all but impassable. Jourdan declared that before he would lead his men to butchery he would resign.

The Committee at this juncture was not quite the group of obtuse civilians and stubborn dictators that some historians have drawn. Jourdan's offer of resignation was waved aside as unworthy of a patriot. He was given more liberty in executing his instructions. On November 17 he was authorized to follow his own plan. The army therefore went into winter quarters to rebuild its strength for the spring. But strained relations continued. When the Committee ordered 15,000 men sent from the north to the Vendée Jourdan was slow to comply, complaining of the weakness of his army and pointing to the danger of an Austrian counter-maneuver. The Committee protested. The Republic, it wrote to him, is paying 140,000 men under your command. Where are they? Jourdan could only reply that whatever the books said in the War Office the number of his men was nowhere near 140,000. Desertions, sickness and fallacious accounting must be to blame. The Committee reprimanded him for not keeping it informed, denounced the prevalence of graft and corruption, observed that enemy patrols were again reaching Saint-Quentin, and on January 10 put Jourdan under arrest. The order was written by Carnot, who had seen Jourdan's merit at Wattignies.

It is hard to see any good reasons for the removal of Jourdan, who was both competent and loyal. Perhaps those are right who say that Robespierre and others wanted to put their favorite Pichegru in his place. On this matter, as on many others, our knowledge comes from rumors and allegations. For the historian, one of the most distressing features of the French Revolution is that the revolutionists, excited, factious, unscrupulous in their use of means, are almost the worst possible candidates for the witness stand.

Jourdan escaped the fate of Houchard. He was sent into retirement at his home in Limoges, promised a pension, and told that he might some day be reemployed. Meanwhile he returned to his dry-goods shop, where, according to the story, he displayed in a prominent place his sword and his uniform as a commander-in-chief, awaiting the day when he should again be called upon to wear them. That day, as it turned out, was not far off.

The battles of Hondschoote and Wattignies put the Committee of Public Safety more solidly in power. The Revolutionary Government proclaimed on October 10 could now enjoy the credit for success. But victory was only beginning; the enemy was still on French soil; the government could still appeal to national emergency to justify its dictatorial methods. Enough had been done to make the Terror seem useful, not enough to make it seem superfluous. After Wattignies the party of the Mountain felt itself less desperately on the defensive. The Mountaineers could proceed to something more constructive than the repelling of invaders. Torn by distractions, fighting among themselves, resorting often to pure expedient, obstructed by counter-revolution and never forgetful of the war, they could still in some measure begin to create the France that they desired.

As the Twelve became more firmly entrenched, and needed less vigilance at the Jacobins and in the Convention, some of them could safely turn their backs on Paris. For a time at the end of October it looked as if only five would be left in the city, though the number never actually fell below six. Couthon had been in Auvergne and Lindet in Normandy since August. After the vote of confidence on September 25 Saint-André and Prieur of the Marne went on mission to Brittany. Carnot was absent during the Wattignies campaign. Upon his return Saint-Just and Hérault-Séchelles departed separately for Alsace. Prieur of the Côte-d'Or was in Nantes for a few days. Collot d'Herbois stormed off to Lyons on October 31. Since Billaud was away at other times, there were only two of the Twelve who never executed a mission in the provinces—Robespierre, who was indispensable for watching over Paris politics, and Barère, who was indispensable in the administrative business of the Committee.

We have observed Carnot in action in Flanders. We shall have to follow the others to their various destinations. There we shall see them as individuals away from the crowded stage of Paris. We shall see also what the Terror of which they were emissaries really meant in some parts of France.

Meanwhile in the next chapter it is necessary to linger with those who remained in Paris, with Robespierre primarily, but with Barère and Billaud also, and the others who at one time or another were with them until the end of 1793.

CHAPTER V

The "Foreign Plot" and 14 Frimaire

B Y OCTOBER the work of the Committee of Public Safety was settling down into something like a smooth business routine. The normal day began at nine o'clock in the morning and lasted until after midnight. Carnot was present virtually all the time; the others constantly came and went. Barère and Billaud spent hours at the Convention, which met in the afternoon. Robespierre spoke there on great occasions. Lindet and Prieur of the Côte-d'Or sat regularly with the Subsistence Commission. Robespierre and Collot d'Herbois were active at the Jacobin society, which met in the evening, usually adjourning at about ten o'clock. All were busy during the day with their own clerks and secretaries. In these circumstances it was late at night before the Committee of Public Safety could formally assemble.

The members had no leisure, hardly enough time for sleep, and practically no home life. Only one, the wealthy Hérault de Séchelles, was an old resident of Paris. The others, coming from the provinces, put up in rooming houses or furnished apartments. Robespierre and Prieur of the Côte-d'Or were bachelors; Saint-Just was engaged; Barère's republican sentiments had lost him his wife; the wives of the others were not all in Paris. Robespierre lived plainly with his friends the Duplays, at 366 rue Saint-Honoré, near the Jacobin club. Carnot, Barère and Lindet were among his neighbors, all three having quarters within a few minutes' walk in the same street. Saint-Just and Saint-André were housed a few blocks away in the rue Gaillon, at the Hôtel des États-Unis.

The day's work was divided into definite stages. Current questions were discussed first. Deputations and petitioners were then received. So far as possible, to save each other's time, the members took turns at this task of meeting the public. Incoming dispatches were read and distributed early in the day. General deliberation followed, in which the important correspondence was reviewed, measures of "public safety" were decided on, and the decrees to be submitted to the Convention on the next day were considered.

Such at least was the program adopted on September 23. How long it proved practicable is not known.

Each member had a particular kind of business to watch over, but their fields were not sharply delimited, and they had to substitute for each other during absences. Responsibility was collective; anyone might sign papers on any subject. It is therefore difficult to determine the real division of labor. By going to the original manuscripts, however, it is possible to discover who wrote, or was the first to sign, each order. Such a study has been made by Mr. J. M. Thompson, an English authority on Robespierre, for 920 documents issued in the four months after September 23. In this period, it seems clear, Robespierre and Barère took the initiative in matters of police, Carnot, Barère and Prieur of the Côte-d'Or attended to matters of war and munitions, Barère and Saint-André to naval affairs, and Lindet to questions of provisioning and supply. Of the 920 documents, Carnot penned or first signed 272, Barère 244, Prieur of the Côte-d'Or 146, Lindet 91 and Robespierre 77. The figures then drop to 29 for Collot, down through 12 for Saint-Just, to only one for Prieur of the Marne.

Each man had his uses, either in Paris or on mission, but if we except Robespierre, who as political expert protected the others from hostile party onslaughts, the most valuable of the Twelve was probably Barère. Like Carnot, Barère drew up a large number of orders and decrees. Unlike Carnot, he gave close attention to many subjects. He was skilful in phrasing the thoughts of others. He excelled at the conference table. With his prodigious memory and ready speech, he could often, late at night, when everyone was tired and the discussion grew confused, bring a whole problem into focus, summarize the arguments, gather up the pertinent facts, and present the issue that had to be decided. He was, moreover, the liaison man between the Committee and the Convention, where he delivered statements of policy and panegyrics on the army, or demanded terrorist measures with a fluency for which he was nicknamed the "Anacreon of the Guillotine." Barère did not usually tell the exact truth to the Convention. He acquired more of a reputation for personal dishonesty than he deserved, for he told the Convention what the Committee had decided it should hear.

The Committee continued to work through the six ministers of the old Executive Council. On October 26 it created a new Subsistence Commission, which became the headquarters of a vast system of economic regulation. The Committee of General Security, the political police of the Republic, remained a partly autonomous power, though its members had been named by the Committee of Public Safety. The two together were called the governing committees. The guardians of Public Safety, as if anticipating the danger from their fellows of General Security, decreed on October 22 that the two bodies should meet together once a week; but the decision was ineffective, for only about a dozen joint sessions took place in the Year Two.

The Committee of Public Safety, with its auxiliaries, grew very fast in October. On the 4th, for example, it created twelve special couriers in addition to those attached to the ministries. Exactly a week later this number was increased to thirty. Six carriages were kept always ready in the courtyard below. The clerical force expanded so rapidly that many new rooms in the Tuileries had to be taken over. The War Office was already an immense bureaucracy, and the Subsistence Commission soon had hundreds of employees.

As the Twelve settled down to the routine of governing France, the need for harmony among them became imperative. Their responsibility was collective; no one was their chairman or even their leader; their important decisions were all reached in conference over the green table. In the end the Committee was fatally divided. But even in October one rift appeared. It was not in itself fatal, but it was an omen.

At this point a poet enters the story, Fabre d'Eglantine.

He was born plain Fabre, but he had once won a literary contest at the Floral Games of Toulouse (where Barère also had been honored), and had received the usual prize, a wreath of eglantine, or dogrose, worked in gold. Thereafter he added "Eglantine" to his name. Thus distinguished he came to Paris a few years before the Revolution. He wrote some charming sentimental verses which give him a lasting place in French literature. To his contemporaries he was known as a dramatist and actor, author of one or two successes *de scandale,* an unscrupulous climber who attacked the reputations of others to gain publicity for himself. When the Revolution came he was soon involved in it. Elected a deputy to the Convention, he sat with the bolder spirits of the Mountain. Meanwhile he showed signs of a new affluence, notable, if not suspicious, in a man of letters.

The poet of the eglantine played a central rôle in politics, but he also found an outlet for his poetic gifts, putting the final touches on the Revolutionary Calendar. This calendar makes necessary a digression.

The Revolutionists from the first had felt the breath of a new era. They had called 1789 the first year of liberty. Then after September 1792 they referred to the first year of the Republic, and after January 1, 1793, to the second year. These expressions, however, were only a manner of speaking. The old-fashioned calendar continued to be used.

The old calendar had the disadvantage of keeping people's minds upon the Christian tradition. It was a framework to the Christian life, almost impossible to escape from. Its Sundays drew men's minds to church, its Fridays to fasting, its saints' days to models of piety, and to superstition. Its cycle of Lent and Easter, Advent and Christmas, set a religious stamp on the passage of time itself. And of course its method of counting years implied that the birth of Christ was the supreme event in human annals.

On October 5, 1793, the Convention abolished the Christian era for public purposes in France. The practical aim was to weaken the influence of revealed religion. Behind this practical aim lay a profound belief that the proclamation of the Republic was the true turning point in man's destiny. There was also the idea of replacing mere custom by institutions rationally planned. This incredible Convention, in the midst of revolutionary terror, in the two months of September and October, began the codifying of the laws, introduced the metric system, and not only launched a new era but even provided a decimal system for measuring the minutes and hours of each day.

Years were now to be counted from the first day of the French Republic, commonly known as September 22, 1792. The Year Two thus began on September 22, 1793. Each year was divided into twelve months of thirty days (with five days left over, in leap year six), each month into three décades (ten-day "weeks"), each day into ten unnamed "parts," and each such part again into ten, "down to the smallest measurable portion of time." This metric system

for the day was not made immediately mandatory for public officials, and never was observed.

For three weeks patriots wrote such dates as "fifth day of the
third *décade* of the first month of the second year." But Quaker-like
namelessness was extremely confusing. Fabre d'Eglantine supplied
the poetic nomenclature by which the Revolutionary Calendar is
best remembered.

Fabre divided the republican year into four parts, each corresponding to a natural season, and made up of three months
named after natural characteristics. The year began with the three
months of autumn, Vendémiaire, Brumaire and Frimaire, named
respectively for the wine-harvest, for fog, and for cold. Winter
followed, with Nivôse, Pluviôse and Ventôse, the months of snow,
rain and wind. Spring began with Germinal, flowered in Floréal,
and spread through the ripening fields in Prairial. Summer was
ushered in by Messidor, named for crops; passed into Thermidor,
named for heat; and ended with Fructidor, the month of fruit and
fruition. After Fructidor came the five extra days, or six in leap
year, which were to be called the *sans-culottides*.

The days of the *décade* were named *primidi, duodi, tridi*, etc., to
décadi, the Republican Sunday. As every Christian day was dedicated to a saint, so every republican day was set aside for the contemplation of a natural object. Most days were assigned to the
vegetable kingdom, but the *quintidis* were specially associated with
animals, and the *décadis* with agricultural implements. The day on
which all this was enacted, for example (October 24, 1793), was
a *tridi*, the day of pears, 3 Brumaire, Year Two.

On one matter Fabre's proposals received an amendment from
Robespierre. How were the *sans-culottides* to be named? It was
agreed that they should be a time of celebration. Fabre recommended that they be called, in order, the festivals of Genius, Labor,
Actions, Recompenses and Opinion. Robespierre objected. There
must, he said, be a festival of Virtue, and it must take precedence
over the festival of Genius. Was not Cato a better man than Caesar,
or Brutus than Voltaire? The Convention, after discussing this
knotty question, followed Robespierre, discarded Actions, and put
Virtue first.

It may finally be said of this calendar, in which the Revolutionary psychology is so openly revealed, that the festival of Opinion

was to be an exciting day in the Republic. Opinion meant public opinion, which in turn meant the opinions of Jacobins and sans-culottes, other opinions being considered merely private. On the day of Opinion the citizens should be free to say what they pleased about public officials. It was to be a day, as Fabre said, of "songs, allusions, caricatures, lampoons, ironic shafts and wild sarcasms" —in short, a very French occasion. Nothing was to be feared, he went on, from personal vengeance or animosity, for "opinion itself will do justice to the bold detractor of a respected magistrate."

This same Fabre d'Eglantine, who spoke so reassuringly of false denunciation, approached Robespierre and Saint-Just one day in the middle of October, intimating that he had an important matter to reveal. These two, meeting with the Committee of General Security, gave Fabre an interview. He proceeded to denounce a vast foreign conspiracy, a network of secret dealings between hypocritical patriots and foreign spies.

The bugbear of the Foreign Plot thus rose up to haunt the Mountain. Let us note the circumstances clearly. The Mountain at this very time was consummating its victory. The Girondists arrested on June 2 were about to be put on trial; they were guillotined on October 31. Moreover, about a hundred more "moderates" had just been expelled from the Convention, including seventy-odd who had signed a petition in favor of the victims of June 2, and whom Robespierre was now trying to save from the guillotine. The Republic was further purged by the execution of Marie-Antoinette on October 16, the day of Wattignies. After long struggle the Mountaineers had triumphed. Party strife, however, far from being appeased, became if anything more intense. The stalwarts of revolution, with their old enemies gone, found much to object to in each other.

The Foreign Plot was a myth, but it disguised a mass of intrigue that is almost beyond the power of historians to unravel.

Robespierre and Saint-Just were both men with a strong tendency to believe evil of foreigners, and to accept as a fact any conspiracy that they heard of. Fabre d'Eglantine found it easy to persuade them. The story had a certain plausibility. Spies were known to be active. The papers of an English agent had been found, showing lists of Frenchmen to whom he had paid bribes. And Paris undoubtedly swarmed with shady international adventurers, many of whom were on friendly terms with leading Jacobins.

Hérault-Séchelles had long cultivated a mysterious Belgian named Proli, who was rumored to be the illegitimate son of the Austrian minister Kaunitz. Proli for a time lived at Hérault's house, and was Hérault's secretary while Hérault was on the Committee. Proli was a member of the Jacobin club, and probably knew its secrets through his friend Desfieux, who was on its committee of correspondence, and who was in turn a protégé of Collot d'Herbois. There seemed, moreover, to be something off-color about the Spanish grandee Guzmán, the Portuguese Jew Pereira, the Englishmen Rutledge and Boyd—not to mention the mysterious Baron de Batz, a Frenchman, but a royalist and a schemer. Two Jewish bankers, the brothers Frei, who had been ennobled by their Austrian sovereign, were intimate with the outspoken radical Chabot. Chabot was married in September to their sister, who brought him a large dowry. It was whispered that Chabot himself had furnished the dowry as a means of concealing his own ill-gotten gains.

In a somewhat different class, among foreigners, were two members of the Convention: Thomas Paine, a naïve Anglo-American radical, who now found himself in revolutionary complications well over his head, and Anacharsis Cloots, a rich Prussian humanitarian, who described himself as the representative of the human race, and preached international revolution.

The presence in Paris of so many ambiguous characters convinced the Committee of Public Safety that there was in truth a Foreign Plot. This belief in turn enabled Robespierre, as the political strategist for the Committee, to discredit opposing factions by calling them the instruments of hostile powers.

What really was behind the Foreign Plot was the animosity of factional chieftains, and a sordid story of systematic racketeering. Certain prominent Jacobins, through such useful friends as the Baron de Batz, were lining their pockets by attacks on private business. Fabre d'Eglantine was one of this group. The East India Company, the life insurance companies, the water companies, the Bank of Discount were unmercifully milked. The technique was to threaten revolutionary legislation, extort bribes, and speculate in stocks for a fall. When stock companies were abolished in August, greedy eyes turned to the profits that might be made from the liquidation of their assets.

The game was dangerous. Exposure would be the more fatal because of the high principles which all professed. Robespierre, the Incorruptible, and the Committee of Public Safety, most of whom were men of probity, could be expected to be severe.

Fabre d'Eglantine became frightened. As an ally of Danton he had to fear denunciation by the Hébertists, though numerous Hébertists were involved in the same kind of corruption. He decided to attack some of the Hébertists first. To compromise them without spoiling his own chance of profits, he brought the old charge hackneyed by years of use—he accused them of conspiracy with foreigners. The Hébertists were thus menaced by the Law of Suspects. Fabre was free to go on with his own maneuvers, for if the Hébertists should call him a grafter he could now represent himself as a patriot insulted out of pure vengeance. Taking advantage of his position on the committee of the Convention charged with India Company affairs, he falsified the decree by which the liquidation of the company's assets was arranged, and gained for himself and his accomplices a booty of 500,000 livres. The scheme was so successful that even when Chabot squealed to Robespierre a few weeks later, and the India scandal came uncertainly to light, Robespierre believed that the financial intrigues were a part of the insidious foreign conspiracy, and Fabre d'Eglantine, along with Danton, went untouched.

The India scandal was the reality, the Foreign Plot the myth. Both contributed to wreck the Mountain, but the myth had the more immediate and pronounced effect. Providing a means for repressing the Hébertists, it marked a turning point in the Revolution. The drift to the left which had swept away every government of the past five years was now slowed down. It was now the radicals who bore the fatal taint of treason. Significantly enough, one of the first men arrested because of the Foreign Plot was the notorious agitator Maillard, who had led the famous march of the women on Versailles in October 1789.

The Foreign Plot momentarily strengthened the Revolutionary Government, at the cost of dividing the Mountain on which that government was ultimately based. It played into the hands of the Committee of Public Safety; but it introduced even into the Committee the poison of distrust. For Fabre denounced one of the Twelve—Hérault-Séchelles.

Robespierre and Saint-Just did not like Hérault-Séchelles. His noblé birth, his wealth, his elegant manners, his flippancy, his irony, his self-assurance and frank love of pleasure inspired in his two colleagues a chill hauteur, a stiff sense of middle-class disapproval. If there was any sincerity in Hérault's character, as there may have been, since he had made sacrifices for the Revolution, it was so encrusted with affectation as to be well hidden from sight; and certainly Robespierre and Saint-Just would not have the subtlety to detect it. Between two moralists and an esthete there could be little understanding.

When Robespierre and Saint-Just heard Fabre accuse their colleague they were probably neither surprised nor pained. Robespierre had long feared treachery in the Committee. It seemed all too likely that Hérault was selling official secrets to the Austrians through Proli. He could be classified as a Hébertist. He was one of the few whom Hébert never attacked. Like the Hébertists, he seemed to favor an expansionist war. He had his own paid agents in Switzerland. He was the friend of Carrier, a radical soon to be famous as the Terrorist of Nantes.

Hérault was too powerful to be abruptly arrested. On the other hand, if Fabre's charges were true, he could not be kept in the counsels of the Committee. He was sent late in October on mission to the department of the Upper Rhine. Mathiez, the chief authority on the subject, declares that the Committee sent him off in order to be rid of him. Barère, in his *Mémoires,* says that Hérault applied for leave. It is hard to see why the Committee, if it believed Hérault a traitor, should purposely send him with full powers to Alsace, a frontier region, near the battlelines, and on the borders of Switzerland where he was thought to be intriguing. It seems likely that Hérault, sensing trouble, asked to go to Alsace, and that the others in the Committee, who had to treat him as an equal, granted his request as an easy means of removing him from Paris.

The almost simultaneous departure of Hérault, Saint-Just and Collot left in Paris only five of the Twelve—Robespierre, Barère, Carnot, Billaud and Prieur of the Côte-d'Or. They were soon joined by Robert Lindet returning from Normandy. These six were virtually the Committee of Public Safety until almost the end of the year. Together they faced the crisis of what was called De-christianization, built up a kind of planned economy, and advanced a little further along the devious road that led from anarchy toward order.

Robespierre took the lead in dealing with Dechristianization. He saw in it the workings of the Foreign Plot, a shameful travesty of Revolutionary principles, instigated by persons who wished to disgrace the Republic before the world. He called it "ultra-revolutionary," by which he meant that it was a form of counter-revolution. The ideas of universal upheaval and an international crusade against tyrants he also branded as "ultra." He used the corresponding term "citra" for those who thought the Revolution was going too far. "Ultra" and "citra" are of course relative terms. Robespierre himself would be "ultra" to Brissot, Brissot to Lafayette, Lafayette to many who thought themselves soundly revolutionary in 1789. For some people Robespierre would be "citra," falling short of the true aims of the Revolution. He was indeed accused of favoring an outworn fanaticism.

Unless we beg the question by seeing in Robespierre the true norm and essence of the Revolution (as Mathiez tends to do), it is hard to see how the Dechristianizing movement was really ultra-revolutionary. It sprang from authentic Revolutionary sources, the Jacobin club and the Paris Commune, and it was a natural outgrowth of Jacobin ideas. When Robespierre opposed it he was opposing something in the Revolution itself, not something "beyond" the Revolution. Moreover, if revolution means change, overturn, innovation, then the Dechristianizers of 1793 were the revolutionists, and Robespierre was an exponent of counter-revolution, or at least of orderly change arrived at under the authority of government.

The abolition of the Christian calendar, the reduction of the salaries paid to bishops, the laws forbidding the clergy to teach school, all coming in September and October, showed that the National Convention was in a decidedly anti-clerical mood. The spirit of the French Revolution since 1789 and before, with its emphasis on the individual and the state, was opposed to the claims of the Catholic church. On the plea that religion was an individual matter, vows had been forbidden, monasticism destroyed, public and collective worship severely regulated. In the belief that political allegiance should come before religious affiliation, the clergy had been elected like other public officials, and were required to swear an oath of loyalty to the state. Most of them refused the oath, and the church became the firmest pillar of counter-revolution. More laws followed, repressing the clergy for political reasons; and, in the general anarchy of the times, religious believers suffered from much persecution that was not endorsed by the national government. In these circumstances the fact that Christianity was never formally outlawed does not seem very important.

The Jacobins of 1793, including Robespierre, saw little difference between revelation and superstition. At most they would consider Jesus a worthy moralist and good sans-culotte. Billaud-Varenne, it may be remembered, wrote a diatribe against the church before the Revolution started. Barère was observed at the Floral Games to have "sucked in the impure milk of modern philosophy." Saint-André, once a Protestant minister, was now a militant deist. Virtually all the members of the Convention were followers of natural religion; they believed in a Supreme Being conveniently distant, dwelt on man's abundant capacity for natural virtue, and regarded priests as charlatans and revealed mysteries as a delusion. Revealed religion, they would say, was in its death throes, soon to expire before the searching eye of reason.

But the Committee of Public Safety had the task of governing the country, and saw the danger of needlessly arousing antagonism to the Republic. Couthon, indeed, down in Auvergne, out of touch with his colleagues, succumbed to the hysteria of Dechristianization. The attitude of the Committee in Paris was very different. It is shown in a letter drafted by Robespierre and signed by him, by Carnot and Collot, and by Billaud-Varenne, author of the *Last Blow against Prejudice and Superstition.*

The letter was to André Dumont, representative on mission in the Somme. "It has seemed to us," it read, "that in your last operations you have struck too violently against the objects of Catholic worship. . . . We must be careful not to give hypocritical counter-revolutionists, who seek to light the flame of civil war, any pretext that seems to justify their calumnies. No opportunity must be presented to them for saying that the freedom of worship is violated or that war is made on religion itself. Seditious and uncivic priests must be punished, but the title of priest must not be openly proscribed. In regions where patriotism is lukewarm or sluggish the violent remedies necessary in rebellious and counter-revolutionary regions must not be applied." Dumont was indignant at this reprimand.

Agitation reached its high point in Paris a few days later. Patriots gave up their Christian names, taking instead the names of classical heroes or of Revolutionary martyrs, such as Brutus, Gracchus or Marat. One enthusiast called himself No-God-the-Father, *Pas-de-bon-Dieu,* implying in the *bon* that he would perhaps accept a Supreme Being. A petition circulated in the city asking the Convention to abolish the constitutional clergy and to stop paying salaries to churchmen. Gobel, constitutional bishop of Paris, with a number of his clergy, came before the Convention, declared that he had seen a new light, abjured his priesthood, handed over his crozier and his ring, and donned ostentatiously the cap of liberty. The Convention applauded; some of its members who had once taken holy orders imitated the bishop. Throughout the city the section committees closed the churches; the Commune forbade their being reopened; and in the provinces, where the same proceedings had begun independently, the example of Paris spurred on the Dechristianizers.

The cathedral of Notre-Dame, standing four-square and ancient amid the hubbub, was invaded by the evangelists of a new religion. On a *décadi,* 20 Brumaire (November 10), it saw the culmination in a popular form of the learned efforts of Diderot and Voltaire. A symbolic Mountain was constructed in the nave. At its summit stood a little Greek temple dedicated "To Philosophy." On a rock half way up burned a Torch of Truth. Girls dressed in white with tricolor sashes, and crowned with flowers and oak leaves, moved up and down the mountainside during the ceremony, while an actress from the opera impersonated Liberty. The Convention (where Liberty was officially embraced by the chairman and secretaries) decreed that Notre-Dame should henceforth be known as the Temple of Reason, and then joined the city fathers and a great crowd of people at the new shrine.

Robespierre regarded this performance as a ridiculous masquerade. He knew that it was impolitic in a nation of Catholics. He had before him the reports of government observers, who declared that the whole movement was superficial, that the same people who were fierce rationalists when in crowds together often relapsed into their old ideas when they went home, fearing the wrath of God or the death of their unbaptized children.

In forcible Dechristianization, besides the principle of religious freedom, was involved a serious political question, the old question of the relative powers of the national government, the Commune and the patriotic societies. The exhibition in Notre-Dame was a trial of strength between the city leaders and the Convention. As usual the Convention yielded in outbursts of applause. Irresponsible radicals in Paris were allowed to open wider the already yawning breach between the church and the Republic. Robespierre conceived it to be the duty of the Committee to bring the Convention back to its senses, and to gain control once and for all over the Commune, and if possible over the Jacobins. To gain this end nothing was more useful than the Foreign Plot.

Revolutionists from that time to ours have availed themselves of foreign conspiracies, but whatever may be said of Hitler or Stalin, it seems to be true that Robespierre really believed in this one.

On the troubled day of September 5 the assemblies of the Paris sections, those hothouses of revolutionary exuberance, had been limited to two meetings a week. Some of them turned themselves into popular societies so as to be undisturbed in their sessions. These societies were then organized under a Central Committee, on the initiative of two Frenchmen, Desfieux and Dubuisson, and two foreigners, Proli and Pereyra. This committee in turn, with other men active in the Commune, and with certain advanced Conventionals including the German Anacharsis Cloots, backed the petition against the clergy, and instigated Gobel to abdicate his priesthood. The same group organized the celebration of 20 Brumaire in Notre-Dame.

These leftists were in sober fact discrediting the Republic in the judgment of the world. Robespierre believed that they deliberately meant to do so. In his eyes they were hired by hostile powers to push the Revolution to a ridiculous and ruinous excess. The people, he said, was not really present in the popular societies. This was true, for the popular societies of Paris were dominated by a few hundred organizers. But, he explained, the real people was present in the Jacobin club of the rue Saint-Honoré.

At the Jacobins he made his main attack, and there, on November 21, he delivered one of the great speeches of his career.

"Some have supposed," he said, "that the Convention, in accepting civic offerings [thus Robespierre chose to interpret the Convention's presence at Notre-Dame] has proscribed the Catholic religion. No, the Convention has not taken this rash step, and will never take it. Its intention is to maintain the freedom of religion that it has proclaimed, and to repress at the same time those who would abuse their freedom to trouble public order. It will not allow peaceable ministers of religion to be persecuted, but it will punish them severely whenever they dare to use their functions for the deception of citizens or the arming of prejudice and royalism against the Republic. Priests have been denounced for saying the mass; they will say it longer if an attempt is made to prevent them. He who would prevent them is more a fanatic than he who says the mass.

"Some would go further. Under pretense of destroying superstition they would make a kind of religion of atheism itself. Any philosopher, any individual may have on that matter whatever opinion he pleases. Whoever would make a crime of atheism is a madman, but the public man, the legislator, would be a hundred times more mad to adopt such a doctrine. The National Convention abhors it. The Convention is not a writer of books, an author of metaphysical systems; it is a political and popular body, charged with protecting not only the rights but the character of the French people. Not for nothing has it proclaimed the declaration of the rights of man in the presence of the Supreme Being. It will be said perhaps that I am narrow-minded, a man of prejudice, even a fanatic. I have already said that I spoke not as an individual or as a systematic philosopher, but as a representative of the people. Atheism is aristocratic; the idea of a great Being that watches over oppressed innocence and punishes triumphant crime is altogether popular."

At this point the Jacobins applauded with vigor, and Robespierre, after praising the belief in God in words not recorded, continued:

"I repeat: we have no other fanaticism to fear than that of immoral men, paid by foreign courts to reawaken fanaticism and give our Revolution an appearance of immorality, characteristic of our cowardly and savage enemies." Foreign courts, he said, maintain two armies. One is on the frontier. "The other, more dangerous, is in our midst; it is an army of spies, of paid rascals who insert themselves everywhere, even in the heart of the popular societies." He named a few, including Proli.

"I demand that this Society purge itself finally of this criminal horde! I demand that Dubuisson be driven from the Society, and also two other intriguers, one of whom lives with Proli under the same roof, and who both are known to you as his agents: I mean Desfieux and Pereira. I demand that a purifying scrutiny be held at the tribune, to detect and drive out all the agents of foreign powers who under their auspices have introduced themselves into this Society."

The Jacobins responded immediately to this powerful address. The men named by Robespierre were dropped. It became evident which way the wind was blowing; arrests of Jacobins had been taking place for more than a month (though Fabre d'Eglantine's part was not generally known); many of the brethren were involved with foreigners in the financial scandals; no one could be sure that the Law of Suspects might not engulf him. No one could afford to seem to fear an investigation; Robespierre's demand for a "purifying scrutiny" was therefore echoed by many, including Hébert. Hébert declared that plotters were trying to embroil him with Robespierre, the "friend of truth." He denied that he was an atheist, affirmed that a good Jacobin must accept the Gospel maxims, and that Jesus Christ was the true founder of the popular societies. Hébert, it must be repeated, was not the head of a party. His name was used later, like Trotsky's among Communists, to describe a "deviation." He was one among many, important because he was an official of the Paris municipality, and editor of a violent paper, the *Père Duchesne*.

The Convention presently passed a law reaffirming the freedom of religion.

At the Jacobins the purifying scrutiny began at once, and lasted for several weeks. Members took turns at the tribune of the society, exposing themselves to the public inspection and free comment of the others. There was something in Jacobin psychology which made this procedure not only a political advantage but a delight. Denunciations were prepared beforehand and virtuously launched.

Members then justified themselves by reviewing their careers, expatiating on their aims and motives, showing that they were neither "new patriots" who had joined the bandwagon late, nor old Girondists or Fayettists now parading a false purity. Hypocrisy was the vice most feared, and with reason, for in these giddy times, when without the appearance of conformity a man might go to jail or to the guillotine, no one could tell what anyone at heart believed.

Those of the Committee of Public Safety who were in Paris passed the scrutiny with success, though Robespierre had to protect Barère, who was branded as a waverer. Robespierre, Collot d'Herbois and Billaud-Varenne were the ones in whom the society most often expressed its confidence—a sign that Jacobin opinion was to the left of the average for the Committee. Couthon passed through the "crucible," as he called it, soon after his return, rejoicing that members had to give account of themselves "in the presence of the people," and "undergo in a way the Last Judgment." Poor Cloots, the visionary from the Rhineland, was assaulted by Robespierre as an agent of foreign tyrants, a preacher of universal revolution and ringleader in the "philosophic masquerade" of Dechristianization. He was expelled. Hébert passed, and also Fabre d'Eglantine, who managed to persuade the brothers that he owed his prosperity to the earnings of his pen. Their time had not yet come.

Two days after Robespierre's great speech, the society, "astonished that there exists in Paris any other society than the Jacobins," decreed that the Central Committee of the Paris patriotic clubs should be investigated and dissolved, because, said a member, it might become "liberticide." Thus the attack on the Commune began. The same attack was meanwhile pushed by the Committee of Public Safety.

It was obviously necessary, if the Revolutionary Government was to govern—if, for example, the Committee of Public Safety was to make its religious policy effective—to control the independent ardors of subordinate officials. Dechristianization was symptomatic: throughout the country there were communes, Jacobin clubs, representatives on mission, all with their own ideas on what the Revolution meant, who, in the judgment of the Committee, were ruining the Republic by irreligious extravagance. Others, even patriots, lagged behind the official views of Paris. Even patriots could not be trusted, and behind the forefront of articulate and demonstrative patriots lay the vast mass of Frenchmen, men and women who did not want a Republic, and who thought of their new rulers as ungodly regicides. When power is in the hands of men who will not take instructions, or when the ruling philosophy is not generally accepted (both of which were now the case), then a government of necessity either falls or becomes a dictatorship.

Unity and efficiency were made necessary also by plans for co-ordinating the economic resources of the country. The government could exist only if the armies were provisioned, and enough food made available, at sufficiently low prices, to prevent the poorest consumers from rising in rebellion. To meet these needs the law against hoarding and the General Maximum had been enacted, and were strengthened by the Law of Suspects; but the economic regulations were at best extremely difficult to enforce, and were often applied, or not applied, or misapplied, to suit the political views of those who, in various places, happened to be influential. Requisitioning led to endless confusion; departments professed themselves poor, to save their produce for themselves; representatives on mission, Revolutionary Armies, agents for the eleven real armies, for the eighty-three departments, for Paris and other communes, roamed the length and breadth of the country, finding their supplies where they could, trying to outwit each other, disregarding, because of the pressure behind them, the needs of the country as a whole. The Subsistence Commission set up in October was authorized to plan production and distribution on a national scale. We may be sure that Robert Lindet, after long sessions with the commission, pointed out, at the nightly conferences of the Committee, the almost insuperable obstacles in the way of economic coordination.

Saint-Just's law of October 10, proclaiming the government revolutionary until the peace, granted the Committee a certain authority over the constituted bodies. But the wording was vague, and the effects rather nebulous. Sporadic progress was made. The Convention decreed on November 25 that its members, when acting as representatives on mission, must exactly obey the orders of the Committee. On December 4 Barère and Billaud won another victory in the Convention, defeating an attempt of the Paris Commune to assemble the revolutionary committees of the sections.

Some control was even won over the Jacobins. The purge initiated by Robespierre served this end. The Committee requested the society to submit a list of its affiliated clubs. Objections arose, but Hébert and Danton both supported the Committee, which, with the list in its possession, proceeded henceforth to deal directly with some thousands of patriotic organizations.

Billaud-Varenne, who had become a kind of minister of the interior, because charged with much routine correspondence with the provinces, took the lead in framing new administrative machinery. This onetime drifter, ex-schoolteacher and ineffectual lawyer, showed himself a different man now that he was in a place of power. In 1789 he had been the most immoderate of the Twelve in his attacks on public authority. Now he demanded that authority be absolute and unquestioned.

On November 17 Robespierre made one of his infrequent speeches in the Convention. It was a challenge to the world. "Should all Europe declare against you, you are stronger than Europe! The French Republic is as invincible as reason; it is as immortal as truth. When liberty has made a conquest of such a country as France, no human power can drive her out." This bold assertion was a confession of religious faith. It was backed up by practical arrangements. Barère, following Robespierre, announced that Billaud-Varenne on the next day would present an important message from the Committee.

Billaud appeared, therefore, before an expectant assembly. He fainted, perhaps from overwork, before his address was finished, but was able to go on.

He began by describing the prevailing anarchy, which he said was characteristic of the infancy of republics. Everywhere the laws were without vigor. In some places they were not even known. Everywhere the wise measures of the Convention were distorted by local officials to promote their own ambitions. "So long as the laws," he said, "to have their full execution, pass through the successive interposition of secondary authorities, each of these authorities becomes the supreme arbiter of legislation; and the first which receives a law at the moment when it is enacted is undoubtedly a more powerful authority than the lawmaker, because it may suspend or stop execution as it pleases, and so destroy the law's existence and effect." Hence came all the troubles of federalism, a

"legal anarchy," a "political chaos," in which counter-revolutionaries of all descriptions could manage their intrigues.

Billaud proposed a rigorous centralization of power. All public
officials were to become mere "levers" for the transmission of a
force; this force was the will of the people, as determined in the
Convention and its Committee of Public Safety. No one, whatever
his position, was henceforth to possess any immunity. Anyone,
even members of the Convention, could be arrested if he obstructed
the public will. "No inviolability for anyone at all!" cried Billaud.
We are called anarchists, he said. "Let us prove that this is a
calumny, by substituting of our own free will the action of revolutionary laws for the continual oscillations of so many interests,
groupings, wills, passions that clash with each other and tear the
breast of our country. Surely this government will not be the iron
hand of despotism, but the reign of justice and reason."

Away with political opposition! In England, of course, an opposition was necessary, because cabinet ministers could not be trusted.
"Here, on the contrary [to quote a speech at the Jacobins two days
before Billaud's at the Convention], the unity of the Republic re-
quires that there be none. Discussion is doubtless necessary, but
only on means of effecting the public good. Is there an opposition
party, a right wing, in the Jacobins and the other popular societies?
Obviously not. Then why should there be one in the Convention?"
Alas, why? Two waves of rightists had been removed from the
Convention in six months. But always another seemed to form.

At the end of the discussion of Billaud's proposal the question
arose of how elected officials, when dismissed by the central power,
were to be replaced. It was agreed that no further elections could be
held. Couthon, just back from Auvergne, found the formula: "The
right of election belongs essentially to the sovereign people. To
impair it is a crime, unless extraordinary circumstances demand it
for the people's welfare. Now, we find ourselves in these extraordinary circumstances. . . . Those who appeal to the rights of the
people mean to pay a false homage to its sovereignty. When the
revolutionary machine is still rolling, you injure the people in en-
trusting it with the election of public functionaries, for you expose
it to the naming of men who will betray it." It was decided that
the Convention, meaning the Committee of Public Safety, should
appoint the successors to elected office holders.

The law of 14 Frimaire (December 4), passed virtually as Billaud proposed it, definitely founded the revolutionary dictatorship. It was the constitution of the Reign of Terror. Nor was it merely ephemeral. It created the *Bulletin des lois,* which existed until 1929, the organ by which French legislation was formally published. Setting up a strong central power, providing channels for the quick flow of authority from Paris to the remotest village, sweeping away all intermediate agencies that could obstruct or twist the policies of government, it recalled the age-old efforts of kings and ministers to bring order out of feudalism, and anticipated the means by which Napoleon organized modern France. The law of 14 Frimaire, "extraordinary" though the circumstances in which it was enacted, proves the profound continuity that joined the Revolution to past and future.

By the new law the Convention became "the sole center of the impulse of government." Counterfeiting the *Bulletin des lois* was to be punished by death. Officials who perverted the laws which they were charged with enforcing were to spend five years in irons and have half their property confiscated. All the constituted authorities, departments, districts and communes, to which the revolutionists of 1789 had given an almost unbounded freedom, were put under the grim inspection of the two governing committees. A swarm of locally elected administrators, or those of them who survived the purge for which the new law provided, became "national agents" removable at the pleasure of the Convention. Administrators were forbidden to assemble under any pretext; they were to correspond only in writing. Revolutionary Armies not authorized by the Convention were dissolved. Committees of surveillance were integrated with the recognized agencies of government. No armed force, tax or loan was to be raised except by national law. No official or official body was to alter or expand its lawfully established functions. The enforcement of all these provisions was handed over to the Committee of Public Safety.

The Revolutionary Government, thus consolidated, was still considered to be provisional. The constitution of the preceding summer, enshrined and venerated in the hall of the Convention, was still looked to as the ultimate basis of government. But the ideas that went into the law of 14 Frimaire were not really provisional. They have contributed as much to the making of modern states as the more liberal philosophy for which the Revolution is better known. Modern states exist by the ideas of unity, order, subordination and efficiency, and by the idea of law as the will of a sovereign power. Twentieth century states, democratic or dictatorial, share these ideas; and these are the ideas of 14 Frimaire, proclaimed at a time when the rest of Europe was largely feudal.

The law of 14 Frimaire, it is hardly too much to say, had as permanent a significance as the Declaration of the Rights of Man. They were poles apart, for they attacked antithetical extremes, anarchy and despotism. Each was a statement of a fundamental demand, one for public order, the other for individual liberty. The dualism that they express is an old one in political science, and the practical commentary is also an old one: that the best state must have elements of both, more order than the men of 1789 arranged for, more freedom than the men of 1793 would allow.

The new organizing law was an instrument of Terror because the government which it strengthened was the creation of a minority, the triumphant leaders of the Mountain, itself a party among republicans, who in turn were only a party among the original revolutionists, who in their turn did not include all the people in France. As in the name of liberty France now possessed the most dictatorial government it had ever known, so, in the name of the people, it now had the political system which, of all systems in its history, probably the fewest people really liked. The ruling group knew that in a free election it would not be supported. It knew that it did not represent, in the sense of reflecting, the actual wishes of actual men and women. It claimed to represent, in the sense of standing for, the real will of the real people, the fundamental, unrealized, inarticulate ultimate desires, the true welfare, of Frenchmen and of mankind, present and future. This was the Revolutionary faith.

Meanwhile actual Frenchmen had to be dealt with, those who did not yet share the faith, or who though sharing it differed in the methods which they recommended. The Terror waxed in fury. Everywhere voices were heard demanding unity, and division multiplied without end; loyalty was praised, and conspiracy flourished; confidence was eulogized as the supreme bond of society by men who trusted no one, and whose every act, and

almost every word, made confidence impossible. Suspects poured
into the prisons, and the guillotines fell more frequently on out-
stretched necks. The more the deaths mounted, the more enemies
the executioners had to fear. The more severe the government became the more opposition it aroused, and the only answer to opposition seemed to be an increase of severity. The longer the Terror
lasted the more deeply the Terrorists were compromised by it, and
the more fearful they became of letting any but themselves control
the machinery of power.

By the end of the year, according to the best figures, 4,554 persons had been put to death by revolutionary courts. Over 3,300
of these perished in December, for it was in December that rebellious Lyons was punished and the civil war in the Vendée put
down. Many of the Vendéans, caught with arms in their hands,
would have been sentenced by a milder government than that of
the Republic. No class escaped; most of the executed Vendéans
were peasants, and three-quarters of all victims came from the
shopkeeping, laboring and agricultural classes. It was not only
aristocrats who felt the sharp edge of a new order.

In Paris, before the year was out, even Mountaineers began to
hint for clemency. The Committee of Public Safety went its way.
The loud voice of Collot d'Herbois, who since his trip to Lyons
had good reason to fear a reaction, rang out over the benches
of the Jacobins:

"Some wish to moderate the revolutionary movement. What!
Can a tempest be steered? The Revolution is one. We cannot and
we must not check its motion. Citizens, patriotism must be always
at the same height! If it drops for an instant it is no longer
patriotism. . . ."

The tragedy of the Terror lies partly in this interpretation of
patriotism.

CHAPTER VI

Republic in Miniature

PUY-DE-DÔME is a department in central France about half the size of Connecticut, forming part of the old province of Auvergne. Across its western part runs a series of mountain peaks, called *puys* in the neighborhood, from one of which the department received its name. Other mountains border it on the east. Between these ranges extends the fertile plain of the Limagne, where, in the eighteenth century, tilled fields alternated with undeveloped woodlands, and vineyards were interspersed among patches of wheat and rye. A guidebook of 1795 tells us that high willows dominated the open country. Some of the highways for which France was famous came together in the Limagne, hard-surfaced roads bordered with walnut trees, avenues of civilization hurrying across this country of peasants, on to the south and the Mediterranean cities, with a branch to Lyons, some seventy miles to the east.

At the western edge of the plain, on a height of land of its own, stood the city of Clermont-Ferrand. In normal times it was a quiet provincial capital. Once in its history it had appeared on the stage of world affairs, for it was the birthplace of Pascal, who, in this city and on the neighboring summit of Puy-de-Dôme, had proved with his barometer that the atmosphere had weight. Travellers commented on the somber appearance of the town, a result of the dark color of its houses, which were built from volcanic rock quarried not far away. The finest building was the college, erected by the Jesuits in the 1730's. The streets were dark, narrow and crooked. Huddled in them were numerous workshops, where, at the time of the Revolution, craftsmen worked at the manufacture of hats, stockings, woolens and paper goods, and at the preserving of fruit for which the town was known even in Paris. The greatest charm of the city was its magnificent location. From its boulevards planted with trees, visitors could look up to Puy-de-Dôme, only five miles away and three thousand feet above the streets of Clermont, or out across the spreading valley to the ridge beyond, whose peaks were usually covered with snow.

Clermont, with more than 20,000 people, was the local metropolis. Its closest rival was Thiers, a busy center where farmers did their marketing, known also for its manufacture of knives and scissors. The peasants in the uplands, where the land was poor, supplemented their meager incomes by working for the hardware dealers in town. Thus had capitalism penetrated the country; the men in Thiers, having money, credit and knowledge of the market, directed the labors of a ring of peasantry, who worked for wages in their own huts and cabins. The same situation prevailed at Riom, the third town of the department, and even at the tiny place called Ambert. So decentralized was industry that even Ambert, hardly more than a village, produced paper, pins, sieves, garters, woolens and laces. The labor was usually done in the surrounding rural areas; the materials, the wages and the instructions came from Ambert, where also the product was sold.

Puy-de-Dôme was like many other of the eighty-odd departments. It was not as isolated or backward as some other parts of the Auvergne. It had a college, three towns of some consequence, an educated merchant and professional class, a handful of urban wage earners, a number of local nobles and gentry, who were usually poor and who were trying to avoid the attention of the revolutionary authorities—and a great mass of peasantry, in itself a group composed of many economic classes. By and large, the peasants were poorer and more ignorant than in some parts of the north, better off than in some regions to the west. There were independent farmers among them, with a larger number who owned pieces of land too small to produce a living, and who, like those who owned none at all, either rented a few acres, or hired out their labor to other peasants, to ex-noble landlords, to landowning townsmen, or to the merchant-capitalists who dealt in cutlery or textiles. The peasants had very little interest in politics, and almost no sense of public life on a national scale. The Revolution had already lightened their main grievances. They wanted now chiefly to be let alone. They were attached to tradition, to the routine of the village, to their age-old methods of agriculture, and to the Catholic church.

Into this little world, on August 29, 1793, came three Representatives of the People.

Some of these representatives on mission have already entered our story. In this and the three following chapters we turn to those who were also members of the Committee of Public Safety.

The representatives on mission, of whom there were more than a hundred, were members of the Convention stationed in the provinces and with the armies, to impose the idea of an indivisible Republic upon a country distracted by cross purposes and civil discord. By the liberal constitution of 1791 there were no regular channels through which national authority might flow. Before the law of 14 Frimaire, which turned certain local officials into "national agents," the representatives on mission were for practical purposes the only men outside Paris who acted in the name of centralized government. Standing for unity in a cooperative national effort, they were equipped before 14 Frimaire with virtually sovereign powers; but the unity that they were supposed to serve was endangered by the very powers necessary to achieve it, for some of the representatives acted as rulers in their own right, threatening to replace the federalism of Girondist departments with a new federalism of deputies on mission. For this reason, as we have seen, the Committee of Public Safety denounced their independence early in October. The legal control won by the Committee in December did not really settle the question. In the end, the conflict between the Committee and the representatives helped to bring the collapse of the Revolutionary Government.

It is difficult to imagine the effect produced in 1793 by the phrase "Representatives of the People." Neither word today sends a thrill through anybody's spine. Both words were then alive with the emotions of a new belief. A Representative of the People, for Frenchmen of the First Republic, was the most august being that could exist on earth.

The representatives embodied the majesty of the nation, and travelled in the reflected brilliance of its glory, like the proconsuls of Rome or the satraps of ancient Persia. Members of the Convention, they were the immediate wielders of sovereignty, the individual agents of the people's might. They stood above all existing laws and authorities, for the source of law flowed through them, a mysterious current that gave their actions the attribute of justice. Plain enough men for the most part, not demanding or wanting to be fawned on, they nevertheless often found that local Jacobins received them with adulation, ordinary persons with marked deference, and counter-revolutionaries with the hypocritical and ostentatious respectfulness associated with royal courts.

The three men sent to Puy-de-Dôme had been specifically granted unlimited powers by the Convention. The 14th of Frimaire being still in the future, they could do as they saw fit. They could make arrests, create revolutionary courts, conduct trials, erect guillotines. They could nullify, extend or curtail the force of any law. They could issue decrees and proclamations on any subject. They could fix prices, requisition goods, confiscate property, collect taxes. They could purge any existing government body, or, if they chose, dissolve government bodies altogether, replacing them with committees of their own nomination. On their arrival, all authority returned to the people, whose direct and immediate agents the Representatives were.

The three who came to Puy-de-Dôme were in an especially strong position, for one of them, Georges Couthon, was a member of the Committee of Public Safety. Couthon took precedence over his two colleagues, Maignet, a lawyer, and Chateauneuf-Randon, a onetime noble. Couthon and Maignet were natives of the department. They had been sent because of their influence in Puy-de-Dôme, Chateauneuf-Randon because he understood military affairs.

The purpose of their mission was to organize forces to take part in the siege of Lyons. In a larger sense, it was to attach Puy-de-Dôme more firmly to the Jacobin republic. Couthon was devoted to his native place. He had protected it, back in Paris, by vaunting its patriotism. He had kept up a frequent correspondence with its revolutionary leaders. Now he wished to turn it into a model for the whole country. Here, at home, he was free for a short while to work out his dream for the Revolution. What he did gives some sign of what the Committee of Public Safety wanted to do for all France. Here we may observe the Terror at close range.

The outlook in Puy-de-Dôme would have discouraged a man of less faith than Couthon. The departmental officials, and a good share of the population, were sympathetic to the rebels at Lyons. The officials had joined with those of neighboring departments in disavowing the leadership in Paris. They were in fact in rebellion against the National Convention; but by hedging and pretext had succeeded in making their position unclear. Couthon was aware of their real attitude; so was the Committee of Public Safety. The Committee had almost pronounced Puy-de-Dôme to be in a state of insurrection; Couthon had interceded to prevent this fateful step; and the Committee, as an alternative, sent Couthon himself to take charge of the situation.

Puy-de-Dôme was recalcitrant in producing soldiers. It had made no real response to the national levies. All that Couthon found on his arrival was 550 recruits with four cannon, a force which the department officials had raised to send to the Vendée, and had then kept at home to protect themselves. In the face of this obstruction, and of peasants who fought conscription with scythes and pitchforks, Couthon had to carry out the Levy in Mass.

Moreover, the harvest was bad. There was almost famine in the summer. Merchants refused to supply the market at the prices fixed. Mobs rioted in the towns. The departmental authorities had done nothing effective.

Clermont was in an uproar when Couthon arrived with his two colleagues. The Jacobin society had been outraged. A terrific scene had just occurred at its meeting; people poured into its hall, struck the presiding officer, shouted that they would not go to fight their brothers at Lyons. The whole town vibrated with excitement. The Representatives of the People had to act at once; they called a mass meeting at the cathedral, "published the dangers of the fatherland," declared that the Lyonnese wanted to undo the whole Revolution.

Two nights later a frightened messenger galloped into Clermont. He came from the Jacobin society at Ambert in the hills toward Lyons. His news was dreadful. A few miles away, in the next department, the Jacobin commander and his troops had been ambushed and captured by a party of Muscadins. Ambert was in a panic. Its Jacobins were threatened; even people of neutral or undecided opinions could fear the worst. The peasants, unconcerned though they might be in the issues, faced the ravaging of their fields and homes. For the first time in two hundred years Ambert looked upon the stark prospect of civil war.

The next morning, September 2, Couthon proclaimed the Levy in Mass. The bells of every church were to sound the general alarm.

COUTHON

Every town and village was to furnish men, armed if necessary with axes, pikes, or pitchforks. Grain and flour, saddle horses and dray horses were requisitioned. Relay posts were established for couriers. Tax collectors were to hold their funds, not remit them to Paris. All government bodies were to remain in permanent session.

That night Couthon sent a glowing dispatch to the Committee of Public Safety, announcing that the whole department was rising spontaneously in an outburst of patriotic emotion, and that the "rocks of Puy-de-Dôme" would soon roll upon the Lyonnese rebels and crush them.

Such language exaggerated the truth. Couthon was undoubtedly self-deceived. It was characteristic of the revolutionary leaders that, with palpable evidence to the contrary, they still believed the people enthusiastically behind them. They lived by faith and hope; they meant by the "people" something higher and nobler than the people that they saw; had they been more swayed by observable facts they would in all probability not have accomplished what they did. Consequently, on matters of public opinion, deputies on mission could rarely make an accurate report to their own government.

The truth was that Couthon ran into almost every possible difficulty. The old resistance to military service continued. Harvest time was at hand, most inopportune for adventures. Ordinary people, hardly able to think on a national scale, did not understand why men from Auvergne should go to help Paris fight against Lyons. At one village the peasants threatened to kill any of their number who answered the call to the colors. At another the tocsin rang for ten days and not a man stirred. The vine-growers proved to be the most willing, not so much for patriotic reasons as because, with their harvest approaching, they wished to have their service over as soon as possible. For grain farmers the harvest was already in progress, and they vehemently protested. Couthon answered by building up a picture of imminent peril, and enemies of the government, in reply, spread the idea that anyone who joined the army would be ruined.

Maignet and Chateauneuf-Randon set up headquarters at Ambert, to assemble the recruits and organize them into a disciplined force. Their problems were multifarious. Their troops melted away almost as soon as they could be gathered. The peasants would not stay at Ambert, idle and useless as they thought, while their fields went untended a few miles away, and brigands, more or less imaginary, threatened their families. The three Representatives were obliged to promise better police protection in the country, and decreed that the wives, children and other dependents of conscripted men would be provided for by the public treasury.

It was vital, of course, to maintain the level of economic production even with so many able-bodied men under arms. This need led to many decisions that bewildered the population. To reassure the farmers Couthon announced that horses needed in agriculture would not be requisitioned; but since the peasants had practically no horses not needed in agriculture, and since horses had already been requisitioned, the result was confusion. Chateauneuf and Maignet proclaimed at Ambert that men over fifty, and all millers, bakers and gunsmiths should be exempt from service. It happened that on the same day Couthon proclaimed at Clermont that exemption would be granted to fathers of families, to "men who were individually responsible for one or several plows," to all bakers, millers and carters, and, at the discretion of local authorities, to any number of shoemakers, tailors, blacksmiths, saddlemakers, harness makers, and others "whose services in their occupations are useful to the Republic." The effect of this decree, with all its possibilities of local favoritism, would be to scatter a third of the little force that Maignet and Chateauneuf were desperately trying to hold together. They pointed out the difficulties to Couthon, who acknowledged his mistake and promptly countermanded his order. Meanwhile everyone was confused, and desertions continued.

By the middle of September there were supposed to be 10,000 men at Ambert, though the actual number was only a fraction of this figure. The two deputies in command were anxious to move on toward Lyons, knowing that desertions would fall off when the men were farther from home. To prepare for their departure, and to leave a reliable base of supply behind them, they dissolved all existing authorities in the district of Ambert except justices of the peace, and replaced them with a local "committee of public safety, subsistence and military administration." This committee, which possessed practically unlimited powers, was made up of local

Jacobins, including some who had just been relieved of their elective offices. Their function was to act as intermediary between the department of Puy-de-Dôme and the expeditionary force at Lyons. With these arrangements made, Chateauneuf and Maignet set out, and reached the scene of operations before Lyons on September 17.

So in spite of all handicaps the Representatives of the People produced a fighting force, however clumsy, inexperienced and reluctant, within three weeks after their arrival at Clermont.

Couthon did not immediately follow his colleagues. His poor health and his paralysis made him physically less active than they. Yet his task was the more exacting. While they went to Ambert to drill their men, and then to Lyons to join forces with the rest of the army, Couthon remained in Clermont alone, responsible for supplying the expeditionary force of the department and for keeping all the obstructive elements under control.

He was working with men whom he knew he could not trust, the departmental governing board of whose disloyalty to the Convention he had written proof. He could at any moment dissolve them as an organ of government and send them as individuals to jail. He could govern, if he wished, through tools and favorites from among the many local radicals who assiduously paid him court. Yet he hesitated. He was not a mean man; he cared nothing for private vengeance. He respected the ability of some of the department administrators; he had known them when he was an ordinary lawyer in Clermont. He needed their experience, and thought them politically harmless while he was present to watch over them. But agitation against them continued. On September 14, in Paris, someone in the Convention demanded that the authorities of Puy-de-Dôme be suspended. Finally on the 22nd Couthon acted. He arrested the fifteen members of the board, but instituted no prosecution against them. A number of faithful Jacobins took their place.

Meanwhile he was tireless in calling the resources of Puy-de-Dôme to life. A cripple, almost physically helpless, his hand yet reached into the farms and workshops. There was a cannon foundry in the neighborhood which fortunately belonged to a good Jacobin. It gave a start. Shops were kept active day and night at the manufacture of small arms. Still there were not enough; it

was decreed that ironworkers, locksmiths and cutlers must combine
to produce 6,000 pikes before the end of September. Tinware and
brassware was requisitioned that the troops might cook their
meals; hatchets, pick-axes and shovels that they might be able to
pitch camp. Shoes were sent on to them, and linen for bandages.
The doctors in Clermont had to give up their instruments to the
army surgeons. In a series of complicated decrees, Couthon specified all the sizes and calibers in which bullets were to be made, in
view of the diversity of equipment with which the recruits had
been sent away. Again, when trouble arose because grain was being
requisitioned in different regions at different prices, so that merchants were beginning to speculate for a profit, he immediately
set a uniform price for the whole department. And repeatedly,
throughout, he appealed to Paris for funds.

Couthon's chief auxiliary was the committee of public safety
set up by his colleagues at Ambert, a body whose short history
shows that not all the work had to be directed from above. This
handful of local Jacobins, politically doctrinaire, behaved in some
ways with the wisdom of a New England town meeting. They
forwarded supplies to the army, and passed on messages from
Lyons to Clermont. They rounded up deserters and watched
suspects. Under their guidance locksmiths were assembled to repair
guns and printers to print general orders. Taverns were regulated
so that the wagoners who carried goods to the front would have
no grounds for complaint. A hospital was organized, and an
ambulance service to bring the wounded home. Armed patrols
kept order in the countryside while the able-bodied men were away.
Finally, since many in the reserve left at Ambert still insisted on
deserting, the committee on its own authority ordered the whole
force out of the department, to get the men far enough away to
keep them from going home. All these measures Couthon had
simply to endorse; the burden of decision was lifted from his
shoulders.

It is on record, however, that even this efficient committee succumbed to the phobias of the Revolution. It began to purge itself;
the orthodox wanted to exclude the politically unsound. The more
sensible members prevailed to the extent that only two were
dropped; but had the life of the committee been longer, its
membership would in the end undoubtedly have been smaller.

Couthon could not long delay going to Lyons, and finally left Clermont on September 28, reaching the encampments near the city four days later. There, as a member of the great Committee, he took charge over a host of somewhat disorganized dignitaries, including army commanders and representatives on mission. Lyons surrendered on October 9. Couthon's activities in this connection form no part of the story of the present chapter—with one exception.

The fate of the fifteen unfortunate officials of Puy-de-Dôme, under arrest back in Clermont, had still to be settled. The fall of Lyons made their plight more critical. Records in the city implicated them more deeply in the rebellion. Couthon knew that Collot d'Herbois, a violent man, was soon to replace him as commandant at Lyons. He therefore ordered that the fifteen culprits be sent to Lyons immediately, there to be tried in the revolutionary court. The court was staffed by men picked by Couthon. The trial of the fifteen was a protracted affair, deliberately drawn out and befogged by the judge in charge, so that in the end only two of the defendants were sentenced to death, and thirteen were acquitted. They made haste to withdraw from the political scene. As for Couthon, before he left Lyons the more overheated patriots were assailing him with charges of moderatism.

He was greeted as a conquering hero in Clermont to which he returned in early November with Maignet and Chateauneuf. Even the peasants, who hardly knew what had triumphed, were joyful at seeing the men come back to the fields. The Jacobins prepared to shower their leader with honors. Men fought for the privilege of carrying the august invalid about. Escorts, dinners and receptions were arranged. The clubs held special meetings at which they might debate under the chairmanship of a Representative of the People, exhibiting their talents in the sunshine of revolutionary power. Excited women joined in the chorus. Among them none was more strange than Suzanne Mignot, a woman who, disappointed in her marriage, had plunged into revolutionary politics, and saw in Couthon a kind of god of the Republic. She was a believer in Mesmerism, through which she tried to cure the many infirmities of her idol. To be near him she had become the close friend of his wife. She followed Couthon and Mme. Couthon to Lyons, haunted them in their home at Clermont. It is said that she eventually went insane. Other women, later called "furies of the guillotine," wild-eyed and not always sober, joined crowds of men to shout "Vive Couthon!" in the streets.

Couthon was exhilarated by these evidences of support. He was expected in Paris, but he was not eager to return. There was still work to do in Puy-de-Dôme. Now that the local crisis was over, now that every effort need not be spent in raising and supporting a citizen army, he remained more free to embark on the task that really absorbed his imagination, the task of turning his home department into a model for France. He remained three weeks longer. The time was sufficient to launch Puy-de-Dôme on the way to becoming a small republic of virtue.

The peasants sang *Te Deums* in their churches on hearing of the fall of Lyons; they little imagined that the Jacobin conquerors were about to prohibit all observance of their religion. Word of the fall of Lyons reached Puy-de-Dôme almost simultaneously with the news that the Christian calendar was abolished. Then came rumors of religious disturbances in other departments, in the neighboring Nièvre under Fouché, further north under André Dumont. Republicans in Puy-de-Dôme had their own religious problem near at hand. Hundreds of priests were hidden in the Auvergne mountains, from which they secretly descended, with heroic determination, to preach the religion of Holy Church and spread agitation against the Republic. A terrific tension was built up, which was discharged in a fierce outburst of Dechristianization.

Couthon joined with enthusiasm in the assault on Catholic worship. Had he not been a member of the Committee of Public Safety he might have got himself into trouble. The Committee had already, on October 27, reprimanded André Dumont for his anti-Catholic violence. Under Robespierre's guidance it was taking the view that Dechristianization was a subtle counter-revolutionary movement instigated by foreigners. The hollowness of this theory is clear from the example of Couthon. Couthon was almost the ideal type of Jacobin, a man above all suspicion of treachery, disinterested, humane, capable of piety, neither a Hébertist nor a demagogue nor a grafter. He became an ardent Dechristianizer because Dechristianization was entirely consistent with Jacobin ideals. He failed to see its political implications, because he had been away from Paris since before the Hébertist uprising of

September 5. He did not realize that some Dechristianizers were less honest than he was, that a few (probably a very few) were converts to atheism, and that the movement had become a test of strength between the Paris Commune and the national government. It is strange that he remained in such ignorance, strange that the Committee, if it was serious in its religious policy, did not caution or inform him. But he received no word from his colleagues during November, at least none of which there is printed record. So, while the Committee fought Dechristianization in Paris, one of its members vigorously pushed it in Puy-de-Dôme. The whole situation shows the confusion that still remained in the government.

Couthon believed, like Robespierre for that matter, that Catholicism was a compound of ignorance, imposture and superstition. He had ceased to see any difference between the constitutional and the refractory clergy—with some justification, for even the constitutional clergy, long loyal to the Revolution, was generally displeased at the régime of the Mountain. But Couthon by this time had passed beyond politics. He opposed the church because he thought it enslaved the human mind.

His repugnance was increased by an incident that happened at Billom, a small town near Clermont. Stopping here on his way back from Lyons, he found that the leading church, of which the inhabitants were very proud, enshrined a vial said to contain some of the true blood of Jesus Christ. Indignant that such things could be, he called out the local Jacobins and held a solemn public assembly, at which a medical man of the neighborhood subjected the contents of the vial to the rigors of chemical analysis. The precious fluid turned out to be a kind of colored turpentine. Loud were the outcries against the dishonesty of priests, and much were the centuries of credulity deplored.

Four days later a decree went out from Clermont to all Puy-de-Dôme. Its preamble was a statement of the philosophy on which the revolutionary leaders had been reared. It proclaimed a religion without clergy or mysterious dogmas, a Rousseauist creed springing from the goodness of men's hearts, directed to a God of nature, who was impersonal, aloof and sublime. Couthon, like Robespierre, frowned no less upon atheism than upon revealed religion.

24 Brumaire, Year II of the
Republic. [November 14, 1793]

The Representatives of the People,

Considering that, if it is in the heart and mind of every man of good faith to recognize a universal Creator, who maintains the harmony of nature and produces the marvels that we wonder at but cannot conceive, it is an outrage to this good and powerful Being to suppose that he wishes any other altar than the hearts of his children, other temple than the world of which he is architect, other worship than that consistent with the reason that he has given us. . . .

Considering that the reason and philosophy which today enlighten France and will soon govern the world, after breaking the scepters of kings should likewise strike unto death the monster of fanaticism, tear aside the veil of impostors and dissipate those images of superstition which hold peoples in error and have both offended the Supreme Being and degraded men;

Ordain . . .

A number of articles followed. The titles of bishop, vicar, priest, etc., were to be abolished. The clergy were to be paid no more salaries; but those dispossessed would receive small pensions. All objects of gold, copper, tin or lead in the churches were to be set aside for the use of the National Convention. Religious vestments were to be distributed through the Jacobin clubs to "young persons of the sex" who had distinguished themselves by their virtue and patriotism. Church bells were to be removed and steeples torn down. All signs of the Catholic cult were to be destroyed. Lastly, in place of priests preaching on Sundays, there were to be patriots, chosen by the clubs for their eloquence, who toured the country on the republican *décadis*.

Thus did the French Republic dare to lay hands on the City of God. It is easy to represent what followed simply as vandalism. So it became when ruffians and half-wits, as happened only too frequently, were turned loose upon the churches. On the other hand, the defenders of the old religion were often mere bumpkins whose habits had been broken. But above this vulgar brawl raged a struggle between two systems of idealism, and the flame of idealism burned at this time more fiercely in the partisans of the Republic. For men like Couthon the true Republic was itself a kind of City of God. Above the republic of cold reality, disrupted by faction and shaken by violence, rose the massive bulk of the Republic One and Indivisible, an ideal commonwealth where men lived in harmony and peace, a classless world of citizens and brothers, a community of men whose minds were free and whose spirits were independent, a society to which men owed their liberty, their dignity and their rights. "Would that I might die," Couthon once said in all simplicity, "seeing my country free and its people happy."

Since a republic of this kind was believed to be dictated by human nature, opposition to it was believed to come only from sinister vested interests, and in particular from the entrenched power of the clergy and of the rich. It was, in truth, a plain fact of politics that the clergy and the rich did not approve of the Jacobin republic, actual or ideal. In addition, Puy-de-Dôme faced the prospect of famine. A census of grain ordered by Couthon in September showed that there was only half enough on hand to feed the population of the department through the winter.

The same day, therefore, which saw the decree on religion saw another on the regulation of the movement of foodstuffs. Commissioners were again to take a census of the available cereal crops. The farmers were required to thresh their grain within one month, and were forbidden to keep in their barns more than they needed for their own consumption for four months. In this way it was hoped to overcome the reluctance of the peasants to exchange their produce for paper money at fixed maximum prices. Grain was thus to be released for the market, but since the merchants would not undertake to distribute it at the prices demanded by the authorities, Couthon's decree further provided that the markets were to be supplied by requisitions. This meant that public officials were to buy farm products at a price at which farmers were unwilling to sell, and pass them on to consumers at a price which private traders were unable or unwilling to meet. Anyone who disobeyed or resisted the law was to be sent to the Revolutionary Tribunal at Paris.

Puy-de-Dôme was thus divided by a kind of class struggle, or, more exactly, by a struggle between the producers and the purchasers of food. The law worked out to the advantage of consumers, especially of poor consumers who were unable to pay what might be termed the bootleggers' prices. The small bourgeois and hired laborers of the towns gave Couthon their support; landlords and merchants, and those peasants who owned or rented their farms, were thrown more definitely into the opposition.

Against the merchants Couthon's feelings were particularly bitter. Some of them were men of means. Many of them, because of their business, had affiliations with the federalists of Lyons. They had once been enthusiastic for the Revolution; hardly more than a year ago they had helped to elect him to the Convention. Now they were estranged from him, alarmed because he consistently took the radical tack. In his eyes they were betraying the Revolution, stirring up party strife, obstructing the only government that could save France from ruin. He commanded them to keep their shops open at the usual hours. If nevertheless they withdrew to their estates in the country, he ordered them back to town, where they could be better watched by Jacobin committees. He applied the Law of Suspects to suit the political situation. The committees of surveillance were granted large powers of discretion: they might denounce as suspects those individuals whom they considered dangerous, even if the law of September 17 did not cover their case; and they might release from suspicion any persons (except nobles and priests) who were involved by the law but whom the committees thought to be devoted to the Jacobin cause. The possibilities of intrigue thus opened up may be imagined.

And still the menace of famine was not removed. No amount of local regulation could remove it, if there was in truth not enough food to carry the department through the winter. Supplies would have to be brought in from outside. Where to find them and how to transport them, as we shall see, remained one of Couthon's chief concerns long after he had returned to Paris.

He was too important a man to linger on as a departmental administrator. Paris called—and those wider vistas seen from the green room in the Tuileries. Yet he hesitated to go. He was very much a family man. Invalid that he was, he liked to live at home; and he did not intend to take his young child to the capital. In Puy-de-Dôme he was a monarch, a maker of law, a symbol of power in all patriotic eyes. Undoubtedly he enjoyed these satisfactions of his proconsulship. He was eager to accept some of the invitations with which the Jacobins plied him. On November 16 he wrote to the Committee of Public Safety explaining his delay, and went up the valley to Issoire to take part in a patriotic function there.

Here he presided over a special session of the club, where, in the majestic presence of a Representative of the People, a number of orations were delivered. Priests came to make a formal surrender of their priesthood, and a few lawyers also repudiated their profession, which had lately fallen into disrepute. Citizens stood up to abjure their Christian names, and to announce the usual substitutes—Gracchus, Brutus, or Marat. Couthon had already been calling himself Aristide instead of Georges for several days. A tremendous banquet was held, with more speeches, followed by a spectacle in the marketplace, where the figures of two hundred saints, all that could be found in Issoire, were solemnly burnt. Couthon then dismissed a few officials, appointed new ones, questioned suspects, released some, detained others, acted the sovereign throughout, and went back to Clermont.

Clermont on 30 Brumaire witnessed the climax of Couthon's sojourn in the department. The day, a *décadi*, was set aside for the apotheosis of Chalier, the Jacobin of Lyons who had been martyred by the enemies of the Republic. Fifty clubs from all the country round had their delegates in Clermont. Never had the somber town seen such a sight.

The ceremonies began at nine in the morning. Wildly cheered, Couthon hobbled to the rostrum. He made an important announcement: a special tax of 1,200,000 livres was soon to be levied on the "selfish rich." As the applause died down he revealed that he was about to present four virtuous young ladies with Republican dowries. The four happy girls were there, chosen in advance through the Jacobin clubs. They came forward, were handed 2,000 livres apiece, and received the "fraternal accolade" (the well-known French embrace used on such occasions) from the conqueror of Lyons and Representative of the People. The crowd then marched to the cathedral (Temple of Reason), carrying a bust of Chalier, which was deposited near the altar. Speeches were heard on the dangers of fanaticism; the country doctor from Billom explained how he had proved the blood of Christ to be turpentine; and the representative Maignet was solemnly rebaptized Publicola. The congregation poured out its feelings in patriotic hymns.

In the afternoon, when a quantity of wine had undoubtedly flowed, less edifying events are said to have occurred. All the images of saints in Clermont were pulled down and piled in the public square. A match was lit, and yelling sans-culottes danced about the flames. Some people walked gaily up and down dressed in chasubles, albs, stoles and other sacred apparel. A high local official was seen dragging a saint through the street with a rope tied about the neck. Possibly our informant on this matter exaggerates; he wrote his account later to show how scandalous the day had been.

The evening was given over to community singing and to more speeches. All joined in a new song, "The Defeat of the Rebels of Lyons." Couthon then favored the others with a solo, "The Foolish Homage to Saints." Maignet followed with a softer number, "The Fond Ties of Marriage." In a final speech, Couthon declared that the churches were henceforth to be used as schools, and that church buildings not needed for such purposes might be torn down by impoverished patriots, who could use the wreckage for building materials. That night the city was specially illuminated, "to enlighten the triumph of reason in the night."

The tax on the rich promised on this occasion was enacted a few days later. Designed to provide the economic wherewithal for a moral regeneration, it was one of the chief means by which Couthon hoped to purify the department, and was decreed in terms strangely compounded of ruthlessness and philanthropy. The rich were to be relieved of their property, according to the reasons given in the preamble, because they were aristocrats who wished to undo the Revolution, because justice demanded and the Constitution recognized the universal right to schooling at the public expense, and because it was to the interest of the wealthy themselves that the poor be sufficiently educated to understand why they must respect the property of others.

The tax took the form of a capital levy. All persons whose fortunes were "presumed to reach 40,000 livres" were liable for payment. Bachelors and suspects were to give up all their wealth not needed for their own maintenance. Each was to contribute a share sufficient to make a total of 1,200,000 livres, and was to pay the whole amount assessed upon him within ten days of receiving notice. Assessment was to be determined by the departmental board, on the basis of lists furnished by district authorities. It thus lay with the most active local politicians, by this time well purged of their more moderate elements, to "presume" who among their neighbors possessed 40,000 livres, and to decide who, as bachelors or suspects, could be subjected to more stringent impositions.

Of the proceeds, 50,000 livres were to be turned over to the Jacobin societies. Schools were to receive 225,000. Classes were to be housed in the churches. Committees of the Jacobin clubs were to decide on the content and methods of instruction, and were, sitting jointly with district councils, to appoint the teachers. The bulk of the fund, 925,000 livres, was set aside for the relief of the indigent. The identity of the indigent was also left for local Jacobins to determine.

This measure was a declaration of class war, though hardly in any strictly Marxian sense. With its highly personal methods of enforcement, it was a terrific weapon against all those whom the reigning Jacobins did not like—not only the wealthy, but the suspects, among whom anybody might find himself, and bachelors, whose existence was an insult to the ideal of correct family living. Couthon was still pursuing the enemies of the republic. He wanted money, and it was the wealthy who had it. He wanted political support, and the poor and middling elements were willing to give it. He looked upon the mass of people not as workers but as patriots, capable of virtue, morally fit to live in the French Republic. His humane nature made him sympathetic to the unfortunate. His political sense told him that he must weaken the leaders of the defeated federalist movement. His levy on the rich was prompted by political need and by generous impulse, not by any considered theory of economic classes.

He signed the decree on November 25, and on the same day left Clermont for Paris.

As if to show that his mind dwelt on other than material questions, he published another edict at the village of Aigueperse, where he spent the night just before crossing the border of the department. It was the last official act of his mission in Puy-de-Dôme. It concerned funerals.

His purpose here was still further to root out Christianity, and to enforce equality in the solemnities of death. The decree, a long and complex one, shows the mania of a man who thought that the world could be suddenly renewed, and expected the most personal habits to be altered by a few scratches of the pen. Exact regulations were provided for the use of hearses and caskets and for the manner in which bodies were to be laid out. No religious symbols were to be allowed. No priest was to be permitted to take part. A civil official would make a few suitable remarks at the cemetery, which was to be known as "the field of rest." The walls of these fields were to be of a prescribed height, high enough to keep out wandering animals, low enough to enable passersby to look within. Lastly, "the body shall be covered with a cloth of the national colors; the same shall serve for all citizens of the commune."

In this way Couthon would have liked to be buried, with the tricolor of the Republic draped about him. Probably he had no belief in immortality. He did not, like Fouché in the Nièvre, require cemeteries to be placarded with signs declaring that "death is an eternal sleep"; he ignored the question in his pronouncement on funerals, as he seems to have ignored it in his life. So far as he associated himself with anything eternal it was with the principles for which he believed the Revolution stood. The Republic, he once said, "is immortal like the Nature on which it is founded." He could be content to be laid in a "field of rest" under the auspices of a "civil official," with the Republican emblems following him to the grave.

Five miles beyond Aigueperse he crossed the border into Allier. He never saw Puy-de-Dôme again, nor his six-year-old son, nor his co-workers among the Jacobins of Clermont. Nor was he buried with the honors of the Republic.

The reader may have been expecting more news of the guillotine. He may have heard that the crippled Couthon was one of the most bloodthirsty of the Twelve. But the fact is that during his mission not one person was executed by revolutionary justice in Puy-de-Dôme. The two officials who were sentenced at Lyons, as against thirteen acquitted, were the only citizens of Puy-de-Dôme to climb the guillotine in these months. Couthon possessed the power of life and death. Puy-de-Dôme seethed with disaffection. Yet the terrible power remained unused. Where the conscription in May had led to half a dozen executions, in September Couthon carried on the Levy in Mass with none.

Except for the half-dozen executed in May, it seems that only seven persons were put to death by revolutionary law in Puy-de-Dôme during the Terror. Their cases rose after Couthon's return to Paris. For their deaths he was indirectly responsible. The charges against them were violations of the policies he introduced, especially the forcible Dechristianization.

After Couthon left, the committees of surveillance, strengthened by the organic law of 14 Frimaire which made them agents of the Committee in Paris, remained actively on the watch for suspects. Patriotic orators toured the department in their attempt to replace the priests. The decree on funerals was to some extent enforced, though with difficulty among the peasants. Lists were drawn up of the worthy poor who were to receive help, and of the selfish rich, suspects and bachelors who were to pay the capital levy. It is not known, however, how much wealth really changed hands through this decree.

Chateauneuf-Randon remained at Clermont as representative on mission in the locality. His most stubborn problem was the religious one. During his tenure church bells were removed and steeples demolished. There were many protests. Citizens in various communes betrayed a sudden concern for the beautiful, petitioning that their church towers be spared as masterpieces of architecture. A few of these requests were granted, usually on condition that in towers left standing the doors should be blocked up, and placards posted announcing "the triumph of reason over the vestiges of error and fanaticism." In some places caps of liberty were hung upon the spires, and statues of liberty placed ostentatiously on the roofs. A church, though standing, was thus signified as belonging to the Republic.

Probably stolid indifference, more than anything else, saved the churches from extensive mutilation. Few patriots could indefinitely keep their feelings at the "level of revolutionary circumstances" urged upon them by so dynamic a leader as Couthon. And the patriots were in a minority. Opinion in Auvergne, for all that the representatives could do, was not very radical.

We may now take leave of Puy-de-Dôme for the time being, with the Phrygian caps hung jauntily upon its spires, and the statues of liberty glaring defiantly from the tops of churches into its hills.

CHAPTER VII

Doom at Lyons

AT the village of Sainte-Foy, on October 2, a long expected coach arrived from Clermont-Ferrand. From it, with difficulty, helped by his wife, emerged the "nimble general," as the paralyzed Couthon jokingly called himself. He was received by five representatives on mission, including Maignet and Chateauneuf-Randon, and by a staff of military officials, who had captured Sainte-Foy only three days before.

The army that he now joined was a large one, but heterogeneous and without unified leadership. It included the contingent from Puy-de-Dôme and other hastily assembled bands, raised by the strenuous exertions of representatives on mission. These raw conscripts, though their arrival had been dramatic, could contribute little in proportion to their numbers. The main operations were in the hands of experienced soldiers of the Army of the Alps, who had to be withheld from the frontier until the civil war could be ended.

The headquarters at Sainte-Foy stood on a hill that rose directly above the confluence of the Rhône and the Saône. Below it was spread out the city of Lyons, built for the most part on a long tongue of land formed by the junction of the two rivers. It was the second city of France, and a population of 120,000 made it one of the principal cities of Europe. For two months it had lain under siege, holding out stubbornly, but the Jacobin army now pressed within gunshot of its last defenses.

Lyons was a great industrial center, known especially for its manufacture of silks. Double the size of Manchester, highly developed on capitalist principles, it was one of the places where the Revolution took on most clearly the aspect of a class struggle. Like Paris it had been shaken by a series of municipal upheavals. At the beginning of the year the Mountain had come into power, led by the local revolutionist Chalier, who drew support from the large wage-earning class. The industrial and merchant aristocracy resisted; and the violence of the Chalier régime, its subordination to the Mountain in Paris, plus the conservatism of a very old, very proud and very Catholic city, threw the bulk of the population into the hands of the upper bourgeoisie, with the result that, on May 29, a new group came into office, imprisoned Chalier, and threw off the authority of the National Convention. Lyons thus became a leader in the federalist rebellion. Chalier was eventually put to death. Thousands of refugees poured across the bridges, mostly silk-weavers and other working-class people. They settled in rude camps under the protection of the besieging army, supported partly by money sent by the government in Paris.

The tricolor of the Republic continued to float in the beleaguered city. The rebellion was predominantly Girondist; its leaders, at least at the beginning, had no wish to make common cause with the Bourbons or with foreign powers. But Girondinism was somewhat confused, a mixture of philosophic idealism with class prejudice and regional assertiveness, and the Girondists of Lyons, once they defied the Convention, found themselves standing shoulder to shoulder with counter-revolutionists. Royalists flocked in to give a knife thrust to the Republic. Enemy powers were encouraged. The English hoped to hold Toulon as long as Lyons, key to the Rhône valley, was in revolt. The Italians from Piedmont found invasion from the east much simplified, until they were thrown back about the first of October.

Couthon, on arriving, immediately summoned a council of war. Some of the representatives, pointing out that the city was on the brink of starvation, and hoping to spare the bitterness of armed conquest, advised waiting for a peaceable surrender. But the instructions from the Committee of Public Safety were explicit. Faced with the problem of revolt in other southern cities, and of driving the English from Toulon, the Committee demanded that Lyons be occupied without delay. It was probably on the day of Couthon's arrival that the representatives received their orders. They were urged to lose no time. The message from Paris was a bad omen for the future of Lyons.

"Let them perish," said the Committee, referring to the rebels, "let the national power, deploying in a terrible manner, wave over this criminal city the sword which too long has threatened guilty heads."

Couthon therefore ordered an assault, though not without more delay, and not until the rebels had refused two ultimatums calling for surrender. On October 9, meeting with feeble resistance, the Jacobin army marched in—in time, fortunately, for the representatives to gratify the impatient Committee, which had meanwhile demanded news of the fall of Lyons by return of mail.

The city was in chaos. It was strewn with the wreckage of bombardment. Its provisions had disappeared. The shops were closed; some of the citizens were in hiding; many came out to receive food from the conquerors, or to cry "Vive la République" as Couthon's carriage rolled by, partly because they believed in the Republic, partly to protect themselves from the wrath to come. Fugitive sans-culottes descended from the hills; prisoners of the late régime issued from the jails. City politics was turned upside down; the high became low, and the low high; the oppressed prepared to do vengeance upon the oppressors. The invading army, meanwhile, conducted itself with restraint and even generosity toward the half-starved and terrified inhabitants.

Lyons was a doomed city, but the horrors that it saw in the following weeks were not the work of the invading army, or of Couthon or the other commanders. The army moved southward in a few days. Couthon, though sufficiently "exalted," was no worshiper of the guillotine.

Couthon on entering the city naturally ordered the inhabitants to disarm themselves. He gave instructions that the shops and factories should return to business, and he requisitioned food from the neighboring country. Hoping to check the excesses of local Jacobins, he forbade the section committees to meet; and when the section politicians began to make arrests and confiscations on their own initiative, he threatened them with imprisonment. He divided the rebels into three classes, those who still bore arms when captured, those who had held civil employment under the rebellious municipality, and those who had simply been "misled"—a category which might include almost everyone in Lyons. Revolutionary tribunals were set up, by which, after due conviction, culprits of the first class were to be guillotined, those of the second shot, and those of the third released after recanting their errors. No one meanwhile was to be imprisoned without examination.

Left to himself, Couthon, in all probability would have reduced punishments to a minimum, and tried to restore the second city to its usual place, an important one, in the economic life of the country. But he faced three kinds of pressure, all irresistible. The local Jacobins would not be stopped in their revenge; they therefore accused him of moderatism, a fatal charge of which he had to free himself at any cost. The clubs in Paris demanded drastic repression. And the Revolutionary Government, for reasons of state, was determined to make of Lyons a horrible example.

The responsibility for what followed lies largely with the Committee of Public Safety, so far as that body, dependent as it was, in October, on the support of the revolutionary elements in Paris, may be held responsible for anything it did.

A week after entering Lyons, on the day of the battle of Wattignies and of the death of Marie Antoinette, Couthon and his colleagues received from the Committee an extraordinary decree. They professed themselves "penetrated with admiration." They wrote back in ironic language: all the wise measures enjoined upon them for disciplining the city had already been taken, except one— *its total destruction.*

The Committee of Public Safety had decided to blot the memory of Lyons from the French mind.

To achieve this end it passed through the Convention on October 12 one of the most remarkable documents of the Revolution. After articles one and two came the following:

3. The city of Lyons shall be destroyed. Every habitation of the rich shall be demolished; there shall remain only the homes of the poor, the houses of patriots who have been led astray or proscribed, the buildings employed in industry and the monuments devoted to humanity and public instruction.

4. The name of Lyons shall be effaced from the list of cities of the Republic. The collection of houses left standing shall henceforth bear the name of Ville-Affranchie—the Liberated City.

5. On the ruins of Lyons shall be raised a column attesting to posterity the crimes and the punishment of the royalists of the city, with this inscription:

Lyons made war on Liberty.
Lyons is no more.
18th day of the first month of the Year Two
of the French Republic, One and Indivisible.

Barère, who presented the decree to the Convention, declared it necessary as a deterrent to other cities which might rebel.

Collot d'Herbois raged in the Jacobin club, lashing out against the Lyonnese bourgeoisie.

"Some men," he said, "are disturbed when this or that other man disappears. 'He gave a living to the poor,' they say. Should any man who has his hands and his patriotism depend on another for his living? Does he need the existence of another man to support his own? The poor will do without the rich, and Lyons will flourish none the less."

Collot, in being fiercely equalitarian, was not exactly socialist. In denouncing the rich he apparently had in mind, not a collective economy, but a country of equally small independent tradesmen, individualistic and free, to the point where one man's existence did not depend on the existence of another. This was a dream. In the real France of 1793, even in the Revolutionary Republic, the slaughter of manufacturers in Lyons would deprive thousands of employment, whatever Collot said, and would certainly not remedy the desperate under-production from which the country already suffered.

It was Robespierre who penned the instructions that the Committee sent to Couthon. His view was less proletarian and more political than Collot's. He reproved his absent colleague for yielding to a false humanity. A great danger remained, he said; rebels escaped from Lyons were carrying their poison to the other disaffected centers in the south. This belief was mistaken, for the escaped Girondists had fled to the east, and had been cut down almost to a man. But the Committee could not be sure, and the belief was some justification for its action.

"We will not congratulate you on your success," Robespierre wrote to Couthon, "until you have done all that you owe to our country. Republics are exacting. . . ." He warned Couthon against being too trustful. Hypocrisy, as always, was to be feared. "Traitors must be unmasked and struck without pity. These principles, adopted by the National Convention, may alone save the country. They are also yours; follow them; listen only to the dictates of your own energy, and execute with an inexorable severity the salutary decree which we are addressing to you." The decree was the order for the destruction of Lyons.

Couthon was undoubtedly embarrassed by this new word from Paris. It is not rare for the man on the spot to find himself given

fantastic orders, or for men at the front to find those at home
outdoing them in savagery of feeling. Couthon was not a weak
man; he showed his determination both at Lyons and in Puy-de-
Dôme. He was not a moderate man; in his political principles he
was always in the forefront of the Mountain. Perplexed historians
usually conclude that he had a divided nature. He lacked the absolute single-mindedness of the men who dominate revolutions. He
was profoundly different from Robespierre. Humorous enough
to jest about his own affliction, dependent upon friendship, a
married man and a father, he did not make his political views the
entire substance of his life, he was not consumed by suspicion,
and he still believed, as Robespierre once had, that killing, whatever its purpose, is in itself an evil. Nor did he think, like Collot
d'Herbois, that intimidation of others was a sign of strength.

Four days after receiving his new orders Couthon asked to be
relieved of his mission at Lyons. He addressed the request, not
directly to the Committee, or to Robespierre, but to Saint-Just.
The letter is one of the few pieces of evidence that allow us to
see the Committee of Public Safety as an association of human
beings.

"You have not written me a line, my friend," he said, "since
we last saw each other. I am disappointed, because you had promised in case of absence to send me news. Hérault has done better
than you have; I have received two of his letters." Couthon did
not know that Hérault, thanks to Fabre d'Eglantine's "foreign
plot," was now on the black books of the Committee. "You know,
my friend, that to console me in the troubles that beset me I need
some expressions of interest from those whom I esteem. Tell me
that you still exist, that you are well, that you haven't forgotten
me, and I shall be content. . . . Embrace Robespierre, Hérault and
our other good friends for me. . . . My wife, Hippolyte [his son]
and myself embrace you with all our heart."

From glimpses such as this we may imagine the spirit of fellowship which, in the fall of 1793, held the Committee together.

The business part of the letter came between the expressions of
friendship. The Lyonnese, said Couthon, would never be good
patriots. Jacobins should be sent from Paris to regenerate them.
Meanwhile, might he be transferred to Toulon? The southern air
would improve his health. And lastly (as if to show the integrity

expected by the Committee in its agents) might he keep for his own use a curious telescope that had belonged to a rebel leader?

Pending a reply from Paris, Couthon launched the new revolutionary courts, which, however, went into operation so slowly that relatively few executions took place before he left. He began also the process of demolition ordered from the capital. At half past seven in the morning, accompanied by a few soldiers and city officials, he drove into the Place Bellecour, one of the showplaces of Lyons, and after reading the decree of the Convention, solemnly struck three strokes with a hammer on one of the buildings, saying, "In the name of the Law I condemn you to be demolished." The inhabitants had been given time to move, and the wreckers did not hurry with the work. Couthon would probably have been content with formalities. Even some Jacobins protested, declaring that a war against sticks and stones was absurd.

Couthon managed to escape from what he could not prevent, leaving Lyons before the real violence began, going, as we know, not to Toulon, but to Clermont. He did not wait to report to his successors.

These successors were two of the men from whom, in all France, the people of Lyons could expect the least indulgence, Collot d'Herbois and Joseph Fouché, sent with the confidence of the Committee, of which Collot d'Herbois was the most stormy member.

Two strange lives here came together for a few weeks. Collot was an ex-actor, Fouché a onetime professor of physics. Collot was a rake, Fouché a respectable family man. Collot was to die within a few years wretchedly in Guiana, Fouché to emerge from his radical phase as the magnificent Duke of Otranto. The ex-actor was inclined to rant; he was an expansive, vehement, emotional and vulgar man, craving the center of the stage, dramatizing and gesticulating and bellowing when excited. The ex-professor was more quiet; he was cold, intellectual, canny; he preferred to work behind the scenes, delighting in anonymous omnipotence; and his manners were carefully governed. Both, in 1793, were furious equalitarians, and both were unscrupulous.

Fouché had long served in various posts as representative on mission. In the Nièvre, where he was stationed at the time of his appointment to Lyons, his policies were much like those of Couthon in the Puy-de-Dôme. He was a little more harsh with people of wealth, a little more radical in Dechristianization. His main aim, like Couthon's, was to mobilize the resources and control the public opinion of the department. He had set up no revolutionary courts, and no one was put to death in the Nièvre during his rule, though some were sent to the Revolutionary Tribunal in Paris. By and large, only one charge led to many death sentences during the Terror—sedition. Even Fouché, who was rabid against both the bourgeoisie and the church, hardly used the guillotine except on those whom he thought to be traitors. The Terror did not kill people for religion, as had once been the practice in Europe, nor yet for the idea of class, as the Bolshevist dictatorship was to do. It was primarily a weapon for enforcing political allegiance.

Collot d'Herbois had shown the bent of his mind in September, when he demanded death for those who gave out false news, and suggested that the Paris prisons, filled with suspects, should be blown up with mines. He especially detested the bourgeoisie of Lyons. Years before, as manager of the theater in that city, occupying a position that was then only partly respectable, he had seen the social pretensions and the snobbery of the moneyed classes. He had grudges and grievances and a sense of dramatic retribution. He was the only member of the Committee of Public Safety who did not come from a comfortable position in society. He was definitely a Hébertist, the chief author of the law against hoarding, and a consistent enemy of the "aristocracy of merchants."

At Lyons the bourgeoisie had risen in political revolt. The disciplining of rebels, which in some parts of the country meant the repression of peasants, here meant the repression of middle and upper class people. The opportunity was one which Fouché and Collot both used and enjoyed.

Robespierre later condemned the activities of Collot and Fouché on their joint mission. In the end, the hostility of these two to Robespierre helped to bring about his fall. Even in October Robespierre probably had no respect for either man. Collot had been taken into the Committee of Public Safety merely for political reasons; Fouché showed the same violence against religion for which Robespierre had already rebuked André Dumont. Some writers therefore conclude that Robespierre and the Committee, under Hébertist pressure in Paris, consented unwillingly to send Collot and Fouché to Lyons. They would in effect transfer from

COLLOT D'HERBOIS

Robespierrists to Hébertists the responsibility for the massacres that ensued.

It is easy to exaggerate this Hébertist pressure, because it is easy to call Hébertist a great many developments, such as the Maximum, the Levy in Mass, the war on the rich, the attacks on revealed religion, to which Mountaineers of many varieties at one time or another gave their enthusiastic assent. Vengeance upon Lyons was a Hébertist cry. It was also the policy of the government. The Committee had once tried conciliation. Robert Lindet had attempted in June to find a peaceable arrangement. He had failed; then came the siege, the long resistance, the hopes given to federalists, Vendéans, royalists and foreigners. Lyons became the symbol of obstruction. It was to be made, therefore, the symbol of Revolutionary justice. The word "city," said Barère, cannot be applied to a nest of conspirators. Robespierre blamed Couthon for moderation. Carnot drew up the order for dispatching the dreaded Revolutionary Army to the scene.

The rulers in Paris sent Fouché because they thought that his ideas, though perhaps too advanced for a quiet region, were suited to a country in insurrection. They formally endorsed his services in the Nièvre when they transferred him to Ville-Affranchie. They sent Collot, not simply as a means of placating the Hébertists, but because they wanted a known terrorist and a member of the Committee on the spot. They did not foresee what their two agents would do. But they urged them to be severe.

"These monsters must be unmasked and exterminated, or I must perish!" This was Robespierre's policy toward Lyons. Who were the monsters? How could one know? Enemies of the people were cunning in their disguise. They were often hypocrites. War, then, upon hypocrisy! But in a war on hypocrisy men may be accused of faults of which they give no sign, denounced for a word casually spoken, for an acquaintance that may be accidental, for an intention that may be only half conceived. The hunt for hypocrites is boundless, and can produce nothing but demoralization.

Collot reached Lyons on November 4. He immediately ordered a new "national tool, otherwise known as the holy guillotine." Fouché arrived almost a week later. It is possible that, to protect himself against an unknown future, he purposely lagged behind, so that Collot might assume the initiative and appear as the senior partner.

Both men brought an entourage of Jacobins who joined forces with the native sans-culottes. One of the first acts was a ceremonial purification of the city. A festival was held to honor the martyred Chalier.

"To purge the earth and the place where the last remains of this great man were to repose, ten heads were immolated yesterday, and perhaps ten more will fall tomorrow." The words are those of an eye-witness who glowed with satisfaction. Another described the event as follows in an ill-spelled report: "The most remarkable facts are first that an ass was dressed as a Monseigneur. A mitre and cross and all the finest pontifical garments were put on him. And church vases of gold and silver were carried before the ass. And along the way incense was burnt for him. And the said vases were broken on the tomb."

These crude impieties, which were continued in a Festival of Reason two *décades* later, were in direct opposition to the wishes of the Committee of Public Safety. Collot d'Herbois did not have the excuse of Couthon, who was taking part in similar desecrations at this time at Clermont. Couthon perhaps did not know the views of the Committee. But Collot had just come from Paris. He had signed his name, on October 27, to Robespierre's dispatch to André Dumont, instructing Dumont to respect the objects of Catholic worship. Since Lyons was full of Hébertists from Paris, who were supposed by Fouché, Collot perhaps could not in any case have enforced the religious policy of the Committee. Certainly he did not try.

There is no reason to believe that Robespierre disapproved at the time of the rest of Collot's program, so far as he understood it. Collot's letters to Paris kept the Committee informed of his general plans. From the same letters we can see the ideas with which he entered upon his work.

He came to Lyons as a man bent on the annihilation of an accursed city. He interpreted the famous decree in a sweeping sense. The decree, after all, beneath the pompous phraseology, specified for destruction only the houses of the rich. Collot meant to go further. He thought that the demolitions under Couthon had been too slow. He prepared to smash the city with mines and artillery fire. "The explosion of mines, etc., the devouring activity of flame can alone express the omnipotence of the people; its will cannot be checked like that of tyrants; it must have the effect of thunder." Collot might have recalled that thunder in itself is only a loud noise, which produces few effects except sometimes to turn milk sour.

Collot believed that there were virtually no reliable patriots in Lyons. He thought of his mission as a visitation of justice, in which men from one city came to work their will upon those of another. He saw nothing improper in giving free rein to the Jacobins and the Revolutionary Army that streamed in from Paris. These men he identified with the "entire people." The inhabitants of Lyons, whose number he estimated at from 130,000 to 150,000, he regarded as "individuals." Individuals, he thought, could be shown no mercy by the Revolution. He hoped, however, that some of the Lyonnese could be saved. It seemed to him that about 60,000 were of the working class. He recommended that these 60,000 (at first he said 100,000) should be uprooted from Lyons, distributed through patriotic parts of the country, and shaped into true republicans by their new environment. "Disseminated and watched, they will at least follow the lead of those who march beside them. Kept together, they would long be a dangerous nucleus, always favorable to enemies of true principles." Collot thus anticipated the methods of mass transportation used by more recent dictators. "You are too philosophical," he wrote to Robespierre, "to let this idea escape you." It is to be remarked that mass transportation had already been used by the British in Acadia.

The rest of the city's inhabitants Collot seems hardly to have considered among the population. "The population once evacuated," he wrote to Couthon explaining the same idea, "it will be easy to make the city disappear, and to say with truth, 'Lyons is no more.'" Even Collot d'Herbois can hardly have proposed to put to death the sixty-odd thousand whom he deemed unworthy to transport. What he thought, if he thought at all clearly on this point, is not known.

The new proconsul was impatient at the leisurely habits of Couthon's courts. Where Couthon had meant to punish only active rebels, Collot held that no one was innocent who had not suffered from the preceding régime. "Indulgence is a dangerous weakness." Scoundrels must perish to assure life to future generations. When he had been in Lyons a month he found that traitors were still not dying fast enough. Twenty executions a day, he said, were not sufficient to frighten the Lyonnese. "Kings punished slowly, because they were weak and cruel; the justice of the people must be as prompt as the expression of its will." He therefore sought more dynamic methods.

To keep passions aroused, he sent on to the Convention a model of the head of Chalier, which had been badly mangled by the Girondist guillotine. It was to be used as a kind of holy relic. "When attempts are made to move your more tender feelings," he wrote to the assembly, "uncover this bleeding head to the eyes of pusillanimous men who see only individuals." To Duplay, Robespierre's friend and landlord, he observed that the humane sentiments of rebels were mere pretense. "On that side are men who affect a false and barbarous sensibility. Our sensibility is entirely for our country." So the line is drawn, the fatal antithesis, "we and they." *We* represent totality, patriotism, sincerity, devotion; *they* represent mere individuals, treachery, hypocrisy, pig-headedness.

Collot d'Herbois thus becomes a political fanatic. His mind is turned by the fundamental idea of the Revolution, the transfer of sovereignty from king to people. In the name of the people he pushes the meaning of sovereignty to its most hideous extreme: absolute will; inhuman, unmoral, illimitable power. He has made himself a new God, the "people," from which he sees his enemies hopelessly estranged. His "people" is omnipotent and wrathful. To glorify it he will blow up whole cities. Humanity, practical sense, even self-interest are forgotten, lost in the frenzy of good intentions, taut emotions and fixed ideas of which fanaticism is compounded.

A fanatic, however unreasoning, may serve an intelligible cause. The cause for which Collot d'Herbois labored was the struggle against the bourgeoisie. In his mind, more clearly than for most Jacobins, the people meant the proletariat. Fouché at this time was of much the same opinion. Lyons offered them a good field of operations, for at Lyons the lines of economic class were clear. The proconsuls had to admit that the masses in the city were not good Jacobins. They would have been embarrassed if asked to state an economic philosophy. They had no real program for the production of goods once the bourgeoisie should be liquidated. Their economic aims were confused by sentimentalism, political expediency and atheistical fervors. Their campaign was blind and spasmodic, but it was none the less a move in a class war.

To carry out their orders they created a Temporary Commission of twenty members. The obscure persons thus raised to power were not above a common frailty: they wished to be recognized. They adopted a uniform, though their office was a civil one, and even forbade the citizens of Lyons to wear their chosen color, blue. The Commissioners were apparently in need of clothing, and their wants were not modest. For each one, out of the public funds, were ordered, to be exact: a blue coat with red collar, blue trousers with leather between the legs, breeches of deerskin, an overcoat and leather suitcase, a cocked hat with tricolor plume, a black shoulder-belt, various medals, six shirts, twelve pocket handkerchiefs, muslin for six ordinary cravats, black taffeta for two dress cravats, a tricolored belt, six cotton nightcaps, six pairs of stockings, two pairs of shoes, kid gloves *à l'espagnole,* boots *à l'américaine,* bronzed spurs, saddle pistols and a hussar's saber.

Thus outfitted, and supplied with suitable mounts, the Commission administered Revolutionary law in Lyons and the whole department of the Rhône. It drew up, with the knowledge of the representatives, an "Instruction to the Constituted Authorities," which has been called the first communist manifesto of modern times. The Instruction laid down as a principle: "All is permitted to those who act in the Revolutionary direction."

According to the Instruction the Revolution was especially made for the "immense class of the poor." The authors found a "shocking disproportion" between toil and income. They assailed the bourgeoisie; and they cried to the working class somewhat in the manner of Marx: "You have been oppressed; you must crush your oppressors!"

Products of French soil were declared to belong to "France." The farmer was to receive an "indemnity" in exchange for his goods. The wealth of the rich was put at the disposal of the Republic. Those who had an annual income of 10,000 livres were to pay a revolutionary tax of 30,000 livres. "There is no question here of mathematical exactness or timid scruples in the levying of public taxes."

The Instruction provided death as the penalty even for those whose connection with the rebellion was indirect. It was strongly Dechristianizing. Declaring (somewhat inconsistently) that priests were the sole causes of the public misery, and that the relations of God and man were purely internal, it confiscated the precious objects in churches, and directed that public symbols of the cult should be destroyed.

To some extent the revolutionary tax was collected. With the methods of administration that were available, it could scarcely be distinguished from plunder. Requisitions were made also on the neighboring peasants. Collot observed that, in view of the competition for food among conflicting powers, the most successful operators were those who travelled with armed forces. The peasants tended to regard this procedure as nothing but rapine. As for lawyers, nobles and priests, they were jailed as suspects without more ado, and their property confiscated.

The machinery of repression was completed at the end of November. On the 25th the Revolutionary Army at last arrived, several hundred men with cannon, commanded by Ronsin, who like Collot d'Herbois was a playwright by profession. The "army" had seen service in the Vendée. It was now to combat a people already defeated. Theoretically composed of patriots who, by age or marriage, were exempt from service at the front, it had in its ranks a medley of draft evaders, drifters, adventurers and toughs, ready to do any strong-arm work that political leaders might require. Collot d'Herbois had impatiently awaited their arrival.

Ronsin had a very low opinion of Lyons, where, he said, there were not 1,500 patriots. He wrote to the Cordeliers club in Paris describing his entrance into the city:

"Terror was painted on every face. The deep silence that I took care to recommend to our brave troops made their march even more menacing and terrible. Most of the shops were closed. A few women stood along our way. In their faces could be read more indignation than fear. The men stayed hidden in those same dens from which, during the siege, they came out to murder the true friends of liberty. The guillotine and the fusillade have done justice to more than four hundred rebels. But a new revolutionary commission has just been established, composed of true sansculottes. My colleague Parein is president, and in a few days grapeshot, launched by our cannoneers, will have delivered us in a single instant of more than four thousand conspirators. It is time to shorten the forms!"

The new commission to which Ronsin referred was the Tribunal of Seven, organized under the chairmanship of Parein by Collot and Fouché on November 27, and destined shortly to replace all the other revolutionary courts in the vicinity.

A few days later (it was the day of the Feast of Reason) the two proconsuls received a petition from the women of Lyons, said to bear more than 10,000 signatures. The petitioners remonstrated against having the destiny of a great city decided by seven judges. They implored mercy for the thousands of men crowded in the jails. They appealed to nature, humanity, posterity. The authorities remained unmoved. "The revolutionary march takes no holiday," said Fouché, though not publicly. "It no more stops than does the will and the justice of the people." The city officials were more direct. "Shut yourselves up in the privacy of your household tasks," they announced to the women. "Let us see no more of the tears that dishonor you!" Jacobins would consider this answer truly Roman in its grandeur and virility.

So preparations went ahead. The people of Lyons were not yet sufficiently frightened. As Collot said, twenty deaths a day were not enough. As Ronsin said, the inhabitants were more indignant than afraid. As Parein said, it was absolutely essential "to impress terror on the brows of the rebels if we do not wish to run the risk of being assassinated ourselves."

The climax came on December 4, the 14th of Frimaire, the day of the great law that made much of what was happening at Lyons illegal.

Sixty persons, condemned by the Tribunal of Seven, were marched out to the Broteaux, an open place across the Rhône from the city. They arrived singing the Girondist hymn, offering, like Jacobins, to die for their country. They were placed between open ditches intended for their graves. Three loaded cannon were directed on the spot. Near at hand stood dragoons with drawn sabers. The cannon fired; the victims crumpled; the dragoons scrambled over the ditches to put an end to the writhing and screaming mass. The process is said to have taken two hours, owing to the inexperience of the swordsmen. Even Collot admitted that it took too long. Two victims who managed to bolt were shot in flight.

On the next day about two hundred and nine were brought to the Broteaux. The exact number is not known, so hasty was the procedure; tradition says that two government employees who happened to be at the prison were herded in with the others despite their protestations. The condemned men were tied together and raked with grapeshot. One, formerly a member of the Constituent Assembly, set free when his hand was shot off, began to run. He was caught and dispatched by Ronsin's men. The others, variously wounded, were killed and their bodies thrown into the ditches. The graves were so shallow that within a few weeks the municipality had to sprinkle them with quicklime to prevent pestilence.

Another hundred were similarly put to death after a pause of two days.

Wholesale execution at Lyons began in this gruesome manner. The guillotine presently resumed its old ascendancy as the means of death. Never again were two hundred massacred in one day. But the totals mounted. The stench and filth about the guillotine became a public problem, with which a special commission had to deal. Degradation reached the point where women and children, for souvenirs, snatched bloodsoaked garments from dead bodies. At this development even the man who had commanded at the massacres of Frimaire was revolted. He thought it "incompatible with republican austerity."

By April 1794 almost two thousand persons had been put to death at Lyons, more than a tenth of all those sentenced by revolutionary courts for all France during the whole period of the Terror. Of the victims at Lyons 64 per cent came from the middle and upper classes. For France outside Lyons the figure for these classes was only 28 per cent. The Lyonnese bourgeoisie paid dearly for its rebellion.

The events of 14 and 15 Frimaire filled the harpies at the doomed city with great joy. The long promised thunder and lightning had at last struck. Presumably the people of Lyons would henceforth be sufficiently afraid.

"May this festival," wrote the judge Dorfeuille to the president of the Convention, "forever impress terror upon the souls of rascals and confidence upon the hearts of republicans!" It was the ultimate fatuity of the Terrorists to believe that confidence could be created by intimidation. "I say festival, citizen president; yes, festival is the word. When crime descends to the grave humanity breathes again, and it is the festival of virtue."

"Still the heads fall, heads every day!" read a letter to Paris written on 17 Frimaire by Achard, whom Robespierre carried on his lists of usable followers. "What delight you would have tasted if you had seen day before yesterday the national justice upon two hundred and nine scoundrels! What majesty! What imposing tone! It was all edifying. How many villains bit the dust in the arena of the Broteaux! What a cement for the Republic!" After a sentimental quiver at the thought of patriots whom the tribunal had acquitted, Achard estimated that at least another thousand heads would roll. "P. S. Greetings to Robespierre, Duplay and Nicolas."

It is unnecessary to quote further from the tidings sent home by these apostles. It is only necessary to observe the combination of blood lust with the jargon of revolutionary idealism. It is necessary to realize that these men inflicted death with a holy glee.

What the Committee of Public Safety thought of the massacres will never be certainly known. Couthon, now back in Paris, must have been sickened. Nor could he have been the only one. To what extent the Committee was taken by surprise is also not quite clear. The procedure used in the Broteaux was exactly outlined by the Temporary Commission more than ten days in advance. It was common knowledge in the inner circle at Lyons. Ronsin predicted it when he wrote to the Cordeliers. But apparently his letter reached Paris at about the time of the massacre itself.

It is significant that Collot d'Herbois, reporting on 15 Frimaire, did not write either to the Committee or to Robespierre, though both were among his regular correspondents. He wrote to Duplay, his friend and Robespierre's. He mentioned the massacres casually, as if they were nothing very unusual. He meant them to be unusual, however; their whole purpose was to frighten the Lyonnese by a spectacular and unparalleled act of justice. Had he believed that Robespierre and the Committee would be as enthusiastic as he was, he would probably have sent a more direct and more glowing account.

The Committee, moreover, it should be remembered, had long opposed the tendency of representatives on mission to become independent potentates. Billaud-Varenne kept the issue alive. He too was a Hébertist, admitted to the Committee along with Collot d'Herbois. The two men developed in opposite directions. Collot remained anarchical, wild; Billaud became the apostle of organization. Billaud tried on October 4, acting for the Committee, to curtail the powers of deputies on mission. The Convention demurred; and the Committee had to be content with what Saint-Just could get, the decree declaring the government revolutionary until the peace. But Billaud persisted. At the very time when Collot was planning his massacres, Billaud was urging upon the Convention the bill, prepared by himself and his colleagues, which became the law of 14 Frimaire. This law gave the Committee the right to appoint, control and recall the travelling representatives.

Clemency, to be sure, was not what Billaud or Robespierre wanted in the provinces, certainly not in the Girondist centers. But the Committee of Public Safety did want agents who would obey its orders. Collot d'Herbois had shown by his Dechristianizing fervors, if by nothing else, that he could not be trusted to carry out the policy of the government.

From the evidence, such as it is, a conclusion may be drawn. The Committee did not know of the massacres in advance (though perhaps some extremists in Paris did); and it did not much like them when they happened. Presented with the accomplished fact, it had to give its approval. No one in authority could afford to bear the stigma of moderatism. No one could seem to befriend enemies of the people. No one claiming to be true to the Revolution could safely seem less advanced than another who made the same claim. This was the reality in what has been called "Hébertist pressure." Until extremists could be branded as traitors, extremism held a whip hand over more moderate counsels. So long as relatively moderate men might be accused of falling short of the aims which all acknowledged, the moderate men would have to accept, endorse and even glorify the acts of the more violent.

The Committee of Public Safety was caught in this predicament with respect to the slaughter at Lyons. Its members had stated their aims. They had used inflammatory language: the sword of the law must wave; monsters must be exterminated; a nest of conspirators is not a city; republics are exacting. They had declared, grandiosely, without meaning it (as the wording of the decree showed): "Lyons shall be destroyed." They believed in the Terror, in creating confidence by fear, and purity by excision. They did not intend to have two thousand persons killed, or to have massacres theatrically staged to the taste of overheated playwrights, or to have a great city pillaged by unscrupulous intruders in the name of public duty. They were surprised when all this happened. Whether they should have been is another question. They were simply taken at their word, by men who shared their high-flown phrases but were their inferiors in practical sense and honesty of purpose. And the actions of these men, at least for the time being, had to be accepted and approved.

On December 20 a deputation of citizens of Lyons appeared in Paris at the bar of the Convention. They announced that the city was repentant, eager to enter again into fraternity with the Republic. But how could the raging fury of the terrorists lead to peace? The Convention, they pointed out, had never wished legal forms to be abolished or cruel and hideous forms of death inflicted. It had never authorized the inhumanity which its representatives were displaying. It had not wished to destroy, but to create a new, loyal, prosperous Lyons in place of the old. With this aim the petitioners professed themselves to be in complete agreement.

Doubtless the petitioners expressed more faith in the Jacobin Republic than they really felt, and in that sense were hypocrites of the kind that the Republican authorities were determined to root out. Nevertheless, there was weight in their plea, which the Convention turned over to the Committee of Public Safety for consideration.

Unfortunately for the Liberated City, Collot d'Herbois had already rushed back to Paris in self-defense. When the petition from Lyons reached the green table, there sat Collot with the others to receive it. What passed at the conference no one knows. But the decision was not favorable to the Lyonnese, for the Committee sent Collot to give its answer on the next day in the Convention. The Committee had to acknowledge Collot d'Herbois. Ronsin, a mere street radical, it could disown; it had arrested him a day or two before. The campaign against Hébertists, begun at the time of the Foreign Plot, was steadily progressing, though thus far no important figure had been touched.

Collot said nothing new in his speech to the Convention. He dwelt on his old idea of dispersing the population of Lyons. He deprecated that members should disturb themselves over the shootings in the Broteaux. He reasserted that the troubles of Ville-Affranchie came from the enslavement of the poor by the rich. He painted a dark picture of conspiracies in an unregenerate city, which only unremitting terrorization could keep down. He described with pleasure the speedy trials held out of doors, in the open fields, without stuffy formalities, "under the vault of nature." And he reminded his hearers that those who died did not really form part of the people.

He succeeded in counteracting the effect of the petition. The Convention did nothing.

That night Collot went to the Jacobins. He passed with flying colors the "purifying scrutiny" which the society was holding. At Hébert's invitation he described his work at Ville-Affranchie. "In my report to the Convention," he admitted, "I was obliged to employ every circumlocution and every resource of art to justify my conduct, which facts alone ought to justify." He reviled the people of the rebel city, especially the women, who he said were "plunged madly into adultery and prostitution." He denounced the arrest of Ronsin, a worthy patriot who had aided in the good work. Collot thus defied Robespierre, allying himself openly with the ultras whom Robespierre was determined to master.

"Men speak of sensibility," he concluded. "We too are men with sensibilities. The Jacobins have every virtue. They are compassionate, humane, generous; but they reserve all these feelings for the patriots who are their brothers, which aristocrats will never be." We and they!

Meanwhile in Lyons, under Fouché, the butchery continued. Plausible reasons for ruthlessness had long since passed. There was no more the first impulse to revenge, for it was almost three months since the city had fallen. The leading rebels were no more to be feared; they had been among the first to die. The federalist movement had long since ebbed; Bordeaux and Marseilles were under control; so was the Vendée. Toulon was retaken from the English on December 19. The foreign menace was no longer alarming; the armies were in a state of semi-hibernation. Class hatred remained, but it was blind hatred, with no real program of economic reconstruction, only a program of plunder and revolutionary extortion. Political disaffection was still much alive, but there was no longer any disaffection at Lyons which endless intimidation would not make worse.

In short, the Terror, which in the preceding summer had had an object, was debased at Lyons in December to an outburst of vindictiveness and fanaticism. What at its best was a reasonable policy of government was here at its worst—a tyranny in the hands of irresponsible and uncontrollable extremists.

Fouché wrote to Collot almost immediately after Collot left for Paris. He had just received news of the capture of Toulon. "Farewell, my friend," he said. "Tears of joy stream in my eyes and flood my soul. . . . P. S. We have only one way of celebrating victory. This evening we send two hundred and thirteen rebels under the fire of the lightning-bolt."

And on the first day of the new year, 1794, the Convention received a hymn to the new era, a message from Fouché, who was fearful that the complaints against his rule might be too favorably heard. The old story was repeated: men who asked moderation were hypocrites and traitors.

"Yes, we dare to admit it, we are shedding much impure blood, but for humanity, and for duty. Representatives of the people, we will not betray the people's will. . . .

"Our mission here is difficult and painful. Only an ardent love of country can console and reward the man who, renouncing all the affections which nature and gentle habits have made dear to his heart, surrendering his own sensibility and his own existence, thinks, acts and lives only in the people and with the people, and shutting his eyes to everything about him, sees nothing but the Republic that will rise in posterity on the graves of conspirators and the broken swords of tyranny."

It is odd to find the Revolutionary faith so warmly expressed by Fouché, known as a cynic and double dealer, famous as minister of police under Napoleon. Was he sincere in 1793? Very likely he was. Perhaps the cynicism of his later years came from disillusionment in a faith once held with absolute firmness. Persons of many kinds saw a vision during the Revolution. Some were lovers of power, men of little scruple in ordinary dealings with others. Their vision was not for that reason less genuinely seen. They were not hypocrites. Fouché may have been one of these men. He was the same Fouché in 1793 and ten years later, a lover of power, a hunter of suspects and user of devious methods. But in 1793 he believed that he served a noble cause, that when he acted with unchecked violence he expressed the omnipotence of the people. Ten years later, like so many who begin by believing that the end justifies the means, he found that the means to which he had grown accustomed had become ends in themselves, good because they produced results; and so he pursued power and hunted suspects, no longer in the name of a humanitarian ideal, but to serve Bonaparte—and himself.

As for Lyons, we must note that the menaces and the maledictions had, after all, less effect than might have been expected. Lyons was not destroyed. Not all the guilty perished. The population was not transported. Relatively few buildings were demolished. In a year or two the city bore few external signs of the Jacobin visitation. But its citizens long nourished a sense of outrage, and thousands believed that members of their families had been brutally murdered. Memories created during the Terror dominated all the later history of France, and indeed of all Europe. We cannot understand that history or those memories without dwelling on events which many modern historians pass over as sensational. As if the sensational, for human beings, were unimportant.

CHAPTER VIII
The Missions to Alsace

ONCE upon a time (so the next episode might begin), while a very young Republic was struggling with an old, old Empire, one of its fairest provinces was in deep trouble. This province was on the border between the warring countries. Its people were mixed; they faced both ways. Bad and designing men stirred them up. Everybody was uncertain, excited, afraid. The soldiers of the Emperor had broken in, fierce Croats and other fighters from the east. All seemed lost, when suddenly two youths appeared, close friends, almost brothers, sent from the capital of the Republic to save the day. The two youths went to work with a will. They punished the bad men, brought back the courage of their troops, gave them shoes, food, guns; and soon the Emperor's army turned and fled. The two youths then departed as quickly as they had come, after taking only a few weeks to perform their task.

This sounds like a story from the never-never land. Serious historians are not supposed to put off their readers with fairy tales. And yet, when the strictest methods of history have been used, when the evidence has been gathered, when conflicting reports have been cancelled out, prejudices allowed for, exaggerations discounted, and enthusiasms watered down, when we have been as critical and as coldly judicial as we please, a certain fairy-tale atmosphere still hangs over the mission of Saint-Just and his friend Le Bas to Alsace—although, to be sure, the good people and the bad people are not so easy to distinguish as one might wish.

It was in Alsace that the danger from the Allies was most pressing in the last two months of 1793. The enemy, as seen from Paris, was like one of those flabby masses which when pushed in one place protrude in another. The Austrians were checked in the north at Wattignies on October 16; but to assemble the force for this victory the French armies in the east had been weakened; the Prussians therefore advanced toward the river Saar, and on October 13, while Carnot and Jourdan were preparing for battle in Flanders, an Imperial host burst through the French lines at

Wissembourg, drove back the French in utter disorder, and streamed into the department of the Lower Rhine almost to the walls of Strasbourg.

The Committee of Public Safety immediately dispatched Saint-Just to the threatened spot. The decision was made on October 17. News of Wattignies had not yet reached the green room. Marie Antoinette had been guillotined the day before; the trial of the Girondists was about to open; the Foreign Plot had just been denounced by Fabre; within the Committee Hérault-Séchelles was suspected by his colleagues. The British and the royalists held Toulon. The war in the Vendée was at its height. Lyons had fallen a week ago, but the Committee feared that the rebel leaders would undo the Jacobin triumph by scattering secretly through the south.

Alsace was therefore only one problem among several, but it was a problem that presented difficulties of its own. The people of Alsace were German in language and tradition. They had belonged to the French crown for more than a century, and had become loyal to France largely because the old monarchy did not use modern methods of assimilation. Before the Revolution, even in France, ideas of sovereignty and national unity were only partly developed, so that many local peculiarities existed. Alsace continued to be mostly German, the substance of its law unchanged, its Lutheran minorities officially respected, its people subject to relatively light taxes and more free than the rest of France to carry on commerce with Germany. In a sense parts of Alsace were still within the Holy Roman Empire from which they had been conquered. Certain German rulers, among them the prince-bishop of Speir and the margrave of Baden, held lands in northern Alsace where they collected feudal rents and kept a vague legal jurisdiction. Law cases were sometimes appealed from Alsatian courts to the higher courts of these German princes. Agents of the same princes were active in Alsatian villages. Many Alsatians outside the cities thought of their German lord as their true ruler, considered the transfer to France as a piece of high politics far over their heads, and, seeing Frenchmen rarely, viewed them with detachment.

The Revolution swept all provincial liberties away. The modern state which the Revolution created could not tolerate such eccentric overlappings as existed in Alsace. The new idea of airtight sovereignty shut out the authority of the German princes. The abolition of feudal dues deprived them of a historic source of income. Thus the old treaties of annexation were violated; the emperor protested as guardian of German rights, and the friction that resulted was one of the first causes of the war. Alsatian peasants were cut off from the lords to whom they had always looked, and from the formless thing called Germany to which they had not ceased to belong. They could hardly help feeling like orphans in the new France.

Alsace nevertheless responded eagerly to the first stirrings of the Revolution. The peasants were glad to be rid of their feudal payments. The educated classes of the cities were already half French—a fact that seems less remarkable when we remember that French civilization at this time permeated the whole German world. The Alsatians had the advantage of belonging to the country which, in 1789, sent a thrill of hope through the unprivileged classes of most of Europe. Alsace therefore produced its contingent of Revolutionary leaders.

But in 1793, when the Allied forces came in from the north, events in France had gone far beyond the expectations of 1789. In Alsace as elsewhere there was much disaffection. Strasbourg was a prey to outsiders, somewhat as Lyons became a few weeks later. The religious troubles were acute. The peasants grumbled over requisitions. The dominance of Paris was especially resented because of the habits of local liberty that had grown up under the Bourbons.

Now the Imperial army, in which nationality counted for nothing, was commanded by an Alsatian, Wurmser, born in Strasbourg. As he moved into Alsace he invited the natives to join him. Some did so gladly. He set about restoring the old régime, had *Te Deums* sung in the churches for his victories, and masses celebrated for the soul of the deceased French queen. With Wurmser came a swarm of civil servants of the expropriated German princes, bent on reclaiming the lands and revenues lost by their masters. Many peasants received them with open arms, hoping to return to the old familiar village life. Moreover in the Imperial army, besides Serbs, Croats, Slovenians, Wallachians and various kinds of Germans, was the force known as the Army of Condé, seven infantry battalions and twelve cavalry squadrons of French émigrés. These embittered Frenchmen brought a turmoil of revenge into the invaded districts. Even so, they were welcomed by many Alsatians who had turned against the Revolution.

The flood of the old régime was rolling into the Republic, and no man could tell where it might stop. Age was personified in the two commanders, for Wurmser was sixty-nine years old, and his Prussian colleague, the duke of Brunswick, fifty-eight. They were both trained in the old-fashioned school of warfare, and were actually much less formidable than they seemed. Unknown to the French, Brunswick was under orders not to disable the Republican army, not to take advantage of its mistakes, and not to give much help to the Austrians, whom the Prussian court continued to regard as its most dangerous enemy. This diplomatic situation was doubtless a greater advantage to the Republic than the youth of its defenders. The contrast remains, however: after the disasters of mid-October the Army of the Rhine was given to Pichegru, who was thirty-two, the Army of the Moselle to Hoche, who was twenty-five, and the supreme civilian power to Saint-Just and Le Bas, who were respectively twenty-six and twenty-eight.

Saint-Just completely overshadowed Le Bas and determined the policies of their joint mission. Their first report to the Committee of Public Safety, written from Saverne in Alsace, has recently been discovered by an American historian, Mr. E. N. Curtis. The manuscript, in Saint-Just's hand, bears a significant correction. Saint-Just in his haste wrote, "I have given you this detail," then catching the error changed "I" to "we." Le Bas did not object to this domination, was perhaps not even aware of it. The two agreed perfectly; Le Bas worshiped Saint-Just as a paragon, almost a saint; they were personal friends, and Saint-Just was engaged to marry Le Bas' sister.

Fiery, peremptory, curt, Saint-Just was the same man who, less than two weeks before coming to Alsace, had prevailed upon the Convention to vote the government revolutionary until the peace. By revolutionary government he meant government that went straight to its objectives without the formalities of law. He detested verbiage, bureaucracy, red tape. It is impossible to govern without being laconic, he said; and some of his dispatches were models of concision. He patterned himself on those men of few words, the Spartans, adopting a stern demeanor that had been foreign to his youth. With the rigidity of a man who knows himself to be right, he could be cordial in the circle of those who supported him, coldly exclusive to those outside. Someone remarked that he carried his head as if it were the holy sacrament.

Saint-Just and Le Bas arrived in Alsace equipped with "extraordinary powers." Nine representatives armed with "unlimited powers" were already operating in the neighborhood. As members of the Convention and Representatives of the People, these men recognized no authority above them, regarding even the Committee of Public Safety as simply a group of their equals. In taking this attitude they followed the Convention itself, which in October refused to invest its main Committee with control over the representatives on mission. Not even Saint-Just, in putting through the decree of October 10, had been able to win that concession from the assembly.

Saint-Just, for his part, came to Alsace with the idea that the representatives already there had failed. He ignored them from the start. One of his first acts was to write to the Committee asking for their recall. Some were recalled, but others were sent in their place. The Committee, however, continued to correspond almost exclusively with Saint-Just and Le Bas, leaving the other representatives to fret and fume, complain of neglect, and declare that the ascendancy of Saint-Just robbed them of all effective authority.

Acute tension developed between Saint-Just and some of the other representatives on mission. Arising from the struggle between the Committee and the Convention, this clash was a significant incident in the growth of the Revolutionary dictatorship. But it showed even more clearly how little of a real dictatorship had yet been established, for it exposed the disorganization and divergency of powers. The conflict illustrated at the same time the differences, which were becoming increasingly real, between Robespierrism and Hébertism, for Saint-Just was the closest in the Committee to Robespierre, and the other representatives in Alsace were inclined to be ultra.

Intertwined and confused with these political quarrels the real purpose of the mission to Alsace worked itself out. Saint-Just and Le Bas were commissioned to the Army of the Rhine. The Army of the Moselle was presently added to their jurisdiction. They were expected to organize the forces by which the invaders could be driven from France.

The weeks from October 22, the day of their arrival in Alsace, to November 16, when they temporarily left Strasbourg for the front, were the most constructive period of the mission. After November 16 the civilian representatives became increasingly involved in party disputes, and the work of driving out the enemy fell more largely to the military commanders, Pichegru and Hoche.

Saint-Just was known from his great speech of October 10 to have definite ideas on dealing with soldiers. The question to him was above all one of morale. The troops must be made to feel that they fought in their own cause, for the salvation of the democratic Republic; they must have faith in the men who ordered their movements both from behind the lines and on the battlefield; and they must believe that the highest officials of government were really concerned about the welfare of common soldiers. The Army of the Rhine in particular, beaten and dispirited, huddled before the walls of Strasbourg, demoralized by the conviction that it had been betrayed, needed above all else to have its confidence restored. Saint-Just did not hesitate to dramatize himself as the long awaited angel of retribution. On his first day in Strasbourg he issued a proclamation.

> The Representatives of the People,
> sent on extraordinary mission to the
> Army of the Rhine, to the soldiers of
> that army
>
> > Strasbourg, 3rd day of
> > the 2nd month of the 2nd
> > year of the Republic One
> > and Indivisible.
> > [October 24, 1793]

We arrive! and we swear in the name of the army that the enemy shall be conquered. If there are traitors or even persons lukewarm to the cause of the people we bring the sword that is to strike them. Soldiers, we come to avenge you and to give you leaders who will take you to victory. We are determined to search for merit, to reward and advance it, and to pursue all crimes whosoever they be who commit them. Courage, brave Army of the Rhine; you shall henceforth have, along with liberty, good fortune and victory!

All chiefs, officers and agents of government whatsoever are commanded to satisfy within three days the just grievances of the soldiers. After this interval we will ourselves hear these grievances, and we will give such examples of justice and severity as the army has not yet seen.

SAINT-JUST, LE BAS

It was to lay a foundation for discipline, not to encourage petty complaining, that Saint-Just invited the men to make their grievances known. On the same day, apparently a few hours later, he issued another proclamation, announcing the victory at Wattignies. Discipline, he said, was the quality to which the Army of the North owed its success. This thesis he many times repeated.

The officers needed disciplining perhaps even more than the men. Many of them were in the habit of spending the nights in Strasbourg. Officers and men alike had been encouraged by other representatives to take part in the Jacobin politics of the city. With the officers setting so poor an example, and keeping such lax control, the morale of the troops broke down, and soldiers wandered aimlessly over the countryside looking for food or adventure.

Saint-Just set about the purging of army officers which for some time had been a feature of national policy. Many were arrested as traitors or aristocrats; the result was to rid the army of a number of officers that the troops distrusted. Saint-Just affirmed that for the good of the army at least one general must be put to death. The victim was Isambert, a man of sixty, who had weakly surrendered his post to a handful of Austrian hussars; he was condemned by a military court, and shot before the eyes of the assembled troops. Half a dozen other officers met the same fate, including one brigadier.

Officers were ordered to stay with their men. Generals were instructed to sleep in their tents. General Perdieu was dismissed for being in the theater in Strasbourg a few hours after his unit, stationed in the extreme front lines, had been attacked by the enemy. A certain Captain Texier, on his way to the theater a few nights later, had the misfortune to ask directions of Citizen Saint-Just himself. The captain was arrested. Army surgeons also felt the hand of the new master. They were ordered to remain with the men in battle instead of withdrawing safely to the rear. They were commanded also to stop the abuse of hospitalization papers, which soldiers were using as an official pretext for shirking.

Troops were forbidden to leave their places in camp; all outstanding permits to go out were canceled; officers were made responsible for full contingents. A cavalry trooper who asked leave to go home to watch over his private fortune was publicly degraded. It was decreed that anyone trying to slip by stealth into Strasbourg would be shot. And repeatedly Saint-Just ordered Pichegru to drill his men.

To the Austrians, when they suggested a parley, he gave one of his laconic answers. "The French Republic takes from and sends to its enemies nothing but lead."

The troops meanwhile had to be fed, clothed and armed. They were as ragged and ill equipped as the Army of the North whose needs drove Jourdan almost frantic. Corruption and graft ran through the whole system of supply. Saint-Just decreed that dishonest purveyors, if convicted, should be shot; if only suspected, sent to the interior to prison. The Law of the Maximum was to be rigorously enforced. The authorities of eight adjoining departments were ordered to furnish grain and fodder within twelve days. Local authorities in places along the roads were required to supply horses and wagons.

In Strasbourg the demands were especially heavy. On October 31 the city officials were told to raise five thousand pairs of shoes and fifteen thousand shirts. On the same day a forced loan of nine million livres was exacted, to be paid by 193 citizens whose names were attached to the order. Four days later the impatient proconsuls were demanding why these levies had not yet produced results. On November 6 the mayor was instructed "to excite the zeal of all citizens" to supply the army with shoes, coats and hats. On the next morning, from ten o'clock to one, the most wealthy of the persons refusing the forced loan was made to sit, as a lesson to himself and to others, on the scaffold of the guillotine. A week later two thousand beds were demanded from the "rich" of Strasbourg, and on the next day ten thousand pairs of shoes from the "aristocrats" of the same city. Every overcoat in the city was also requisitioned. Since Strasbourg had hardly more than 40,000 inhabitants, it is evident that the tribute of beds (if ever collected) was not paid by the rich only, and that the ten thousand pairs of shoes were not all from the feet of aristocrats—except so far as "aristocrat" was a mere political expression.

To enforce such sweeping ordinances, and to deal with suspects, revolutionary courts were needed. Saint-Just and Le Bas, on their second day in Alsace, created such a court to travel through the department of the Lower Rhine. They extended the authority of the old military tribunal, giving it jurisdiction over persons charged with favoring the enemy or with dishonesty in the furnishing of supplies. It was impossible to separate, in any clear cut way, violations of military discipline or of economic regulations from the larger question of treason against the Republic. In Alsace, as we have seen, there were many who sympathized with the invaders. It is a moot question whether such sympathies were nationalistic, whether Alsatians were attracted to the invaders because the invaders were German. There is not much reason to think so. Throughout France there were people who hoped the Allies would win. Those who took this stand did not mean to be traitorous to France; they believed that the French government was in the hands of a clique of radicals to whom they owed no allegiance.

There was, however, a group in Alsace which, in the name of liberty, wished Strasbourg to return to its ancient status as a free city in the Empire. At the end of October a letter was seized at the French outposts. It was addressed to an unnamed citizen of Strasbourg, whom the bearer was to recognize by his stammering and his spectacles. Edelmann, one of the department administrators, fitted this description. The letter was signed by an émigré, the marquis of Saint-Hilaire, and it announced that within three days a party of disguised émigrés would slip into Strasbourg and take possession of the city.

The letter was actually a forgery, written by a certain Metz to ruin Edelmann, a personal enemy. Saint-Just assumed that it was genuine. He did not in any case trust the departmental administration or the other constituted authorities. These bodies had long ceased to be made up of their original elected members. They had been purged in the past by earlier representatives on mission, and were now full of political appointees not especially sympathetic to Saint-Just and Le Bas.

Saint-Just acted immediately on the Edelmann affair, either because he believed the letter authentic or because he saw in it a means of compromising political adversaries. He ordered every house in Strasbourg searched for outsiders, and invited the inhabitants of the city to denounce all suspects. On October 30 he asked the Strasbourg Jacobins for their frank opinion on the administrators of the Lower Rhine. Three days later he dissolved both the departmental administration and the municipality of Strasbourg. The Strasbourg Jacobins, taken by surprise, protested. Saint-Just defended his action by throwing doubt on the loyalty and the competence of the ejected officials. It was necessary for him to play up the dangers of treason in order to staff the government with men whom he could trust. He was involved in the old vicious circle: so little could the Mountaineers cooperate with each other, so far was France from that great surge of fellow feeling which some historians have depicted, that when a man assumed a heavy responsibility, as Saint-Just did in Alsace, he felt obliged to surround himself with a picked band of adherents, enlarging, in the process, the number of suspects, non-cooperators and political opponents.

Contending leaders had to assure themselves of popular support. More than factional rivalry was at stake; Saint-Just had definite ideas on the improvement of society, and believed that more economic equality was a necessary step to moral regeneration. The working class suffered from high prices and uncertain employment. Fear of leaving their families destitute deterred men from serving in the army. Political leaders, as people of wealth became estranged from the régime, looked with increasing favor on the poor, seeing in them the most patriotic and republican element in the country. Saint-Just, therefore, from motives drawn from both principle and expediency, sought to protect the working classes. For this purpose as well as to supply the army he rigidly enforced the requisitions and the maximum prices. Going a step further, he ordered that, from the proceeds of the forced loan levied on the 193 well-to-do citizens of Strasbourg, two million livres should be set aside for the "indigent patriots" of the city. The sum was increased by more than half a million livres by later decrees.

Saint-Just thus adopted in Alsace the same program for redistributing wealth which Couthon was introducing in Puy-de-Dôme. They aimed at helping the needy, without, however, going to such lengths as the Temporary Commission set up by Collot d'Herbois at Lyons. Collot d'Herbois was a Hébertist; Saint-Just and Couthon became the staunchest of Robespierrists. These latter two anticipated in November, in the regions committed to their charge, the social program which issued a few months later in the laws of Ventôse.

Saint-Just and Le Bas left Strasbourg on November 16. That night the Prussians tried to surprise the garrison at Bitche, a town on the frontier where four roads came together. They were repelled, and Saint-Just and Le Bas, from Bitche on the 21st, announced that the Republic was victorious from Saarbrücken to the Rhine. But the enemy was by no means yet driven from Alsace.

Meanwhile the political crisis came to a head in Strasbourg in the absence of the two proconsuls. Local affairs for some time had been dominated by two outsiders. One was Monet, the mayor of Strasbourg, who had survived Saint-Just's purge of the municipality; he was even younger than Saint-Just, came from Savoy, held everything German in contempt, and was a Hébertist. The other was Euloge Schneider, a German from beyond the Rhine, a round-shouldered ex-monk and an authority on Greek literature; he had crossed into Alsace in 1791, became vicar to the constitutional bishop, edited a stormy sheet that was a kind of local *Père Duchesne,* and was now, at the end of 1793, public prosecutor of a revolutionary court. This court was not the one established by Saint-Just and Le Bas, but had been set up by other representatives on mission shortly before Saint-Just arrived.

Monet and Schneider detested each other, and were detested by the great majority of Alsatians. Neither was French in background, though Monet was French in language. They were foreign adventurers of the kind dreaded by Robespierre, seeing the Revolution partly as the local maneuvers in which they were engaged, partly as a world-wide movement in which men of all nationalities might share. They had little sense of solidarity with the rest of France, or of allegiance to the National Convention.

On the very day of Saint-Just's departure a number of French-speaking strangers appeared in the streets of Strasbourg, fierce looking men with bristling mustaches, wearing red caps and armed with sabers. They were high-pressure patriots, some sixty in number, recruited by Monet among the Jacobins of neighboring departments. They called themselves the Propaganda, and, housed in the deserted college, organized and given a military guard, they set about promoting advanced Revolutionary doctrine. Monet intended to use them for two main purposes, to make the Alsatians forcibly French, and to exterminate the revealed religions, Catholic, Protestant and Jewish, all of which were heavily represented in Strasbourg.

Strasbourg, like other provincial towns, saw its Feast of Reason on 30 Brumaire, the 20th of November. A great procession formed at nine o'clock in the morning, made up of Propagandists, girls dressed in white, local Jacobins, public officials and a miscellany of citizens. Bearing a bust of Marat, the crowd marched to the Temple of Reason, the erstwhile cathedral, over whose portals were placed a large tricolor and a placard reading "Light after darkness." More flags draped the interior, and in the nave stood the usual symbolic mountain, with statues of Nature and Liberty at the summit. On the mountainside were portrayed "monsters with human face, reptiles half buried in fragments of rock," symbolizing the frustrated powers of superstition. An orchestra played, and the gathering (alleged to number ten thousand) sang a "Hymn to Nature":

> Mother of the Universe, eternal Nature,
> The People acknowledges your power eternal;
> On the pompous wreckage of ancient imposture
> Its hands raise your altar. . . .

Monet then made a speech in praise of reason. The surgeon-general of the Army of the Rhine denounced priests, tyrants, rascals, aristocrats, intriguers and moderates. Euloge Schneider abdicated his priesthood; many other clergy also renounced their errors. A fire on the altar consumed "the remains of saints beatified by the court of Rome and a few Gothic parchments," and outside in the street fifteen cartloads of legal and historical documents from the archives of the diocese went up in flames.

These Dechristianizing activities, and other operations of Monet and the Propaganda, were supported by certain representatives on mission. Two of them, Milhaud and Guyardin, decreed on November 7 the suppression of all outward signs of religion. They had been recalled four days before by the Committee of Public Safety; probably they had not yet received the message, but in any case representatives sometimes stayed on, wielding their powers, long after being asked to return to Paris. The representative Baudot was in Strasbourg on the day of the Feast of Reason. He mingled freely with the marching crowd, and made a speech in the cathedral, "congratulating the people," according to the contemporary report, "on its arrival at that happy time when all charlatanism, under whatever form it might take, was due to disappear." Baudot was a physician by vocation, and medicine had made rapid strides in the eighteenth century; but Baudot, taking his cue from Schneider, "abjured a profession which owed its repute only to credulity and imposture."

Baudot, Lacoste and some of the other representatives believed that the Alsatians were more sympathetic to the Austrians than to France. They denounced the German character of the region, whose language they could not speak, and whose people filled them with aversion. Lacoste spoke of guillotining a quarter of the population. Baudot, on one occasion in Strasbourg when two speeches were to be delivered in French and one in German, forbade the German speech to be made. Both Baudot and Lacoste sympathized with the imported Jacobins of the Propaganda, who, wandering among a people of whose language they were totally ignorant, introduced into Alsace the new horror of nationalistic persecution.

The unfortunate Alsatians had also to put up with Euloge Schneider, who could at least speak their language, but who was a foreigner without sympathy for them as a people. Schneider travelled through northern Alsace with his revolutionary court, trundling along a guillotine, ferociously punishing those whom he convicted. He was apparently not an exceptionally bloodthirsty man, since he put to death only about thirty in several months, but he spread terror by his loud talk and noisy threats, and by the impossibly high fines and long prison sentences which he imposed. A woman whom he found guilty of selling two heads of lettuce at twenty sous, and thus depreciating the purchasing power of the assignats, was condemned to pay a fine of 3,000 livres, spend six months in prison, and be exposed on the scaffold of the guillotine for two hours. Schneider was moreover a man of decidedly loose morals. Probably he did not, as some said, levy a tribute of girls in the places where he passed, but his arrival in a town or village was not an event at which the local families could rejoice.

Saint-Just and Le Bas were back in Strasbourg by November 24. In view of what had happened during their absence, it was increasingly difficult for them to ignore or compromise with the extremists. Yet they had to act warily; they were virtually alone, opposed by all the representatives on mission except one, Lémane, and dependent for getting anything done on the very local politicians that they meant to control. They made concessions, not unwillingly, because they favored in principle some of the objectives for which the more violent parties were working. They had already, just before leaving Strasbourg, signed a decree that the anti-German party would favor. By it the women of Alsace were "invited to give up their German fashions since their hearts are French." Soon after returning, finding the anti-religious excitement at its height, they ordered the destruction of statues "around the Temple of Reason" (not *in* it or *on* it, the expression being perhaps intentionally vague), and decreed that a Republican flag should be flown on the steeple.

Their purpose was undoubtedly to save the cathedral from further mutilation. Saint-Just shared the religious policy of Robespierre. Both men had in them a strain of reverence that was stifled at the sight of Catholicism in practice, but awakened at the sight of vandalism and "philosophic masquerades." Charles Nodier, a French man of letters who was a boy in Strasbourg at this time, and who saw Saint-Just occasionally, declares that the stern young Representative of the People, pleading on the floor of the Jacobins of Strasbourg, broke into tears at the thought of violations of religious freedom and outrages against the holy sacrament.

After an idyllic interlude, a quick trip to Paris, Le Bas to see his new wife, Saint-Just his fiancée, whom they brought back to Alsace and installed at Saverne behind the lines (for the two young Spartans were human), and perhaps (though there is no evidence) after a hurried conference with the Committee of Public Safety, Saint-Just and his colleague set about repressing Hébertism in Alsace.

The Propaganda was dissolved. Its members were ordered to go home. Word went out that the imprisoned Strasbourg officials should be treated with humanity. Saint-Just demanded from Schneider a public explanation of his conduct. Schneider replied on December 7. "The sans-culottes have bread, and the people bless the guillotine that has saved them." To acquire a new respectability Schneider then suddenly married a girl at Barr. On December 14 he returned to Strasbourg riding in a carriage full of furniture belonging to his wife. Six horses drew the carriage, because of the weight of the load, according to some; and a group of sympathizers rode on horseback with drawn swords beside the newly married pair. Saint-Just, aided in this matter by Monet's party, saw a chance to bring about Schneider's ruin. He accused him of entering Strasbourg with insolent and aristocratic pomp, and condemned him to exposure for four hours on the scaffold of the guillotine. Le Bas wrote a note to the Committee, announcing the sending of Schneider to Paris for trial. "Let us have no faith in cosmopolitan charlatans," he said, "but trust only to ourselves." The Revolution had become a national enterprise; foreign enthusiasts were not wanted.

Saint-Just had more difficulty with the rival representatives on mission. The bickering and recrimination continued; conflicting orders on the same subject issued from different headquarters; the army was distracted by civilian chiefs who would not deign to communicate with each other. Baudot accused Lémane of making his decisions while drunk; Lémane denounced Baudot for living in scandalous ostentation. Each asked that either himself or the other be recalled. Lémane complained that agents from the War Office encroached upon his jurisdiction. Baudot was indignant because one of his colleagues had once been a priest. The Committee had decided upon Pichegru for the combined command of the Armies of the Rhine and the Moselle; Saint-Just and Le Bas were about to make the appointment; Lacoste and Baudot anticipated them by appointing Hoche instead. Saint-Just, though he accepted Hoche, protested sharply to the Committee. The Committee reprimanded Baudot and Lacoste, but could do nothing; indeed Lacoste had been recalled two weeks before. Lacoste and Baudot excused themselves by saying that the Committee kept them uninformed and that Saint-Just and Le Bas refused to recognize their existence. In short, the harmony among the representatives, during the whole period of Saint-Just's mission, remained nil.

The disagreements were no doubt heightened by personal vanity, and fed by revolutionary psychology, for each representative thought himself supreme, believed his policy the only correct one, and distrusted both the achievements and the intentions of those not of his own faction. But there was a far more substantial basis of difference.

Baudot and Lacoste were extremists, who exaggerated the dangers because they delighted in repression. Alsace was no better than Toulon, according to Lacoste; even the Army of the Rhine was full of pro-Austrians. Counter-revolutionists, he said, had been cheered by Saint-Just's punishment of Schneider. The Propaganda should have been supported and enlarged. Four thousand sans-culottes from outside Strasbourg should be stationed in the city to overawe it. All constituted authorities must again be purged, for the earlier purges had all been unsuccessful; sound Jacobins must be brought from outside Alsace to fill all the public offices. German institutions must be suppressed, and the use of the German language forbidden. Unflinching terror must attach Alsace to the Republic. Unity of power must be established among all authorities. Lacoste and Baudot of course would not be averse to exercising this power themselves. But Saint-Just's predominance was, said Lacoste, "a veritable dictatorship and a monstrosity."

Had Baudot and Lacoste had their way, the department of the Lower Rhine would have met the fate of Lyons, or even worse, since at Lyons there was no question of violent denationalization. As it turned out, only about 120 persons were put to death during the Terror in Alsace, about half of them by the court established by Saint-Just. Considering the extent of disaffection, the nearness of the enemy, and the huge totals accumulated in other places, where men like Baudot and Lacoste were in the saddle, the figure for Alsace was not high.

Meanwhile in southern Alsace, in the adjoining department of the Upper Rhine, another of the Twelve was serving as representative on mission. Hérault-Séchelles was one of the most prominent of Jacobins. He was the main author of the Jacobin constitution. He had twice been president of the National Convention. In August 1793, as leader of the ceremonies that commemorated the fall of royalty, he had been the cynosure of Republican France. But he went to Alsace under a cloud. He tried there to open a correspondence with Saint-Just. Saint-Just ignored him, having heard Fabre d'Eglantine's denunciations a few weeks before. Saint-Just explained his attitude in a hasty postscript to Robespierre. "Confidence no longer has value when shared with corrupt men; in that case [apparently meaning when confidence is *not* shared with the corrupt] a man does his duty from love of country alone, and this feeling is purer."

This cryptic remark, written unthinkingly as the confused wording shows, is perhaps for that reason more psychologically revealing. Saint-Just was a political puritan. He could not willingly work with men of whom he morally disapproved. He judged men more by their motives than by the contributions they might make to a common achievement. He feared that the good cause would be tarnished if dubious characters were allowed to promote it. This was not practical politics. Nor was it practical politics, if Saint-Just thought Hérault guilty of the charges against him, to refuse all association with him and so leave him to his own devices.

Hérault was in truth no exemplary character. He was so affected that it was almost impossible to tell what he believed. Some of his writings, the *Theory of Ambition*, the *Reflections on Declamation*, composed in aristocratic leisure before the Revolution, might make one wonder whether he could be sincere. He was a nobleman by birth; the fact may well have led him, in self-defense in 1793, to proclaim more advanced doctrines than he really favored; in any case even his most patriotic acts might be thought hypocritical by other Jacobins. In Paris he was involved with certain foreign hotheads, and in Alsace he took with him, as his mistress, a woman whose husband and brother-in-law were émigrés. It was factional politics, however, that led Fabre d'Eglantine to accuse Hérault of conspiring with foreigners against the Republic.

There is no reason to believe that Hérault had any intentions of treachery. But he was out of favor with Robespierre, and is therefore out of favor with the modern Robespierrist writers, who hold, briefly, that Robespierre was always right. Albert Mathiez, the head of the Robespierrist school, took especial pains to prove Hérault a Hébertist and an ultra. Professor Mathiez in these erudite researches was not indifferent to the temptations of faculty politics, for Professor Aulard, holder of a choice chair at the University of Paris, had had the misfortune to call Hérault a Dantonist, thus revealing to the sharp eye of his rival a distressing ignorance of the subject.

Alsace offers a laboratory for estimating Hérault's extremism. What Hérault did in the Upper Rhine can be compared with what the Robespierrist Saint-Just did in the Lower Rhine. Mathiez recites the story of Hérault's "excesses": he cashiered certain constituted authorities, he instituted house-to-house searches, he created a revolutionary tribunal, he regretted that the Alsatians were slow in making denunciations, he arrested suspects and deported them to the interior of France. Saint-Just did all these things at the same time fifty miles away. According to Mathiez, Hérault surrounded himself with the friends of Schneider. But Hérault arrested the Schneider of Upper Alsace, a man named Müller, an admirer of Schneider's, and like Schneider a radical ex-priest from across the Rhine. Nor did Hérault grant funds to poor sans-culottes on any such scale as Saint-Just did, not to mention a real Hébertist, Collot d'Herbois, with his Temporary Commission at Lyons.

Hérault used language that might be thought extreme. Reporting on his mission, he took unconcealed pride in his rigorous methods. He declared, quoting the famous phrase of an unknown speaker: " 'Make terror the order of the day!' What he said I have done!" Mathiez calls this effusion "a debauch of useless and even harmful civic spirit." But who among the Revolutionists might not have said as much? And probably it would not have occurred to Hérault to utter the terse dogma of Saint-Just: "The French people is composed of patriots. The others are helots or nothing."

The significant differences between Hérault and Saint-Just in Alsace reduce themselves to three. Hérault, like Baudot and Lacoste, insisted that the number of patriots was almost infinitesimally small. This attitude advertised one's own super-patriotism, and might become, as it did at Lyons, an incentive to almost limitless terrorization. With Hérault, however, it issued in the death of only two or three persons in the Upper Rhine, where there were only twelve executions during the whole Terror.

Secondly, Hérault, again like Baudot and Lacoste, created a Revolutionary Army to regenerate the peasants and townspeople

HÉRAULT DE SÉCHELLES

of the department. These organizations were frowned upon by the Committee of Public Safety, and all except those authorized by the Convention (which meant the one set up on September 5 under pressure of insurrection) were prohibited on December 4 by the law of 14 Frimaire.

Thirdly, Hérault actively supported Dechristianization. He was more definitely a *philosophe* than any other of the Twelve; he had once talked with the eminent Buffon, had travelled far and wide to see the manuscripts of Montesquieu and Rousseau; he shared the ironic spirit of Voltaire, the faith in pleasure preached by Helvétius, the doubts on God which had made the baron Holbach's name a scandal. He entered with enthusiasm into the business of relieving people of their religious persuasions. This was enough to embroil him with Robespierre. As a matter of fact, however, Hérault showed less impatience of Catholicism in the Upper Rhine than Couthon did in Puy-de-Dôme. Yet Couthon succeeded in becoming an irreproachable Robespierrist.

Hérault is doubtless to be classified as a Hébertist. He showed some of the earmarks, without being a really violent man. Hébertism in any case was not primarily a body of doctrine or set of policies. It was a faction, a shifting combination of persons who were inconvenient or dangerous to the government. Hérault was connected with some of these persons, though perhaps no more so than other Jacobins whom the fatal stigma did not touch.

Some kind of factional plot against Hérault developed while he was in Alsace. A mysterious letter was brought to the representative Lémane, who was in charge at Strasbourg in Saint-Just's absence. It was addressed to the mayor of Strasbourg, Monet. The signature was again that of the "Marquis of Saint-Hilaire," now ostensibly writing from Colmar in the Upper Rhine. "I am only here," said the pretended marquis, "to have a talk with our friend Hérault, who has promised me everything." This letter was undoubtedly fabricated to compromise Monet and Hérault. Could it have been inspired by Saint-Just himself? No one knows. Conceivably Saint-Just may have caused both the Saint-Hilaire letters to be written, for both played into his hands. The first, compromising Edelmann, had given him a chance to purge the authorities of the Lower Rhine; the second helped to discredit Monet, against whom he was still struggling, and provided evidence to support the charges against Hérault made a few weeks earlier by Fabre d'Eglantine. But this is pure conjecture, and conjecture proves nothing.

Lémane arrested Monet, and set out for Colmar to interview Hérault-Séchelles. But, so he said, his carriage overturned on the way; he was obliged to return to Strasbourg, where, on further reflection, deciding that Monet "enjoyed the confidence of Saint-Just" (this was not true, in view of the difference between Saint-Just and Monet on the Propaganda), he released Monet, put his two coachmen in jail, and sent the incriminating letter without comment to Hérault. Whatever the plot was, it therefore came to nothing.

But Hérault's name was linked politically with the Hébertists. On December 11 the Committee of Public Safety recalled him, along with Lacoste, Saint-Just's foe, and Javogues, who had been a thorn in the side of Couthon.

The Committee tried to pacify its quarrelsome and factious agents. Robespierre himself penned a letter to Saint-Just, signed also by Barère and Billaud-Varenne, breathing the spirit of cooperation and broadmindedness. The complaints of Baudot and Lacoste had poured into the green room, and were definitely Hébertist in their tenor. Robespierre, who at this time (December 29) needed the support of the ultras against the citras, ignoring the obvious opinions of the two complainants, declared to Saint-Just that Baudot and Lacoste were inspired by as pure a zeal as he was. We must sink our differences in a higher patriotism, he said. It is not quite clear, even in view of the political situation, why Robespierre, in a confidential dispatch to Saint-Just, should deal so blandly with the matter of extremism.

By this time, the end of 1793, the enemy forces were driven from Alsace, through a combination of maneuvers that need not be described. Saint-Just's restoration of morale had its effect. Hoche and Pichegru emerged as military heroes. Not until twenty years later was this quarter of France again to be threatened.

But along with the disappearing Austrians went a pitiable host, refugees from the victorious Republic, estimated at from twenty to fifty thousand, perhaps numbering thirty. Men, women and children, families and whole villages, encumbered with bags and bundles, they hurried along with the retreating Imperial columns, riding on the artillery caissons, improvising seats on the supply trains. They were Alsatians, plain people of German language, terrified by this French Republic which they could not understand. Their lives had been disordered by the deluge of new laws, their Lutheran or Catholic religion had been repressed, their language and their costume denounced, their substance taken by requisitions or by exaggerated fines. They had been thrown into panic by undisciplined French soldiers, by their own Jacobin clubs, by Schneider, by the Propagandists, and by Saint-Just, whose moderating influence was not apparent in the confusion.

All these "aristocrats" were pronounced to be émigrés by the Convention. Their lands were confiscated, and they were not allowed to return. The repatriation of the fugitives, who found no warm welcome in Germany, and who soon were looking longingly across the Rhine like the shades in Hades across the river Styx, was a problem long debated in Paris and not settled until years later. Alsace in its way suffered as much as Lyons from the events of 1793.

The French troops pressed northward, reasserting their ephemeral conquest of the preceding year, relieving the French garrisons which had been left as islands by the advancing flood of the Allies. As the Republicans returned, some thousands of Germans abandoned their homes, imitated the twenty-odd thousand Alsatians, and fled with the defeated army.

On December 30 Baudot and Lacoste (it was now three weeks since Lacoste had been recalled) sent a report to Paris that was full of anticipations of the future. They questioned the value of the law of 14 Frimaire by which their authority was diminished. Such unruliness of representatives on mission was in time to undermine the Committee of Public Safety. Writing from Germany, Baudot and Lacoste declared that the German towns had no idea of the Revolution; they asked for more powers in order to spread the Revolutionary ideas; and they said that they were arranging to have the French army supported by the German population. The formula of the late Republican and Napoleonic years was sketched by the two enthusiastic deputies: maintain the French armies by drawing upon the resources of foreigners, and reorganize the occupied countries by applying Revolutionary principles. A new kind of civilization was coming to Germany and to Europe.

Saint-Just and Le Bas returned to Paris in the first week in January. Saint-Just had accomplished his main purpose with brilliant success. The Austrians were out of France. He had perhaps also prevented the Terror from becoming in Alsace the mad slaughter that it became at Lyons. But he had not exactly reconciled Alsace to the Republic. He ignored the mass migration in which his mission ended. Were not the refugees, by his definition, "helots or nothing"? Nor had he attached the other representatives in the region to the Revolutionary Government. He left behind him a group of disgruntled men who were influential enough to be dangerous. Their dissatisfaction came from important differences of opinion, but it was aroused also by Saint-Just's haughty and exclusive spirit.

Hérault-Séchelles returned in the middle of December. He came back only to his ruin. He was the victim of Fabre d'Eglantine's false denunciation, suspected of belonging to a non-existent foreign conspiracy. The Dantonists in the Convention attacked him for partisan reasons; certain Hébertists spoke in his favor. Couthon feebly interposed, but Robespierre was determined to put an end to the matter. From its agent in Constantinople the Committee of Public Safety received a document, purloined from the Austrians, which showed that the proceedings of the Committee on September 2 had become known to the enemy. The Committee assumed that the leak had occurred through Hérault. On December 31 Robespierre, Barère, Carnot, Billaud-Varenne and Collot d'Herbois, in a letter written by Robespierre, offered their colleague his choice: he could submit to investigation, or he could resign. Hérault never again attended a meeting in the green room, and in three months he was dead.

Probably Robespierre really believed that Hérault was guilty of treason. The evidence against him would not convince a judicial mind in time of calm. The charges of Fabre d'Eglantine were mere assertions, and Fabre's reputation for honesty was low; the document received from Constantinople was so inadequate that it had to be altered before Hérault was put on trial. But with Robespierre the idea of treachery had become an obsession. It does not make

Robespierre the less deluded to argue that the victims of the Foreign Plot deserved their fate because they were Hébertists.

In a way, however, Robespierre was by no means deluded.
Hérault did, after all, have friends among a faction that threatened
the government. He was sacrificed, like many others, not so much
to wild revolutionary frenzies (which conservatives are apt to
exaggerate), as to the principle of governmental stability, which
in the circumstances meant keeping Robespierre and the rest of
the Committee of Public Safety in office. And in the low state of
public cooperation, with the eternal tendency of the Mountain to
split, a governing group, to remain stable or to execute any con-
tinuous policy, had to become smaller and smaller, purging and
purifying itself of those on whom it could not rely.

And how could Robespierre, or the others in the Committee, rely
on Hérault-Séchelles? He had not limited himself in Alsace to
executing their collective policy. How could anyone be sure what
this scion of the old régime, with his arts of the dancing master
and the rhetorician, was really aiming at? Hérault was more a
connoisseur of ideas than a believer in them, an opportunist and a
lover of excitement, a philosopher of the salons who attempted,
with an antique literary republicanism, to take part in the overwhelming reality of the Republic. The real Republic was a turbulent and revolutionary thing, embodying class demands, drawing
strength from a moral earnestness that reached the point of fanaticism. Hérault was a skeptic, an ironist, a scoffer, easygoing,
amiable. There is surely a place in the world for Héraults, but
not by the side of Robespierres, and probably not in revolutions
at all.

With Saint-Just back and Hérault gone, the Committee of
Public Safety took on early in January the form which it kept
until the following summer. Nine of its members were henceforth
usually in Paris. Two were away, Jeanbon Saint-André and Prieur
of the Marne, except that Saint-André spent the month of Pluviôse
in Paris. The nine were later called, with sufficient numerical
accuracy, the Decemvirs.

CHAPTER IX

The Missions to Brittany

MOVING out from the green room in the Tuileries where the Twelve had their headquarters, we have travelled north with Carnot to Flanders, east with Saint-Just and Hérault to Alsace, south with Couthon and Collot d'Herbois to Clermont and to Lyons. In the west also, in Brittany, two members of the great Committee were at work. We must round out the circle before returning to Paris. And we must begin again with the troubled month of September 1793.

It was in September that the Twelve came together in the Committee of Public Safety. In September the Republic passed the turning point from anarchy toward dictatorial rule. September saw the organization of the Levy in Mass, the proclaiming of terror the order of the day, the passage of the Law of Suspects, the adoption of the General Maximum for the control of prices. With the Hébertist uprising of September 5 the Committee of Public Safety was pushed to the left, and from the crisis in the Convention on September 25 it emerged more closely knit, as a kind of cabinet with a prospect of continued power. In these weeks the Committee was already working toward the restoration of central authority made official two months later in the Law of 14 Frimaire. In September also occurred the battle of Hondschoote, which marked the beginning of victory over the Allies.

Since no one at the time knew that September was a turning point, the atmosphere of the month was scarcely one of triumph. The revolutionary leaders viewed each other with fear and suspicion. The foreign enemy was still on French soil. With its internal enemies the Republic was fighting civil war. The country was threatened by famine; farmers and merchants were opposed to the government; the restless masses in the cities, especially Paris, were exploited by agitators of both left and right. The army was in appalling condition, with the officers either untrustworthy or untried, and the troops demoralized, turbulent, unarmed, ragged and barefoot.

In September also the navy fell to pieces. The fleet which had long rivalled the English, which only fifteen years before had helped to break up the British Empire, landing an expeditionary force three thousand miles away in the War of American Independence, was now not even protecting the coast of France.

It was in the first days of September that Paris heard the news from Toulon. There the royalists had thrown open the port to the British, and the French Mediterranean fleet had given itself up to Admiral Hood. Only the Atlantic fleet remained. It was assigned to guarding the western coast. But the sailors aboard certain ships mutinied in Quiberon bay; the officers yielded to prevent armed rebellion; and the squadron, at the demand of the insurgents, sailed back to its headquarters at Brest. So the sea was left open to the British.

The governing Committee acted with its usual speed, and with something more than its usual audacity. It decreed on September 22 that 100,000 men should be made ready for an invasion of England. On the same day, to make feasible this idea, which in the circumstances was fantastic, it selected two of its members, Jeanbon Saint-André and Prieur of the Marne, to restore order in the Atlantic fleet. Not till October 1 could the two commissioners depart. Then six days in a lumbering carriage brought them finally to Brest.

There in the great harbor took place a memorable scene. Twenty-two ships of the line rode at anchor, intermixed with frigates and lesser vessels. The Representatives of the People, accompanied by a party of admirals and civilian authorities, made a systematic inspection. The most mutinous crews were visited first. They saw emerge from the mists of a dismal morning, as from a remote world which they had incautiously forgotten, the brass buttons and red sashes that betokened supreme power in the Republic; the voice of Paris spoke on the decks, answering the sullenness of the seamen with cold phrases of authority, questioning officers and men, ordering punishment for the guilty. The next day was clear, and in radiant sunshine the representatives boarded the ships whose spirit was more sound, leaving the most loyal to the end. Ships of the line became temples of patriotism; the representatives delivered lay sermons on the gains of the Revolution, whereby the lowest seaman could aspire to the rank of admiral; everyone joined in singing the "Marseillaise," representatives, officers and men, on the decks, on the masts and spars and on neighboring ships, until the harbor rang; and at the last couplet, "O holy love of father-land," hats came off and all went down reverently on their knees.

Was Saint-André reminded of his past? It was thus that the French Protestants had worshiped when they were outlawed, meeting outdoors, hearing sermons, singing hymns, kneeling and praying in the fields. Now, in October 1793, in the Republic which was itself a church with a new message of salvation, among a forest of masts and ropes filled with men cheering and waving their caps, Saint-André and his companions were rowed back to the dock in a tumult which, as one of the party wrote, did homage to "the divine character of the French which will soon be that of the world."

To inspect the ships and revive the spirit of the seamen was only the first step. With the first shouting over, Saint-André and Prieur began to face the real difficulties of their task. They began also to disagree. Saint-André objected to Prieur's using convicts from the hulks as witnesses for the government. The two men were of different types both of which contributed to the Revolution. Both believed in equality as proclaimed by the Republic. But Prieur was a firebrand, little governed by policy, trusting to the strength of feelings. Saint-André was a man of affairs, a lover of order and efficiency, born with the gifts of the administrator, which he had shown before the Revolution and was to show when the Revolution was over. They did not clash seriously, for on October 20 Prieur went off to Vannes to prepare for operations against the Vendée. Saint-André remained at Brest to reorganize the fleet.

Even after separating, and though engaged in very different work, Saint-André and Prieur, along with a dozen other representatives on mission, were attacking the same general problem, the total situation in the west of which the naval situation was a part.

This total situation had very deep roots. Brittany was a long peninsula, with poor roads, not strongly attached to the rest of France. It had enjoyed certain provincial liberties under the kings; its clergy and nobility were therefore influential; the peasants were not used to central government, and looked for leadership to their gentlemen and their priests. The same was true in lesser measure in the adjoining department of the Vendée. When the

Revolution came the plain country people objected to the new demands of central government, to its taxes, its religious policy, its conscription of soldiers. Their stubborn displeasure turned into fanaticism, until the country teemed with secret messengers, nocturnal councils, inflammatory sermons, visions, martyrdoms and holy apparitions. In this atmosphere grew up, in the Vendée, the Catholic and Royal Army, a host of peasants fighting to preserve their old way of life, which meant also the old way of life of the king, the nobility and the church.

All around the French coast from Cherbourg to Nantes it was only in some of the seaboard cities that the Republicans had any hold, and even here they were usually federalist and Girondist. Saint-André at Brest, Prieur at Vannes, Carrier at Nantes, were almost like men stationed in a foreign country. For a Republican naval base there could hardly be a worse location than at Brest, at the extreme tip of Brittany, shut off by days of travel from a reliable hinterland, with provisions hard to obtain among a disaffected peasantry, and seamen largely recruited from this same insurgent region.

On October 17 the Vendéans began to cross the Loire and move into Brittany. Some eighty thousand in number, half of them women and children, fleeing before the Republican troops, they spread out formlessly for miles, ravaging and foraging as they went, committing atrocities which were repaid in kind, an anarchic horde without purpose or destination.

The British government had for some time considered assistance to these insurgents. Downing Street was importuned by French émigrés, beset by agents of the counts of Artois and Provence, Louis XVI's brothers. The royal princes wished to restore the absolute rule of the Bourbon house, the refugee French nobles to regain their privileges and their estates. Artois declared with great fanfare that he longed only to set foot on the Vendéan coast, to share in the heroic miseries of his loyal subjects; the émigrés raised the cry for a holy war against atheism and anarchy. But Artois expected to be transported and maintained by His Majesty's Government in a manner befitting a royal highness, and the émigrés in London, when asked to form an army, were noticeably backward in volunteering. All were dependent on the British, whom

they repelled by their voluble lightheadedness. The British government had no interest in restoring either absolutism or feudalism in
France, but wished to end the war, defeat the revolutionary régime,
preserve the old balance of power on the Continent, and win territory in the colonies. Finally, after much bickering and negotiation,
George III on October 29 issued a manifesto to the French people.
Realistic in recognizing certain facts of the Revolution, it promised
that purchasers of confiscated property should not be disturbed,
and that the French people might select their own form of government, though "moderate" monarchy was strongly recommended.
At the same time the British promised aid to the Vendéans, and
asked them to seize a port at which an expeditionary force could
be landed.

If, however, by British help, the émigrés and the Bourbons
were to triumph in France, nothing would remain of the Revolution, however much the British may have wished to check the
excesses of reaction.

The Committee of Public Safety, though without knowledge of
details, was aware of the relations among the Vendéans, the royal
princes, the émigrés, and the British. They knew that the insurgent
west gave allegiance to men outside the Republic. They believed,
however, that England also suffered from internal divisions. Believing that peoples everywhere were waiting to be freed from
tyrants, they thought that if French forces could invade England,
English sans-culottes would rise to support them. Both governments were counting on what today would be called fifth columns.

The Committee demanded therefore, for both offensive and
defensive reasons, that the fleet at Brest be made ready to go to
sea. There was also another reason. France faced a shortage of
food. To bring the needed imports a flotilla of merchantmen was
assembling in Chesapeake Bay. The French fleet had the responsibility of convoying these ships through the British blockade. As
the months went on, and the scarcity in France became more acute,
the safety of the convoy from America became the chief concern
of French naval operations.

First of all, before the ships could return to sea, the dissensions
among the officers had to be quieted. These dissensions showed the
difficulty of reconciling moderate methods with revolutionary
aims. The revolutionary authorities, since 1789, knowing that

naval officers could not be easily improvised, had refrained from violent purges of the naval commands. At the same time, to assert the new principle of equality in careers, and to fill in the many gaps left by emigration, they had given commissions in the navy to officers of the merchant marine. These men were experienced seamen, for no such tyros could command a frigate as might successfully lead a battalion. But the new officers were the social inferiors of the old. They lacked the prestige of a fighting tradition; their manners were often rough; their attitude toward their men and toward politics was not that of aristocrats. Old and new officers did not mix; cliques and coteries were formed, so that any issue however trifling might split the staff of any ship; and some of the new officers, to heighten their influence, encouraged personal followings among the seamen.

For this situation the only cure was to make the corps of officers more homogeneous, which, in a Republic, meant the dismissal of some of the nobly born. Considering the clamor of denunciation and backbiting in which he worked, Saint-André proceeded with as much prudence, though not with as much brilliant success, as Carnot and Bouchotte in the matter of army appointments. Saint-André found no Bonaparte, though some of the men he promoted came to hold important positions under the Empire. He retained as vice-admiral in command at Brest a commoner, Thévenard, who had risen by exceptional talents to high rank under the old régime; and as vice-admiral in command at sea he kept an ex-nobleman, Villaret-Joyeuse, in spite of Jacobin outcries. Five new rear-admirals were created, all commoners, all captains at the time of promotion, all trained both in the merchant marine and in inferior posts in the old navy, and all, unlike most Republican generals, over forty years old. Of the captains a number of the incumbents were carried over; the new ones were advanced in regular fashion from the ranks below. Dash and untutored genius were not sufficient for a naval officer. There were no cases like that of Jourdan, who became a general in chief in three years.

To strengthen morale Saint-André used much the same methods as Saint-Just with the Army of the Rhine. Like Saint-Just he insisted on discipline, "by which alone armed forces are invincible," but a republican discipline, firm without harshness, respecting the dignity of the common seamen. Officers were told to set an example of ready obedience. They were deprived of traditional luxuries; no longer were French naval officers to enjoy dainty pastries at sea; the special cooks and special ovens came off the ships. Packets of Jacobin newspapers went aboard. So did a small army of schoolmasters to teach the sailors to read and write and to conduct republican propaganda. For the newcomers raised by the Levy in Mass instruction in seamanship was given on the ships; men of promise were enabled to study technical subjects and so put themselves in line for promotion. The teachers, Saint-André fondly imagined, would replace the Catholic chaplains who had been abolished by the Convention, and whose absence made the crews extremely restless.

Brest and its environs underwent a drastic purging to prevent a repetition of what had happened at Toulon. The Jacobin society and the constituted authorities were purified of all but unswerving Mountaineers. In the arsenals and shipyards a strict military rule was introduced. Even in normal times the city existed largely by the navy. It now became an industrial machine organized totally for war.

Day and night shifts relieved each other in the workshops. Holidays were done away with. Workmen began and ended their labors by a common signal, a cannon shot in the harbor. All production was managed by public officials, for private enterprise in the circumstances either would not or could not act. Saint-André had to agree to a higher wage level than the Maximum allowed, but all wages, hours and prices, together with the distribution of food, raw materials and finished products, were dictated by administrative decree. The life of the inhabitants was taken over completely by the Republic, not only their working hours, but their hours of leisure, which were spent in political meetings and demonstrations, or in seeing patriotic plays at the theater, reading patriotic news in the newspapers, or engaging in patriotic conversation, carefully spied upon, in the cafés.

"To work in the manner of despots does not suit republicans," said Saint-André; "the negligence of a sleepy tyrant or of somnolent ministers does not agree with our principles." So the easygoing habits of the old régime gave way to modern efficiency. Mass enthusiasm, ungrudging sacrifice, hard work, coordination of effort, enforced moral unity—a combination of faith and dictatorship, in short—were the means by which European nations were henceforth most successfully to exert their power. The French Revolution established its doctrines because it tapped sources of national energy never used by the old monarchies. With the First Republic emerged the lineaments of a modern state at war. Nowhere were they more clear than at Brest under Saint-André.

All resources, human and natural, were drawn on. It happened that at Brest lived the foremost naval architect of the day, Sané, builder of a remarkable ship of one hundred and thirty guns, once known as the *Estates of Brittany,* now called the *Mountain* and serving as flagship for Villaret-Joyeuse. Sané was put in charge of construction and repairs. The drydocks were never empty; within six weeks twelve ships of the line, three frigates and five corvettes were reconditioned. New keels were laid down. Rope works, sail factories, munitions plants were taken over by the state. Muskets and pistols of private persons were commandeered, and food requisitioned from the peasants. Bronze for cannon was extracted from church bells, saltpeter gathered by a special commission, lead mined in eastern Brittany, and a newly found deposit of coal surveyed by Saint-André's order.

Gradually and cautiously the Republic began to assert itself on the sea. Fast ships went out singly, to raid British commerce and keep a lookout for the expected invasion. Six ships of the line issued forth under one of the new rear-admirals, Van Stabel, who, however, was soon driven back to port by the superior force of Lord Howe. The prospect was not very encouraging. The officers were untried in war, the crews were often clumsy, collisions took place in the harbor, the *Convention* bumping the *Mountain,* to the distraction of Villaret-Joyeuse; and so scanty was the supply of telescopes that they had to be divided up, one to each ship.

In this uncertain state of naval affairs Saint-André was called away, ordered by the Committee of Public Safety to go to Cherbourg and the Cotentin peninsula, near which, it now appeared, the Vendéans and the British would effect their junction. He left Brest on November 13.

Meanwhile Prieur of the Marne was busy in the towns along the south coast of Brittany, in the department of Morbihan, discharging the usual functions of a representative on mission, arresting suspects, purging the local authorities, purifying and invigorating the popular clubs, making speeches, presiding at festivals, raising troops and levying supplies. His work was like that of dozens of representatives elsewhere. In the Morbihan, however, about the only partisans of the Jacobin government were some of the working people in the maritime cities of Lorient and Vannes. The peasants were generally royalist, the commercial and professional men generally Girondist. Class antagonisms were plain, and Prieur acted accordingly.

Prieur was at first agreeably surprised by what he found, no doubt because it was the Jacobins who came out to greet him on his arrival. He was soon disillusioned. Within a week he discovered that, at Vannes, "the people show no favorable attitude to the Revolution," that "in a city of 12,000 only 200 accepted the constitution," that "the countryside is given over to fanaticism," that "the poor hide themselves to shed their tears," and that "the despotism of wealth and rank still presents the hideous image of the old régime." He therefore proclaimed terror the order of the day, surrounded the city with troops, and by house-to-house searches began to track down the aristocrats in their lairs.

He appealed for popular support in a Feast of Regeneration held at Vannes on November 3. The celebration began with a salvo of cannon, at which the Representative of the People left his house and marched to the public square, flanked by files of soldiers bearing a tricolor. In the square, to the sound of the second salvo, he set fire to a heap of legal documents, "the titles and registers of feudal rights and other marks of the old régime." The crowd, led by Prieur, then moved on to a statue of a sans-culotte, where, to a third blast of artillery, Prieur presented to the throng a mother of four children whose father had died for liberty. From this demonstration the sans-culottes profited little. The documents which Prieur burned were mere symbols, since feudal payments had already been abolished by law. We hear nothing of any such real transfer of wealth as Saint-Just, Couthon and Collot d'Herbois attempted on their missions. Indeed, the very workmen who labored to make the ceremonies possible did not receive their wages, for the Jacobin municipality had no funds.

Prieur, though a whole book has been written to prove him a wildman, did not really do anything very violent in the Morbihan. He was more adept at arousing revolutionary feelings than at satisfying them, more interested in hunting suspects than in taking their property, more alert in filling the jails than in providing victims for the guillotine. Others of the Committee of Public Safety exceeded him both in organizing ability and in their concern for the lowest classes. Prieur was an average representative on mission, an average republican, vehemently hostile to kings, nobles and priests, concerned more with a political than with an economic redistribution of advantages.

He loved stirring music, oratory and symbolism, and it was by these means that he was most effective. Fascinated by martial airs, he made a specialty of furnishing the troops with bands. He delighted in forcing nuns to sew for the patriotic cause. "How they will cross themselves over the pants of a sans-culotte!" The chagrin of the nuns seems to have pleased him more than the gain of the trousers. It symbolized the triumph of reason over fanaticism, of the nation over the church.

One step taken by Prieur was exceptional among the republican missions, and prophetic as only the twentieth century can know. He organized a Republican Youth. Boys between nine and sixteen were grouped in battalions, armed with "muskets and pikes proportioned to their size and the strength of their years," drilled by citizen soldiers, and given a flag inscribed "Hope of the Fatherland." The boys of one of these battalions, on a certain civic occasion, placed their hands in Prieur's and swore to emulate their fathers in the service of their country.

In a speech to the Jacobins of Lorient, Prieur lashed out against the English, not without reason in view of the imminence of an English landing in the west, but in language that anticipated both Napoleon and Adolf Hitler. The theme was the conflict of manly virtue with the money power.

"London must be destroyed, and London shall be destroyed! Let us rid the globe of this new Carthage. There we shall have peace, there we shall be masters; no, not masters, but avengers of a world oppressed. We shall chase from the Indies and from Bengal these ferocious English, so insatiable for gold that, in selling necessities to the people of those countries, they demand such high prices that a mother has often been seen to give up her child for a handful of rice. . . ." Prieur noted with indignation that the Americans and the Dutch sympathized with Britain. "Everywhere in short is the triumph of Pitt's despotism and of gold. Very well, we will make a triumph of courage and of iron. Soon, next spring I hope, for all arrangements for the project are ready, we shall go to visit the banks of the Thames. Those who wish to be in the expedition must ask priority of inscription. Meanwhile let us show Pitt how a free people deliberates. I move that a sentence to the guillotine be dispatched to Pitt." The Jacobins of Lorient passed this resolution with shouts of joy.

Tangible results of Prieur's passage appeared in the Morbihan contingent of the Levy in Mass. Yet even this body was more a symbol than a reality. Nothing could overcome the obstinacy of the Breton peasants. The troops were miserably equipped. "We have neither shoes nor stockings nor bread nor guns," cried Prieur. The recruits were so unreliable that service against the Vendéans was out of the question, and they were sent instead to the far-off Army of the North. Of 2,879 who departed three hundred were missing at Dol, twelve hundred at Tours, and still others deserted in Flanders. Some of these desertions, it is true, were simply the undisciplined wanderings of men who presently returned.

Prieur bade farewell to the Morbihan on the day of Saint-André's departure from Brest, November 13, without prearrangement with his colleague, and anticipating instructions from Paris by several days. The approaching crisis with the itinerant Vendéans was apparent. Men many miles apart came to the same decisions to meet it. For Prieur the Morbihan was henceforth a minor worry, although it relapsed into counter-revolution as soon as he left it, so that troops had to be detached from the campaign against the Vendéans to guard Republican authority at Vannes.

No one knew which way the nomad insurrection would spread, least of all for a long time its own chiefs. The Republican Armies, badly led, were repeatedly worsted early in November. But what could the rebels do with their victories? Some advised moving further into Brittany to rouse the peasants there, some preferred Normandy, many longed for their homes south of the Loire, some talked of threatening Paris, a few bold strategists suggested marching to Flanders to catch the Army of the North in the rear. Then on November 10 came a bit of drama. Two royalists disguised as peasants slipped into the Vendéan camp, and produced from a hollow stick the manifesto of his Britannic Majesty, countersigned by Pitt, promising the long awaited support, and asking for the seizure of a port on the Channel.

So the Vendéans flocked down to the sea and attacked Granville, at the corner of the coastline near the border of Brittany and Normandy. Granville, republicanized and defended by the representative Le Carpentier, withstood the onslaughts, to the dismay of the Catholic and Royal Army, which imagined that the citizens would rally joyfully to the cause of the throne and the altar. There was no sign of English sails—why should there be, since the Vendéans, too eager, had left no time to communicate with their allies, or to tell them which city they proposed to capture? Perplexed, isolated, long preyed upon by deceptive hopes, too unstable to contemplate an extended siege, the peasants, and their aristocratic leaders as well, were demoralized by the resistance of Granville, and on the very day after their arrival in high enthusiasm at the Channel, they turned inland and flung themselves in a vast confusion toward the Loire. This retreat began on November 15.

On the same day Jeanbon Saint-André and Prieur of the Marne, hurrying to the scene, met at Dinan. The rout of the Vendéans had taken place without them. But the elements of the problem still remained. It was still impossible to tell which way the "brigands" were moving, nor could the representatives know to what a wretched state they had sunk. The vagabond Vendée had still to be reckoned with. And the British were still planning a descent. After a conference, Prieur went to Rennes to take charge of military operations, and Saint-André proceeded with his tour of the coastal towns, heading for Cherbourg. As he moved along the shore on land, British vessels did the same at sea, vainly signalling to their allies, at first not knowing of the reverse of the Vendéans at Granville, then hoping to find them elsewhere along the coast.

As a matter of fact, if the Vendéans lost their chance by acting too soon, the British blundered in acting too late. The expeditionary force, delayed by the haggling of British statesmen with the count of Artois, held back by difficulties in assembling the Frenchmen and Hessians who were its chief components, and who in the end numbered only half the total planned, did not leave Portsmouth until December 1, more than two weeks after the repulse of the Vendéans at Granville, and more than a month after the decision to send an expedition had been made. The squadron, commanded by Lord Moira, when it reached the Norman and Breton coasts, found therefore only blank inattention (or was it Republican laughter?) when it signalled.

The Republic had in western Normandy a small force known as the Army of the Côtes de Cherbourg. Saint-André put an end to its separate existence, joining it with the other Republican troops in the west under Rossignol. Here again he came independently to a decision made a few days later by the Committee of Public Safety—a sure sign that in his mission the Committee was well represented. There was, however, a difference of opinion on the important matter of the qualifications of Rossignol. Saint-André believed him incompetent; Prieur defended him as "the eldest son of the Committee of Public Safety." Both men were right: Rossignol was a political appointee, unfit to command an army, but backed by the Hébertists in Paris, and favored by the Committee as a radical Republican useful in fighting Vendéan brigands and fanatics. The resulting disorganization of the Republican troops in the west was the main reason why the Vendéans roamed at will, continuing to win victories even after the defeat at Granville.

Cherbourg at that time was not yet a developed seaport, only a bleak town at the end of the Cotentin peninsula. Saint-André found it almost stripped of defenses, though Moira's squadron had been sighted off the coast. If the Vendéans, after Granville, had entered the peninsula, running the risk of being caught in a cul-de-sac, and if communication between them and the English had been established, the Republic might have faced in this corner of Normandy what Napoleon was to face in Spain—a "peninsular war" against the combined forces of insurrection and foreign intervention.

As it was, the main significance of Saint-André's stay at Cherbourg was political. He arrived early in December, when the

Hébertist movement was running at full tide over France. So thoroughly had Cherbourg been purged by preceding representatives on mission that only a handful of extremists remained in power. Entrenched in the Jacobin club and controlling a force of cannoneers, they dictated to the helpless local authorities, denounced all their opponents as suspects, and pushed a rabid program of Dechristianization.

Saint-André was a Christian minister by vocation. But he was a very modern minister, who, even before the Revolution, valued little in religion except its teachings of social morality. He favored in principle the Hébertist cult of Reason. He approved of Dechristianization in the long run; he objected to the means used by Dechristianizers, the violence, vandalism and vulgarity which disgraced the Republic in the eyes of a people still Christian at heart. Like Robespierre, he wanted toleration of religious beliefs; but, like Robespierre and most members of the Convention, Saint-André believed that such toleration would be only an interim measure, necessary and just for the time being, until the Republic should bring its mission of enlightenment to completion.

His actions at Cherbourg were therefore ambiguous. He joined in the cult of Reason, but tried nevertheless to enforce the program of the Committee of Public Safety. He wrote a proclamation to the citizens of Cherbourg, which was circulated as a pamphlet.

Here, in eight printed pages, was reflected most of the progressive thought of Europe since the Middle Ages. Religions, so the argument ran, were merely relative and concerned with unintelligible matters; they were by rights only private and internal persuasions, and as such would be tolerated; but believers who tried to apply their religion to public affairs would be disciplined, for their differences of opinion, in themselves of no importance, would, by causing discord over useless questions, break up the unity of the state, which had the true care over man, and the mission of emancipating his human faculties. What religion a man professed was of importance to no one but himself, but it was vital to the community that everyone should be "faithful to the Republic." The pamphlet concluded with a number of ordinances, outlawing violence against religion, requiring religious services to be held indoors, forbidding priests to appear on the

streets in clerical costume, providing a means of civil burial without Christian forms. Lastly it enjoined upon good citizens "to
develop the principles of social morality whenever they find occasion, so as to prepare the triumph which it deserves."

The cult of Reason, for Saint-André, was indistinguishable
from the cult of country. It was a religion of patriotism, but
patriotism did not mean a narrowly national pride; it meant public
spirit, good citizenship, social morality, or what Robespierre referred to as virtue; for the idea of country, *la patrie*, merged
imperceptibly with the idea of society itself. The society of the
Republic was a moral community, deeply committed to a gospel
of its own, concerned for human dignity, competing actively with
the Christian clergy for the uplifting of human souls. But it did
not compete on equal terms. Convinced that the new gospel of
country should be shared by all, that it was in the nature of man to
be a "citizen" but that religious faith was a mere acquired and
variable characteristic, the leaders of the Republic shut up the
older religions behind closed doors, and for processions in the
streets, for public ritual, for mass demonstrations, granted a
monopoly to the civic cult.

These high-minded and philosophical conceptions were beyond
the interests of the average man. Saint-André was no more successful in establishing them at Cherbourg than Couthon was in
the Puy-de-Dôme. The average peasant continued to be more impressed by what his priest told him than by the language of
strangers from Paris. The average man in the towns might be
a vehement revolutionist; reading Saint-André's own words, he
would gather that the religion of Rome was error, fanaticism,
superstition, lies, a mere crutch for feeble minds; he would then
wonder why such an obvious evil should not be immediately uprooted. Some Hébertists, moreover, were men of the anti-social
and even criminal types which in settled societies do not usually
wield power.

Saint-André therefore found himself, like Saint-Just in Alsace,
acting as a defender of the Catholicism which he scorned. He had
to save the organ in the church at Cherbourg from being wrecked
for cannon shot, and the confessionals from being transformed
into sentry boxes. And since, moreover, rejecting the flattery of

the local Jacobins, he tried to break the hold of the club over matters of provision and defense, the upshot of his visit to Cherbourg was that he pleased no one, for the reactionaries were antagonized beyond conciliation, and the revolutionary vanguard complained that he was a moderate.

At Brest, when he returned there in mid-December, Saint-André found the same situation. These were the days when Collot d'Herbois was abetting the radicals at Lyons and Saint-Just suppressing them at Strasbourg, and when both policies, as we have seen, received the endorsement of the Committee of Public Safety. The stand taken by the Committee toward the outbursts in Brittany was similarly equivocal. Saint-André opposed violence at Brest; but at Nantes, at the same time, the representative Carrier, not without official encouragement, drowned thousands of victims in the Loire.

It was the same story reenacted in a hundred places. The Representatives of the People, after silencing federalists and other laggards, everywhere risked falling into the hands of implacable and imprudent zealots. At Brest, while Saint-André was away, the representative Bréard, left in charge and fearing to lose control, yielded to the demands of his ungovernable followers. He authorized a revolutionary tribunal against the known wishes of Saint-André. He allowed the local Jacobin society to force incompetent small politicians into responsible offices. And he dispatched parties of agitators into the neighboring districts to preach republicanism as they understood it.

One of these is a good example of what is meant by an extremist. His name was Dagorne, and he held the office of inspector of the national domain, in which his corruption was no secret. Sent with two others to revolutionize Quimper, he threw the town authorities into jail, replaced them with persons as shady as himself, looted the churches and smashed the images of the saints. Selecting a market day when the peasants were in town in great numbers, he stationed himself in the marketplace, and there, surrounded by loaded cannon pointed toward the onlookers, subjected certain holy vases to an act described as "the most obscene and most disgusting profanation." The spectators stood in helpless horror, hardly able to believe their eyes, and took back into their homes a loathing of republicanism which the next hundred years could hardly overcome.

Saint-André, back in Brest, lost no time in committing Dagorne to prison. He forbade the functioning of the revolutionary tribunal that had been extorted from Bréard. And somehow while stemming the torrents of radicalism he found time to resume his constructive work, building lighthouses, arranging for the faster transport of timber for shipbuilding, tightening the regulations by which the criminals in the galleys at Brest were kept in order. Finding graft in the supply of food he instituted at this time a simple system of which no one had thought before: the amount of supplies taken from the stores on land was to be counter-checked against the amount received on board ship. So, in all the confusion, the progress of efficiency continued.

But the war played into the hands of the terrorists. The Committee of Public Safety clung to its project of attacking England. By the end of 1793, with the continental enemies driven from France, French strategy was passing from a defensive to an offensive phase. On January 2 the Committee wrote a significant letter to Saint-André: France must have dominion of the oceans, "France which alone of all European states can and should be a power on both land and sea." The modern Carthage remained the true enemy of mankind, and especially of Frenchmen. France through all its avatars, Bourbon monarchy, revolutionary Republic, military empire, carried on its modern Hundred Years War with the nation of shopkeepers. This resolve to take the offensive at sea, according to M. Lévy-Schneider, the authority on the naval affairs of the Revolution, was a main reason why the Committee of Public Safety, at the beginning of 1794, made its fateful decision not to mitigate the Terror.

The Committee in January transferred to Brest a representative on mission, Laignelot, who had distinguished himself elsewhere for vigorous methods. Laignelot insisted on setting up a revolutionary tribunal at Brest. Saint-André objected. Laignelot brought with him cannoneers from the Commune of Paris. Saint-André disapproved. At the Jacobins of Brest, waving a naked sword, Laignelot screamed out the famous words: "The peoples will not be truly free until the last king has been strangled in the bowels of the last priest!"

Saint-André was now in the position of Couthon two months before at Lyons. He solved his difficulty in the same way. Unable to prevent this new outbreak of terrorism, and unwilling to seem to approve of it by his presence, he simply departed. On January 25, the 6th of Pluviôse, he was back in Paris at his old place in the counsels of the Committee. What protests he may have made there no one can say. Nor can it be said exactly what his influence was in the determination of naval policy. During Pluviôse, however, the Committee shifted its attention from the idea of invading England to the more manageable enterprise of an assault on the Channel Islands. French warships, previously kept together in view of the projected invasion, dispersed to prey upon British commerce. And a squadron was dispatched to meet Van Stabel, who, sent ahead in December with a few speedy vessels, was to escort back to France the great convoy from America.

Laignelot's revolutionary tribunal, as it turned out, was not particularly bloodthirsty. The Terror at Brest remained relatively mild. By the end of February Saint-André was back at Brest continuing his work; and Laignelot, at Saint-André's express demand, was gone.

But elsewhere in Brittany repression raged with a fury equalled nowhere in France, not even at Lyons. As the Vendéans grew more desperate their treatment of captured Republicans became more atrocious, and as the war prolonged itself seemingly without end the Revolutionists abandoned their last scruples. The battle of Savenay, on December 23, finally broke up the Vendéans as an organized force. Unknown numbers were executed on the spot for bearing arms against the government. Thousands were sent to the prisons, which already bulged with federalists, aristocrats, priests, dismissed officials, rich merchants and other suspects. It was unsafe to send the captured rebels back to their homes, for they could not be trusted to refrain from further violence against the state, especially with a network of secret organizers still active throughout the west, and the possibility of British assistance not yet ended.

The Committee of Public Safety resorted to methods which less revolutionary governments have used in similar circumstances. To Prieur of the Marne went an unenviable distinction. He set up a special court for dealing with the rebels, the *Commission mili-taire Bignon* (named after Bignon, its president), which, first following the army, then sitting at Nantes, pronounced death sentences upon 2,905 persons, more than any other revolutionary court in the whole country, not excepting the Revolutionary Tribunal of Paris. Other agencies of revenge and prevention were at work at the same time. Into the Vendée poured the "infernal columns" of Turreau, who, by order of the Committee of Public Safety, systematically devastated that breeding place of insurrection. Great numbers of Vendéan peasants, some months later, were resettled in more soundly republican regions.

The most notorious of all aberrations of the Terror took place at Nantes, in the famous *noyades* or wholesale drownings conducted by the representative Carrier. Over these affairs much learned controversy has spent itself, Carrier being depicted as a monster by reactionary and humanitarian writers, condemned even by historians most partial to the Revolution, and yet subject to attempts at rehabilitation, on the whole not very successful. Carrier, it may safely be said, was a normal man with average sensibilities, with no unusual intelligence or strength of character, driven wild by opposition, turning ruthless because ruthlessness seemed to be the easiest way of solving a difficult problem.

Our concern is with the relation of the Committee of Public Safety to the drownings. On September 29 Hérault-Séchelles read aloud to the Committee a letter from Carrier, who, writing from Rennes, declared, after recounting his other operations: "I propose at the same time to make up some cargoes of unsworn priests now piled up in the prisons, and to give control of them to a mariner from Saint-Servan known for his patriotism." The Committee heard Carrier's letter "with a lively satisfaction," according to Hérault, who wrote back to Carrier on the same day. Hérault praised Carrier in the name of the Committee, observed that "we can be humane when we are assured of being victorious," and said that the representatives on mission should leave the responsibility for their acts to the subordinates charged with execution.

Later events made Carrier's reference to cargoes of priests seem very ominous. Whatever may have been in Carrier's mind, the phrase itself, vague at best and lost in a lengthy communication, could convey little to the men in Paris. Possibly Carrier only meant that he intended to transfer priests to prison ships in the river at Nantes, though why he should need a "mariner" for this purpose is not clear. In any case, Hérault's advice that responsibility should be transferred to others may have impelled the unsteady Carrier to extremes. Carrier, however, subsequently denied having received Hérault's dispatch.

A few days later Carrier conferred with Saint-André and Prieur of the Marne as they passed through Rennes on their way to Brest. They found him a patriotic and reliable representative. Moving on to Nantes Carrier met Prieur of the Côte-d'Or, who took back to Paris an account of Carrier's views. Carrier himself reported to the Committee, on October 7, that the prisons at Nantes were full of partisans of the Vendée. "Instead of amusing myself by giving them a trial, I shall send them to their places of residence to be shot. These terrible examples will intimidate the evil wishers. . . ." The Committee, in reply, urged Carrier to "purge the body politic of the bad humors that circulate in it."

In the following weeks the Vendéans, retreating from Granville, moved back toward the Loire and toward Nantes. The Revolutionists in the city fell a prey to hysteria. Horrible congestion reigned in the prisons, from which it was feared that the enraged inmates would break out. The prisons were full of fever and disease; it seemed that the hated aristocrats would culminate their evil influence by bringing pestilence to the city.

Carrier bethought himself of his idea of dealing with counter-revolutionists in "cargoes." Accepting the proposal of two local Revolutionists, who showed how boats could be equipped with removable hatches, Carrier proceeded to clear the prisons, without formalities of trial, by drowning their occupants in the Loire. The number of *noyades,* or boatloads of prisoners scuttled, was estimated by an overwrought "witness" (there were few witnesses to these nocturnal performances) at twenty-three; exact historical study can prove the occurrence of only four, but since they were carried on in an atmosphere of secrecy it is entirely possible that their number was greater. The drowning of children is well established, and also the sadistic cruelty of one of the men engaged in the work, who hacked off the arms of victims struggling to leave the boats.

The Committee of Public Safety knew before the end of November that ninety priests had been drowned at Nantes. Carrier, in his reports to Paris, alluded with brutal sarcasm to the repeated "miracles" in the Loire. He gave no details, however, and it was only when the *noyades* were over, at the end of December, that the authorities in the capital were informed of the ingenuity and deliberate planning by which they were accomplished. No one knew then, and no one knows now, the number of the victims. It may have approached two thousand. Most of them were captives from the Vendéan army.

The Committee at first did .nothing. That some of its members were shocked we can well imagine; Couthon, in particular, is known to have raised his voice at the green table in favor of pardoning the rank and file of Vendéans who had been "misled." But the full horror of what had happened in Brittany was not soon realized in Paris; horror, like terror, was pretty much the order of the day; the *noyades* at Nantes, like the *fusillades* at Lyons, seemed in the circumstances hardly more than incidental. In any case, at the turn of the year, the Committee was counting on the support of the Revolutionary vanguard; and so, though a few Hébertist representatives were recalled in December, others, including Fouché and Carrier, were left for a while in office.

But the Committee had a special agent in the west, Marc-Antoine Julien, a youngster only eighteen years old. Some have regarded him as a mere spy for Robespierre; actually he represented the Revolutionary Government, corresponded not only with Robespierre but with Barère and the Committee as a whole, and in his tour of the war-torn area worked in close cooperation with Prieur of the Marne. He reported on the conduct of the generals and the representatives on mission, dissolved illicit Revolutionary Armies, gave instructions to local administrators, tried to combine the worship of Reason with a measure of decorum and toleration. In short, his assignment was to coordinate revolutionary energies in the west, and to keep them within the bounds prescribed by his superiors.

Young Julien began to complain of Carrier's actions on December 19. Writing from Vannes, fifty miles from Nantes, he either did not know of the *noyades* or thought them of slight importance. His objection was only to certain of Carrier's satellites, who he said were terrorizing true patriots. He was willing to believe that Carrier had simply misjudged his men. But on the 1st of January he wrote urgently to Barère and to Robespierre demanding Carrier's immediate recall. By this time details on the *noyades* were known in Paris. Still there was no mention of them in Julien's dispatches. The issue raised was the old question of conflicting authority: Carrier refused to recognize another representative on mission; his agents were factious and violent; they "pillaged, killed and burned" without restraint, and were stubbornly defended by their master.

A month later, now much excited, Julien again wrote to both Barère and Robespierre. He had been to Nantes and seen Carrier, against whom the charges were now infinitely multiplied. The Vendée was rising again; Carrier and the generals showed gross unconcern; they wished to prolong the crisis; Carrier was a satrap, a despot who killed liberty; he kept aloof from good Republicans, abandoned in private orgies; his secretaries were haughty and inaccessible; real patriots could do nothing. Yet Julien tried to be fair, admitting that Carrier had been of great service, before he went astray, in crushing the influence of the wealthy businessmen at Nantes.

Now, on February 3, Julien at last said a word in passing on the *noyades*.

"I am assured," he wrote to Robespierre, "that he had all those who filled the prisons at Nantes taken out indiscriminately, put on boats, and sunk in the Loire. He told me to my face that that was the only way to run a revolution, and he called Prieur of the Marne a fool for thinking of nothing to do with suspects except confine them."

A few days later the Committee of Public Safety recalled Carrier to Paris. Was the recall due to Julien's news of the drownings? Hardly. The drownings were not news in Paris. There was little pity for the victims, who, after all, were mostly "brigands" and "fanatics." Julien himself gave the matter no special emphasis. The drift of thought, both in Julien's mind and in the decision of the Committee, was only incidentally humanitarian. Carrier had called a member of the ruling Committee a fool. He was hounding as counter-revolutionaries men whom the Committee classified as patriots, and defending as patriots men whom the Committee considered, and who often were, the dregs of society, rascals with criminal records, or brutal and unprincipled rowdies with no aim except to perpetuate confusion. Carrier was not cooperating with the government. He was discrediting and crippling the Republic. By revolution he meant lawlessness; he would not recognize that, since 14 Frimaire, even the Reign of Terror had an explicit constitution.

In February, therefore, Carrier returned to Paris, where he was soon joined by Fouché and other disgruntled representatives on mission, who in their disgrace formed a subtle menace to the Revolutionary Government. Robespierre, the political strategist, carried on his campaign against the "factions," which meant, in effect, a campaign to bring unity of purpose and acceptance of authority to men schooled in five years of revolution. Young Julien continued on his travels in the west. Jeanbon Saint-André went back to Brest to rule the navy. Nantes was turned over to the man whom Carrier had derided, a man not noted for mildness, but who at least could act in harmony with the national government—Prieur of the Marne.

CHAPTER X

Dictated Economy

TWO ideas gave purpose to the struggles in France during the Revolution, the rights of the individual and the sovereignty of the nation. Revolutionary philosophers saw no conflict between them. Through the sovereignty of the nation the individual made his rights effective, freeing himself from the old restraints of customary law, monarchy, class, church, guild and corporation, as well as from domination by foreign powers. Individual liberty depended on national sovereignty. The balance of the two produced the liberal and democratic states whose ascendancy lasted until our own time. But the balance is not easy to achieve. It was never achieved during the Revolutionary generation in Europe. The forces from which the nation-state was to liberate the individual, especially the forces of the deposed monarchy, the dispossessed nobility, the outraged church and the foreign governments with which the Republic was at war, remained so powerful and so threatening that Revolutionists more and more made the nation the object of special glory, and granted to the national government an authority which, had it been effectual, would have left the individual almost totally unfree.

The French Republic became for a while in the Year Two a totalitarian state, an enlarged likeness of Brest under Saint-André. It was not militaristic in the full sense, for the power remained in the hands of civilians. It did not persecute races held to be inferior. But it attempted to nationalize the whole life of the country. It arrested and detained tens of thousands of suspects. It used religion, education, the press, the theater for its own ends. And it regulated economic affairs down to the most minute detail.

There were certain principles, said Barère in October, which the Committee of Public Safety wished to be clearly understood: "that products of our territory are national property, that all real property belongs to the State, that the Revolution and liberty are the citizen's first creditors, and that the Republic should have preferred status when it wishes to purchase."

The generalities in this statement were more sweeping than the specific proposals. Private rights were not denied but only restricted. The state did not contemplate the management of economic enterprise, but only the right of non-competitive purchase. Preemption became the foundation of the new economic régime. Hardly distinguishable from requisition, it meant that government agents, paying in assignats at the legal maximum rates, might buy up without question whatever commodities they wished. This right, with the right of requisitioning labor which the Committee also exercised under the Levy in Mass, might well lead to an economy resembling socialism; but what was later called socialism was far from the intention of the Committee, which repeatedly proclaimed its reliance on individual enterprise. "Public management in general does not suit the interests of the Republic," wrote Carnot and Prieur of the Côte-d'Or for the Committee, "because public administrators do not observe the same economy as owners, because experience demonstrates that technical improvements are introduced much later or not at all, and because such establishments in the hands of an ambitious man are a means of power which may be very dangerous to the liberty of the nation." The members of the Committee knew, even during the months when state control was at its height, the dangers in identifying economic with political power.

The economic regulation grew up piecemeal, imposed by circumstance, with no foundation in theory except a general sense of the sovereignty of the nation. In the summer of 1793, as we saw in an earlier chapter, rising prices and scarcity of provisions reduced thousands in Paris to misery. The price of bread was fixed in May, but little benefit followed. Collot d'Herbois and Billaud-Varenne, not yet members of the Committee of Public Safety, put through in July the law against the hoarding or engrossing of daily necessities. Two months later, on September 29, the Convention enacted the General Maximum, which fixed prices and wages throughout the country. Price regulation was an alternative to the unlimited printing of paper money.

By October, with the creation of a new Subsistence Commission much more powerful than the old, the Committee of Public Safety found itself conducting a planned economy more thoroughgoing than anything seen in Europe until the twentieth century. Robert

Lindet, recalled from Normandy, was the liaison between Committee and Commission.

The economic rule was more than the control of production and distribution assumed by modern democratic governments in time of war. Brought into being by pressure from the Hébertists, it had elements of a proletarian attack on private business—until the month of Ventôse, in the spring of 1794, one of the decisive turning points of the Revolution. It had elements also that recalled the mercantilism of the old régime and anticipated the autarky of the twentieth century. It aimed at economic independence within political frontiers, and at destroying the English commercial supremacy, in this respect foreshadowing Napoleon's Continental System and the National Socialism of modern Germany. But above all, perhaps, it was a dictatorship of distress. Had private enterprise been able to function, the needs of war could have been fulfilled with much less governmental control. But private enterprise was at a standstill. Businessmen had for the most part turned against the Revolution, and even those still faithful to it could hardly operate in such turmoil. It was the collapse of private enterprise, fully as much as the war or the demands of the working class in Paris, that obliged the Committee of Public Safety to undertake the economic government of the country.

In the summer of 1793, to counteract the growing scarcity, the Convention laid an embargo on the export of French goods. To prevent the flight of capital it forbade the transmission of funds to foreign countries. It thus became impossible to pay for imports, and since foreign loans were out of the question importation virtually ceased. In June, moreover, the British declared grain and raw materials contraband of war. It was the first time that the British sea power, acting through the blockade, had been directed against the whole civil population of an enemy country. The blockade was not in reality very effective, but it added to the difficulty of importation. France by September was almost completely shut off from trade with the rest of the world.

Since domestic production continued to decline, France was desperately in need of imports. At first nothing was done to increase them. National power seemed more desirable than economic advantage. Temporary economic inconvenience was to be endured for the sake of ultimate economic strength. The relative position of France among the states of Europe would improve, if its economic isolation could be made a means of undermining their prosperity.

This policy of autarky, later modified, was adopted by the governing Committee in the autumn, coinciding in date with the upsurge of xenophobia in which Fabre d'Eglantine denounced the Foreign Plot. On October 9, after a speech by Barère, the Convention prohibited from French soil all objects manufactured in the British empire. On September 21 Barère piloted a Navigation Act through the Convention. Modeled on the English Navigation Act of 1651, the new law forbade foreign vessels to engage in coastal trade between French cities, or to import any goods other than products of their own countries. Foreign vessels for the first time were defined to include those which, even if under French registry, were owned or manned by persons not French. A blow was thus aimed at the shipping of England, and to a lesser extent of Holland, to the detriment of France, which had always used the services of foreign vessels in addition to its own.

Such strong protection for French manufactures and shipping had been unknown in Bourbon times. The trend in the last years before the Revolution was toward economic liberalism. The movement toward freedom of international trade was checked by the Republic, at a time when the Republic was dominated by Hébertists, when its philosophy was most democratic and when the influence of businessmen was at its lowest ebb. The Republic was in truth more a national than a liberal state. It was on the day after the passage of the Navigation Act, we may recall, that the Committee ordered 100,000 men to be made ready to invade England, and sent Saint-André to Brest to reconstruct the fleet.

Barère was the Committee's expert on foreign trade. He had learned much from a certain Ducher, an obscure but influential writer on economic questions, who had been for years French consul in the United States. The ideas of Ducher, which in September were those of the government, were presented to the Convention by Barère in support of the Navigation Act. His speech was significant. This was the time when machine industry was expanding across the Channel, England becoming the workshop of the world, the philosophy of free trade making converts among statesmen. Barère was aware of these facts. He saw the antithesis between the cosmopolitanism of a freely ranging commerce and the nationalism of separate and protected states. He preferred the latter, giving arguments that are worth summarizing, for they have been repeated ever since, by Germans among others.

The freedom of the seas, he said, was the aim of French legislation. He pointed to a future in which, in place of English commercial ascendancy, each nation should have its own economic system. The English Navigation Act was the work of tyrants; the French, "decreed in the midst of a democratic revolution," was a step toward liberty and equality. It would make the nations equal by destroying "the maritime empire usurped by England."

"Are we not yet weary of being tributaries to a foreign industry?" So long as we buy English manufactures or use English shipping we live by the suffrance of the English government, we put our vital reserves in the keeping of a foreign people. We must produce everything ourselves that we can. "Let us close our frontiers and extend our shipping. That is the whole theory of the proposed act."

The fact that England could manufacture certain goods more cheaply than other nations was for liberal economists a good reason why other nations should buy such goods in England. Not so for Barère. Free trade, he said, was a system invented by English theorists, who, knowing very well that England would be the gainer by it, tried to persuade other countries to enslave themselves by accepting it.

The island kingdom, according to Barère, was the pest of the modern world. It wanted to "constitutionify" Europe to suit itself. It aimed at destroying rival commerce; it outraged the flags of friendly nations; it monopolized the produce of the earth to starve the French people. But the day of reckoning approached. "The other peoples of Europe, awakened by the sound of their own chains, will see Europe entirely free when the influence of England shall be weakened or destroyed, its policies impotent, its Indian commerce diminished, its rôle reduced to the trade of broker or maritime agent."

To French merchants Barère issued a warning. Too much had they intrigued against the Revolution.

"But commerce will at length see that its cosmopolitanism must cease, that it too has its cargo on the ship of the Republic, that liberty is not calculated at five per cent, and that democratic government has always been more favorable than monarchy to the prosperity of commerce and welfare of merchants, as well as to the equality for everyone which the merchants up to now wish only for themselves!"

The representatives applauded Barère's address, and the Navigation Act became law. A few days later the customs administration was transferred to the department of foreign affairs. This step signified that international trade was to be an instrument of international politics. About the same time the Convention decreed that all Englishmen living in France should be put under arrest. No allowance was made for English democrats or political refugees who had come voluntarily to the land of promise. Poor optimistic Tom Paine, scarcely more appreciated by Revolutionists than by Tories, busy composing his *Age of Reason,* was among those menaced by the law against Englishmen, though his membership in the Convention kept him out of prison until the end of the year.

The discrimination against the persons and commerce of Englishmen raised a curious debate in the Convention on October 16, the day on which Jourdan won the battle of Wattignies and Marie Antoinette went to the scaffold. An unimportant member, asking why the English were singled out among foreigners for special treatment, had let slip the suggestion that the government was "nationalizing" the war. The Committee of Public Safety chose to make an issue of this remark. Saint-Just prepared a speech. Robespierre and Barère went to the Convention to support him.

"It is important to the Committee," cried Barère, when the legislators showed signs of becoming unruly, "to prove that it has not nationalized the war. . . . I demand that Saint-Just be heard."

Saint-Just then gave a long explanation, worth careful study by anyone interested in the growth of nationalism.

He declared in substance that the French had no quarrel with the English nation, but aimed only at its government, its aristocracy and its businessmen. This line of argument, though startling then, has become commonplace for us; we have all heard of liberal states that make war only on the autocratic governments of other countries, and of revolutionary states that make war only on their propertied or plutocratic interests. The argument assumes that the true lines of conflict run horizontally across the boundaries of nations, dividing rulers from ruled, or employers from employed. Saint-Just took this view, seeing the nation as the governed but not the government, and as the mass of the people but not the aristocracy or the upper levels of business. In this sense there was no clash of interest among nations.

But another element had come into Saint-Just's thinking, a feeling that very real lines of difference run vertically through society, making the significant units not classes, but nations.

"The Committee, in prohibiting [English] merchandise, had in mind only our own economy. . . . It is impossible that relations under the law of nations should always be mutually useful. It was our duty to consider primarily our own land.

"A man may wish well to all peoples of the earth, but he can really do good only for his own country. Your Committee, convinced of this truth, has limited its view of the world to the French people.

"Too long has philanthropy served as a mask to the criminal projects that have torn us. Philanthropy has buried a hundred thousand Frenchmen and twelve hundred million livres in Belgium." By philanthropy Saint-Just meant the broad-minded internationalism of the eighteenth century liberal.

Nevertheless, according to Saint-Just, the idea that the war might become nationalized was a delusion. If the English revolted against George III the French would be their friends. If the new French laws ruined British merchants and manufacturers the English people should be grateful. In short (such was the implication) one might attack the political or economic structure of a country without warring on it as a nation; if a people clung to its old political and economic masters it could expect no sympathy from Republican France. This was a formula for world revolution.

Yet Saint-Just set a high value on national patriotism. He refuted the idea that an Englishman domiciled in France, who had shown himself well disposed to the Revolution, should be exempted from the action of the law. Persons who forsook their native land were not to be trusted. A man's heart remains with his native country—"otherwise he is depraved." Foreigners were suspect by the mere fact of being foreign.

It is clear that the Committee of Public Safety was nationalizing the war without intending to do so. What the members of the Committee believed was that there was no conflict between *free* nations; but a free nation was one which overthrew its king and its nobles, and which also, according to the somewhat temporary doctrine of 1793, attacked its rich business class. A nation which persisted in not imitating France was not free, and so not exactly a nation; the war therefore, though the Committee by its own admission consulted only the interests of France, was not a national war.

In fact, however, whatever the theory, the Republic in the fall of 1793 was on the verge of becoming a closed economic state. The volume of foreign trade had not been so low in generations, having dropped in 1793 to a fifth of what it was when the Revolution began. The policy of self-sufficiency was a gloss on the brute fact of isolation. It was impossible for France to take part in world commerce through the ordinary channels. The story sounds very modern. Internal conditions, inflation, the disorganization of enterprise, the needs of war, the operations of speculators and profiteers, the demands of the impoverished masses, resulted in the Maximum regulating prices. Regulation of prices necessitated government supervision of exports, which if left in private hands would drain off French products into countries where prices were higher, and of imports, which could not be sold in France by private dealers except at a loss.

Only under state control could France enter the international market without ruining itself. Such control became possible after October 10, when the government was made "revolutionary until the peace." From this time on, the Committee of Public Safety, equipped with new powers, multiplied its functions, and while not abandoning economic independence as a desirable aim, sought to draw from foreign commerce such advantages as it could. The new Subsistence Commission received jurisdiction over imports and exports. Almost from the moment of its foundation trade began to increase, and much of the exclusivist legislation to break down. By a paradox of the whole economic régime, not limited to foreign trade, exceptions in enforcing the laws became more common as state control became more efficient. The reason is not hard to see: the laws, enacted in haste for conflicting political ends, often jeopardized the public welfare as responsible officials understood it. The consequence, equally clear, was a system run by administrative discretion, which in a country where the laws were in any case not much observed, was at least a basis for order.

In foreign trade much of the legislation became less necessary as private merchants were brought under supervision. Trade could be encouraged if exports were offset by useful imports, rather than by deposits abroad to the credit of individuals. Neutral shipmasters were allowed on November 7 to make sales in France, to government agents, at prices above the Maximum. On December 10 the Committee suspended the Navigation Act for the duration of the war, ambitious distant objectives giving way to practical needs. During the winter the Committee allowed the export of specie to pay for grain and other necessities; and merchants were permitted to send out luxury articles in exchange for useful goods. The Subsistence Commission, through agents all over the country, requisitioned wines, laces, silks, tapestries, jewelry, fine furniture and art objects of small importance (the Republic, even under heavy material pressure, keeping its masterpieces at home), to be exchanged for foreign copper, wool, wheat or horses.

French citizens having credits abroad were obliged to yield them up to the government, receiving assignats in return. The mails were searched to prevent the export of currency. Merchants had to open their books to government inspectors, who scrutinized them for foreign balances, which were confiscated and paid for in assignats. The Paris bankers had to raise fifty million livres in foreign currencies for the Committee of Public Safety, which agreed to protect them, in these operations of high finance, from molestation by the revolutionary committees of the Commune. An exception was made in the law forbidding export of French funds to permit payments in Genoa, which, then a small neutral republic, was in effect the chief Mediterranean port of France. Yet with all the requisitioning of foreign exchange and of exportable surplus goods, the balance of trade was not made up, so that the Committee of Public Safety, in a country well drained of hard metal by departing émigrés, had to consent to the export of gold and silver to the value of at least forty million livres.

Attempts to convert the debt owed by the United States into cash were not successful.

The revulsion against "philanthropy" suggested that importation could be supplemented by plunder. On September 15 Jeanbon Saint-André persuaded the Convention to adopt the "ordinary laws of war," in reprisal, he said, against barbarous conduct of the enemy. The Committee then circularized its generals, instructing them to take hostages when they entered enemy territory, to levy taxes and requisition goods, and to send back to France what they did not need for themselves. Among the items specified were food, forage, cattle, draft animals, iron, coal, wood, cloth, wool, leather, cordage, silver from churches, public moneys and all public property that could be carried. Loot, however, though it helped to supply the armies after the victories in Flanders and Alsace, was not of much economic significance in the Year Two, because not enough enemy territory was yet occupied to make it so. It was an incentive in turning the war into one of conquest. It was not an answer to the internal difficulties in France.

The main problem was to increase domestic production. Upon its solution depended not only foreign trade and the maintenance of the armies, but the calming of the hungry crowds in Paris, and hence the continuance in office of the Committee of Public Safety. To increase production the Committee followed the principle, laid down in the law of the Levy in Mass, that labor, capital and technical knowledge could be conscripted for the service of the country.

Some of the most eminent scientific men of France were called to the Tuileries. Prieur of the Côte-d'Or, by vocation an army engineer, dealt with them most directly, but all members of the Committee were aware of the value of their services. Lavoisier, indeed, the greatest chemist of the day, was guillotined—without much reason, except that he had held an interest in the tax-farm before the Revolution. To chemists as such the Committee gave a warm welcome. No government had ever before made such an attempt to associate itself with science. Working ardently for the Republic, through the worst days of the Terror, were men then prominent in the scientific world: Berthollet, Monge, Vandermonde, Guyton de Morveau, Fourcroy, Hassenfratz. With their assistance the Committee of Public Safety filled the museums with rare plants from the estates of émigrés, enlarged the library of the old School of Mines, and created the germ of the famous Polytechnic by transferring to Paris, to save them from the hazards of war, the books and instruments of the engineering school at Mezières. Inventors plied the Committee with ideas for new machines, until steps had to be taken to distinguish the men with real ideas from the impostors and the cranks. We find the Committee, on April 17, 1794, requisitioning the services of two men not forgotten in the history of science, the mathematician Lagrange and the biologist Lamarck. The purpose was probably to protect them from disturbance. We hear also of an unfortunate astronomer to whom the Committee sent 6,000 livres when he was detained by the Spaniards at Barcelona. He was travelling to measure an arc of the meridian in preparation for the metric system.

The Republic, in a word, hoped to draw upon the achievements of the age of Enlightenment, carrying on the idealism of the philosophical century (somewhat shorn of its "philanthropy"), and inviting its savants to make useful their vaunted knowledge of nature.

In the matter of production, the most urgent need was for food. Agriculture was disorganized by the drafting of men into the army, by the transfer of property rights, by the low fixed price of farm produce, by the recurrent and sporadic requisitions of crops and cattle. Large parts of the country were threatened by famine, while in some places the farmers gorged themselves on what they would not sell. The south, moreover, a vine-growing country, was even under normal conditions somewhat less than self-sufficing in food.

French agriculture at best was not very productive by the highest standards of the time. The Committee of Public Safety, looking beyond the temporary crisis, conducted a systematic program of education. Never before had agricultural reformers had so free a hand. Pamphlets were issued on the improvement of crops, care of the soil, diseases in horses. Ponds were drained, woods cleared, barren lands reclaimed. Peasants were urged to turn their vineyards and pastures into wheatfields. The Committee fought to popularize the potato. At the Jacobin club certain patriots frowned upon its use, lest Europe think that France was starving.

But the scientists pronounced it to be edible by man, and the Committee trumpeted its merits. Great beds of potatoes were sown in the gardens of the Tuileries and the Luxembourg, as a means of advertising the new vegetable to the citizens.

Most such measures could not be expected to relieve the food shortage immediately, certainly not in the winter of the Year Two. They show the direction in which the government was looking. They did not remove the immediate menace of hunger.

Discoveries had recently been made by French chemists on the chemical composition of steel. The Committee ordered that the new processes be taught to workmen. The scientists drafted a booklet of instructions, of which fifteen thousand copies were put into circulation. At Meudon, in on old chateau outside Paris, secret experiments in the manufacture of munitions were carried on. An incendiary cannon-ball was designed for the navy. It was supposed to burn up the enemy's ships, but the furnaces necessary to heat it were so dangerous to French vessels that it had to be abandoned. Meanwhile the War Office was experimenting with balloons, and Chappe, with money furnished by the Committee, was building his "telegraph" to Lille.

The shortage of gunpowder was acute. Before 1789 government agents had the right to search barns and sheepfolds, though not homes, for deposits of saltpeter. This right had been taken away during the liberal phase of the Revolution. Importation was no longer possible. In August 1793 the army had only fourteen million pounds of powder on hand, instead of the eighty million which it needed. The right of search reappeared, including access to homes; the price of saltpeter was raised to encourage production; and private persons were set to work hunting in houses, shops, barns, stables, caves and cavities wherever the precious material could be found.

Coal was increasingly important at the end of the eighteenth century because of the dwindling of the wood supply. The Committee, following the old royal government, tried to encourage its use. The Paris munitions plants required almost four thousand cubic meters a month. The Committee had to offer premiums to mining companies, or operate them dictatorially at a loss. The worst difficulty in supplying coal was in transportation, since horses and wagons were needed in agriculture or requisitioned for the army, and the canals were low because of drought in the preceding summer. The Committee took upon itself, or rather handed over to its Subsistence Commission, the regulation of canal boats and wagon trains.

Copper was the more necessary because cannon were still cast in bronze, iron being too brittle and too heavy. The Committee therefore had to deal with the copper magnates, the Perier brothers, founders of a famous family in France. There being no copper mines in the Republic many expedients were resorted to. Kitchen utensils were confiscated from émigrés and from victims of the guillotine, patriots gave up their pots and pans, the churches lost their ornaments and bells. Copper was brought in through Switzerland, much of it surreptitiously from far-off Hungary, which being a Hapsburg domain was of course at war with France.

The fundamental weapon of land warfare, before the "armament revolution" of the nineteenth century, was the smooth-bore, muzzle-loading flintlock musket, with its extension, the bayonet. It was not exactly a primitive weapon; the French model of 1793 required the labor of sixty-four men for its manufacture; but it had not changed in principle for a hundred years. All Europe combined had never produced as many as a thousand a day. This was the figure that Prieur of the Côte-d'Or and Carnot set as their goal in August at the time of the Levy in Mass. It was decided to centralize the production of muskets in Paris, for the established plants were in places threatened by foreign or civil war.

Putting aside its preference for private ownership, the government went itself into the business of manufacturing muskets; and seems to have turned out more than two-thirds of all those produced in the Year Two. On the day after enactment of the Levy in Mass, the Committee of Public Safety requested the sections of Paris to submit lists of metal workers living within their boundaries. Only half the sections replied, and those not promptly; such was the negligence and inefficiency that the Committee had to combat. Gradually workmen were found. Those who had their own workshops were put under contract with the arms administration. The far greater number who had no shops or tools went directly into public employment. Forges were erected on the esplanade of the Invalides and in the Luxembourg Gardens not far from the potato

beds. Paris rang by day and glowed by night with the hammering
and forging of guns.

Results came slowly. It was not easy to transport heavy ores
to Paris. Both labor and management presented a problem. The
workmen under contract, after receiving their fuel and material
from the government, would all too often use them for their own
purposes or sell the product to private dealers. The Committee
had to discover and prosecute these swindlers as best it could. In
the public shops the labor was clumsy. Workmen and foremen
were alike untrained, and "the clerks of the War Office," as Barère
admitted, "having no knowledge of this kind of production, often
issued notes that made no sense." It became necessary to decree
that anyone obstructing the orders of the Committee in matters
connected with the manufacture of arms should be punished with
two years in irons.

On November 3 the first batch of muskets was completed and
presented to the Convention. Carnot made a detailed report on that
day. He declared that France, once dependent on foreigners for
the means of its defense, would soon not only be self-sufficient, but
would serve as a storehouse where all peoples could arm themselves against tyrants. And in truth beginning with November
production rapidly increased. In the public shops the number of
workers rose from only 633 on November 3 to more than two
thousand at the end of the year, and more than five thousand in
the following summer. At that time, in Thermidor, about five
hundred muskets a day were produced. The number was only half
that hoped for by the Committee, but it was large by the standards
of the eighteenth century, and in the circumstances it represented
an extraordinary achievement. In the summer of 1794 the nationally owned workshops of Paris were probably the greatest arsenal
of small arms in the world. They were abolished soon after reaching their maximum output, during the reaction after Thermidor.

Distribution is the familiar antithesis to production in the
language of economics. It is not really an antithesis, of course,
for distribution is a part of production. The apportionment of labor
and of resources among different industries, the amount of reward
which workers in different industries receive, even distribution in
the simple sense of moving goods physically from one place to
another, are of the utmost importance in determining what is

produced, how much is produced, and where and when production is to take place. These problems are even more subtle and unmanageable than the problems of material exploitation or manufacture. The Committee of Public Safety never satisfactorily solved them.

The Maximum of September 29 caused trouble from the start. Virtually no one—neither merchant nor manufacturer nor farmer nor laboring man—was pleased with what the law entitled him to receive. Production was therefore paralyzed, and had to be galvanized into action by various methods, including the Terror. The members of the ruling Committee had no real belief in the fixing of prices and wages. Even Billaud-Varenne, who was something of a Hébertist, had said publicly that he disapproved of it. But the law was backed by the Hébertists and the Commune. Indeed there seemed to be no alternative to it; prices would soar if uncontrolled, the government would issue more assignats, and the vicious circle of inflation would be complete. This is precisely what happened after Thermidor. The assignat, after remaining stable during the rule of the Robespierrist Committee, crashed precipitously after Robespierre's fall. There was distress in the Year Two, but widespread misery in the Year Three.

The English and the greedy aristocrats, said Barère, were responsible for the failure of the Maximum to function smoothly. This was political talk; Barère and all competent observers knew what the real trouble was. A month after its enactment, the Convention, on motion of Barère, voted that the law be amended. Prices henceforth were to be calculated, not only by adding one-third to the price of 1790 (as provided on September 29), but by including the costs of transportation and a five per cent wholesaler's and ten per cent retailer's profit. It was hoped that dealers with this incentive would see fit to remain in business. But the task of finding the values for 1790 for scores of commodities, with all their grades and qualities, in every part of France, was exceedingly complex. It took until the following spring to compute the new rates, and meanwhile the country lived under a law that was generally admitted to be unworkable.

The Maximum of September 29 limited wage rates to a fifty per cent increase over the corresponding rate for 1790. Had the legal commodity prices been uniformly enforced, without loss to production, wage earners would have enjoyed a slight advantage. In reality their position was precarious, for the amount of illicit bargaining, carried on especially by women, was enormous. Wages were in some cases lowered by the law of September 29. In the preceding months, labor being scarce, wage rates had risen in many lines of employment. Agricultural laborers in the summer of 1793 frequently earned three times as much as in 1789. The law of September 29 allowed them only about half the new amount. Workingmen obstinately resisted this provision of the Maximum.

For the system to be successful the price and wage levels had to be enforced equally. Most officials and Jacobins, being predominantly middle class people, tended to watch over wage rates more strictly. Such discrimination did not represent exploitation of the mass of the people by a small minority. Even in Paris (in 1791), according to a trustworthy estimate, the number of bourgeois, small merchants and small craftsmen whose income was determined by prices was about equal to the number of laborers whose income depended purely on wages. In most other towns the proportion of proletarians was smaller. In rural areas the situation was confused, but the numerous peasants who owned or rented land would prefer high prices to high wages. In the economy of the eighteenth century, the working class and the wage-earning class were by no means the same.

In Paris, under the Hébertist Commune, the price level was emphasized and the maximum for wages virtually ignored by the authorities. Wage-earners had a brief moment of self-indulgence. There are records of men earning five and ten times their usual income, while the prices of goods they purchased remained rigidly controlled. Cab-drivers, offered the maximum fare by naïve bourgeois patrons, extorted larger sums by abusive language and revolutionary threats. Workmen refused employment, preferring to live for a week or so on their savings. Working-class women bought the finest fowl in the markets, while the wives of government clerks whose salaries were fixed, or of shopkeepers whose income depended upon sales, could afford only the toughest and leanest birds.

Workmen in the government arms shops were worse off than those in private employment, for the government could not be intimidated as easily as private employers. While a water-carrier in Paris might make twenty livres a day, a first-class mechanic in the arms manufacture was limited to sixteen. The Committee of Public Safety intended, to be sure, to pursue a fair and democratic policy of collective bargaining. A meeting was held in October, when the public shops were being organized, at which representatives of the workmen were present; it was agreed that payment should be by the piece, with a daily minimum of three livres and maximum of five—hardly munificent when a carter might charge eight livres to move half a cord of wood. Exceptions had to be made for certain types of skilled labor, as of the first-class mechanics mentioned above; but the Committee refused requests for a general upward revision of the scale.

The government, however, requisitioned its labor, which in any case many were willing to give in a spirit of sacrifice. Every man in Paris competent for such work was required to report to 4 Quai Voltaire, the seat of the Arms Administration. Once employed in the arms manufacture, no one could change his job. Troublemakers were regarded as suspects. Two years in prison awaited anyone hampering the production of materials of war. Labor was to be carried on in a spirit of patriotism, with the corollary that it was subject to a semi-military rule.

The Republican authorities faced the same problem of discipline which the early factory owners were trying to meet at the same time in England. On December 12 the Committee issued a kind of factory code. Workers were required to enter and leave the shops at the specified hours; they were fined for tardiness; their product was inspected; they were forbidden to form any organizations whatever; spontaneous "trooping together" was also prohibited and when it occurred was to be immediately broken up; but if workers felt themselves aggrieved they might peaceably and reasonably lay their complaints before the public authorities. Managers were made responsible for the good behavior of the men. Inspectors were created to visit the shops unannounced, call the roll of workmen present, and compare it with the manager's record; the purpose was not only to see that employees were regularly at work, but to prevent graft in the wages bills, for the manager had to pay a fine for every absentee whom he recorded present.

Hours were long, running to fourteen a day, and no holiday was allowed except the *décadi,* one day in ten. Workers in industries for national defense, according to a ruling of November 12, must think of themselves as soldiers. They must not relinquish their work "for the observance of any cult or the ceremonies of any brotherhood, religion or association whatever"—that is, they must work on Sundays, saints' days and Christmas. In this dawning age of modern efficiency laboring men were not accustomed to such severe restraints. Many persisted in their old ways, wasting time by talking during working hours, or going for walks, or running out to cafés. The Committee of Public Safety, overwhelmed though it was by more momentous affairs, had repeatedly to take action against these easygoing habits. When a hundred men in one of the government shops planned a hunting trip of several days, they were forbidden to go. When the Perier brothers complained that they could not continue production unless their workmen were disciplined, the Committee came to the support of the Periers.

The Committee, in short, was on the side of production, as most effective governments of whatever social philosophy apparently are. The labor policies of the revolutionary Republic and of the early industrial capitalists had much in common. The Committee punished strikes severely, and regarded agitators among the workmen as criminals at common law. Sometimes a more kindly spirit prevailed. In some individual cases leaves of absence were granted for reasons of health, and payments were made to sick or incapacitated workmen. In the spring of 1794 workers in the same shop were allowed to assemble, to formulate grievances and to make suggestions directly to the Committee. But the tempestuous Year Two was no time for humanitarian reform. The workers in the government shops remained restless and intractable.

Keeping men at work in the war industries was only part of the larger problem of allocating the labor supply of the country. The Committee of Public Safety, especially before 14 Frimaire, had great difficulties with the local authorities, who, usually in an excess of zeal, tended to draft all available men into the army. It was largely to save them from recruiting agents that the Committee requisitioned workmen for its shops. Private operators of basic industries, and also the farms, had to be furnished with labor. Young men were especially in demand because of their quickness in learning new jobs, the very men who by the Levy in Mass were to go to war. Thousands of them were withdrawn from military service. Searches had to be made in the ranks for soldiers skilled in industrial processes. In February, facing a shortage of fuel, the Committee recalled from the army all those who, six months before the Levy in Mass, had worked at the production of wood or coal. Conversely, civil employment sheltered many young men evading the conscription, bad patriots, ill disposed to the Republic, causing all sorts of underhand sabotage.

Conscripted labor, rewarded at relatively low wages, was supplemented by compulsory labor pure and simple. The corvée reappeared in some regions, the obligation incumbent on the peasants of working on the roads. It had been one of the chief grievances of country people under the old régime, and the humanitarian philosophy found it shocking, but in truth, as the Committee observed, it was no worse, now that it became a patriotic act, than compulsory service in the army. Many, indeed, conscripted for the army, found themselves stationed on the home front, working in agriculture under army rule. Prisoners of war and deserters toiled on the highways and canals. Barère, many years later, remembered a suggestion made by Saint-Just, who proposed that the ex-nobles be forced to do common labor on the roads. The whole Committee, says Barère, heard this proposal in stony silence; it had not abandoned all scruples of decency.

Many observers were of the opinion that scarcity was due not so much to physical shortage as to a blockage in distribution. This view must be accepted with reservation, since it expressed the popular prejudice against farmers and middlemen. The higher Revolutionary authorities, as we have seen, acted in the belief that production itself was inadequate. But it was certainly true that such goods as existed were not all being passed on to consumers. The attempt to keep down wages was by no means the main cause. More important was the unwillingness of farmers to part with their produce and of commercial men to undertake to distribute it. Revolutionaries saw counter-revolution in this attitude, which, however, was probably prompted less by political philosophy than by an elemental desire for self-protection.

To force the circulation of goods seemed to most contemporaries more feasible than to regulate prices. Hence the law against hoarding preceded the General Maximum by two months. It ordered all the thirty-odd thousand communes to create "engrossment commissioners." The law was rarely applied in the rural communes, where the commissioners would have had the unneighborly duty of forcing farmers to disgorge their barns. In Paris and other cities the commissioners, recruited from the working-class sansculottes, were inclined to regard all merchants, small and large, with suspicion. They searched private homes to prevent the laying up of future supplies, obliged retailers to sell off their stocks from day to day, and interfered with the operations of wholesalers whose large stores were subject to confiscation. The law was Draconian, prescribing death for anyone withholding goods from the market, though only eight death sentences on this charge are known. The net contribution of the engrossment commissioners, though in sporadic cases they doubtless helped the city population to relieve its wants, was to handicap the merchants by whom these wants were still chiefly supplied, and whose services the Committee of Public Safety was not prepared to dispense with. Collot d'Herbois, the main author of the law, obtained its modification in December, and after Ventôse it was abrogated entirely.

Another means of forcing circulation, often used by municipal authorities, was to buy goods with public funds and sell them to consumers at the legal price regardless of loss. In Paris, for example, in January 1794, women were demanding that the Commune relieve the shortage of soap. The Commune purchased a large quantity in Marseilles and sold it at twenty-three sous a pound, at a loss of 45,000 francs, since soap was unobtainable at Marseilles except at much higher prices. At this rate, said a contemporary, the Commune would lose 1,140,000 livres a year if it tried to furnish all the soap in Paris, as it would have to if it entered the business at all, since no private dealer would compete on such terms.

What was needed was that both government and private merchants be able to purchase, as well as sell, at controlled prices. Even persons critical of the Maximum agreed that so long as it existed it must be uniformly enforced. But not all the police agents, Jacobin clubs and section committees in the Republic could enforce it. Even if enforced it would not always be fair, for the rates were badly adjusted to each other, full of discrepancies and contradictions. And of course French maximum prices would buy no imports abroad.

The main function of the new Subsistence Commission was to bring the circulation of goods under national control. Decentralization had led to chaos. Men literally took the food from each other's mouths. The Army of Italy, stationed in the extreme south, requisitioned its needs at the doors of Paris. The Paris Commune swept up provisions under the eyes of the Army of the North. Coastal cities, to get food for themselves, carelessly exported resources without regard for national interest. Supplies levied for one city, army or district, were stopped on the road and requisitioned by the agents of another. Farmers were distracted by a competition more furious than that of commerce. Merchants found their property immobilized, and some petitioned the Committee of Public Safety to override local Jacobin orders.

The Commission gradually brought about a kind of system. In the end, after Ventôse, it remained the only body having the right to levy requisitions. Meanwhile it assigned to each army a definite area in which to provision itself. It dispatched its agents throughout the country—the right of sending authorized agents being restricted, by the law of 14 Frimaire, to the Subsistence Commission, the Committees of Public Safety and General Security and the vestigial council of ministers. Through these agents the Commission began a census of the national food supply. A law of August 17 punished with ten years in irons anyone convicted of making a false declaration. Tables were drawn up in Paris showing which departments had an excess of food and which were in need. With these differentials established, the Commission faced the problem of transportation. Boats and wagons were commandeered, the centralized maintenance of highways was brought back from the old régime, and at this time, in January, the corvée again became legal.

The Subsistence Commission was thus one of the vital organs of the régime. Beginning in a few unused rooms at the Ministry of the Interior, it expanded until it occupied the whole of the Hôtel de Toulouse, and had clerks and officials numbering over five hundred. It was apparently not free from the faults of bureaucracy. The three Commissioners had at one time to send a message to the outer office—"in view of the complaints made of the rude-

ness of several employees and junior clerks, the Commission
reminds everyone that all republicans are equal, but that equality
does not exclude courtesy and consideration."

It is impossible to leaf through the vast records of the Subsistence Commission without respecting the men who faced such a
colossal task. The Commission brought a boon to the country in
making requisition somewhat less arbitrary. It helped to hold the
Revolutionary Government together. Beyond that, its operations
were not very successful.

The difficulties were enormous, even apart from underproduction
and the dislocations caused by war. Fundamental in the problem
was the immemorial local-mindedness of the peasants. Country
people for centuries, living near the edge of subsistence, always
in dread of famine, hated to see grain withdrawn from their
localities. Free trade within national frontiers was a bourgeois
idea. The uncertainties of revolution intensified the age-old fear.
Local political officials, haunted by the same specter, exaggerated
the needs of their districts or attempted to conceal the true extent
of their resources.

Paris was more nationally minded, but intolerant toward country
people. The Hébertist Commune, hard pressed by scarcity, declared
that rich peasants should be guillotined, and sent out its Revolutionary Army to gather food. During the winter the Commune
forbade meat, wine, candles, soap, sugar and such goods to be
taken from the city, thus working hardships upon neighboring
farmers who were used to purchasing them in Paris, and who re-
taliated by refusing to bring in their produce. One woman, after
carrying some eggs to market, and having the herring for which
she had traded them confiscated at the city gates, swore that in the
future she would keep her eggs for herself. Both sides suffered,
and the peasants complained that Paris cared nothing for the rest
of the country. Such localism, as observers noted, was the negation
of "fraternity." It was a sign that the French people were not yet
fully educated into acting together as a nation.

In these circumstances the Commission found it difficult to plan
on a national scale. It suffered from a dearth of competent personnel. The census of grains was unreliable, the laws against false
declarations could not be enforced, and in some cases soldiers had
to be quartered on farmers to induce them to yield up their produce.

LINDET

Improvidence spread in the wake of five years of disturbance. Animals were slaughtered before attaining their full growth. Pasture lands fell into decay, and the arable fields were too frequently left unsown. The Commission ruled against the slaughter of lambs (by which meat, wool and new generations of sheep were lost); yet lamb was to be seen in the butcher shops of Paris.

As an example of what happened we can reconstruct from the archives of the Commission a little story about Andelys, one of two rural districts set aside for the provisioning of suburban Paris. The Subsistence Commission repeatedly directed Andelys to send grain to Saint-Denis. The peasants remained deaf. New orders from the Commission. Grumbling in Andelys. The local agent, named Baillif, is thereupon invited, on November 24, to denounce the recalcitrants. Three days later a special decree goes out from the Commission on the provisioning of suburban Paris. Agents are again urged to activity on December 12. Complications: a wagon-load of flour from Andelys appears by mistake at the doors of the Commission. Explanations, new orders, reprimands. The unfortunate Baillif is then denounced in turn by the surveillance committee of Maintenon. He is transferred by the Commission to another post. More pressure on Andelys, December 23; Andelys petitions against requisition; the Commission decides that Andelys must share with Paris. On February 15 Andelys is ordered to send seven thousand quintals of hay to Bernay. More requisitions follow. Baillif, now back in his old office, reports "fermentation" in Andelys. He is summoned on February 28 to explain the disturbance directly to the Committee of Public Safety. The Subsistence Commission also submits a report on the same subject. It seems that the irate people of Andelys want their old mass and their saints. They are assigned to making shoes for the army. More uprisings, more obstruction, and more reports of the Commission to the Committee. So Andelys passes from our sight.

Another example is offered by the correspondence of Georges Couthon with the governing board of Puy-de-Dôme. Couthon, within a month after returning from his mission at Clermont-Ferrand, took up a burden that remained with him the rest of his life—interceding with the Subsistence Commission for his home department. His personal influence had apparently no improper effect; the case of Puy-de-Dôme remained typical enough; and

Couthon's reports on his comings and goings throw a beam of light into a forest of complexities. Here is a synopsis from his letters:

December 21: Couthon confers with the Commission, which listens with politeness and understanding, but shows him the comparative statistics of other departments, and concludes that Puy-de-Dôme has provisions to last four months, if consumption be reduced from six to four quintals of grain per person a year, the scale adopted for the army. Conditional promises of aid are given. Much depends on future imports from the Barbary Coast and from the United States.

December 31: The Commission has granted Puy-de-Dôme 30,000 quintals to be furnished by the adjacent department of Allier.

January 11: Allier has protested; the Commission stands by its decision, but is authorizing Allier to receive 30,000 quintals from the next department, Cher.

February 13: Cher is making difficulties. The Commission is to take new steps.

February 25: Unfortunately, writes Couthon to the board in Clermont, the representatives on mission at Lyons have requisitioned the grain assigned to you by the Commission.

March 1: Couthon has again been to see the Commission, which has designated Bourges, in the department of Cher, as a source of supply for Puy-de-Dôme. The board at Clermont is empowered to send its own inspectors to Bourges.

March 22: New orders have been sent to Cher to enforce the requisition.

March 29: A delegation from Clermont is in Paris. Couthon has given them a letter of introduction to the Commission, and has spoken privately to Lindet. But, he adds, I must ask that you recall your agents from Bourges, for we have decided, in the Committee of Public Safety, that no local authorities shall send missions under penalty of twenty years in irons. However, you may send to Bourges some members of your Jacobin club. "Thus there will be no inconvenience."

April 5: What we have been unable to get from Cher will be made up elsewhere. We are promised 60,000 quintals from expected imports.

April 10: "The Subsistence Commission is having embarrass-ments in replacing what we lack of the 30,000 quintals that the department of Cher has not been able to furnish us completely."

April 15: Though Lindet promised me 60,000 quintals of im-ports, the Commission has convinced me that no grain arriving in southern ports can possibly be spared for Puy-de-Dôme, because the wants of the departments of the Midi, and of the armies of Italy, the Alps and the Pyrenees, are extremely urgent. We are granted instead 125,000 quintals of arrivals in Atlantic ports be-tween Brest and Sables d'Olonne. Atlantic ports are advantageous because they receive more captures than those of the Mediter-ranean. The Commission also promises 14,000 quintals from the department of Deux-Sèvres. "It is a bit distant, but the Commis-sion says it is *certain*." We do not lose by these arrangements the right to receive what we have coming from Cher. Meanwhile Clermont may levy 8,000 quintals on Riom (in Puy-de-Dôme itself), which, according to calculations of the Commission, can supply 45,000, and so has no grounds for complaint.

May 20: "I am thinking of your needs. . . ."

May 31: I enclose a requisition allowing Clermont to draw 600 quintals from Riom and 600 from Billom. (Both these towns were in Puy-de-Dôme, and the figures seem to have shrunk.)

July 2: I have not lost sight of your problem. All grains in the Midi still have unchangeable destinations. "Considering that the help granted to us from Cher, Deux-Sèvres and other places has not had its full effect," I have made further representations with the Commission. Lately I have been kept at home by a slight accident, but "my first step on leaving my bed will be directed toward the Subsistence Commission. You may count on me, my dear *concitoyens*. . . ."

So end Couthon's letters to the board at Clermont (for Thermi-dor was only three weeks off) with Couthon, ailing as usual, still preparing himself to be carried to the Hôtel de Toulouse.

Not all the extraordinary measures that the Committee of Public Safety adopted could remove the evils of scarcity. In principle the dictated economy foreshadowed the twentieth cen-tury. In practice it remained clumsy and erratic. The political disorder blocked the economic planning, which, however, as con-ceived by the Committee, would have been difficult to realize in the best ordered state of the time. Effective regulation was not easy with industry decentralized in hundreds of thousands of cottages, statistics undeveloped, reports brought in on horseback, computation all done mentally and all records laboriously kept in longhand.

A great crisis came toward the end of the winter, as the Republican Calendar moved into the month of Ventôse, which began on February 19, 1794. Ventôse, in a way, was more a turning point than Thermidor.

Privation can be met either by acceptance, which leads to Spartanism, or by discontent, which, when exploited for political aims, may lead to revolt. The Committee of Public Safety became increasingly Spartan, lauding the virtues of discipline and sacrifice. The reason was not simply that it was the government in office. "Virtue" was a favorite idea among the more honest Revolutionists; it meant a patriotism blended with a good deal of the old-fashioned morality of unselfishness. Of this quality Robespierre was the almost official spokesman; it was he who had put Virtue in the Revolutionary Calendar. Saint-Just was a Spartan of severer type, a warrior, an "athlete" of the Republic. Couthon, though gentle and generous, was by no means soft; physical suffering had confirmed him in fortitude.

"Meat," wrote Couthon from Paris on 7 Ventôse (February 25), "is very rare here. Since the day before yesterday it is furnished only to the sick. Once a day I receive a bit of beef from which soup has been made. It is enough, for republicans must be sober. Sobriety is the mother of many other virtues. If I had the police power in my hands I would do as the general council of the commune of Angers has done: I would make privation the order of the day. . . ."

But not everyone was so philosophical, and the increasing divergence between those who were willing to accept "virtue" and those who demanded more tangible satisfactions was perhaps the main difference between the Robespierrists and their opponents.

"The situation now prevailing in Paris is really alarming. The almost total lack of provisions is irritating and inflaming most of the people." These words were turned in to the government on 5 Ventôse by one of its most accurate observers. Most butcher shops, he said, were closed. People had been fighting in the streets for food, and it was the strongest who obtained it. Merchants bringing supplies into the city were attacked and plundered by maddened women. On 6 Ventôse, according to the same observer, there was no meat even for the sick; and milk, of which the poor used a great deal, was running short. The same was true of other commodities.

Disorder was spreading among the workers in the manufacture of arms. On the morning of 16 Ventôse a placard fastened at the door of one of the government shops was found defaced. It was a statement of regulations concerning hours, signed by six members of the Committee of Public Safety. Under Barère's name was scrawled *cannibal*. Under those of Lindet and C.-A. Prieur, who had the most direct charge of the economic régime, was written *cheaters of the people, foolish and stupid as it always is*—and also, in red crayon, *robbers, murderers*.

Matters had been made worse rather than better by the Maximum of September 29. The publication of the new Maximum on 23 Ventôse, allowing higher rates to encourage commercial distribution, did nothing to calm the agitation in Paris. For weeks ordinary men and women had cried that merchants and shopkeepers should be guillotined. This clamor was the voice of Hébertism. Others denounced a plot to starve the people and to overthrow the Convention, which was dominated, so they said, by foreigners and politicians of the Commune. These charges bore the earmarks of Dantonism—or perhaps of government propaganda. The factions were maneuvering furiously to take advantage of the popular unrest. Another insurrection seemed imminent, another day like September 5, another attack on the Committee of Public Safety, another collapse of authority, perhaps an experiment in unvarnished proletarian rule, or a disintegration into anarchy with no rule, regulation, or intelligent purpose whatever.

The events of Ventôse therefore were decisive.

CHAPTER XI

Finding the Narrow Way

THE new colossus of government was to be used for a political purpose. The ruling Twelve, though they spent most of their time in administration, were more than administrators in the usual sense. All were ardent Jacobins, very much alive politically, not wholly absorbed in simply running a machine. This was as true of Lindet, sitting all day and half the night in his busy back office, as of Robespierre, who passed many hours quietly thinking and writing in the vine-covered home of the Duplays. All asked themselves the questions which we too must ask. What was the purpose of the Revolutionary Government, with its corollary, the Terror? For what reason did virtually everyone lose his freedom? To what end were whole classes vilified, intimidated, hunted, and in their own eyes robbed?

"To assure the national defense," is the answer given by one school of historians. But France at the beginning of 1794 was no longer on the defensive. The Republicans had the upper hand in the north, in the Rhineland, at Toulon, Lyons, Bordeaux and in the west. The spirit in Paris was one of attack, a determination to humble the enemy, especially England. Yet military aggression was not the true aim of the Revolutionary Government. It is obvious from the records, and not the most prodigious learning can obscure the fact, that the great aim of the government in 1794 was to establish and perpetuate the French Republic. That is what Robespierre and hundreds of others thought they were doing. In their minds victory in the war was only a necessary step toward consolidating the Republican rule. Robespierre, like Abraham Lincoln, thought not only of the war but of the peace that was to follow, the kind of country for which he was asking men to die.

It is not hard to explain why some of the greatest French experts on the Revolution have laboriously shunned this seemingly flattering conclusion. Men still quarrel in France over the Revolutionary principles, and ever since 1792 influential persons have believed that republicanism was forced upon the country by the blade of the guillotine. The favorite reply of those who would justify the Third Republic is to interpret the violence of the First Republic as a means of national defense. Now the exigencies of modern French politics have nothing to do with what really happened in 1794. If the purpose of the Terror was to assure national defense, it was national defense with special Jacobin overtones, expressed by Saint-Just when he declared that the French people was composed of patriots, the others being "helots or nothing." National defense was inseparable from the active promotion of a political system, because patriots, in the eyes of the authorities, were those who wholeheartedly supported the government of the Mountain. And in this sense, at the end of 1793, even a great many Mountaineers were ceasing to be patriots.

The Mountain was splitting as every Revolutionary group, when it took its turn in power, had split before it. Holding together to liquidate more conservative elements, the Revolutionary vanguard could never agree on what to do with success. Citras and ultras, as they were now called, persons somewhat behind or somewhat ahead of those who had enough power to lay down the standard, were as old as the Revolution, indeed older, being apparently coeval with politics itself. There was nothing new, and in itself nothing unhealthy, in such division between citras and ultras.

The new features at the end of 1793 were several. A strong government was now in office, willing to maintain itself by vigorous repression, and able to point to spectacular successes against foreign and domestic foes. The idealism of earlier years was beginning to fade; much of the factional dispute was aimless and petty, and much of it prompted by personal egotism. Repeated fragmentation, continued emergence of newer and more limited groups from older and larger ones, had resulted in making the contending factions extremely small, hardly more than fluid associations of personalities, all claiming to represent the true course of the Revolution, all denouncing their enemies as false patriots, and all asserting their identity with the people. Whoever won out, France would be governed by a minority many times subdivided. The practical question was whether, for the purpose in hand, the best minority was the existing Committee with its adjuncts.

We have seen evidence of these quarrels within the Mountain in preceding chapters—Fabre d'Eglantine involving his enemies in a trumped up Foreign Plot, Chabot denouncing accomplices in the India Company scandal to save himself, Baudot and Lacoste making trouble for Saint-Just in Alsace, extremists at Cherbourg accusing Saint-André of moderatism, Carrier ridiculing Prieur of the Marne as a fool, the Hébertists in Paris (Hébert holding office by fifty-six votes) misapplying national legislation on economic matters, and trying to organize the Paris sections against the governing Committees. And we have seen how Robespierre brought the government to disavow violent Dechristianization, and acting upon Fabre's revelations put a number of Hébertists in jail.

The situation was complicated by the return of the great Danton to Paris. Danton was the only surviving Revolutionist whose personal ascendancy was equal to Robespierre's. But the two could no longer cooperate. Danton had refused on September 6 to serve on the ruling Committee, declaring that he would join no committee but would be a spur to them all. Then he had gone off with his new wife to the country, to enjoy the ease of a retired politician, earning the reputation among radicals of being a man from whom all Revolutionary vigor had been drained. Chabot's exposure of the India scandal revealed some of Danton's friends as grafters. Danton's own record in money matters was not above reproach. He returned to Paris in an unfavorable light, seemingly as a defender of corruption. Since he was the strongest figure outside the government a motley following gathered about him, composed of men who had something to gain by the fall of the Committee of Public Safety, and who looked to him as the most likely successor to Robespierre. By December a Dantonist party had been formed.

Ideas were of subordinate importance in holding the factions together. They existed largely by opposition to each other. The Hébertists were the party of the Commune; the Dantonists drew their strength from the Convention. Hérault-Séchelles, long thought a Dantonist, is now considered a Hébertist. Bourdon of the Oise, a Dantonist in December, was a Hébertist a few weeks before. The Dantonists were indeed generally "citra," but Chabot had supported the Enragés, Fabre d'Eglantine in framing the Republican Calendar had given comfort to the Dechristianizers, and Baudot in opposing Saint-Just in Alsace had conducted himself as an extremist. The Hébertists were generally "ultra," but Hébert had helped to crush the real radicals of the preceding summer, Anacharsis Cloots had a hundred thousand livres a year, and the Dechristianizing ardors of Chaumette were scarcely more heated than those of Couthon or Saint-André at the same time.

Danton himself wished to moderate the Terror. He was in truth an exhausted volcano; like Leo X with the papacy, now that he had the Republic he wished to enjoy it. He saw no more need for wholesale guillotinings when Republican armies were victorious at home and on the frontiers. He considered that the war had come to a draw, and that peace might be made, especially if France took on a less fiercely revolutionary appearance. It is arguable that his judgment was correct: that the Terror was no longer needed for national defense, in the sense of protecting the country from the inroads of foreign powers. The great difficulty was the failure of Mountaineers to agree. Danton would solve it by creating a vague and broad Republic, in which men of all kinds, good and bad, sound and tainted, might, after disposing of irreconcilable extremists, join together by not arguing over principles. The Republic after Thermidor, disfigured by cynicism, loose-living and peculation, would not have shocked him.

Danton indicated a broad and comfortable way. Robespierre preferred the straight and narrow. Robespierre was still the idealist, after five years during which, in wave after wave, men had become disillusioned with the Revolution. To Robespierre it was unthinkable that after all the risk and the suffering, all the struggle and the eager anticipation, all the dreadful decisions already made, the responsibilities bravely assumed, the execution of the king and the queen, the proud challenge to the crowned heads of Europe, the shootings and guillotinings of men who after all were Frenchmen, and who if less obstinate could be brothers—that all this should issue in a world no better than the old, a Republic in which vice, hypocrisy, irreligion and egotism should be laughed at.

Robespierre used a good deal of political realism in judging the Dantonist party. Danton was surrounded by men unworthy of him. There was Camille Desmoulins, a kind of child in politics, a man known familiarly as Camille at a time when few were called by their first names, treated by others with an affectionate levity, so little respected that, with quantities of work to be done by members of the Convention in committees and on mission, he was never entrusted with duties of any consequence—useful however as a temperamental pamphleteer, his great triumph being a work that had helped to ruin the Girondists. There was Fabre d'Eglantine, poet and forger, whose complicity in the India scandals and brazen fabrication of the Foreign Plot came to light early in January. There was Chabot, a licentious ex-Capucin friar, hoping to hide his own dishonesty by exposing his confederates to Robespierre, married to the sister of a foreign banker, as a means it was said of explaining his new opulence of living. There was Philippeaux, who had been on mission to the west, and who repeatedly denounced the blunders of certain Hébertist generals in conducting the Vendéan war; he was remembered years later by Prieur of the Côte d'Or as a scatter-brained and self-pushing opportunist. And there was Bourdon of the Oise, who cared little which party he belonged to if only it showed signs of strength, and who delighted in embarrassing a government that had remained unappreciative of his merits.

The Convention was disposed to listen seriously to these men. Some of the more estimable members formed a kind of fringe to their party. Dantonism had in it the seed of a parliamentary opposition, by which members of the Convention, without being treasonable to the Republic, might discuss and criticize the work of the government. That it never developed in this way was not entirely the fault of individuals. Organized parties were frowned upon by eighteenth century liberals, including the American Founding Fathers. The Jacobins in particular saw no need for political opposition. Criticism was often a cloak for intrigue. Discussion of policy almost always passed into denunciation of motives. The ablest men in the Convention were busy with executive work; the hall was usually filled with second-raters, vain in their majesty as Representatives of the People, restless under the leadership of their colleagues on the committees, inclined to magnify trifles because important decisions were no longer made on the floor of the house. In the Convention still survived the old claim of legis-

lators to be more important than the executive, the old suspicion
of liberals toward the power of government, the old dislike of
revolutionists for persons in authority. The character of individual
Dantonists added a last increment of political ineptitude. If anything was certain it was that men like Camille Desmoulins and
Fabre d'Eglantine had little notion of how to govern France.

Danton's program for mitigating the Terror was the most important of all political issues in December. It was discredited by
the low repute of its most outspoken supporters. It was unrealistic
in not candidly presenting the probable consequences. It was of
course vehemently denounced by the Hébertists, who would have
to be disposed of before terrorism could cease. The Committee of
Public Safety was not sympathetic to Hébertism, but it did not
wish, by crushing the Commune, to fall into the hands of an unruly and exultant Convention.

Shortly after returning to Paris Danton prevailed upon Camille
Desmoulins to take up his pen in the cause of Indulgency. Desmoulins was a friend of Robespierre's. They had been at school
together, in this same Paris, twenty years before. Maximilien
looked on Camille, who was two years his junior, almost as on a
younger brother who must be protected from his own caprices.
It seemed that whatever Camille did or said would be forgiven.
Camille began to write with his usual heedlessness, the Dantonists
reaped their advantage, and Robespierre, within a few weeks,
faced one of the cruelest personal difficulties of his life.

In the first number of his new journal, the *Vieux Cordelier,*
Desmoulins struck out against the Hébertists, calling them the
tools of foreigners and extolling Robespierre as the great monument of Revolutionary infallibility. The second number deplored
the evils of atheism, and was harmonious with Robespierre's
views. Robespierre in fact had seen these two numbers before
publication; they were useful propaganda against the Commune.
The third number, appearing on December 15 and not shown
to Robespierre beforehand, was the bombshell. Pretending to be
a translation from Tacitus, it drew a gripping picture of society
under the Caesars, a society driven frantic by suspicion, uncertainty, fear, delation, duplicity and violence. The application to
France was clear. Only in 1933 was it revealed that Camille's

"translation of Tacitus" was modeled on a French translation of an English adaptation of the Latin original.

Childish pretensions to learning, however, do not necessarily invalidate a writer's ideas. Even babes may speak wisdom. Desmoulins undoubtedly portrayed a régime of terror with telling strokes. Was the picture true to life? When the Indulgents began their campaign hardly a thousand persons out of twenty-five million had been executed by revolutionary courts. The repression at Lyons and in the west was only beginning, and little news of it had yet come to Paris. Yet actual bloodshed is not the only measurement of terror. Nervousness, apprehension, fear of secret denunciation haunted thousands whom the guillotine did not touch. Among these were certain corrupt politicians, the Fabres, the Chabots, though we need not believe that Indulgency aimed at nothing higher than the saving of scoundrels. Whatever their motives, the Dantonists found public favor. The third number of the *Vieux Cordelier* was snatched from the newsstands, and created an enormous buzz in the cafés.

What were Camille's ideas? They were summarized in one revealing sentence.

"I shall die in the opinion," said Camille, "that to make France republican, happy and flourishing, a little ink would have sufficed, and only one guillotine."

This belief must be pronounced mistaken. The conflicting forces in French society were not to be resolved by the propagation of words. France could not be made a republic by ink, not even by ink plus one guillotine. This fact was apparent to Robespierre. If the Indulgents really wanted a republic they were deluding themselves in suggesting that the prisons be opened and the guillotines taken down. If they did not want a republic, or wanted only republican forms, behind which dishonest, weary or frightened Revolutionists could retire, then they were guilty, it seemed to Robespierre, of counter-revolution.

Meanwhile the Hébertists carried on a kind of leftist agitation from the Commune and the Cordeliers club. Socialists have judged this faction as unfavorably as conservatives, refusing to recognize it as part of the socialist tradition, preferring to look back to Babeuf, who led an abortive proletarian movement a few years later. Babeuf had nothing to do with the Hébertists, being at the time an obscure employee of the Subsistence Commission; but continuity was not wholly wanting, for some disciples of Babeuf in 1796 were followers of Hébert in 1793. Hébertism gave an outlet for sporadic proletarian discontent, which, since the leaders were not men of ideas, hardly went beyond blind fury against shopkeepers and peasants, clamors for the guillotine, and detestation of the Christian religion.

The Hébertists were on the defensive in December. Their attempt to regain control over the police powers of the Paris sections was foiled by Barère and Billaud-Varenne. The rise of Indulgency threatened them with extinction. Anacharsis Cloots, who claimed that the People was God, was driven from the Jacobin society by Robespierre. Vincent, assistant to the war minister, Ronsin, commander of the Revolutionary Army, and Maillard, a well known political thug, went to prison.

Then on December 20 Collot d'Herbois came back from Lyons. "The giant has appeared," wrote Hébert in his *Père Duchesne,* "and all the dwarfs that have been annoying the best patriots have scurried a hundred feet underground." In Collot the Hébertists had a supporter on the Committee of Public Safety. He denounced the arrest of Ronsin, his helper at the Liberated City, thus breaking openly with Robespierre. The Hébertists took heart.

Robespierre and the Committee, with the possible exception of Billaud-Varenne, would undoubtedly have preferred to be rid of Collot d'Herbois. Men of education and principle, they could hardly enjoy having this gesticulating ex-actor and loud-talking butcher of Lyons in their midst. Yet he was useful in holding the adherence of the Commune, and in any case, especially with the exclusion at this time of Hérault-Séchelles, it was difficult to drop Collot without raising the whole question of the membership of the Committee.

This question it was extremely impolitic to raise. It was an issue on which Hébertists and Dantonists could come together. Guardedly and furtively both factions, with many confusing contradictions and disclaimers, were trying to subvert the Decemvirs, each looking to a time when it should succeed to power. Members of both factions, with due circumlocution, had demanded that the constitution of the preceding July be put into effect. This would mean dissolving the ruling Committee and dismantling the whole

Revolutionary Government, and would have led straight back to chaos. France could not be governed under a republican constitution until the war was over, and until the more perfervid revolutionaries were either liquidated or disillusioned. Before the constitution must come the Terror.

The Dantonists, playing upon the restiveness of the Convention, carried on a continual skirmish with executive officials. Bourdon took the lead. He moved that the six ministries be abolished, and that the Committee govern without them. Robespierre and Barère succeeded in having the motion shelved. Bourdon recurred to the same theme; Robespierre explained that under a Republic the old distrust of ministers was needless. Bourdon aimed his guns at the War Ministry, which Vincent had filled with Hébertist appointees; Philippeaux added his refrain, an endless tale of bungling in the Vendéan war. Bourdon demanded the arrest of an agent of the Committee of General Security, who during a fracas had seized a member of the Convention by the collar. Others in the assembly complained that, while travelling on missions, they were stopped by police officials to have their papers examined. Others said that employees of the ministries defamed the Representatives of the People. So it went: the Convention was made to listen to grumblers who, far from constituting a parliamentary opposition, kept pecking at the government as a means of preserving their sense of importance.

The monthly grant of power to the Committee of Public Safety expired on December 10. Barère asked two days later for a renewal. Bourdon objected, declaring that certain members of the Committee were not trusted by the Convention. Someone else proposed that a third of the Committee be retired each month. Cambacérès (who was to be arch-chancellor under Napoleon) diverted this attack on the government by having the question postponed to the following day. At the next session, after what political huddles we do not know, a member asked for a roll call, to discover who those were who mistrusted the Committee. This proposal was turned down; no roll call was held; it would have proved nothing anyway, for deputies would have feared to reveal themselves so openly as belonging to the factions. After a warm speech by an unimportant deputy the existing Committee, by unanimous vote, was continued in office for another month.

The reasons given were not that France still faced a desperate peril. The Convention reconfirmed its Committee because it thought the worst peril overcome. No doubt memories lingered of the turbulent session of September 25, at which the Committee had threatened collective resignation. Whoever sought to divide the Convention, Robespierre had then said, was an enemy of the country, "whether he sits in this hall or is a foreigner." The Convention was undoubtedly cowed. But it was not yet terrorized. Its members were not afraid of the guillotine in December; they did not expect to follow the Girondists to the scaffold; they could hardly conceive that they, the residue of the faithful, might in their turn be purged as aristocrats and traitors. The main reason why they retained the Committee was not fear, but the reason offered: "Only since the existence of the present Committee has the Revolution been on the march."

But the malcontents did not accept the decision of December 13. Three days later, when Couthon proposed the recall of an inefficient representative on mission who happened to be an ex-priest, and when the Convention impulsively decided to recall all representatives who had been clergymen or nobles, the indefatigable Bourdon insisted that the same principle be applied to the Committee of Public Safety. He attacked Hérault-Séchelles by name, pointing to his Hébertist connections. The Committee, for reasons not known to Bourdon, dropped Hérault two weeks later. Bourdon's proposal also implicated Jeanbon Saint-André, without whom the Revolutionary Government would have no significant navy. The absent Jeanbon found defenders, and Bourdon's whole maneuver came to nothing. The Convention reversed its decision to recall nobles and ministers of religion. One more piece of evidence was added to show that the Convention was being agitated by an anti-government faction, and that in any case it had difficulty in seeing beyond the impulse of the hour.

Meanwhile the third number of Desmoulins' *Vieux Cordelier* had appeared, on December 15. A government spy reported that it was being read aloud in the cafés, concluding that at the Café de la Montagne, "it was universally applauded." The manuscript of this confidential report still exists, with its final sentence underlined in ink, probably by the hand of one of the Twelve, during a nightly session of the Committee.

Menaced by opposing factions which joined in a common obstructionism, caricatured by the Indulgents as nothing but Caligulas and Neros, yet needing virtually unlimited power to discharge the enormous responsibilities that they had undertaken, the Committee of Public Safety decided to lay before the Convention a reasoned justification of their position. Robespierre carefully prepared an address "On the Principles of Revolutionary Government." Delivered, in the name of the Committee, on Christmas Day—5 Nivôse, a mere *quintidi* for Republicans—it was one of the first answers to the insistent question: What is the purpose of the Terror?

The speech of 5 Nivôse was also the first important statement in modern times of a philosophy of dictatorship.

It would be easy enough, Robespierre began, for Republican valor to overcome Englishmen and common traitors. It was more difficult to confound intrigue and to make the principles of general prosperity prevail. He then launched into his subject, the theory of revolutionary government, which, he said, quite rightly, was something new in human affairs, not treated in books.

"The function of government is to direct the moral and physical forces of the nation toward the purpose for which government is instituted.

"The aim of constitutional government is to preserve the Republic. The aim of revolutionary government is to found it.

"The Revolution is the war of liberty against its enemies. The constitution is the rule of liberty when victorious and peaceable. . . .

"Constitutional government is chiefly concerned with civil liberty, revolutionary government with public liberty. Under constitutional rule it is almost enough to protect individuals against the abuses of public power; under revolutionary rule the public power is obliged to defend itself against all the factions that attack it."

It is clear that Robespierre had the utmost respect for constitutional government. The essential liberalism appears plainly—the belief that it is the government against which individuals normally need the most protection. That Robespierre regarded dictatorship as an interim phase, necessary rather than desirable, is beyond possibility of question.

Faction, he went on, is the chief menace to the Revolution, and is represented by two deviations, weakness and rashness, moderatism and excess—"moderatism which is to moderation what impotence is to chastity; excess, which is to vigor what dropsy is to health." Both have the same purpose and effect, to break down confidence in what the government is doing.

"Who then will disentangle all these differences? Who will trace the line of demarcation between excesses contrary to the love of country and of truth?" Who will be pilot between Scylla and Charybdis? Who will find the narrow way? He did not answer, but he believed it could only be himself.

"The founding of the French Republic is not child's play. It cannot be the work of caprice or indifference, nor the chance outcome of individual ambitions and of all the elements of the Revolution. Wisdom as well as power presided at the creation of the universe." The Republic, in short, must be planned. Like the God of Newton constructing a world to run by natural laws, the Revolutionary Government was to build a state which, when once created, held together by its own law and constitution, not by force.

At this point Robespierre began to see his vision. The enemies of the Republic, he said, have great advantages, all vices being on their side, only the virtues being for the Republic. We hear, speaking in the statesman, the voice of the provincial lawyer from Arras, the lonely and unworldly dreamer, who could not have loved the common man so much had he thought him capable of evil.

"Virtues are simple, modest, poor, often ignorant, sometimes gross; they are the appanage of misfortune and the patrimony of the people. Vices are surrounded with riches, adorned by the charms of pleasure and the snares of perfidy; they are escorted by all the dangerous talents; they are escorted by crime."

And from his vision Maximilien passed to his obsession, the Foreign Plot. Austria, England, Russia, Prussia, Italy, he said, have established among us a secret government that rivals the government of France. They too have their committees, their treasury, their agents. Foreign spies sit in our clubs, in our government offices, in our section assemblies, in the Convention itself. "They gnaw all about us; they take our brothers by surprise; they caress our passions; they try to sway our opinions; they turn our own resolutions against us." Everywhere, urging some patriots to be violent, others to be lukewarm, inciting our clergy to sedition, agitating our workingmen, sabotaging our industry, betraying our plans, is this elusive, numberless, invisible swarm of foreign spies.

Robespierre certainly exaggerated. Spies were of course active in France, but it was not the intrigue of foreign courts that brought dissension among Revolutionists. Robespierre was succumbing to the temptation of all governments to blame trouble on causes outside the country. He was preparing to attack factionalism by attributing it to treasonable conspiracy. Probably he believed what he said; men believe strange things in time of tension, especially when strange reports are politically convenient. Moreover Robespierre had Fabre d'Eglantine's charges to keep in mind, and the recent news from Constantinople that proceedings of the Committee were known to the enemy. And yet, in his account of foreign machinations there was a tone of almost psychopathic delusion, very different from the sober and sensible explanation of the difference between constitutional and revolutionary government. It is doubtful whether the whole Committee of Public Safety believed in the foreign menace as much as Robespierre did. But the others were willing to follow his lead.

Both factions were warned on 5 Nivôse. They were attacked directly at their common rallying point, their plea for constitutional rule. It was clear that the government intended to suppress them both, that it would not falsely flatter one while proceeding to destroy the other. But the opposing chieftains, Hébertist and Dantonist, were by no means silenced by the warning, nor could they combine in any effective way for joint defense.

The next great clash occurred at the Jacobins early in January. Collot d'Herbois assaulted the Dantonists on the 5th, vehemently opening a Hébertist counter-offensive. He accused Philippeaux of sowing strife by criticizing the generals in the Vendée, and Desmoulins of holding principles that were not those of the society. Desmoulins jumped up, brandishing some papers, which, he said, proved that Hébert in selling copies of the *Père Duchesne* for the army had cheated the government out of 43,000 livres. Hébert tried to reply; Robespierre's younger brother interrupted, deprecating petty personal squabbles. Hébert stamped his feet and rolled his eyes, crying, "Do they wish to assassinate me? . . . Oh, God!"; and someone else shouted "Tyranny!" Then Maximilien himself arose, rebuked his brother, supported Collot d'Herbois, said that the question must not be deflected, that the present inquiry was not against Hébert but against Philippeaux and Camille Desmoulins.

At the next meeting, on the evening of January 7, Robespierre tried to pacify the excited brethren. There are no more factions, he boldly said; only the French people against its enemies. To lift the level of debate he proposed a new subject as the order of the day, "The crimes of the English government and vices of the British constitution." The society consented with applause, and did in fact spend the rest of January exhausting the riches of this congenial theme.

But just as Robespierre's motion was carried Camille Desmoulins, arriving late, came into the hall. He sped to the tribune to answer the charges of Collot two nights before. He was vacillating, confused, gropingly contrite; he admitted perhaps having erred in supporting Philippeaux, whom he was now willing to forsake, for there was no mutual loyalty in the factions. Someone called out for him to explain the *Vieux Cordelier*.

The time had come for Robespierre to pass judgment on his boyhood friend, to choose between personal attachment and political conviction. To this dilemma, which thousands had faced during the Revolution. the Jacobin faith had an unswerving answer: the love between parent and child, man and woman, brother and brother, friend and friend must if necessary be foregone for love of country. The Incorruptible, more than most Jacobins, could observe this rule. Yet he wished to save Desmoulins, and in any case he was coming to believe, for political reasons, that it was best to suppress dangerous ideas without making enemies of the men who held them. Rising to confute Camille, he spoke completely as the pontiff, inflexible toward error, yet hoping not to split his church.

"Camille had promised," he declared, as a hush settled over the assembly, "to abjure the political heresies, the erroneous and evil sounding propositions that cover the pages of the *Vieux Cordelier*. Camille, puffed up by the prodigious sale of his journal and the perfidious praise which the aristocrats showered upon him, has not abandoned the path traced for him by error. His writings are dangerous, they give hope to our enemies, they favor public malignity. . . .

"Camille's writings are certainly to be condemned, yet we must distinguish between the person and the works. Camille is a spoiled child, who had good inclinations but has been misled by bad companions. We must use rigor toward his paper, which even Brissot would not have dared to acknowledge, and yet keep him in our midst. I demand that as an example his issues be burned in the society."

"Well said, Robespierre, but I reply with Rousseau—burning is no answer!"

The impish Desmoulins had aimed his dagger well. He intimated plainly that Robespierre was abusing him as an archbishop once abused a man now sainted by good Jacobins. Robespierre lost his temper.

"How can you dare to justify a writing that is the joy of the aristocracy? You must learn, Camille, that if you were not Camille you would not be treated so lightly. The way you try to justify yourself proves to me that your intentions are bad. 'Burning is no answer!' How can that quotation have any application here?"

"But Robespierre, I don't understand. How can you say that only aristocrats read my paper? The Convention, the Mountain have read the *Vieux Cordelier*. Are the Convention and the Mountain composed only of aristocrats?"

The altercation was finally stopped by Danton, who told Camille not to be alarmed, and urged that nothing be done to kill the freedom of the press.

Desmoulins was of course right in point of fact; the Mountaineers did read his paper. That fact constituted the danger; the *Vieux Cordelier* was raising doubts in the once reliable vanguard of the Revolution. He was right also in thinking that burning was not exactly an answer. It was Robespierre, however, who adopted the only method for creating the kind of Republic in which all Mountaineers, whatever their conduct, professed to believe. By the methods of Desmoulins a kind of Thermidorian republic might be created, constantly in danger of relapsing into monarchy

and reaction; but neither Desmoulins nor anyone else would admit
that such an outcome was what he wanted.

The Dantonists were badly discredited in the next few days.
Fabre d'Eglantine, the full depths of his roguery discovered, was
expelled from the Jacobins, denounced by Robespierre, who however continued to believe in the Foreign Plot. Fabre, Chabot, two
other Dantonists guilty of embezzlement, together with Hérault-
Séchelles, were turned over to the Revolutionary Tribunal on
January 17.

Desmoulins, after being driven from the Jacobins, was formally
reinstated at Robespierre's demand. Dealing with criminals and
supposed members of a foreign conspiracy was one thing. Dealing
with old stalwarts who might be only temporarily misguided was
another. Robespierre's careful distinction between Camille's doctrine and his person no doubt arose from friendship, but it expressed also, or precipitated, a new wisdom in his ideas. Six weeks
before, in setting the Jacobins on their "purifying scrutiny," he
had given his approval to an orgy of recrimination. Now, in January, he objected to the naming of names. He realized at last that
attacking personalities only made factiousness more bitter. We
must, he said, "discuss intrigue, but not any intriguer in particular." We must fight faction, but not attack the factious as individuals. Only in this way can we be sure that our charges spring
from love of country. Robespierre was trying to lift denunciation
to the level of politics, to generalize arguments which the Jacobins
(the more so perhaps because they were Frenchmen) insisted
upon making personal. It was a statesmanlike idea, though in the
circumstances it could not serve its purpose, for threats do not
become less terrible by becoming vague and nameless.

As the Dantonists were checked, Hébertism enjoyed a revival.
Vincent and Ronsin were released from prison. Billaud-Varenne,
behind the closed doors of the Committee, was attacking Danton
himself as a traitor, to the embarrassment of Robespierre, who
did not yet believe in such a perversion of the truth. Hébert,
toward the end of January, opened an economic propaganda more
vitriolic than ever, calling for an increase of the Revolutionary
Army, screaming for the guillotine, vilifying grocers, tavern-
keepers, butchers, shoemakers, farmers, declaring in his usual
language that he would spare small merchants no more than large

ones, "for, f——, I see a league formed of all sellers against all buyers, and I find as much bad faith in the small booths as in the big warehouses." Meanwhile, throughout the country, the Dechristianizers were still rampant, undeterred by the Convention's decree of December 6 forbidding violence against religion. The Convention itself, and its representatives on mission, showed little interest in enforcing the decree, which had been issued only at the demand of Robespierre and the Committee.

But the government, in rejecting Indulgency, did not mean to encourage extremism. In Paris, where scarcity made the population restless, it was dangerous to attack too openly the seeming friends of the poor, yet already, at the close of his speech of 5 Nivôse, Robespierre had held out promises of relief, hoping to win for the Committee the favor that the Hébertists were receiving. In the provinces, while the Subsistence Commission struggled to prevent famine, the Committee redoubled its efforts to control the representatives on mission, and to protect law-abiding religious worshipers from the Carriers, the Fouchés, the Baudots.

An old circular to the representatives, drafted on December 24 but not yet sent, was taken from the files and dispatched on January 23. It commanded action, unity, speed; tolerance in dealing with sincere "fanatics," unflinching rigor toward "those who only preach heaven the better to devour the earth"; and above all it urged the representatives to stay within the limits of their legal powers. It is to this time, late January, that we should attribute a rather famous letter of the Committee. The letter is undated, but it was signed by Jeanbon Saint-André, who only reached Paris on January 25, and it was taken notice of in Strasbourg on February 2 and at Lyons on February 13. It was therefore probably not written in November, at the time of the first outbreaks of Dechristianization, as has previously been thought. The exact dating is of some importance, for, if written at the end of January, the letter shows that the Committee moved against Hébertism simultaneously with the ebb of Indulgency, and that Robespierre, at this advanced period of the Terror, had by no means lost all sense of proportion.

Written by Robespierre himself, and signed by every member of the Committee then in Paris, the letter was a circular to all the revolutionary clubs. It urged Jacobins everywhere, in disseminating enlightenment, to avoid the pitfalls of overzeal. As with Saint-André's proclamation at Cherbourg, the language was not flattering to the religious, but the purpose was toleration.

"The more violent the convulsions of an expiring fanaticism are," declared the Committee, "the more caution we must use. Let us not give it new arms by substituting violence for instruction. Keep in mind this truth: there is no commanding of consciences. Some are superstitious in good faith, for weak minds exist. . . . They are sick persons that we must prepare to heal by winning their confidence, and who would be made fanatical by a forced cure."

This was the most sensible advice that could have been given in the circumstances. Robespierre believed in freedom of religion— so long as religion confined itself to another world, and did not affect political allegiance. He favored conversion by persuasion— though among means of persuasion he would include some fairly intensive propaganda. To Camille he had been inquisitorial, incensed by Camille's cutting rejoinder, sternly committing his writings to the flames. Now he said, "There is no commanding of consciences." The inconsistency was in part that of a frustrated idealist who found his principles and his policies unavoidably in conflict. But Robespierre would argue that suppressing Desmoulins did no violence to liberty or to conscience either, for he did not believe Desmoulins sincere. He expected more conformity among the Jacobins upon whom the founding of the Republic depended, than among outsiders who had yet to be raised to the Republican level.

The circular to the Revolutionary clubs at the end of January, like Robespierre's new theory of impersonal denunciation, was part of the wider strategy of placing the Revolutionary Government on a foundation of principle. The Committee decided to give out once again a public statement of its aims. The initiative perhaps came from Robespierre. But what Robespierre should say, in this new address to the Convention, was agreed upon over the green table.

At this point we must again direct our darts at those towers of scholarship, MM. Aulard and Mathiez, who have held that the men of 1794 acted as they did almost entirely under pressure of circumstances. This argument of "circumstances" is supposed to excuse the violence and repressiveness of the Terror. It is like the argument of "national defense," the chief "circumstance" being the need of winning the war, to which Mathiez adds the need of satisfying proletarian demands. Now a man who acts only from circumstance is a man without settled purpose, swayed by forces outside himself, responding to nothing but the immediate and momentary stimulus of environment. Robespierre, in this picture, reached his decisions because of Hébertist agitation or last week's insurgency at the Jacobin club, or because the clergy and aristocrats made trouble, or to meet the demands of war, or, more vaguely, to assure the "public safety."

All these things the Revolutionary Government did do, but they are not all that it did. The Committee, and especially Robespierre, wished to escape from the confinement of mere circumstance. They wished to clarify the issues, to overcome the bewilderment into which a long troubled people had fallen, to rise above the short-sightedness, the cross purposes, the wrangling, the personalities, the day-to-day decisions and hand-to-mouth expedients which too often had to be adopted. They wished also to free themselves of the charge of being only lovers of power. Robespierre was already called a dictator; he wished to justify his position. As Mr. J. M. Thompson, the English authority, puts it, he had become by January an inquisitor without a creed, striking out in all directions, ruining his own best friends, in the name of an ideal which he had not yet made explicit.

So the old question renewed itself: What is our aim? What is the purpose of the Terror? What *kind* of Republic do we want? The answer was given in Robespierre's speech of February 5, the most memorable of all his addresses. M. Aulard, in a work of 400,000 words on the French Revolution, seems not to have mentioned this speech at all; M. Mathiez, in one of 250,000, devoted five sentences to it, being of the opinion that his hero was better justified by certain principles of class struggle than by the ideas which Robespierre himself never tired of expounding. This silence of the officially accredited historians of the Third Republic, a silence the more remarkable among the thousands of facts, details and minutiae which they introduce, is an odd commentary on democracy in modern France.

ROBESPIERRE

The speech of February 5, 1794, was not only the best expression of Robespierre's real ideas, but also one of the most notable utterances in the history of democracy.

The speech was called a "Report [from the Committee of Public Safety] on the principles of political morality which should guide the National Convention in the internal administration of the Republic."

Too long, Robespierre began, have we acted in difficult circumstances only from a general concern for public good. We need "an exact theory and precise rules of conduct."

"It is time to mark clearly the aim of the Revolution." Today we announce to all the world the true principles of our action.

"We wish an order of things where all low and cruel passions are enchained by the laws, all beneficent and generous feelings awakened; where ambition is the desire to deserve glory and to be useful to one's country; where distinctions arise only from equality itself; where the citizen is subject to the magistrate, the magistrate to the people, the people to justice; where the country secures the welfare of each individual, and each individual proudly enjoys the prosperity and glory of his country; where all minds are enlarged by the constant interchange of republican sentiments and by the need of earning the respect of a great people; where industry is an adornment to the liberty that ennobles it, and commerce the source of public wealth, not simply of monstrous riches for a few families.

"We wish to substitute in our country morality for egotism, probity for a mere sense of honor, principle for habit, duty for etiquette, the empire of reason for the tyranny of custom, contempt for vice for contempt for misfortune, pride for insolence, large-mindedness for vanity, the love of glory for the love of money, good men for good company, merit for intrigue, talent for conceit, truth for show, the charm of happiness for the tedium of pleasure, the grandeur of man for the triviality of grand society, a people magnanimous, powerful and happy for a people lovable, frivolous and wretched—that is to say, all the virtues and miracles of the Republic for all the vices and puerilities of the monarchy.

"We wish in a word to fulfil the course of nature, to accomplish the destiny of mankind, to make good the promises of philosophy, to absolve Providence from the long reign of tyranny and crime.

May France, illustrious formerly among peoples of slaves, eclipse the glory of all free peoples that have existed, become the model to the nations, the terror of oppressors, the consolation of the oppressed, the ornament of the universe; and in sealing our work with our blood may we ourselves see at least the dawn of universal felicity gleam before us! That is our ambition. That is our aim."

Maximilien could hardly have made it more clear. Nor could he have shown himself better as a child of the Enlightenment. He wanted a state founded upon morality, and by morality he meant not a sentimental goodheartedness, but the sum total of the qualities which he listed. His program was doubtless utopian; he expected a sudden regeneration of mankind, a complete transformation, seeing in the past no index, except negatively, to the future. This expectation he shared with the most reputable French thinkers of the eighteenth century.

Democracy alone, he went on, can assure the kind of society that we aspire to. "A democracy is a state in which the people, endowed with sovereignty, guided by laws of its own making, does for itself whatever it can do for itself well, and through delegates what it cannot." We must therefore find the principle of democratic government.

This principle, he explained, expressing the best political science of the day, is virtue, the love of the laws and of one's country, which in a democracy means the love of democracy and equality. He then argues, as Montesquieu did, that to strengthen a form of government one must strengthen its principle, in this case virtue.

"We do not pretend to cast the French Republic in the mold of Sparta. We do not wish to give it either the austerity or the corruption of the cloister. We have just laid before you in all its purity the moral and political principle of popular government." Fortunately, he added, virtue is natural to the people, which to love justice need only love itself. The people can be governed by reason, its enemies only by terror. Shall it be only the enemies of democracy that use force? And he recurs to the distinctions laid down on 5 Nivôse:

"If the basis of popular government in time of peace is virtue, the basis of popular government in time of revolution is both virtue and terror: virtue without which terror is murderous, terror without which virtue is powerless." Terror, the intimidation of enemies of the people, is only inflexible justice, and "so is an emanation of virtue."

The tragic misconception was Robespierre's idea of the people, which he shared with certain *philosophes* who, living in calmer times, should have known better. The French people was nothing like what Robespierre imagined. It was not all compact of goodness; it was not peculiarly governable by reason; it was not even a unitary thing at all, for only a minority was even republican. Robespierre's "people" was the people of his mind's eye, the people as it was to be when felicity was established, and which he now, by a kind of bootstrap philosophy, made the actual and operative cause of what it was finally to become.

The misconception led him to state what Saint-Just had already so well expressed. "The only citizens in the Republic are the republicans. Royalists and conspirators are foreigners, or rather enemies, in its eyes." So the people in reality became the nucleus of the pure. Others, not being citizens, had no rights. In France as it really was no permanent state could be established on such principles. A Republic so conceived must remain at war with a large part of its own population.

Such a Republic was committed also to remain at war with Europe. A fatal confusion had arisen. By law, and in the general understanding, the government of France was "revolutionary until the peace." The Revolutionary Government existed to win the war. But it existed also to found the democratic and constitutional Republic, to which the chief danger was internal faction. Peace, by ending the Revolutionary Government, would destroy the narrow pathway to a democratic and moral world. War and democracy were joined by an iron bond, fused in the essential dualism of the Revolutionary Government itself. History is full of ironic situations, and this surely is one of them: the war, begun in 1792 against the opposition of Robespierre and the sincerest democrats, became indispensable in 1794 to the fulfilment of their program, was kept up, enflamed and made glorious by their military successes, only to be inherited after 1795 by men who also needed war to maintain their position, but whose position was no longer democracy. Of course the Committee of Public Safety in the Year Two asserted many times its love of peace. But what peace?

"Peace and the Republic, peace and the ruin of tyrants, peace and the awakening of peoples!"

These words, and others even more bellicose, spoken by Barère on February 1 in the Convention, were published in the *Moniteur* and could be read everywhere in Europe. The Committee did not want an early or a conciliatory peace. Danton's ideas of negotiation were branded as defeatism—today we should call it "appeasement." The feelers put forward by enemy governments were rejected with derision. To further the doctrine that peace was impossible, as well as to stop party recrimination, Robespierre launched the Jacobins on their discussion of the crimes and vices of the British government. Couthon proposed that the society celebrate fittingly the anniversary of Louis XVI's death. The Jacobins drew up "an act of indictment against all kings," and appointed, as a special committee, Robespierre, Couthon, Billaud, Collot and one other "to bring together the particular crimes of the tyrants." In the Convention, on the anniversary, portraits of the kings of France and of Prussia were publicly burned and the ashes stamped fiercely underfoot. Thus did Frenchmen secure their national defense, hurling maledictions to the established order of Europe.

Could peace have been made except for the intransigence of the Republic? Could a French Republic, kept within its own frontiers, have been recognized in 1794 by the other powers? Could the war have been ended before the French army, by brilliant achievement, became a vested and controlling interest in the state? Perhaps not. But Danton thought the questions worth asking. The Committee of Public Safety suppressed all discussion of them. It could not bear to look upon the questions, because it would not accept for France the relaxed and morally equivocal Republic which Danton's policies would introduce. Here again the bond between war and democracy was joined.

The great oration of February 5 was a menace to many, and gave a new direction to the Terror. Robespierre's own ruin was implicit in it. He was henceforth pursuing the impossible, building up to a terrific climax that could only be his fall. Step by step, as he discovered in others weaknesses of character or differences of purpose which he did not believe were natural to humanity, and which he therefore attributed to conspiracy or perversity, he isolated himself from those who had been his companions in guiding the Revolution, to the point where not the staunchest Republican could feel safe, and the majority of the Committee of Public Safety turned against him.

The fact that his aim was impossible does not mean that his diagnosis was incorrect. Who would not agree that France in February 1794 could well use a little more "virtue"? Let us not forget the grafters, liars, hypocrites, false denouncers, political toughs, swindling contractors, party leaders who would not see beyond party, individuals on whom even party had no hold, the men to whom patriotism meant self-advancement, and liberty a chance for agitation and self-indulgence, the people who would not pay taxes, or serve in the army, or accept the wages and prices prescribed by law, the Revolutionists who had come to want a perpetual revolution for their own advantage, the others who secretly hoped that their earlier work might be undone. Robespierre in demanding virtue was not simply yearning for a vague abstraction found in books, but demanding something that the Revolution sadly needed. Had he been able to compromise a little more with reality, had he been more free of the flaws which he saw in others, he might have accomplished more in the end. As it was, the debasement that followed his fall showed that his reading of the signs was not mistaken.

Nor does his pursuit of the impossible deprive his aim of significance, or imply that it is not worth even approaching. Since 1940 it is no longer so laughable as it once was to say that democracy is founded upon virtue. As we read through the catalogue of changes which Robespierre announced that the Revolutionary Government wished to see in France, we sense a certain similarity to what we might have read in the morning paper, a disconcerting resemblance, disconcerting because the words were spoken in the midst of dictatorial terror, to the scheme of things which in our own day is sometimes called simply "civilization." Maximilien, with all his faults, which were many, was one of the half-dozen major prophets of democracy.

CHAPTER XII

Ventôse

VENTÔSE, the month of wind and storm, produced a tempest of peculiar fierceness. The factional rivalries traced in the last chapter combined with the economic crisis described in the chapter preceding. The revolutionary heavens rocked; when calm returned, deceptive and unwholesome, many old faces were missing, but the Committee of Public Safety seemed to stand more firmly than ever.

The Committee was unusually depleted when the disturbances began. Robespierre and Couthon were at home sick. Saint-André returned to Brest on 30 Pluviôse, and Billaud-Varenne went to Saint-Malo to prepare for the attack on the Channel Islands. Hérault was in disgrace, and Prieur of the Marne had not been in Paris since September. At the Tuileries Carnot, Lindet and the younger Prieur remained at their rather specialized labors, and Barère was as tireless as ever, but the politics of the Committee were largely in the hands of Saint-Just and Collot d'Herbois, the most positive, self-willed and single-minded of the Twelve.

The nature of Robespierre's illness is not known. He fell sick a few days after the great speech of February 5, and for over a month was absent from the Committee, as well as from the Convention and the Jacobins. He was able to receive visitors, to think and to watch. Perhaps his withdrawal was not wholly involuntary. Taking no pleasure in the daily maneuvers of politics, delighting in nothing but the ideal ends for which he worked, and which stubbornly failed to come nearer, Robespierre was disappointed, puzzled, sometimes almost disillusioned. He dropped remarks about buying a place in the country. He may have thought of abandoning a turmoil in which men of virtue were so little heeded. But from such ideas (if we may reconstruct his inner life) he would always be called back by his sense of duty; his imagination would go out to the people, by nature good, exploited by the rich and the ambitious, the people whom some honest man must lead into happiness.

So in his semi-retirement he watched and waited. He wished to see whether his last speeches, laying down government policy, would have the effect intended, whether the quarreling Revolutionaries would rally to the banner of virtue, whether the threat of terror would make the use of terror less necessary. At the worst he would let the situation mature, and if the factions remained obstinate do the duty to which he had bound himself. Meanwhile he nursed his health and remained on the sidelines, not in the grand aloofness of a tyrant, but in the lodgings at the Duplays for which he and his brother paid the middle-class sum of about eighty livres a month.

Collot d'Herbois had a rare opportunity to push himself forward while four of the most powerful personalities among his colleagues were away. His position was strengthened by the return of Carrier on 3 Ventôse. Carrier was responsible for the *noyades* at Nantes, Collot for the *fusillades* at Lyons. If the drownings were too much, so were the shootings; if Carrier was in danger, so was Collot. At the Jacobins, therefore, where Carrier immediately submitted himself for the "purifying scrutiny," Collot welcomed him with a speech of congratulation. Collot at the time was the only member of the Committee habitually at the club, where even Saint-Just seldom spoke. Carrier was approved in a wave of applause.

With the return of Carrier and with the spotlight on Collot d'Herbois, the Hébertists took heart. They loudly demanded their old remedies. The peasants being afraid to bring produce to Paris, the Cordeliers club voted for an increase of the Revolutionary Army. Meat being so scarce that even Couthon was reduced to a soupbone, there was talk of invading the prisons and roasting and eating the prisoners. The Commune wanted more enforcement of the law against hoarding, so ruinous to trade that even Collot d'Herbois had lost faith in it. Labor was restless, the workers in the public arms shops were unruly, not less so because the Ministry of War was a hotbed of Hébertism. Attempts were made to transfer the War Office to the Luxembourg, where it would be entrenched in one of the most radical quarters of Paris. And the old cry against moderatism grew more furious. Why was Fabre d'Eglantine still at large, the denouncer of the virtuous Ronsin and Vincent? Why were seventy-five Girondists still in prison, protected by Robespierre? If they were in prison they were guilty, and if guilty why should they live?

Meanwhile, on 3 Ventôse, Barère laid before the Convention the new tables of the Maximum, allowing dealers a higher mark-up on their goods. They had been three months in preparation, and were endorsed by the Committee of Public Safety and the Subsistence Commission. The bill passed after long discussion and some objection. It was clear that the government was trying to reach a better understanding with business and agriculture. It was moving directly away from the clamor and intimidation which constituted the economic program of the Hébertists.

Collot d'Herbois was involved in the Hébertist machinations, which if successful might conceivably make him master of the Republic. Against him in the Committee was pitted an extremely dangerous adversary, the boyish and too beautiful Saint-Just, the regenerator of armies, the man of emergencies and twin pillar to the absent Robespierre.

Saint-Just was to dominate, if anyone did, the hurricane of Ventôse. Never before had his influence run so high. What was he thinking of? A clue exists—his *Fragments on Republican Institutions,* a series of observations jotted down at intervals about this time, and published after his death. Only the great speeches of Robespierre throw as much light on ultimate aims.

Saint-Just's ideas were Robespierre's ideas sharpened, simplified, exaggerated, schematized and turned into aphorisms. Robespierre had in him a broad streak of average human befuddlement, even mediocrity; Saint-Just was a specialized machine of revolutionary precision. Robespierre denied that Sparta was his model; Saint-Just harped continually on the ancients. Robespierre was self-righteous, Saint-Just more so: "God, protector of innocence and virtue, since you have led me among evil men it is surely to unmask them!" To Robespierre the straight and narrow way was plain enough; to Saint-Just it was terrifyingly obvious: "I think I may say that most political errors come from regarding legislation as a difficult science." Or more laconically: "Long laws are public calamities."

The low opinion of civil law was the starting point of the *Republican Institutions.* It may be remembered that Saint-Just was a lawyer by education. Schooled in the intricacies of a deca-

dent feudalism, he emerged, like many others, with a strong contempt for the subject. There would be no lawyers and few courts
in his ideal state. The Republic could do with few laws because
of the civic virtue and simple habits of the citizens. Even the
conservative Montesquieu, as well as Robespierre and Jefferson,
had this idea of a democratic republic. Saint-Just went further—
further in the direction of liberty, for in his society no legal contract was binding when either party wished to break it; and further in the direction of authority, for in the name of individual
freedom he deified the state. Saint-Just, of all the Twelve, would
have been the most at home in a twentieth century revolution.

Institutions (this is the main point of the *Fragments*) were to
be the means of establishing the French Republic. They would
reduce laws to a minimum, and also protect the state against
the influence of mere personalities. Saint-Just used the word
"institutions" in a peculiar sense. They were the social means for
producing good individuals. Bad societies such as monarchies had
no institutions; only republics could possess them. Friendship was
such an institution: men were to declare their friends in the
temples, fight beside them in war, be buried with them in the same
tombs; and those who did not believe in friendship were to be
banished. Old age was an institution: the aged of blameless lives
were to wear white scarfs. Civic festivals were an institution,
with the people burning perpetual incense and singing hymns to the
Eternal in the temples.

But the institutions of most importance were three: education,
censorship, and property.

Education? Its function is to make republicans. Boys over five
belong to the state. No parent may interfere with his child's wishes.
Boys are to be organized in legions, battalions and companies,
taught martial exercises, and assigned to farmers to work in
the fields. They are to be brought up in the love of silence, under
stern discipline, wearing a uniform of coarse cloth, eating vege-
tables, and sleeping on mats of straw. At sixteen they became
workers, at twenty-one, soldiers, "if they are not magistrates."
Teachers must all be over sixty, for "respect for age is a cult of
the fatherland." Girls do not matter. They stay with their mothers.

Censorship? "In every revolution a dictator is needed to save
the state by force, or else censors to save it by virtue." Magis-

trates must be created whose function is to set an example. Why should there not be six million of them in France? They are to expose the misdoings of public officials, but are forbidden to use their power against the people. Saint-Just's "censorship" was the patriotic denunciation with which he was familiar, clothed in a dignity derived from the censors of ancient Rome.

Property? "I defy you to establish liberty, if it is possible to raise up the unfortunates against the new order. I defy you not to have unfortunates, unless you arrange for every man to have his piece of land." Opulence is infamy. "Beggary must be destroyed by the distribution of national property to the poor." More conservative advice is also given: French finances are shocking, and the quantity of paper money must be reduced. But the main message is clear. The needy are to receive land so that they will not revolt against the government. Whether the city working class really wanted farm lands remained to be seen.

Saint-Just's ideas on education and censorship were fairly current among the Revolutionary leaders in 1794. His proposals for dividing up property were more definitely his own. The majority in the Committee of Public Safety did not share them. Augustin Robespierre, who was very close to his brother, stopped about this time at Lyons, where he found Fouché encouraging the extremists. "A system exists to make the people level everything off," wrote Augustin to Maximilien on 3 Ventôse, adding in alarm, "if we are not careful everything will be disorganized." The majority of the Committee were not more radical than the younger Robespierre.

From whom in the Committee did Saint-Just find support for a program of dividing up the property of enemies of the Revolution? It is not really possible to answer this question decisively. The late Professor Mathiez thought that Robespierre and Couthon were Saint-Just's chief backers. But a number of doubts stand in the way. Neither Robespierre nor Couthon was present when the Committee accepted the program, though Saint-Just had certainly conferred with Robespierre in his home. Neither Robespierre nor Couthon, in public utterances during the following months, made any clear statements on the redistribution of wealth. Robespierre and Couthon were mostly concerned with religion; they worked for a spiritual renewal and purification of society. The time came when Saint-Just, at the wish of Billaud-Varenne, agreed to keep quiet on matters of Robespierrist religion. There is evidence that Saint-Just, in Thermidor, was no longer quite in harmony with Robespierre.

Collot d'Herbois and Billaud-Varenne, on the other hand, had both shown favor to the idea of social revolution. Collot, with Fouché, had authorized the "communistic" Temporary Commission of Lyons. Billaud, in 1793, wrote a book, too little known, called the *Elements of Republicanism,* which presented a far more developed argument for redistribution of wealth than Saint-Just's *Republican Institutions.*

Billaud here held the right of property to be sacred, so sacred that all should enjoy it. The welfare of the people is the highest law, he said. "This law," he then declared, in his involved way, "this law which for the public good is unsparing to persons and with greater reason to property will not justify any valid complaint by the capitalists, if, without taking from them at present the excess of a fortune whose magnitude is evidence only of ancient usurpation, we limit ourselves to measures for lessening the corrosive effects by an accelerated redistribution, without leaving the possibility of further accumulation." He recommended therefore that the property confiscated by the Revolution be divided up with a view to equality, that no one be permitted to own more than a fixed quantity of land, and that the right of inheritance be abolished. Moreover, no one should be allowed to live without working, and everyone should have a right to employment. All this he deduced from the social contract, for without such provisions, he said, society was a contract of the few against the many. After Thermidor Billaud said no more of these ideas of 1793. But he probably believed in them in Ventôse of the Year Two.

The three in the Committee most sympathetic to the division of wealth, as a proper aim of the Revolution and not merely as a tactical maneuver, were probably therefore not a Robespierrist triumvirate which had little real existence—not Robespierre, Saint-Just and Couthon—but another trio composed of Saint-Just, Collot d'Herbois and Billaud-Varenne. This trio was even less a triumvirate than the other. Personal and factional differences prevented cooperation. Saint-Just, we can well believe, thought Collot d'Herbois an unscrupulous ruffian and Billaud-Varenne somewhat turgidly violent. Differences of emphasis notwithstanding, Saint-Just was still drawn most strongly to Robespierre. Economic ideas had no clear ascendancy in Saint-Just's mind. He feared the office-holders at least as much as the property-holders. He was suspicious of the wealthy, but still more so of corrupt or uncoordinated officials in the Revolutionary state. Like Robespierre, Saint-Just aimed first of all at purifying the Republic through the police power.

The others present in the Committee in Ventôse—Barère, Lindet, Carnot, Prieur of the Côte-d'Or—were no lovers of social revolution. All four, before the Revolution, reckoned their assets in five figures. They were (in normal times, and except for Hérault-Séchelles) the most comfortably situated of the Twelve. For poverty they felt a humanitarian concern, for property a philosophical respect. But with the property of enemies of the Revolution they could be severe. On the preceding September 4, before Collot and Billaud joined the Committee and when Saint-Just was inactive in its counsels, the Committee had ordered the goods of the rebels of Marseilles divided among "the persecuted patriots of those regions." When serving political aims, redistribution of wealth was acceptable even to Barère and the others.

The question now, early in Ventôse, was above all political. The problem, as Saint-Just had written, was to prevent uprisings against the new order of liberty. The Committee was on the point of crushing the Hébertists, whose followers it wished to placate. It was making concessions to the business interests, whom it did not wish unduly to encourage. It was still struggling with enemies of the Revolution, whom it wished to deprive of the means of resistance.

The Committee therefore agreed to Saint-Just's proposals, and arranged for him to make a speech in the Convention, a continuation of Robespierre's warning against the factions, to which an announcement of the new economic policy should be added. Saint-Just prepared his oration; his colleagues discussed it with him all night in the green room, never tiring, according to Collot, of listening to its pointed phrases. It is important to note that the whole Committee debated and assumed the responsibility. The new program was not especially "Robespierrist," the less so because both Robespierre and Couthon had been ill at home for weeks.

The next day was 8 Ventôse. Saint-Just, president of the Convention for the fortnight, spoke for half an hour, summarizing parts of his *Republican Institutions,* attacking the old régime with a mendacity unusual even in the oratory of the day (Louis XVI had 8,000 persons killed in the streets of Paris in 1788!), and laying down the principle that no enemy of the Republic could own property within it, and that no one had civil rights who had not helped to make France free. The Convention then voted to sequester the property of enemies of the Revolution. Five days later, 13 Ventôse, after another speech by Saint-Just, it was voted that all communes in France should submit lists of the "indigent patriots" for whose benefit the new confiscations were to be made.

Thus were enacted the famous laws of Ventôse. How they worked out is a subject for the next chapter, where they can be seen alongside the other interests of the Committee.

The Ventôse laws could do nothing toward immediate relief of hunger in Paris, nor in any case satisfy demagogues who counted on discontent to maintain their position. The Hébertists became more active than ever. Ominous placards still appeared in the streets. Agitators circulated among the workingmen. The Cordeliers club seethed with repressed excitement. A new journal dedicated to the principles of Marat was projected—always a bad sign. Some apparently inferred from Saint-Just's speeches that he and Robespierre would support an uprising; others looked to Collot d'Herbois; others planned to make a clean sweep, setting up in place of the Committee a "grand judge" as dictator, or so at least it was charged at the trial which followed.

At the Cordeliers, on 14 Ventôse, agitation reached its apex. "I denounce to you a new faction. . . ." So cried Vincent.

"I have been alarmed since returning to the Convention at the new faces I see in the Mountain. . . . There is a desire, I see it, I feel it, to make the Revolution go backward. . . . Monsters! They want to break up the scaffolds. . . ." This cry of rage was from Carrier.

"You will shudder when you know the infernal projects of the faction. . . ." Hébert spoke cautiously, feeling his way, urged on by the others, taunted for losing his old fire. He reminded his hearers of the affair of Camille Desmoulins at the Jacobins. "Remember that he was driven out, eradicated by the patriots, and that a man, misled surely—otherwise I would not know how to describe him—was there very conveniently to get him reinstated, against the will of the people, which had expressed itself clearly on that traitor." No one could denounce more unmistakably, in a public assembly, Maximilien Robespierre.

The Cordeliers proclaimed a state of insurrection, throwing a black crêpe over the Declaration of the Rights framed in their auditorium. Only one of the forty-eight Paris sections rallied to the summons, the Section Marat, composed largely of members of the Cordeliers club. These zealots proceeded to the city hall and announced that the people was risen. If the Commune supported them there would be an uprising like that of September 5.

But the Commune was under watchful eyes in the green room. The mayor of Paris, only a few hours before, had received an order from the Committee, written by the hand of Saint-Just, instructing him to report every day on public opinion in the city. The Commune officials greeted the insurgents coldly. Chaumette, who had led the march into the Tuileries on September 5, spoke in favor of the government. Others pointed to the laws of Ventôse, which, they said, showed that the authorities had the welfare of the sans-culottes at heart.

The insurrection was abortive, but the government struck back. Barère took his turn at denouncing the factions, on the very day after the scene at the Commune. Collot d'Herbois, unwilling to countenance a revolt against a body of which he was a member, perhaps deciding at the last moment that the existing Committee was the best shield for his conduct at Lyons, denounced the rebels. He brought about a reconciliation of the erring Cordeliers with the Jacobins. He alone of the Committee being then active in the clubs, he may have been trying to consolidate a personal following. While he was addressing the Cordeliers, Hébert's wife whispered to her neighbor, "It's all a play." Did the Hébertists have reason to know that Collot was only staging an act?

The restlessness in the city did not subside. Prieur of the Côte d'Or tried to appease the workers in the armament shops. If they really knew what the government was doing, he said, they would not fall victims to agitators. Carnot took steps to keep deserters from foreign armies at least ten leagues from Paris—a safeguard against the "fifth column." Hanriot, commander of the Paris national guard, gave orders to prevent looting. Meanwhile the Cordeliers showed new signs of unruliness, Hébert and his friends again raising anti-government talk. In all this uncertainty the legal powers of the Committee of Public Safety expired. They were extended by the Convention for another month on 22 Ventôse, at the request of Couthon, just returned from his sickbed.

That evening Robespierre rejoined the Committee. For the first time in over a month all nine were present, the full number in view of the permanent absences. The meeting was a momentous one. Saint-Just had prepared another speech, a final and terrible damnation of the "factions." All discussed it, and Saint-Just became the spokesman for his colleagues.

The 23rd day of Ventôse (March 13) was a fateful day in the short annals of the First Republic. Saint-Just stepped into the tribune of the Convention with his bulky manuscript, called a "Report on the factions of foreign inspiration, and on the conspiracy plotted by them in the French Republic, to destroy representative government by corruption, and to starve Paris." For its laconic author, the speech, like its title, was long, repetitious, rambling and wordy. The speaker meant to leave no loopholes.

The Revolution, one gathered, was to go unflinchingly forward. Yet there was another element in the picture that Saint-Just drew. On 23 Ventôse the Republic definitely put on a few scanty and ill-fitting garments of conservatism. Ever since the preceding summer, since the rise of the Committee of Public Safety, the merits of order, obedience, and authority had been advanced. Now more than ever the language of men in power could be heard.

Saint-Just began by discussing the right of insurrection, affirmed in the Declaration of Rights and recently invoked by the Cordeliers. Insurrection, he said, is of course a right, a guarantee for the people; but government also has its guarantee, the people's justice and virtue. Whoever corrupts this virtue makes government impossible, and public virtue is corrupted when confidence in the government is lost. The present sovereign is not a tyrant; it is the people. Whoever opposes the present order is therefore evil, and insurrection, once a useful recourse, is now counter-revolution. Opposition does exist—furtive, clandestine—because no one ever opposes an established order openly. Opposition always disguises itself; subversive elements always pretend to be loyal.

There is in fact, he said, a great secret intrigue afoot in the land, instigated by foreign courts, which are frightened by our confiscating the goods of enemies of the Revolution. There is a plot to starve the French people. (How more conveniently could a member of government explain the food shortage?) The Allies do not wish to fight; they plan to leave us to famine and to our internal dissensions. (Was the war, then, necessitated by the internal politics of the Republic?) Countless Frenchmen are the tools of this nefarious enterprise. Their masks are hard to penetrate. Some cry loudly that the government is too sluggish, others wring their hands and call for moderation. (Hébertists and Dantonists, of course.) We can detect them by their perversity, their fickleness, their falsity, their hypocrisy. Those who did not believe yesterday what they believe today are our enemies. (Who, in these times, had not often changed his mind?) We cannot even be sure of the revolutionary clubs; they are full of officeholders who have a vested interest in deceiving the people. (To correct this evil Saint-Just had included censorship in his *Republican Institutions.*) There is no modesty, no acceptance of humble station. "Everyone wants to govern, no one to be just a citizen."

What to do?

"If the people loves virtue and frugality, if effrontery disappears from men's faces, if a sense of shame returns to the commonwealth and counter-revolutionaries, moderatists and scoundrels to the dust, if we are terrible toward enemies of the revolution but loving and affectionate to the patriot, if officeholders bury themselves in their offices and set themselves to doing good without running after notoriety, content with the witness of their own hearts, if you give lands to the unfortunate and take them from rascals, then I will admit that you have made a revolution. But if the contrary happens, if the foreign interest wins out, if vices triumph, if a new upper class replaces the old, if punishment does not pursue the hidden conspirators, then let us flee into the void or to the breast of the Deity, for there has been no revolution, and is no happiness or virtue to hope for on the earth."

Nothing more concrete was charged against those whom Saint-Just had entered the Convention to accuse. Division itself was the crime.

"Every party is then criminal, because it is a form of isolation from the people and the popular societies, a form of independence from the government. Every faction is then criminal, because it tends to divide the citizens; every faction is criminal because it neutralizes the power of public virtue.

"The solidity of our Republic is in the very nature of things." Alas, nature was something higher than what eyes could see. "The sovereignty of the people demands that the people be unified; it is therefore opposed to factions, and all faction is a criminal attack upon sovereignty." This was the Rousseauist doctrine of the general will. It is not to be lightly dismissed. Faction is in truth a disruption of sovereignty, if faction means disagreement not only on policy but on the fundamentals of political order, not only criticism of the government but refusal to accept the form of government established. In that case there is actually no general will at all, and the attempt to enforce one leads to trouble.

France since the eighteenth century has been in this uneasy predicament. Since the days of the *philosophes,* important political differences have meant changes of régime, i.e. revolution, with its accompaniment of persecution, retaliation and forced conversion. Politics in some countries have rested on a bedrock of underlying agreement, so that remodeling can be done in relative peace. In the underlying rock of France is what geologists would call a fault, a fissure. Years pass calmly, then the rock slips, structures come tumbling down, and heads are likely to fall. Such a time was the year of the Terror, but there have been other such years, 1816, 1848, 1871, and apparently 1940. If we judge by intentions, rather than consequences, it is important to add that the Terror of 1794 was conducted in the name of democracy.

In Ventôse of the Year Two matters had reached the point where the slightest "independence from the government," in Saint-Just's phrase, was a menace to the existing order. The Mountaineers, who at a distance look so much alike, had so little general will even among themselves that critics of the government could not be distinguished from enemies of the state. For the good of the Revolution the Revolutionists had to be decimated. The phrase, "revolutions devour their own children," had already been coined by a Girondist, now dead. To repeat it was regarded as counter-revolutionary by the government. Revolutions, it was explained, devour none but their enemies.

Hébert, Ronsin and Vincent, with two others, were seized during the night following Saint-Just's speech. Fifteen more were rounded up in the next few days. The Committee stood firmly together in the crisis. Robespierre marked his return to politics by a discourse at the Jacobins, on the night of the 23rd, backing Saint-Just; Couthon did the same, and Billaud-Varenne the next day. Barère on 24 Ventôse ordered 200,000 copies of Saint-Just's speech from the printers. Lindet granted two million livres to the Commune to provision the city and quiet the Hébertists' sympathizers.

Collot d'Herbois doubtless had mixed feelings. He had an interest in securing approval for Ronsin, his co-worker at Lyons, and Carrier, his fellow butcher of Nantes. Ronsin he could no longer defend, but his intervention probably saved Carrier. Though among the most notable in fomenting insurrection, Carrier was not among those arrested. It is likely that the Committee passed him by as a means of rallying Collot d'Herbois to their common front.

The twenty defendants were soon hustled before the Revolutionary Tribunal. They were a miscellaneous lot. Hébert was national agent in the Commune, Ronsin commander of the Revolutionary Army, Vincent assistant to the minister of war. The Belgian Proli, supposed accomplice of Hérault-Séchelles, was with them. The group included a Dutch banker, a French general, a hairdresser, a bookseller, a tobacconist, a doctor, a surgeon's apprentice, an ex-peasant woman, and someone described as a man of letters. Most of these were also in the public service. The only member of the Convention was Anacharsis Cloots, German by birth, who boasted of rising above nationality. The throwing together of natives and foreigners was to give color to the charges of foreign conspiracy.

The trial was brief, with the accused arraigned in a body, and the evidence consisting chiefly in recollections of witnesses who had heard chance remarks of dubious import. The jurors soon stated that their consciences were satisfied, and the presiding judge condemned all twenty to death, except one, a police spy who had been shut up with the others. On 4 Germinal (March 24), at five o'clock in the afternoon, Mme. Guillotine put an end to eighteen of her warmest admirers—the ex-peasant woman having declared herself pregnant, and so receiving a delay.

With the fall of the Hébertists more happened than could be easily realized. If the Revolution was not over, at least the first step in reaction had been taken. For five years revolutionary elements in the city had guided events. Paris had stormed the Bastille, marched the king and queen from Versailles, overthrown the monarchy, purged the Girondists from the Convention at the point of its bayonets. Its power had been felt in the preceding summer—the Levy in Mass, the Revolutionary Army, the economic dictatorship were the result. The Committee of Public Safety itself, and the whole machine of the Revolutionary Government, had sprung from demands made effective by organized radicalism in Paris. The capital had repeatedly pushed the Revolution onward, by forcing the central government to its will.

On 23 Ventôse, for the first time in over five years, central authority asserted itself, and instead of yielding to insurgents put them in jail. The Revolution would henceforth be the work of government, not an upheaval from below. To threaten established rule had again become treason.

The Committee of Public Safety had no intention of checking the Revolution. In official eyes the Hébertists were only agitators, representing no legitimate public interest, a mere body of plotters who had deviated from the true course. Every government since 1789 had taken that view of the forces that menaced it. So the partisans of peaceful reform regarded the crowds who overthrew the Bastille, the constitutional monarchists the mob that unseated the king, the idealistic Girondists the rioters who brought the Mountaineers to power. In each case the program of the successful party became the recognized course of the Revolution, and the persons driven from office fell into the limbo of tyrants and aristocrats—where Robespierre and the others would have been if the Hébertists had succeeded.

Did the Hébertists then differ from earlier insurgents only in that they failed? If so, then their fall marked counter-revolution. It would be odd to portray Robespierre as a kind of early Metternich. Nor is any such wild revision needed. But the problem is not as obvious as might appear. Only a very convinced Robespierrist could, without more ado, accept Robespierrism as the true Revolution, and Hébertism as the deviation.

Hébertism, the complex of practices and ideas labeled ultra by Robespierre, was undoubtedly a powerful tendency, popular with the sans-culottes and favored by many members of the Convention when they served as representatives on mission. In opposing it Robespierre was, in a real sense, going counter to the Revolutionary torrent. But Hébertism as a political party, aiming at overthrow of the men in power, was very weak, so weak that one wonders whether it was necessary for the government to put the leaders to death. The uprising of the Cordeliers was a fiasco. Neither Chaumette nor Carrier nor Collot d'Herbois nor the Paris sections nor anyone in the Convention would, in a showdown, support it. Very different in this respect was the revolt which drove out the Girondists, to say nothing of that which destroyed the Bastille. The Revolutionary spirit was ceasing to be a popular rebelliousness in the streets and the cafés. The great political leaders were either dead, or in power; they were no longer raising sidewalk agitation. Hébert, Ronsin, and the rest were in any case men without ideas, living by mere confusion. They had no solution for the economic crisis on which they thrived. There was no such political reason for their insurrection as there had been for previous ones: the Revolution was in no danger of extinction in March 1794, as it had been from the royalists in July 1789, from the foreign powers in August 1792, and from its own forces of anarchy in May 1793.

The Hébertist chieftains, in short, were a faction or medley of factions, as the Committee held. They were mostly functionaries and public jobholders, revolutionaries on the lower rungs of the ladder, the "officeholders" whose refusal to subordinate themselves Saint-Just repeatedly denounced. Representing the anarchical side of the Revolution, they were a nuisance, even a menace, to the organized Revolutionary state. It does not follow that they were purposely conspiring with foreigners against the Republic.

All this is only to say that the Revolution was now in the government, not in the populace. As a thing of government, controlling the apparatus of sovereignty, the Revolution was to sweep Europe for twenty years.

The fall of the Hébertists was the beginning of the general liquidation. Only their attempt at insurrection made the Hébertists the first to go. Few others could have felt any security from Saint-Just's or Robespierre's speeches since December. Indeed, the ruling Committee, determined to concentrate Revolutionary vigor in itself and its adjuncts, had even less tolerance for moderates than for the too hasty patriots whom it had just put to death. On 25 Ventôse, in an order written by Barère (the distribution of responsibilities is to be noted) the prosecutor of the Revolutionary Tribunal was authorized to recruit as many spies as he needed to get convictions.

Unfinished business was pushed through. Hérault-Séchelles was at last imprisoned; the elegant littérateur went to the Luxembourg, leaving his beloved manuscripts, the *Émile* and the *Nouvelle Héloïse,* in Rousseau's own hand, to be confiscated by the Arts Commission. The grafters, Fabre d'Eglantine, Chabot and two others, were packed off to trial. According to Saint-Just's report of the 23rd, corruption was an intrigue against the state. Not everyone in the government seems to have understood the new doctrine. In the Convention, when the Committee of General Security reported its findings, the speaker, Amar, dwelt only on the sordid facts of financial fraud. Robespierre and Billaud-Varenne jumped to their feet, exclaiming that the main point had been missed, that the question was political, that in lining their own pockets the culprits were promoting the Foreign Plot. Amar accepted the rebuke; the greater committee won another victory over the lesser. There is some evidence for the Robespierrist allegation. The grafters had worked through a certain baron de Batz, who had meanwhile escaped, but who was a royalist trying to disgrace the Convention by luring greedy deputies into a scandal.

On 30 Ventôse Robespierre publicly warned the "remaining" faction. It would be absurd, he said, to suppose that there was only one—the one already disposed of. Camille Desmoulins had had the audacity to publish another tract calling for moderation. Bourdon was lashing out against the Commune: Why was the city of Paris so slow to express delight at the fall of the Hébertists? So called Indulgents vented their fury upon discredited extremists. Danton tried to calm the vengefulness of his friends, without much success. Yet the Convention was sympathetic to Danton. He was still dangerous to the government, being out of office and yet in a position of leadership, enjoying a tremendous reputation not weakened by the misdoings of corrupt friends nor by his own love of money, attracting men by his virile self-confidence, his hearty good fellowship, his easy back-slapping habits, beside which Robespierre seemed the pale preacher of an uncomfortable rectitude. Danton liked people; only *the* people could touch the feelings of Robespierre.

If Dantonism remained, with Hébertism crushed, the Committee would lose the advantage of its central position. The rank and file of sans-culottes would think the government plunging into moderatism and reaction. For the moderatists in Danton's camp the governing Committee would soon seem the extreme of radical frenzy. Moderates were sure to object to much of the Ventôse property program; many of them even made light of Republican virtue. On the other hand, as we shall see, the Committee was about to adopt certain policies which the moderates favored. It would not do to seem to yield to their pressure. And down beneath such rational calculations were the fundamental aversions, ranging from Collot d'Herbois' violent hatred for those he feared, to Robespierre's moral repugnance for those he thought frivolous or tainted.

Danton stood in the way, and even Danton, titan of yesterday, was to go. There are stories of last-minute attempts to bring a reconciliation. A dinner was given in the suburbs at which Danton and Robespierre were present. Danton, it is said, cautioned his old colleague against playing the dictator, warned him that the average Frenchman would not tolerate such rule, implored him to reaffirm their old friendship for the good of the Revolution, and finally, as Robespierre sat by unmoved and suspicious, broke into tears. We may believe that Danton wept, for Robespierre later noted the tears themselves as a sign of his treachery. The two were beyond hope of agreement. Danton's argument for all to make common cause was to Robespierre a blind defense of the unfit.

Not very pleased, for he had once trusted Danton, but with his mind now more than half made up, Robespierre was brought by his fiercer colleagues to take a stand. Saint-Just eagerly drafted another report. Robespierre went over the manuscript with care, conscientiously correcting one or two of Saint-Just's wilder claims, adding voluminous notes of his own. The notes doubtless expressed what Robespierre considered the strongest possible case. An odd one it was by any normal standards. Danton, years ago, it seems, had consorted with persons since fallen into discredit. Danton had praised patriots now known to have been false. Danton had always avoided denouncing the real conspirators. He had taken money from Mirabeau. He had once advised dissolving the Convention and putting the constitution into effect. He had never been in true harmony with the Revolution. He had said severe principles in politics frightened people away. He had called public opinion a harlot and posterity foolishness, and the best virtue, he had actually declared, was conjugal intercourse!

Robespierre's picture was a travesty on Danton. Yet who of the Revolutionists was not travestied before, and after, he went to the guillotine? Robespierre himself was to suffer even worse misrepresentation from those who survived him.

Not all of Robespierre's notes were adopted at the discussion in the Committee from which Saint-Just composed a final draft. Some items that Robespierre had scratched out appeared in the final report. Others that he let stand were not made use of. For example, Robespierre charged that the petition from Lyons against Fouché and Collot d'Herbois, presented in December, was a Dantonist maneuver. The Committee thought it wise to suppress that allegation. The incident shows that Robespierre had by this time absorbed the massacres at Lyons into the stream of Revolutionary orthodoxy—they had happened, they were therefore right. Violence was not so deplorable to him as it once had been. The change was ominous.

On the evening of March 30 the Committee of General Security was called in for a joint conference. A warrant for the arrest of Danton, Desmoulins, Philippeaux and Delacroix was drawn up and presented for signature. A turbulent scene followed among the twenty men present. Turning deaf ears to pleas for unity, Robert Lindet refused to sign. He is supposed to have said that he was there to feed the patriots, not to kill them. One member of the lesser committee also refused. All the others, one by one, beginning with Billaud-Varenne, finally affixed their names. Saint-

Just and Robespierre asked postponement of the arrest until after Saint-Just's delivery of the report the next day. They wished Danton to be present, scorning, apparently, to seem afraid. The others objected, pointed to the risk, said the Convention might rebel, warned that they might themselves be guillotined. It was decided to seize the victims that very night. Saint-Just was so annoyed, we learn from an eye-witness, that he threw his hat into the fire and stormed out slamming the door.

To send to death Representatives of the People, prominent figures in the Convention and the Mountain, was in truth more hazardous than the operation against the Hébertists two weeks before. It was by no means certain to succeed.

When the Convention opened on March 31, Legendre rushed in crying that four members had been locked up during the night. Danton was one; he did not know the names of the others. "Citizens, I am but the fruit of the genius of liberty. . . . My bringing up is not the work of men but of nature alone. . . . Citizens, I declare that I believe Danton as pure as I am. . . ." Murmurs and signs of disorder greeted this apology. The chairman thundered that he would preserve freedom of speech. Legendre went on. He demanded that Danton and his fellow prisoners be brought into the hall. All members of the two governing committees were also summoned. The aim was to confront accusers with accused, in the hope that the Convention, asserting itself in a surge of enthusiasm, would refuse to ratify the arrest.

Robespierre at last gained the floor. He defended the seizure of Danton unheard, doing his duty by the Committee, but with a warmth that makes one wonder whether he had really been of the opposing opinion the night before. Was Danton, he asked, a privileged being? Should he have a right denied to Chabot and Fabre d'Eglantine? Must not equality among deputies be preserved? Was the people's freedom to be jeopardized? The same argument was taken up by Barère, who continued:

"There is talk of dictatorship. This word has rung in my ears for a quarter of an hour. It is essential to destroy such an idea. I notice that the friends of the accused are the only ones trembling for liberty. . . .

"What? Dictatorship in committees removable every month, every minute! . . . Can you talk of dictatorship where committees are constantly responsible, draw their authority from the Convention, report to it what they do?"

Saint-Just at this point entered the room and marched silently to the tribune. No more was said of fetching the prisoners. The representatives settled down to hearing the report. Saint-Just droned it off, with no gestures except to saw the air by raising and dropping his hand—as if it were a guillotine, someone said. Perhaps he was moody because his quarry was not there to hear him.

The speech (it was the last of Saint-Just's series against the factions) was a kind of history, almost a philosophy, of the Revolution. There was nothing very new in it. Its thesis was stated at the end. "Those I denounce have never been patriots, but aristocrats more adroit and more guileful than those at Coblentz." For proof the speaker reviewed the preceding years. The trouble, he said, had first grown up in the extreme decentralization of powers, which gave a swarming-place for intrigue. Public officials had always been especially dangerous. There had always been factions, or rather the faction, for there was only one, the faction inspired by foreign interests, which appeared now as the Orléanists, now as the Brissotins, again as the Hébertists, and finally as the cronies of Danton. Evidence of their handiwork was the fall of the currency, upheaval in the colonies, loss of trade, hoarding of goods, bad advice, suspicious language, federalism, etc. In short, so Saint-Just would have his hearers believe, every difficulty that France had faced during its Revolution was caused by treason, and all revolutionaries who had not anticipated the government doctrine of March 1794 were traitors. In comparison the falsehood about Hérault-Séchelles was a trifle. Hérault and Saint-Just had been together on the committee that wrote the constitution ten months before. Hérault had written more of it than anyone else, as Saint-Just knew. But the orator now declared that Hérault had stood by in "mute witness" to that performance. The reputation of everyone considered dangerous was to be smeared.

At the conclusion was a forecast. With the rout of the Dantonists there would be an end to purges. "Intrigue will no longer touch this holy spot; you will give yourselves up to legislation and government; you will sound the depths and snatch the fires from heaven to give life to the still lukewarm Republic, to enflame the love of country and of justice. Then there will remain none but patriots. . . ." A halcyon time, but would it come?

Not a word of question or criticism followed Saint-Just's reading. The assembly accepted the report with the usual unanimity and applause, and delivered up the Dantonists without further protest.

The battle shifted to the Revolutionary Tribunal, where, two days later, Danton and those arrested with him were herded in with Hérault-Séchelles, the four grafters, and five foreigners presumably agents of the Foreign Plot. The accused, it can at least be said, were given a hearing. The government felt none too secure, though there was little real doubt of the outcome. The trial was public; the patriots who jammed the galleries, and even the jurors, might be stirred to sympathy for their old hero. And although members of the Committee of General Security were present to watch the proceedings, the worst did in fact happen. Danton, when his turn came, unloosed the powers which had been denied him in the Convention, roaring like an infuriated lion, bellowing his defiance and his indignation and his denials, until the noise could be heard in the street, and a crowd collected to listen. The other defendants also managed to parry the attack.

Danton called by name for sixteen members of the Convention, including Robert Lindet, to be summoned as witnesses. So favorable was the impression that he created that the judges and the public accuser had to accede; and—terrified themselves at the thought that their own heads depended on getting a conviction—they sent a note to the Tuileries stating Danton's wish, and asking helplessly what they should do. The Committee was not to be outmaneuvered. Within a few hours Paris learned that a revolt was being plotted in the prisons, from which the inmates were to stream forth wreaking murder and revenge, assassinating the members of the Committee, who bravely announced themselves willing to die for the fatherland. Danton's eloquence was branded as insolence and perversity. "What innocent man," asked Saint-Just, "ever revolted against the law?" The temerity of the accused, he added, was in itself enough proof of their guilt.

The docile Convention ordered that prisoners who "resisted or insulted" the national justice should be silenced. Defense therefore ceased. The judge and prosecutor worked upon the jurors,

SAINT-JUST

showing them secretly at the last moment a mysterious but incriminating letter. It is possible that a letter now at the Library of Congress was the document produced on this occasion. The Library of Congress letter, a scrawl in Danton's hand, was written in August 1793 to protect Marie Antoinette, then in prison. At that time Robespierre himself had not intended violence to the queen. The letter none the less, in April 1794, would be acceptable proof that Danton had conspired to restore the throne.

The death sentence was pronounced on the fourth day of the trial, which, it need hardly be emphasized, had been an outrage to civilized procedure comparable only to certain political trials of our own time. The prisoners were executed the same afternoon.

All died with fortitude except Camille Desmoulins, who had mocked at others in the same plight, and who now struggled until the clothes were torn from his chest and shoulders. On the whole the group was quiet, dejected and thoughtful, but Danton kept his buoyancy, and tried to cheer the others. Camille seems to have been surprised that the "people" hissed at him as he passed. At a café along the route David, functioning as artist, not as member of the Committee of General Security, stood making his sketch of Danton which can still be seen.

In the procession rode one of our original Twelve, the first to perish, Hérault-Séchelles. Three forgeries, it appears, had been necessary in the documents used to convict him. He had disdained to say more than phrases in his own defense. Sitting alone in the rear seat of the death cart, he appeared, from all accounts, perfectly at ease, eyed the spectators with detachment, nodded to friends in the rue Saint-Honoré. At the Place de la Révolution he was the first to descend, and he remained inscrutable in that scene of anguish and derision. He calmly observed the fate of those dispatched before him. When his name was called he turned to embrace Danton, but was pulled away. He then mounted the scaffold without loss of poise. His death was the triumph of his life: affectation became dignity. Six years ago he had noted in himself a "republican" temperament. It would be interesting to know the image in his mind at these last moments. Was it the republican martyr, the skeptical philosopher, or the aristocrat showing the vulgar how to die?

The events of Ventôse (the Dantonists were guillotined on 16 Germinal, April 5, but "Ventôse" can conveniently be extended as a symbol) were momentous both in the short run and in the long. The fall of the Hébertists left the small Revolutionists, the sansculottes, in a state of bewilderment. It was necessary for the Committee of Public Safety to give them a sense of direction. The fall of the Dantonists frightened the Revolutionary leaders, especially the members of the Convention. It would be wise for the Committee to give them some reassurance. To what extent it did either we shall see. The difficulties were forbidding, for Robespierre's narrow way had become a tightrope, which stealthy hands were waiting implacably to cut.

And a century and more later, when France was again a republic, the old divisions were still plain. All modern republicans looked back on the Revolution with favor, but by no means with agreement. No one wanted to idealize Hébert; the creation of a socialist legend in the nineteenth century made it useless to do that. But some idealized Danton, and some Robespierre, for Dantonists and Robespierrists were still alive. There were easygoing republicans, good livers, not always above scandal, and more rigid and absolute republicans, radical democrats, quick to tear the mask from ordinary bourgeois society. The two groups distrusted each other almost as much as each distrusted, and was distrusted by, the monarchists. Practical Frenchmen argued over their past with a sectarian fervor incomprehensible in the United States. Nor is the end in sight, unless in the France of the future all serious argument is to be ended. That solution, too, had an early trial, under Napoleon.

CHAPTER XIII

The Culmination

THE Committee of Public Safety, as the true governing body of France, survived the death of the Dantonists by one hundred and thirteen days. They were a Hundred Days more illuminating than those of Napoleon, for during them the Revolution reached its climax. The Committee, having disposed of its enemies, now ruled with a free hand. Robespierre stood at the pinnacle of his career. Vistas opened upon the new and longed for world. In Belgium the Jacobin army won the great victory patiently prepared for in the green room; and at sea the navy, Jeanbon's patched up middle-class squadrons, challenged the domination of the British. Floréal and Prairial brought not only the maturity of the Revolutionary dictatorship, but the springtime of the democratic Republic, a brief moment, for the best Jacobins, of optimism soon cut short.

The period is much argued about and little understood. Over it hangs the cloud of the Grand Terror, the spasm of guillotinings that preceded the fall of Robespierre. In the two months before 9 Thermidor about twenty-five hundred persons were put to death, the majority by the Revolutionary Tribunal of Paris, which received in May a virtual monopoly over Revolutionary justice. Most of these executions could scarcely be justified, as earlier ones could, even under the ample doctrine of reason of state. They arose less from political calculation than from panic. The Grand Terror was a psychological fever, like the Great Fear that had gripped the peasants five years before.

It would be wrong to disregard the crescendo of terrorism. The numbers of actual victims may indeed be made to look small. During the whole Terror, running over more than a year, only one Frenchman in fifteen hundred, and only one in over three hundred nobly born, was sent to the guillotine. Half the victims were taken in armed rebellion. In large parts of the country executions were unknown, especially after Ventôse. But it is necessary to see beyond the scaffolds, to remember the three hundred thousand declared suspects, the hundred thousand political prisoners, the degradation of judicial process, the spying and tale-bearing and denunciation, the distrust of friends and self-righteous ruthlessness toward foes, the moralized debasement of common human relations. The Terror was a disease that left a lasting disfigurement in France.

Even so, we shall not dwell much on the Grand Terror, which in fact was by no means entirely the work of the Committee of Public Safety. The Hundred Days before Thermidor were not primarily a time of destruction. They were a time of creation, of abortive and perhaps visionary creation, nipped by the fatal blight of the Revolution, the inability of the Revolutionists to work together. Had the Jacobins been a revolutionary party of the modern kind, drilled to a mechanical obedience, the whole French Revolution would have been different.

To found the Republic, and to create the institutions thought necessary to a democracy, was the chief aim of the victorious Committee after Ventôse. The war was also to be fought, no longer defensively, though the Austrians were still at Condé and Valenciennes. And for both purposes, to win the war and to establish the Republic, the Revolutionary Government was still to be strengthened.

Though the Revolutionary Government was held to be provisional, its consolidation involved, as has been seen, many decisions of permanent importance. The principles of 14 Frimaire were applied in new ways after Ventôse. Subordinate organizations lost what was left of their independence. The Paris Commune was filled with government appointees, the Cordeliers club closed, and the Revolutionary Army disbanded. Soldiers in the real armies lost their right to petition the Convention. Local authorities, such as departmental and municipal boards, were forbidden on pain of twenty years' imprisonment to send deputations to each other. The Committee recalled a great many representatives on mission, preferring to work through the national agents, or through special inspectors like the young Julien who had denounced Carrier, men whose allegiance was directly to the Committee. The revolutionary courts set up by representatives on mission were dissolved, political prisoners thereafter being tried in Paris. The two famous provincial courts of the late Terror, those at Arras and at Orange, were authorized by the Committee of Public Safety.

On April 1 Carnot made one of his rare appearances before the Convention. He proposed to abolish the six ministries of the Executive Council, which, with their semi-independent personnel, had sometimes been out of step with the Committee. To do their work he recommended twelve executive commissions, on the model of the Subsistence Commission and thus practically departments of the Committee of Public Safety. The idea had been heard in the Convention before, as had some of Carnot's own arguments, viz., that ministers were a tyrannical invention of kings. The Committee in the past had regarded criticism of the ministers as a factious attack upon itself. Now that the factions had fallen their ideas could safely be adopted. No time was lost, for Danton had been arrested less than forty-eight hours before Carnot's speech, and was not yet even on trial.

The suppression of the ministries (which the Convention voted without comment) put an end to the theoretical separation of executive and legislature. Carnot sketched clearly a cabinet form of parliamentary government. At the top, he said, was reason, which the people always obeyed; then came the people, then the elected representative body; then, "direct emanation, integral but changeable part of the National Convention, the Committee of Public Safety," which was to direct administration, determine policies and represent the executive in the assembly. Carnot observed that the new arrangements were to be temporary, like the Revolutionary Government itself. Yet he presented the scheme in the light of general political philosophy, and seemed not to feel that it was of limited application. It is noteworthy, in any case, that despite the authority of Montesquieu and all prevailing doctrine, the Committee of Public Safety, to meet realities of politics, outlined the only form of representative government that has ever been successful in France. The Committee was henceforth a cabinet, though a very autocratic one, since no elections were to be held in the visible future, nor any parties or free discussion allowed in the Convention. Carnot continued to take the lead in planning details of the reorganization.

The trend of development, by which the political debris of 1793 was built into a pyramid of organized authority under the prin-

ciples of 14 Frimaire, made it increasingly awkward for the
pyramid to have two peaks—the two governing committees of the
Convention. The men of Public Safety looked with a certain disapproval on their colleagues of General Security. The coordinate
status of the two bodies meant that the political police operated
independently of the rest of the executive government. The lesser
committee sometimes made arrests not desired by the greater, and
sometimes brought inadequate zeal to cases which the greater
committee considered vital. In September Public Safety had
gained the right to name the members of General Security, but
no true subordination had followed. The former continued to
cut down the sphere of the latter. The report against the Dantonists was a supreme act of political police. Yet the lead had
been taken by the superior committee, acting through Saint-Just.

Ten days after the death of Danton, Saint-Just again made a
speech in the Convention. The result was an elaborate police act.
The two committees now had equal rights in pursuing conspirators. The greater committee alone was to inspect and purge the
personnel of government. Two new commissions, under the two
committees jointly, were to execute the laws of Ventôse. Nobles
and foreigners were banned from Paris. Persons talking against
the Revolution or living idly were to be deported. And a committee
of the Convention was to design a body of civil institutions for the
Republic. The whole act bore the clear imprint of Saint-Just.

A new General Police Bureau was now organized in the offices
of the Committee of Public Safety. It, too, was Saint-Just's work :
its head was a friend of his, its employees were instructed to be
laconic, and its chief labors were to be supervision over all officeholders in the state. The new bureau embodied the censorship that
Saint-Just called for in his *Republican Institutions*. Its function
was primarily surveillance over public administration, though in
practice it dealt also with other affairs.

The Police Bureau, like other bureaus of the Committee, was at
bottom a clerical staff. It prepared matters for the consideration
of the Committee, which so far as possible made all the important
decisions. The Committee deputed one of its members to superin-
tend the work of the bureau, and this member was supposed to
bring up for discussion at the green table all business that was not
obviously routine.

At first Saint-Just was in charge of the bureau, but five days after its inception he went on mission to the Army of the North, and for the next two months, all of May and June, the Police Bureau was in the charge of Robespierre. Thereafter, until Thermidor, Saint-Just and Couthon took turns in overseeing its work. How these three used the position entrusted to them is an important question, for they were later accused of forming a triumvirate, and of plotting largely by means of the Police Bureau to subject the whole Republic to themselves.

The man directing the bureau wrote instructions on the documents it put before him. From these notes much can be deduced. Saint-Just was severe, often ordering arrests; Robespierre was more inclined to ask for further information. Saint-Just, however, in the first days of the bureau, turned several cases over to the Committee of General Security. Robespierre, during his two months' tenure, referred only four cases to the rival committee. It is clear that Robespierre wished a state police independent of the Committee of General Security. That committee, however, continued to handle four times as many cases as the Police Bureau, and since some of these were of importance it remained the chief organ of political police. The work of the bureau was enough to aggravate the friction between the two committees, but not enough to remove it.

Did Robespierre and the two others, while thus encroaching upon the Committee of General Security, try also to build themselves a separate power within the Committee of Public Safety? It does not appear so. Orders issued by the bureau were orders of the ruling Committee, whose members had to sign them. A quarter of these orders were drafted, and half were signed, by members not in the "triumvirate." The other half were signed by Robespierre, Couthon or Saint-Just alone. Important arrests seem to have been discussed by, or at least known to, the whole Committee. The very regularity of the procedure probably made the others suspicious of decisions made privately by the member directing the bureau; yet many decisions had to be so made, for the Committee had no time to discuss jointly all the details assigned to each man's care. Confusion was bound to result, as when Carnot found two of his clerks arrested without his knowledge.

The Police Bureau, in short, was an instrument of the Committee of Public Safety, not of a Robespierrist coterie; and its activity was harmonious with the whole development of the Year Two, a step in subordinating the Committee of General Security, and a means of bringing the army of officeholders to the views of the government in Paris. Had Barère, Billaud or Collot been in charge of it its work would have been no less inquisitorial. But it was a contribution of the Robespierrists to the power of the Committee; it was designed, manned and operated by them, and if the Committee should disintegrate into a mere collection of individuals, the Police Bureau would appear as a Robespierrist machine.

The Committee was a fully grown dictatorship after Ventôse. Yet its authority was not absolute. It depended on the Convention for the strength of its position. The purging of the Convention, by an odd paradox, showed the importance of that body—had the Convention been entirely nugatory its members could have been let alone. If the Convention should withdraw its mandate the dictatorship would collapse, the more so because the Committee itself was destroying the organs of popular revolution, and because the nine who sat in the green room were held together more by respect for the Convention than by loyalty to each other. Moreover the Committee of General Security stubbornly maintained itself. As early as March 16 the United States minister to Paris wrote to Jefferson that the two committees would probably come to open blows. He observed also, soon after the fall of the Hébertists and the Dantonists, that the next faction would rise in the Committee of Public Safety itself. To show the truth of his prophecies would anticipate the end of the story.

Reorganizing the ministries, extending the principles of 14 Frimaire, setting up a new agency of police, were all merely means to an end. The question remains of what the Committee wished to do, what precisely the democratic Republic was to mean.

An indication was given on April 14, when the Convention, on its own initiative, ordered the remains of Jean-Jacques Rousseau to be borne to the Pantheon. The new state, so far as it came from books, was to draw its inspiration from the *Social Contract*. It was not to be the liberal state that emerged in the nineteenth century. Jacobins were far from wishing to leave the individual to his own devices. Their democratic Republic was to be unitary, solid, total,

with the individual fused into society and the citizen into the
nation. National sovereignty was to check individual rights, the
general will prevail over private wishes. In the interest of the
people the state was to be interventionist, offering social services;
it was to plan and guide the institutions of the country, using
legislation to lift up the common man. It was to resemble more
closely the states of the twentieth century than those of the
nineteenth.

Democracy, in short, as early as 1794 dissociated itself from
the theory of pure liberalism and laissez-faire. It identified itself
with a very wide exercise of sovereignty, or, to put it more con-
cretely, of the power of government. "The function of government," Robespierre had said on 5 Nivôse, "is to direct the moral
and physical forces of the nation." To what end? How did the
Committee, possessing a relatively free power after Ventôse, conceive of its function of direction? How did economic aims compare with other more "moral" ones?

No one can doubt that the government of the Year Two regulated economic affairs with unparalleled thoroughness. We have
devoted a whole chapter to describing that regulation. Most of
the control, however, was regarded as temporary, to last only
during the war and the internal political crisis. A modified economic
policy set in after Ventôse. Made feasible by the fall of the Hébertists, and adopted in the light of experience, the new policy expressed the real drift of economic doctrine within the Committee.

Regulation became less hostile to merchants and manufacturers.
The new policy was to invite their cooperation without giving them
a free hand.

The Committee granted premiums and subsidies, transferred
certain munitions plants to private enterprise, removed the last
vestiges of the law against hoarding which Billaud and Collot
had sponsored in the preceding July. Price controls were relaxed.
No one in the Committee had ever had much faith in the Maximum; authorized exceptions now became more frequent, the law
being used as an instrument of discipline, available on occasion to
check profiteering or counter the demands of labor. Export trade
was encouraged, though exporters were required to import useful
commodities or to turn over foreign exchange to the government.
The Subsistence Commission, renamed the Commission of Com-

merce and Supply and constituting one of the twelve new executive departments, continued and even expanded its functions of supervision; it alone now possessed the right of requisition, and it set up new agencies, such as export boards in the ports where its representatives and those of the merchants deliberated together.

It was clear after Ventôse that the Revolutionary Government had no intention of driving the "aristocracy of merchants" from the state which it was laboring to establish. Neither did it intend to allow private business to interfere with the national interest. Its faith was overwhelmingly in private enterprise, but not in absolute laissez-faire. Even moderate regulation, however, suffered from association with the repressiveness of the Terror. After Thermidor, in the reaction against terrorism, all regulation of business was abandoned.

What the Revolutionary Government proposed to do for the lower classes in the economic scale is a highly debatable question. The Committee, as has been seen, tried to make known new scientific ideas to the population. It distributed pamphlets on agriculture among the peasants, and descriptions of new technical processes among metallurgical and other craftsmen. Probably it regarded such public enlightenment as a duty of government irrespective of the emergency of war. Plans also were drawn up for universal education and for the relief of many kinds of distress—policies which waited a hundred years for approximate fulfilment. The debatable question is to what extent the Revolutionary Government, going beyond the enlightenment and relief of its citizens, contemplated an extensive redistribution of wealth. Much wealth had already changed hands during the Revolution. Previously, however, property confiscated by the state had been acquired only by persons able to pay for it, because the confiscated property was used to support the paper money.

The laws of Ventôse marked a new departure. They provided, or were thought to provide, that "indigent patriots" should receive lands free. Such was Saint-Just's original intention as expressed in his *Republican Institutions*. It was never carried out.

The laws of Ventôse, as framed by the Committee and enacted by the Convention, did not in fact state that real property was to be divided. They stated that it was to be confiscated from suspects, and an indemnity paid from the proceeds to the poor. The newly confiscated wealth, like the wealth already confiscated from the clergy and the émigrés, could be used to uphold the financial structure of the Revolutionary state, and the poor could be relieved, as formerly, by receiving an "indemnity" in paper money.

To this outcome Saint-Just's own generalities contributed. Saint-Just, like most other middle-class leaders of the Revolution, had almost no real knowledge of the problems of working-class people. He saw an undifferentiated mass of indigent patriots to whom it would be both humane and expedient to give land. He failed to distinguish between those who could use land and those who could not, between able-bodied landless agricultural laborers and the rest of the needy, the small artisans and city wage-earners, the not-quite-landless peasants, the old, the widowed, the orphaned, the crippled. Barère and others, who put serious thought into the relief of suffering but who objected to overturning the property system, nullified the Ventôse laws by absorbing them into the very different, but still ambitious, program of public charity. No one in the Committee offered effective opposition to this development. Billaud and Collot were not interested in a social revolution not initiated by themselves. The thoughts of Robespierre and Couthon were on other things. Saint-Just himself underwent a change of heart. In a notebook seized on his person on 9 Thermidor he had written: "Don't admit division of property but only of farms," farms (*fermages*) apparently meaning the large tracts leased by owners to middlemen who either sublet them to peasants or worked them with hired labor. The abolition of these "big farms" was much more generally demanded by the peasants than the redistribution of property rights. Saint-Just's shift was therefore in the direction of real rural opinion, but it reduces the probability that the Robespierrists, when they fell, were on the point of sponsoring a great social revolution.

The fact is that Saint-Just, if he wished to rally the lowest classes to the Republic, had very little idea how to do so. We have seen how the attitude of the Committee toward urban wage-earners resembled that of the early factory owners during the industrial revolution. Of the four-fifths of the population who were peasants the problems were even less understood. Among all the reforming writers of the eighteenth century the peasants possessed no authentic spokesman, and nothing in the experience or education of the Revolutionary leaders could fill the gap. The idealism of the Revolution helped the peasants, removing their feudal burdens, granting them land on instalment payments, promising them education, taking steps to relieve their poverty, endowing them with rights of citizenship which they were not prepared to exercise. After these initial reforms the peasants' economic demands went largely unheeded. Peasants petitioned that the Maximum be applied to rents. No one in the national government supported them, for to regulate the terms of leases would be an acknowledgment that the Maximum was permanent. The peasants objected to the share-cropping system of *métayage;* they were still objecting in 1913. They wished the right to join in collective purchase of confiscated land, and to buy it without competitive auction. No one supported these requests. They wished to keep their old communal methods of agriculture, which were officially frowned upon. It was thought feudal and counter-revolutionary for a village to exercise communal authority over individual property.

The Ventôse policy in the end, far from winning support for the government, hardly amounted to more than another measure of Terror. The Jacobins in various parts of the country who compiled lists of suspects, usually on their own initiative, showed more the old zeal for hunting enemies of the Revolution than a new ardor for providing property for the poor. The corresponding lists of indigent patriots, ordered by the Committee, were never completed. The indigent were not eager to declare themselves. After clashing with the government over religion, military service, corvées and the Maximum the country folk remained suspicious, and they were not likely if destitute to announce themselves to the authorities, since a recent law threatened habitual mendicants with deportation to Madagascar. The Committee in enforcing the Ventôse laws issued vague, fragmentary and sporadic orders, and at times discouraged subordinates who seemed too willing to take action. Of the six commissions provided for in the act of 23 Ventôse only two were set up, and these were ignored by the Committee of Public Safety until a week before the 9th of Thermidor.

On the whole, though the intentions of the government were favorable, the laboring classes had much to resent. The Committee began to worry about the harvest with the coming of spring. Fear of depriving agricultural laborers of economic incentives was one argument for shelving the laws of Ventôse, and fear that prosperous farmers would monopolize labor by paying high wages led to a policy of strict enforcement of the Maximum. On May 30 the Committee requisitioned agricultural workers, proclaimed a uniform wage, and threatened recalcitrants with the Revolutionary Tribunal. Illegally high wages were nevertheless paid by farmers, so that, to discourage city workers from migrating during the harvest, the Committee forbade them to leave their shops without permission.

In Paris the new national agent was Payan, a personal friend of Robespierre, and the new Commune was entirely subordinate to the Committee. Meat was still scarce, fuel hard to get, candles almost non-existent. Beggars walked the streets despite the stern laws against begging; it was complained that they asked alms "superstitiously," that their afflictions were pretended, or that they offered change for fifty franc notes. Under the Hébertists the Commune had held down the price of commodities but not of labor. The reverse was now more nearly true. On April 21 two hundred tobacco workers, coming to the city hall, asked for an increase of wages. Payan, calling them tools of the nobility, victims of agitators and an emetic to the body politic, turned over their case to the General Police Bureau. When workers in one of the public shops complained against their fourteen-hour day, two of their leaders were arrested by the Committee. The assemblies set up for collective bargaining in the national arms factories were reorganized; henceforth representatives of the government formed a majority, and the workingmen found themselves outvoted.

The Committee took the view (embodied in the Levy in Mass) that work of every kind was like service in the army, a patriotic duty requiring discipline and sacrifice. Spartanism ruled economics. To understand the difference between Athens and Sparta, said Billaud-Varenne, constituted the whole science of government. Labor was not placated; agitation spread and deepened into the summer. Since Ventôse the common workman could look for support nowhere except to the government. The government, made up of middle-class men impatient of the demagogy and quack cures of Hébertism, pursuing ultimate aims upon which the hard-pressed workman found it difficult to concentrate, gave no answer except to appeal to his virtue.

The Committee of Public Safety, in these fateful Hundred Days, succeeded in attaching no class to itself by economic interest. It did not replace the Hébertists in the affections of the sans-culottes, who consequently grew disillusioned in the Revolutionary leadership and were ceasing to be an effective political force. Businessmen had their labor requisitioned for them by the authorities, and were no longer under such suspicion as a few months ago; but they were allowed only limited profits, or had at times to operate at a loss, and they were not free to run their affairs independently. Those who if unwatched would be unscrupulous found much to complain of. Labor and capital could agree that the régime of regulation should be not only temporary but short-lived.

But not all interests are economic, nor do human beings function simply as labor and capital. Fear of the guillotine is a pronounced form of self-interest; and the most overwhelming interest of all is that of the man who can lose himself wholly in a great cause. To these interests the Revolutionary Government appealed—to fear of its power, and to love of its aims, that "virtue" which meant devotion to the Republic. The polity announced by Robespierre in February was at hand, the rule of virtue and terror.

The Terror turned increasingly into vengeance. Chaumette was guillotined, though in Ventôse he had supported the government. The widows of Hébert and Desmoulins followed him. Officials of the old monarchy were dragged from retirement and dispatched, including Malesherbes, one of its great reforming statesmen. On May 10 was created the dread Commission of Orange, which stripped prisoners of all pretense of defense, and foreshadowed the use of similar methods in Paris. The Commission of Orange was administered by the representative Maignet, who with Couthon in Puy-de-Dôme the year before had shown himself a reasonable man. But even reasonable men now succumbed to the contagion. A spirit was abroad which contemporary conservatives truly described as satanic. The bodies of two fugitive Girondists were discovered in the south in June. The local club moralized, holding that men who had led such wicked lives deserved their gruesome death, with "their corpses hideous and disfigured, half eaten by worms, their scattered limbs the prey of devouring dogs, and their bloody hearts the pasture for wild beasts."

At the same time went forward in perfect sanity the routine attention to business that was organizing the country, and in high hope and idealism those creative labors that were to regenerate the Republic. The government would inculcate virtue in the widest sense. It would give the nation new feelings, make it into a new people. Robespierre was most interested in the teaching of a pure religion. There were many other ways of working toward the same end.

Crude propaganda was not overlooked. The famous David, for example, presented two caricatures to the Committee on May 18. One showed an army of louts led by George III, whom in turn a turkey led by the nose. The other represented the British government as a horrible and nightmarish monster. The Committee paid him three thousand livres, and ordered a thousand copies of each.

The press was rigidly controlled, there being no more journals like those of Hébert and Desmoulins, and indeed few journals at all. The theater became entirely official. There were fewer radical plays than in 1793, especially fewer diatribes against religion, a development due partly to official policy, and partly to the waning of revolutionary spirit outside the government. In attacks upon tyranny, once the common stock of the patriotic stage, the authorities now scented counter-revolution, as the seasoned revolutionist M. J. Chénier learned to his cost.

Chénier wrote a tragedy called *Timoléon* to revive his literary reputation. The scene was laid in ancient Hellas, but the characters spoke such lines as:

> I, friend of the Republic, can it be
> That I aspire to found my tyranny?

and:

> Before the Terror, worthy men retreat:
> Kindness dies, and virtues grow discreet.

and:

> Now may a dagger, wet with tyrant's gore,
> Hang over every speaker evermore.

The Committee of Public Safety, warned by Payan, decided that the play must be submitted to a "preliminary scrutiny of con-

noisseurs." The literary jury included Payan himself, and Barère
and Saint-Just were present at the reading. The embarrassed
Chénier won some applause at the end. "I doubt, however," remarked Saint-Just, "if the government committees can permit
many performances of his *Timoléon*." None at all were permitted,
for it was stopped in rehearsal by an officially arranged rebellion
in the audience. Perhaps Collot and Billaud, playwrights themselves (indeed even Couthon had written a play), took a professional satisfaction in crushing the most eminent of Revolutionary dramatists.

Of literary men of any distinction, even those who had gone
farthest in supporting the Revolution were now outdistanced.
Condorcet, caught after months of concealment, committed suicide
at the end of March. Chénier and Volney, who had accepted the
fall of the Girondists, looked with no favor upon the existing
régime. Yet the Committee of Public Safety was determined to
enlist writers, and all practitioners of the arts, in the task of
creating the new state.

A series of decrees in Floréal, all written by Barère though
signed by others, were Napoleonic in conception. They suggest
also more recent dictators.

27 Floréal, Year Two
[May 16, 1794]

The Committee of Public Safety calls upon poets to celebrate
the principal events of the French Revolution, to compose hymns
and poems and republican dramas, to publish the heroic actions of
the soldiers of liberty, the courage and devotion of republicans,
and the victories won by French arms. It calls also upon citizens
who cultivate letters to transmit to posterity the most noteworthy
facts and great epochs in the regeneration of the French, to give
to history that firm and severe character appropriate to the annals
of a great people conquering the liberty attacked by all the tyrants
of Europe. It calls upon them to compose classic books, and to in-
fuse a republican morality into the works destined for public
instruction, pending the proposal by the Committee to the Convention of the kind of national award to be decreed for their
labors, and the date and form of their competitive contest.

B. Barère, C. A. Prieur, Carnot,
Billaud-Varenne, Couthon

Not content to demand "classic books" the Committee invited painters to glorify the Revolution on canvas, and summoned all musicians and teachers of music to a contest for civic chants and martial airs. Architects were called upon to create a Republican style, the Committee specifying as objects of attention "the places destined for the exercise of the sovereignty of the people in the primary assemblies, the ceremonies devoted to the festivals of the *décadi,* the town halls, law courts, establishments of justices of the peace, prisons, houses of detention, national theaters and public baths and fountains."

The Committee intended to beautify Paris, established contests for sculptors, ordered a bronze statue of Rousseau, brought some sculptured horses from Marly to the Champs-Elysées, authorized David to choose, from among the works in various palaces, figures to adorn the bridges over the Seine. It sketched a rearrangement of the Tuileries gardens, transferred trees from Versailles to Paris, sponsored the Museum of Natural History and the Institute of Music, planned two arches of triumph, and organized a zoo. It directed that a statue by Houdon, representing Philosophy grasping the Declaration of Rights and the constitution, should be installed in the hall of the Convention. Existing only in plaster and never finished in marble, Houdon's statue was a good expression of the Committee's brief régime.

The peasants were not forgotten. A contest was opened "to all artists of the Republic," meaning apparently architects and builders, "for the amelioration of the lot of inhabitants of the country, by proposal of simple and economical means of constructing more convenient and healthy farms and dwelling places, taking account of the geographical features of the different departments, and drawing material from the demolition of castles, feudal structures and nationalized buildings whose preservation shall be judged unnecessary."

David was a busy man in these weeks, for in addition to the commissions just mentioned, and the duty of planning the civic festivals, and his functions in the Committee of General Security, he was instructed to design a new attire for Representatives of the People sent to the armies, and to report on means of improving the dress of the nation, "adapting it to republican manners and to

the character of the Revolution." The Committee would revolutionize even clothes.

Language also fell within its purview. On June 4 the Convention issued an Address to the French People, signed (and possibly
written) by Prieur of the Côte-d'Or, who was serving his turn
as president of the assembly. All the leading ideas except one
had been anticipated by the Committee of Public Safety, and
presented in a speech by Barère, during the past winter. The one
exception signified the new concentration upon virtue. Prieur's
statement deplored swearing and obscenity, reproved the coarse
phrases of the fallen Hébertists, and affirmed that only decent
and respectful language reflected the majesty of the French people.

Prieur and Barère both held that a uniform people must have
a uniform speech. They inveighed against the niceties of pro-
nunciation by which aristocrats sought to distinguish themselves.
They attacked four languages in the Republic that were not
French: German, Breton, Basque and Italian. The existence of
these languages, they pointed out, produced a linguistic federalism,
a division in the community, for the people who spoke them could
not understand public events. Barère averred that the Bretons used
the same word for "law" and "religion," so that the Bretons
thought every change in the law a violation to religion. He noted
the exodus of twenty thousand Alsatians in December, attributing
it only to their speech, which, he said (showing the new importance
of nationality in the modern state), made them more sympathetic
to Germany than to France. No one could be a citizen, obey the
laws or participate in the commonwealth without commanding the
common medium of expression. Barère in his peroration reviewed
the tongues of Europe—Italian suited to effeminate delights, German the organ of militarism and feudality, Spanish the cant of
the Inquisition, English once glorious and free, now the patter
of despotism and the stock-exchange. "As for us, we owe it to
our fellow citizens, we owe it to the strengthening of the Republic,
to have spoken throughout its territory the language in which is
written the Declaration of the Rights of Man."

The Convention therefore authorized an army of schoolteachers
to bring the language of reason, justice, liberty and equality into
Brittany, Alsace, the Basque regions and Corsica. In practice not
many such teachers appeared. But a kind of linguistic terror broke

out in some places, spread by local Jacobin zealots. Fanatics were
not wanting who demanded the extermination of German culture
in Alsace. The authorities in Paris refused to countenance such
extremes, but on 2 Thermidor, July 20, independently of the Committee of Public Safety, the Convention ordered that all official
and legal documents must be written in standard French.

Over education the Committee of Public Instruction had authority. The ruling Committee interfered relatively little, for
Jacobins on this matter were agreed. The aim was to universalize
literacy, and so to cure the masses of prejudice and fanaticism,
that is wean them away from the monarchy and the church. Emphasis fell upon the making of citizens, in the expectation that
free individuals would emerge; but the educational doctrines of the
Year Two, which Saint-Just's Spartan ideas hardly exaggerated,
were the negation of individualism. The child was to be brought
up for the state, practical subjects were favored, and all subjects
were to be given a Revolutionary angle. History was to portray
kings as cruel, imbecilic and hypocritical, eulogize the sub-noble
classes, and include study of the American Revolution, "the first
philosophical revolution." By study of the heroism and constitutional liberties that the French Revolution had produced, young
people would acquire "that national pride which is the distinctive
character of free peoples." But except for a program the Revolutionary years contributed almost nothing to popular education, for
in the absence of funds, and in the confusion and preoccupation
with other aims, the old church schools were not replaced. It is
extremely doubtful whether more Frenchmen could read in the
reign of Napoleon than in the reign of Louis XVI.

The Committee of Public Safety took note of the ignorance in
which young people were growing up. At the same time its members were convinced, as Barère said, that the Revolution was to
the human mind as the sun of Africa to vegetation. They gave
thought to founding a normal school for teachers, but a Hundred
Days were too short—the *École Normale* dates from 1795. The
Committee had obtained good results in initiating young men into
certain practical arts. Delegates had been brought to Paris from
all France to learn how to make munitions, then sent to their own
localities to teach others. It was decided now to found a military

school, on the same regional principles, for boys of sixteen and
seventeen who were just under the age of conscription.

This institution, known as the School of Mars, was not in
operation until the eve of Thermidor and was abolished soon after,
but the plans were laid in May, and they show the methods by
which the Committee hoped to weld the French nation into a
democratic and republican people.

The three thousand pupils came equally from all parts of the
country. Contingents from each district were broken up on arriving in Paris, so that each boy would lose his localism and learn
fraternity with the nation. Almost all were from sans-culotte
homes, their fathers being peasants or artisans, in many cases also
volunteers in the army. The school was to correct, said Barère,
that indiscipline of youth which was such a problem; it would
turn out not merely soldiers but citizens and men of virtue, patriotic, robust, frugal, serious-minded and clean-living young men
who would be a credit to the Republic. The boys lived in tents,
ate beef twice a *décade* and pork on other days, slept on straw
mattresses and arose at five o'clock in the morning. They learned
to maneuver, to use firearms and to understand something about
fortification. No time was wasted on mere theory, as in the old
royal schools; the cadets were taught to charge straight ahead with
the bayonet. They were also taught hygiene. Some came from
such humble parentage that the use of the latrines had to be
explained to them.

There was no Republican education, said Barère, unless a boy
belonged to the Republic before belonging to his family. Yet on
completing his course each was to return home, lest he think
that education raised him above the persons among whom he was
born. Those who distinguished themselves would receive other
opportunities, for the "incalculable advantage of revolutions is
that merit obtains the rank that is due to it, and that each citizen
discharges the functions devolved upon him by the kind of talent
he has shown." This advantage of course not only benefited the
individual but increased the collective efficiency of the state.

Three thousand in number, encamped just north of the Bois de
Boulogne, drilled and organized and armed, almost frantic with
Revolutionary patriotism (for they were chosen from among
thousands who had clamored for admission, by local authorities

who wished to show off their most creditable youngsters in Paris),
the cadets were a potential weapon of great power in the politics
of the city and of the nation. At the head of the school was Le Bas,
Saint-Just's friend, one of two members of the Convention
appointed to direct it. He was young himself, only twenty-nine,
tested in Alsace and in the north, grave in demeanor, with blue
eyes and blond hair that one student long remembered. The object
of boyish hero-worship, he was in a position to become the leader
of a Republican Youth. No modern dictator would have overlooked such a chance. Yet the Robespierrists made no attempt to
use the School of Mars for their own advantage. Couthon publicly
opposed its very existence.

For despite all the Grand Terror the government of these Hundred Days did not rely chiefly on force. Not marching bands, any
more than quick economic returns, were to draw people to the
new order. The Committee, in eighteenth century fashion, put its
hopes in the diffusion of enlightenment, which meant less a cold
persuasion of the intellect than an emotional surging toward truths
that make men free. The Revolution was a religion, which reached
its apogee on June 8, 1794, when Citizen Robespierre, in the name
of the French People, conducted services in honor of the Supreme
Being.

Robespierre on this occasion was more priestlike than ever, and
the eminence he thus attained, together with whispers that he was
planning a personal theocracy, hastened his fall. But the worship
of the Supreme Being only realized a common dream. Robespierre
was never more representative of the Revolution, never less swayed
by an ambition private to himself, than when officiating as hiero-
phant of the Republic.

There was much in the Revolution recalling the Protestant
revolution of the time of Luther and Calvin. Couthon cried out
for a religion of God not of priests. Extremists smashed images
in churches. Jacobins generally thought well of Jesus, but considered most of Christianity since the first century a corruption of
simple truths. Like early Protestants they held religion to be internal, but the doctrine of man's natural goodness relieved them
of much wrestling with the soul. Religious individualism expressed itself rather, as with Rousseau and Wordsworth, in a love
of solitary walks, in reverie at evening, hearkening to the inner

voice, musing on nature, yearning for the absolute and the sublime. Robespierre often held such quiet sessions with himself.

But it was not meditations on the Supreme Being, which could be shared by conservatives, that made the Jacobins a group of religious apostles. It was their burning faith in things human, their absolute certainty of being right, their passionate and absorbing devotion to the indivisible Republic that was their church, their willingness to die for a cause without whose triumph life would be empty. It was their sense of world-renewal, their hope of regenerating mankind, their feeling of standing at the barricades of eternity to save all future generations. It was their craving for brotherhood, for a fraternity of common will, first of all among themselves as the choice spirits of the elect, but also for the nation and for humanity: the psychology of purging the heretic drew strength from this very yearning for cohesion.

A strict code of morality was generally added, especially by the group represented by Robespierre. The element of Puritanism in the Revolution was very strong. Under the Robespierrist Commune prostitution was suppressed, salacious pictures were banned, and soldiers were forbidden to bathe in the Seine where they might be seen. The Robespierrists set a high value on frugality, not alone because material goods were scarce; on discipline, not alone because France was in a state of confusion; on chastity, not alone because promiscuous sex habits might take the patriot's mind off his civic duty. They believed that these virtues were good and adequate ends in themselves. They identified them with a particular structure of society, the democratic Republic. We have it from Grégoire, no Robespierrist in politics, that there were no truer synonyms in the French language than republic and virtue, or monarchy and vice. We have it from Thuriot, a Dantonist if anything, that man would not be free until he was as pure as he came from the hands of nature. The virtues of democracy in those days were austere.

Revolutionary religion expressed itself spontaneously in many ways, with the forms usually patterned on the Catholicism in which the revolutionaries were brought up. The most passionate Jacobins called the Revolution the "sacred sickness," meaning no irony, and spoke of Republican temples, martyrs, preachers, hymns, sermons,

catechisms and decalogues. One republican decalogue went as
follows:

> To the people only shalt thou swear
> Obedience religiously.
> On every king thou shalt declare
> Hate and war eternally.
> The laws the people shall ordain
> Thou shalt observe most faithfully.
> Thy liberty thou shalt maintain
> As long as life in thee shall be.
> Equality thou shalt keep dear
> By practising it constantly.
> From selfish acts thou shalt keep clear,
> Done thoughtlessly or purposely.
> For offices thou shalt not plead,
> To serve in them improperly.
> Reason only shalt thou heed
> To guide thee in futurity.
> Republican thou strict shalt live
> That thou mayst die as worthily.

The verses are anonymous, and probably arose from genuinely
popular sources, though possibly from one of the writers whose
services the Committee of Public Safety meant to enlist.

These ardors produced the Temples of Reason and the Dechristianizing ceremonials of the Year Two. The manifestations were
diverse, having arisen from local enthusiasms or the conflicting
policies of representatives on mission. In some Temples of Reason the Supreme Being was taken note of, in others only Reason
and Nature. In some regions the Jacobin clubs officiated on the
décadi, in others the local government bodies. There were places
where Marat and Brutus were venerated, but elsewhere Republicans thought such practices superstitious. The Republican catechisms that sprang up far and wide did not all instil the same
doctrine. Republican services for baptism, marriage and burial
varied from spot to spot. In one department Catholic worship
might be severely repressed, while going on almost as usual across
the river.

The Committee of Public Safety would not have been true to
its character had it viewed such variation with a friendly eye. Nor

would Robespierre have been Robespierre, had he felt any confidence in what thousands were doing independently without his
knowledge.

Robespierre had never objected to Dechristianization in principle. Couthon, who with Maximilien was the most religious
member of the Committee, had been a fairly extreme Dechristianizer himself in Puy-de-Dôme. He fell in with Robespierre's
ideas after returning from Clermont-Ferrand. He rallied to Robespierre's belief that there should be no crude violence against
peaceable Catholics. He accepted Robespierre's view that much of
the anti-Christian activity was the atheism which they both
abhorred. Real atheism was rare even in those Temples of Reason
where the Supreme Being was not worshiped, but the accusation
was useful in discrediting the Hébertists. When the Hébertists
were disposed of Robespierre and Couthon pushed their own
Dechristianizing program, without the abruptness and the vandalism of the Hébertists, with explicit denials of atheism and
explicit assurances to law-abiding Catholics, but looking in the
long run to the disappearance of revealed Christianity from
France. The intensity of their own revolutionary faith made them
think Christianity on the verge of extinction.

The Committee shared their beliefs, and wanted religion systematized under the eternal principle of 14 Frimaire. There was
to be a uniform, national, established Republican religion. Established churches existed almost everywhere at the time, even in
New England. The theory that the state should be indifferent to
religion was remote from Revolutionary ideas, and in any case
is perhaps not expedient in a country predominantly Catholic.
Over against the hierarchy of Rome the Revolutionary Government would set up its own church to bring spiritual unity to
Frenchmen, a church in which even Catholics might participate
since the being it worshiped was divine, and in which the more
advanced patriots who needed no superstitions might also find an
outlet for their fervors.

On the day after the death of the Dantonists, Couthon, in announcing to the Convention what the Committee meant to do next,
included hints of forthcoming changes in religion. His correspondence shows that the matter was discussed in the green room
during the month that followed. On May 7 Robespierre came

forward with the new policy, delivering a great speech on the moral and religious ideas of the Republic. Couthon proposed that the address, with the attached law, be translated into all languages and disseminated throughout the universe. It was Couthon who drafted the order, five days later, for the words "Temple of Reason" to be removed from the churches, and in their place written: "The French people recognizes the Supreme Being and the immortality of the soul."

These words constituted the first article of the law of May 7. They were intended to persuade the world that the Jacobins were not, as they seemed to outsiders, materialistic and cynical barbarians bent on the destruction of all human values. Conservatives were not convinced: it seemed absurd that the authority for believing in God should be the will of the French people or the oratory of Robespierre.

The new law set up thirty-six festivals, one for each *décadi*, on each of which the citizen, in communion with his fellows, was to absorb the ideas on which the new order must be founded. The festivals would draw his thoughts, on successive *décadis,* to the Supreme Being and Nature, to the human race, to liberty and equality, to love of country, to hate of tyrants and traitors, to truth and justice, to various virtues, to youth and age, happiness and misfortune, agriculture and industry, ancestors and posterity.

The feast of the Supreme Being and Nature was set for 20 Prairial, the 8th of June. Preparations went busily ahead: national agents read aloud Robespierre's speech and the accompanying law in the buildings once called churches; Jacobins everywhere planned arrangements for the great day; and in Paris, under David's direction, an army of artists, carpenters, song-writers and costume-designers set to work. To all appearances the enthusiasm was general. Even Sylvain Maréchal, who had vaunted his godlessness, composed a hymn to the Supreme Being. So did the disgruntled Chénier, though his hymn was rejected; he also wrote some new words for the "Marseillaise." Catholics felt a little hope, for the law of May 7 reaffirmed freedom of worship. At the Paris Jacobins it was even suggested that persons not believing in God and immortality should be driven from the Republic. Robespierre, favoring toleration, and also suspecting a plot, answered that the ostracism of atheists was a truth best left in the writings of Rousseau.

If Robespierre believed that spiritual unity was at last about to prevail, events soon occurred that might well disturb his confidence. On May 23 an assassin named Admiral fired on Collot d'Herbois. He had meant to kill Robespierre, but not finding him had shot at Collot instead. On the very next day a girl of twenty, Cecile Renault, after suspiciously insisting on seeing Robespierre, was found to have two knives on her person. She said she had come to see what a tyrant looked like, and confessed to being a royalist. The Committee of General Security soon warned Couthon that a mysterious stranger was looking for him, probably an assassin. Couthon, it is refreshing to learn, refused to be alarmed, saying that the stranger was probably an unfortunate who wanted to ask him a favor.

Couthon's humanity had few imitators. He himself was outraged at the attempts upon Robespierre. The authorities were terrified, sensing their insecurity. They enlarged the two cases into the vast system of the Foreign Plot, a confused thing in which dead Girondists, Dantonists and Hébertists were implicated with the British government and forty persons hastily rounded up by the police. The forty, including most of the family of Cecile Renault, were packed off to the guillotine in a body, wearing the red shirts of parricides by special order of the Committee of Public Safety. Thirty-seven years before, the man who stabbed Louis XV was tortured to death, to the sadistic delight of the spectators; but no assortment of persons unconnected with the crime had been put to death.

The great day came, 20 Prairial, lovely with all the radiance of June, for the Supreme Being seemed to smile on the efforts made to adore him. Every man, woman and child in Paris had a part to play. David's instructions were extremely minute, and demanded the most exact study, prescribing every move to be made, and anticipating the moments when the throngs were to break into applause, and when, in the fashion of the times, they were to let tears well up in their eyes from tender joy.

At daybreak, as martial music broke out all over the city, housewives bestirred themselves to adorn their windows with flags and flowers. Families then proceeded to the headquarters of their sections. Each of the forty-eight sections marched as a unit on hearing the signal, streaming in from all directions to the Tuileries Gardens, the men and boys walking in one column and carrying branches of oak, the women and girls in a column beside them, wearing flowers. Between the two columns of each section marched the boys from fourteen to eighteen formed in a square and carrying swords.

Meanwhile the National Representation assembled in its hall in the Tuileries, awaiting notification that the people had arrived. When word came the deputies filed out into the garden, led by their president, who happened during this fortnight to be, not accidentally, Maximilien Robespierre. Since their new costume was not yet designed, some deputies wore the uniform of representatives on mission, others, who had never been on mission, merely added to their civilian clothes the tricolored sashes and high plumes of the others. The august body took seats in a kind of grandstand specially prepared.

At the foot of these seats, and surrounded by the respectful citizenry, stood an artfully contrived figure of Atheism, among smaller figures of Ambition, Egotism, Discord and False Simplicity. On these figures was written "Sole Foreign Hope."

Robespierre, as president of the Convention, made a speech which, though brief, was more of a sermon than any he had ever given. He spoke of the power of God who too long had seen a world given over to tyranny, but who had planted in the hearts of men those qualities that made them fight for freedom and justice, and who at length looked down upon a great people celebrating its happiness. Interrupting his discourse, he approached the symbolic figures and applied a torch. Atheism with its satellites disappeared "into nothingness." From the ashes rose up an image of Wisdom, a little discolored by the flames of expiring evil.

Resuming his address, Robespierre reached a height of moral grandeur and national leadership.

"Let us be grave and discreet in all our deliberations, as men who determine the interests of the world. Let us be ardent and stubborn in our wrath against the confederated tyrants; imperturbable in danger, terrible in adversity, modest and vigilant in success. Let us be generous toward the good, compassionate toward the unfortunate, inexorable toward men of evil, just toward all. Let us not count on prosperity without admixture, nor on triumph without obstacles, nor on anything that depends on the fortune or perversity of another. Let us rest only in our own constancy and our own virtue. Alone, but infallible guarantors of our independence, let us crush the wicked league of kings even more by our greatness of character than by the force of our arms."

The closing words, invoking the Being of Beings, were lost in the cheers of the enormous congregation, which immediately prepared, under the eyes of hundreds of marshals, to move off to the Champ de Mars. The procession was a work of art in itself, combining classic balance with the emblems of patriotism and sensibility.

First rode a squadron of cavalry preceded by trumpeters and followed by cannoneers. A hundred drummer boys and pupils from the Institute of Music marched behind them. Then came twenty-four of the sections, in alphabetical order, with men and women in their parallel columns, bedecked with their oak-leaves and flowers, and with a band playing between the twelfth section and the thirteenth. Behind another band, and in the exact middle of the procession, the several hundred members of the Convention had their place, led by their president. Each carried a bouquet of wheat, flowers and fruit, and the whole body, vivid with sashes and plumes, was enclosed in a long tricolor ribbon borne by citizens of all ages from small children to gray-headed elders. The Convention was divided in the middle to make room for a car drawn by eight oxen with gilded horns, hauling miscellaneous objects of symbolic purport—a plow, a sheaf of grain, a printing press, a young oak tree and a statue of liberty. A hundred more drummers followed the representatives, leading the twenty-four remaining sections, at whose midpoint, corresponding to the band further ahead, was a carriage filled with blind children singing a hymn to the Deity. More cavalry brought up the rear.

Defiling into the Champ de Mars, renamed the Champ de Réunion, the concourse beheld one of the artificial Mountains that had become familiar symbols in the Republic. This one was exceptionally high and commodious, and executed with careful naturalism, a tree of liberty sprouting at the peak, and rocks, shrubbery and pathways lining the sides. The National Convention ascended

to the summit. Selected citizens of all ages and both sexes occupied
the lower levels. The throngs below were estimated at half a
million; however exaggerated the number, most of Paris was
probably there.

The multitude surrendered itself to the intoxication of music.
Another hymn to the Deity was played by the bands, also "a grand
symphony." The occupants of the Mountain, specially chosen and
rehearsed, sang the "Marseillaise" with Chénier's words, beginning,

> Mighty God, of a people intrepid
> It is thou who defendest the walls.

With trumpets giving the signals from the top of a high column—
the problem of organizing a mass meeting in those days was not
easy—the whole host joined in the refrain, swearing annihilation
to crime and tyrants. During the last stanza, if we may believe
contemporary reports, which often confused what was supposed
to happen with what actually did, mothers raised their male infants
in homage to the Author of Nature, girls threw their flowers in the
air, and the teen-age boys drew their swords and presented them
to their fathers, who, "sharing the enthusiasm of their sons," laid
hands upon the young heads in paternal benediction. Then to a
loud salvo of artillery, "interpreter of the national vengeance,"
the French People dispersed into their homes.

Doubtless many of the participants were only excited by a holiday spirit. Doubtless many "aristocrats" were present, fearing to
remain away, and giving only a hollow cooperation. It is known
that some members of the Convention thought the whole proceeding ridiculous. The rest of Europe could see little but hypocrisy
in the piety now publicly displayed. It is easy today, when tastes
have changed, to make the apparatus of the occasion, the bouquets,
the feathers, the jack-in-the-box Wisdom, seem absurd.

Yet however much planned by art, and imposed by the government, the doings of 20 Prairial expressed something deeper, and
were a climax to those festivals that had arisen spontaneously
for five years. They were indeed a consummation to the century.
Was it not the aim of the *philosophes* to make wisdom arise from
the ashes of error, and to free the Supreme Being from the disguises of the God of priests? The *philosophes* would not have
enjoyed the festival of Prairial; they would perhaps have found

it vulgar and rather noisy, or complained that in detail it was not precisely what they expected. Whether they would have found it naïve is more doubtful, and it is certain that the ideas expressed were theirs.

Something more potent and portentous than philosophical deism revealed itself in the Champ de Mars, something that Rousseau, of all eighteenth century writers, would have understood best. Gathered in mass, Revolutionary Paris forgot for a moment its privations and its grievances against the authorities, lifted itself above immediate politics, sensed the thrill of constituting a people, a great kindred of the aged, the blind, the vigorous in years, the girls bashful and unused to appearing in public, the boys who shortly might be dead or mutilated in Belgium. Only a dull eye could miss the fervent humanity in the feast of the Supreme Being. It was a humanity of close brotherhood, fraternity, cohesion, of a social body dedicating itself to a mighty cause, and so was transformed into glorifying of the nation and fierce antagonism to everything outside. Revolutionary France felt a tremendous confidence in itself, sensing itself to be the equal of the combined forces of Europe. Liberty and equality had become matters of national prestige.

The Committee of Public Safety could organize and excite these feelings, but it could not dominate them, or turn them into specific loyalty to itself. Robespierre could be the leader of the Revolutionary religion, but he could not be its pope; he could express the sentiments of thousands, but he could not dictate what thousands should believe. The Revolution was greater than any of its leaders, and the faith that impelled it was never a faith in persons. The enthusiasm of 20 Prairial was no measure of allegiance to the individuals operating the government. It was so far above politics as to have no effect on the political situation. Robespierre did not become supreme because the Supreme Being was acknowledged, and the surge of fraternity did not exclude quarreling, or that of humanity the guillotine.

Robespierre himself, it is more than likely, had never been so happy as on that day. It was the great experience of his life to stand as president of the National Convention, escaped from the assassin's hand, hated by all the wicked, calling the French people to the true God. The eloquence and the brevity of his address

reveal the depth of his feeling. His face is said to have lit with
an unusual expression of pleasure, and certainly he enjoyed his
rôle, but there is no reason to accept the theory that what he
most enjoyed was a new grasp upon power. Maximilien's thoughts
soared far over politics as he committed atheism to the flames.

But the day turned all eyes upon him, giving him a dangerous
preeminence, which his enemies tried to accentuate. It is said that
certain members of the Convention, marching with their president
in the front row on 20 Prairial, purposely lagged so that Robespierre would seem to be hurrying forward in a desire to march
alone. Admirers also singled him out: zealots called him the
Messiah, the restorer of God, the foreordained savior of the French
people and of mankind. British news reports spoke of the soldiers
of Robespierre and the decrees of Robespierre, perhaps from
ignorance, perhaps (as Barère said on May 26) to spread the belief that France suffered from a personal tyranny. If the American
minister, however, Gouverneur Morris, a conservative and sensible
observer, thought Robespierre a dictator, he failed to say so in
his communications to the State Department.

Robespierre possessed, in truth, more the appearance than the
reality of individual power. His attempt to lend more reality to
the appearance, to increase his influence in the Committee of Public Safety, hastened his fall. He would himself disclaim, of course,
any merely personal ambition or intention of dictatorship. But
it was his weakness, more than with most men, to confuse intention with fact, and to have no conception of how he appeared
to others, or of what solid ground such appearance might have.
Preaching to the multitude on June 8, he could not understand
why he should be thought a pontiff. Suspicious himself, he could
not comprehend why others suspected him. Popular with the small
revolutionaries (as even his enemies admitted), and counting on
this popularity to strengthen himself against rival political leaders,
he could not see why his popularity should be feared. After the
fate of Desmoulins and Danton, whom he had often supported,
he could not see why his support inspired no confidence. He deplored factionalism, but inflamed it by his ceaseless accusations
of faction. He spent hours poring over the papers of the Police
Bureau, and wondered why he was not trusted. He wanted more
Frenchmen to become good Republicans, but he regarded "new

patriots," persons more orthodox in 1794 than in 1793 or 1790, as most probably hypocrites.

There was in Robespierre himself, apart from other causes of his ruin, something that produced complete political frustration. His narrow way led to a stone wall. Spokesman of democracy he could be, and apostle of principle; but builder of a political society he could not be, because his character and his experience made him, in actual practice, exclusive and sectarian. The chasms in the new France were not to be bridged by Robespierre but by a man with no open party commitments, sufficiently cool toward Revolutionary ideals to compromise with conflicting interests, arriving as it were from another planet—Bonaparte returning from Egypt.

CHAPTER XIV

The Rush upon Europe

THERE is a curious story about Mme. de Montgerout, the most famous woman pianist of the eighteenth century. She had been arrested, but having influential friends she was brought before the Committee of Public Safety for questioning. The Committee was dubious of her, until one of its members pointed to a piano in the corner of the room and asked her to play the "Marseillaise." She complied gladly, eager to prove both her republicanism and her talent, elaborating and enriching the theme with variations of her own. Her examiners were so impressed that they finally began to sing. Mme. de Montgerout, also singing, pounded the keys with added vigor. Clerks and secretaries rushed into the green room, stood amazed, and joined the chorus. Soon hundreds of voices could be heard from all parts of the Tuileries, in the halls, through the windows, from back rooms and attic offices, raised in the marching song of the Revolution.

> Aux armes, citoyens!
> Formez vos bataillons!
> Marchons. . . .

When the commotion subsided Mme. de Montgerout received her freedom, and the excited bureaucrats went back to work. The moment was revealing. It showed how at the very center of government routine labor was stirred by a tremendous faith.

The French Revolution, because it embodied a social faith, was, like the German revolution of the twentieth century, a menace to the constituted order of Europe. It threatened everything held dear by beneficiaries of the old order, the familiar balance of power in Europe, the respect paid to monarchy and aristocracy, the privileges of class, church, town and province, the deferential obedience of inferiors to their betters. The Committee of Public Safety in its last Hundred Days opened those onslaughts upon the old Europe which ended only with another Hundred Days, at Waterloo.

The old order yielded in 1794 to the power and fanatic determination emanating from the Tuileries. But it crumbled also from
its own weakness. The old society, faced with a crisis, could not,
or would not, put up enough defense. To understand the triumph
of the Committee it is necessary to see the conditions in Europe
which made that triumph what it was. And the condition of
Europe in 1793-1794 was disturbingly similar to the condition of
Europe in 1938-1940.

There was a general belief that the normal state of affairs ought
to be reestablished in France—in this case monarchy. There was a
general feeling that law and civilization must be saved from
brutality and violence. But the European governments, beneath
all their protestations, had no real sense of running a danger in
common. They would not rally their utmost forces, or even realize
the vastness of the upheaval before them. A French émigré in
October 1793 (it might have been a German refugee in 1938)
denounced the ineptitude of European statesmen—"the same lack
of foresight for the future, the same refusal to believe in dangers
however near, the same aversion for bold measures, the same hope
for a change for the better, which yet has always brought a worse
state than the preceding." The Swiss conservative Mallet du Pan
demanded a Committee of Public Safety for the whole continent,
equipped with full powers to annihilate the common peril. Others
made the same proposal. Nothing was done; no international
force existed except the coalition, the old-fashioned diplomatic
alliance against France.

Unity of feeling had not yet disappeared from Europe, but in
the exercise of power the strongest forces were those of division.
To preserve monarchy meant preserving the old rivalries of the
dynasties. To preserve civilization, as previously known, was to
preserve old and rooted conflicts, and frequently meant practising
the old barbarities according to the old rules. Every European
government would prefer, other things being equal, to see the
Revolution crushed in France, but none wished another government than itself to emerge stronger from the process.

The states in the coalition remained preoccupied with their own
affairs. Each put down within its own borders everything thought
to resemble Jacobinism. Domestic reforms came to an end, lest
radicals be encouraged. Governments refused to imitate the Re-

public by raising their own peoples in a Levy in Mass, though the suggestion was heard; they feared to arm the opposition against themselves. None but the British could make a national appeal to its people. To minimize the true meaning of the Revolution they exaggerated the figure of Robespierre, portraying him as a superman, a dictator who swayed the world by his individual desire. Little was said of deeper causes for the unprecedented convulsion in which Europe found itself. "Fear," as Albert Sorel puts it, "overshadowed intelligence."

Each power, having its own ambitions, saw in the disorders in France as much an opportunity as a menace. The British as always wanted colonies and command of the sea, in both of which France had long been the only significant rival. Russians, Prussians and Austrians were more interested in eastern than in western Europe, and the courts of Berlin and Vienna played against each other for influence in Germany. The Dutch were more vitally concerned with keeping the French out of Belgium, but fearful also of letting others in—except the Austrians, the actual owners, who were harmless to Holland because their real attention was further east. Spain and Sardinia, though dreading French aggression, hoped mainly to gain something by being on the winning side.

Russia remained apart from the coalition, technically at peace, annexing a large part of Poland while the German powers were engaged in the West, shutting Austria out of the Second Partition, yielding a fragment to Prussia to assure the deal. In March 1794 Kosciuzko made his last stand for Polish independence. The cause was hopeless; Poland was not a nation, but a split society where the rebels could not call upon their own population, which was in a state of serfdom. The French Republic, with much practical wisdom, declined to aid so unpromising a rebellion, and the three eastern powers made plans for the Third Partition, each eager to put down the revolt, and each afraid to let either of the others take the lead. Prussia therefore refused to expend its forces against France, and in Vienna the reinforcements destined for Belgium were transferred to Galicia. In 1794, as in 1793, the agony of Poland added to the strength of France.

Each ally suspected the others of intriguing for a separate peace, not without reason, for dissatisfaction with the war existed in every country. Interested parties, often French émigrés, fought

against the psychology of appeasement, filling Europe with wild
rumors and imagined terrors. A supposed speech of Saint-Just to
the Committee of Public Safety was printed in several languages;
it was probably concocted by a French royalist, and revealed,
ostensibly, that the Committee was spending millions to promote
treason throughout Europe. The truth is that the gold exported
from France went mostly to buy food and raw materials. From
its envoy in Basel the Venetian government heard alarming news.
A Venetian spy, it seems, had dinner with Robespierre and
Couthon, who told him that France needed the wealth of Italy,
that the Republic would attack the Austrian possessions in Lom-
bardy to speed its victory in Belgium, that the French would not
openly violate Venetian neutrality but would stir up trouble as
a pretext for intervention. The Committee, so the report runs,
was relying not on force of arms but on money and espionage,
and on the attractiveness of Revolutionary principles for the
Italian people. Why Robespierre and Couthon should describe a
fifth column so frankly is not clear. It is possible that the Venetian
envoy at Basel invented the whole story, for he wished to be
transferred to Paris, and may have chosen this means to prove
his knowledge of French affairs. The Venetian government paid
little attention to the alleged revelations.

Opposition to the war persisted. In England some Whigs were
cool to the anti-republican crusade. Fox asked vainly for a plain
statement of war aims, pointing out that to restore the Bourbons
would put France in the condition of 1789, "from which all the
misfortunes are derived that now make war necessary and peace
impossible." Pitt answered that there could be no peace with
fanatics, and Burke stated the purpose of the war simply—"the
complete destruction of the horde of scoundrels who brought the
struggle on." In Prussia some of the king's advisers proposed
an understanding with France, digestion of Poland, and "protection" of the north German states in a league of neutrality led by
Prussia. In Spain there were complaints: Spain could fight only
with help from England, which in return demanded free trading
rights in Spanish America, and so virtually the dissolution of the
Spanish Empire. In any case the collapse of France would signify,
for the Spaniards, unchecked control of the Mediterranean by the
British. This danger was apparent also to the Italians in Sardinia,

who were obliged moreover, pending their conquests in France, to cede some of their Lombard territories to Austria. Of all parts of Europe northern Italy was most sympathetic to the Revolution, being full of educated and anti-clerical middle class people. These were inclined to think the Revolution inevitable, and to oppose the alliance with Austria against it. The Austrians themselves had little heart for the war, fighting as they were in Belgium, the least valued of their provinces, alarmed by Prussian designs in north Germany, and mortified by the thought of not getting their share in Poland. When a French adventurer claiming to be a secret agent of the Committee of Public Safety talked with Austrian diplomats and was received by the emperor, rumors flew over Europe that even the Hapsburgs, to whose stock Marie Antoinette belonged, were contemplating peace.

The Allied preparations for the campaign of 1794 were therefore not the most formidable that could be imagined. The English expressed a willingness to pay Prussia a sufficient subsidy to maintain 100,000 men on the western front. The Austrians killed this proposal, fearing to increase the power of their rivals. Their aim was to keep the Prussian army small, and to occupy it with minor diversions; for as an Austrian statesman said, if the Austrians defeated the French with the support of the Prussians, then Berlin would hold a whip over Vienna. The Viennese government therefore not only failed to reinforce Coburg, its commander in Belgium, but opposed also any close cooperation between him and the Prussians. The Berlin government in any case was not disposed to risk its precious army, which in Prussia was a bulwark of the state, in impolitic campaigns in western Europe. Meanwhile everybody depended on the British, Berlin and Vienna both asking London for subsidies in cash, and relying heavily on the British sea power to reduce France to starvation.

Against the fumbling of the coalition the Committee of Public Safety acted with decision, profiting from dictatorial advantages which no foreign ruler except Catherine of Russia possessed, and dependent on no allies, for Poland was left to its fate and the negotiations with Turkey came to nothing. The labors of the fall and winter brought their fruit in the spring. The national army, 800,000 strong, was ready to act. The recruits from the Levy in Mass were trained, and were being gradually fused with the older

men, through the brigading of two battalions of conscripts with
one of the old army. Suspects and incompetents had been weeded
out of the officers' corps; the old clashes between plebeian and
aristocratic officers, like the old misunderstandings between conscripts and professional soldiers, were disappearing. The troops
were armed, for in nothing had the Committee been more successful than in producing munitions. A navy existed, and plans were
made to increase it. Where Parliament in February voted to raise
the British fleet to 80 ships of the line and 100 frigates, the Committee of Public Safety, in May, resolved to build up to 100 ships
of the line and 160 frigates. It is understandable that the French
naval plans were not carried into effect as well as the British,
since the British were supporting a land army of only 60,000, at
least under their own flag.

One gathers from the reports of the representatives on mission
that the French forces were as well fed as in the preceding autumn.
Lindet and the Subsistence Commission had at least warded off
actual starvation. But provisions were still scanty and uncertain.
Not even the Decemvirs could make crops ripen in the winter. No
large break in the British blockade had occurred.

A government little loved by its own people, struggling against
famine, possessing the strongest army in the world, surrounded
by wealthy and disorganized enemies who had tried to invade
and partition the country in its moment of weakness, was a government peculiarly liable to the temptations of plunder and revenge.
The Committee, to win over the mass of Frenchmen to the new
order, had to relieve them of the heavy burden of supporting its
armies. To show the average man that the Terror produced results,
it was necessary to win victories in the field. But with victories
won, and the armies living on foreign resources, Frenchmen would
demand a stop to the Terror and to the Revolutionary Government,
which according to Robespierre were the sole means by which constitutional democracy could be founded. The Robespierrists were
aware of the paradox, and their foreign policy was therefore ambiguous. They claimed not to want conquests, but they meant to
occupy foreign soil. They needed military successes, but Saint-Just
warned Barère against glorifying French victories in his speeches.
They wanted early triumphs, but not an early peace.

The idea of invading England persisted. Prieur of the Marne was mentioned as representative of the French people among the English. Young Julien, a lad of high-school age, hoped to continue in England his travels as political inspector. Billaud-Varenne, when at Saint-Malo, received instructions to make the Isle of Wight his next objective after the Channel Islands. But nothing was accomplished; the French fleet was needed elsewhere, the British overawed the Norman coast, and the Republic, like Napoleon eleven years later, had to defeat its Continental enemies before assaulting the modern Carthage.

Adjacent Continental territories, in the official view, were to be not annexed but exploited, stripped of portable wealth and left useless as bases of attack on France. On May 13 the Committee created four "evacuation agencies" over the sole signature of Robert Lindet. These bodies, operating with the armies, carried out the policy of plunder adopted in the preceding September. Rapine upon civilians was of course not a new form of barbarity— the Majesty of Austria, foreseeing defeat in Belgium, ordered his generals to levy forced loans before retreating and to leave nothing valuable for the French. But the methods of the French were far more thorough. The Revolution, which modernized so much else, modernized also the technique of exploitation.

From all fronts, in April and May, encouraging bulletins reached the green room. Civil disturbances in the West were subsiding; the commanding general was turning to clemency, and no longer using cannon against the brigands. From the North came word: "We have found vast resources in and around Courtrai"—Courtrai being in Belgium. From the Army of the Moselle: "We are finding hay and forage." From the North again: "Do not be alarmed." From the Rhine: "You may be reassured." From the Eastern Pyrenees news arrived in May that the Spanish army was destroyed and the French streaming into Catalonia, where the people seemed ripe for revolution, and where the victors captured enough munitions to supply all the armies in that part of the south.

The Army of Italy presented more of a problem. It entered the territory of the king of Sardinia in April, forty thousand people fleeing before it, according to the younger Robespierre, who complained that the villagers thought the French would eat their babies and desecrate their religion. Not much booty was obtainable in these highland regions. The Army of Italy was not very well fed. It was heavily in debt to the Republic of Genoa, the small neighboring neutral state through which it imported much of its food. The Genoese in May were raising difficulties over credit. Genoa had long been belabored by the British. Now, with the rest of northern Italy, it ran afoul of France.

Ever since November Augustin Robespierre, who was representative on mission with the Army of Italy, had urged the invasion of Genoa as a means both of feeding the army and of coming to grips with Sardinia. The French government found it more useful to keep Genoa neutral as a channel of trade. But the Genoese, squeezed between Sardinia on land and the British at sea, were scarcely their own masters, and by June they were giving so little service to France that the elder Robespierre inclined toward his brother's opinion. He expounded his views in a note to the Committee's secretary for foreign affairs—an insignificant person since the abolition of the ministries, and considering that the Republic had virtually no diplomatic affairs to attend to. The Genoese, said Robespierre, must be intimidated. If the Committee is firm, then Genoa "will not persecute the friends of humanity and will find itself committed to maintaining the rights of man." Augustin Robespierre was directed to lay plans with his young friend General Bonaparte. The general drew up a scheme for invading Italy, which was brought to Paris by Augustin. The Committee summoned the Genoese envoy and berated him for hours. But it took no action.

The Committee of Public Safety did not in fact carry the war into Italy beyond Sardinia. Nevertheless the conditions for an Italian campaign were maturing. The very general who in two years was to become famous by conquering Italy had already submitted his plans. Let the hand of civilian government be relaxed, the prestige of the army increase, the war with the Hapsburgs be prolonged, the distress of the Army of Italy become more urgent—and General Bonaparte, with a horde of Republicans, would descend into the Lombard plain.

But in the spring of 1794 the eyes of the Committee were directed mainly to two spots, one at sea and one on land, both vital in political and economic strategy, and both watched over by a member of the Committee on mission, Saint-Just with the northern armies, Jeanbon Saint-André with the Atlantic fleet.

All other naval operations yielded before the need of protecting the great convoy from America. For almost a year vessels had been gathering in the Chesapeake. There were more than a hundred of them, loaded with the produce of the United States and the West Indies. Agents of the Committee had spent millions of livres in gold in the United States, storing their purchases in the waiting ships. The Subsistence Commission counted on these supplies. Should the food-bearing argosy, as Barère called it, fall into the hands of the British, the resulting bread riots in France might endanger the government.

Van Stabel, one of Saint-André's new rear-admirals, had sailed for America with four warships in midwinter. He was expected to appear off the French coast with his long train of merchantmen about the end of May. The British were on the alert; the usual squadrons patrolled the Bay of Biscay, and Lord Howe ranged at large with the main British fleet. The French force at Brest, hastily refurbished in the past seven months, was not ready for a major action. Yet it had to go out. The blockade had to be broken.

On May 16 Prieur of the Marne, the most betravelled of the Twelve, arrived in Brest after many conflicting orders, for the Committee had hopes of using his services in Paris. He was to rule the shipyards while Saint-André was at sea. He reached Brest barely in time. After weeks of contrary winds the day of May 16 was fair, ending in a grand sunset, toward which, at 6:00 p.m., the fleet began to move, twenty-five ships of the line led by the 120-gun *Mountain,* one of the most powerful war machines afloat. All Brest watched the departure with profound emotion. To make it possible the whole city had worked day and night since the mutiny in Quiberon Bay. Every resource of the Revolutionary Government, all the enthusiasm of the Republican faith, were built into the reconstituted navy, now exposed to the seasoned seamanship of the British, who cruised watchfully somewhere off Ushant. Prieur remained with his colleague until the last moment, sailing with the flagship to the mouth of the harbor, where he took leave with fervid embraces and heartfelt good wishes, hurrying back to town to send word to the Tuileries that the fleet had sailed.

The orders for the expedition were explicit. Protecting the convoy was laid down as the "sole rule of action." The admiral, Villaret-Joyeuse, was to avoid battle unless he positively knew the convoy to be in danger. For, as the Committee wrote to Saint-André, the fleet must be kept intact for the invasion of England.

But on reaching the high seas Saint-André and Villaret entered the world of guesswork and accident in which all mariners before the days of wireless had to act. They hoped to join Van Stabel five hundred miles west of Brest, but they had no news from him, and he had in fact not received the message fixing the meeting place. All parties, Villaret, Van Stabel, Howe, the minor British squadrons and two small French flotillas that were to unite with Villaret, operated in varying degrees of ignorance of one another's whereabouts. Villaret presently fell in with some vessels that had once sighted the convoy, but its present and future course could still only be conjectured.

None of the French captains was schooled to command a ship in naval formation. All were by past experience either under-officers in the old royal navy, or captains in the merchant marine, as Saint-André himself had once been. They practised maneuvers as they went. Saint-André, who kept a journal of the expedition in which as a member of the government he noted the performance of the officers, found little to reassure him. The maneuvers were clumsy, the signals were not always understood, the ships drifted apart in night and fog, and the frigate commanders, having more zeal than discipline, chased isolated merchantmen instead of co-operating with the admiral. The captains discovered miscellaneous weaknesses and damages in their equipment, and some of the masts proved to be unsound even without unusual strain. The haste of the past few months revealed itself in unreliable construction.

The morning of May 28 disclosed the long line of Howe's fleet in the distance. Following orders, Villaret and Saint-André tried to withdraw. Howe moved up to force a battle; he could not establish full contact, but succeeded in cutting off the rear ship in the French line. The trapped vessel fought till its chief officers were dead, and was then let go by the British, to be picked up by a French captain who was shocked at the anarchy in which he found its crew. The survivors, when back in France, as might be expected, denounced Saint-André for incompetence and bad faith.

At dawn on the 29th the French lookouts again sighted their stubborn pursuers, this time only two or three miles away. The two fleets, after groping through the night, found themselves running parallel in the same direction. They veered toward each other in sporadic but destructive combat. Again the encounter was inconclusive. The French losses were greater, but were made up in a few hours by the arrival of one of the expected flotillas.

Villaret and Saint-André, who fortunately were in perfect agreement throughout the expedition, set their course to the north-westward, hoping to draw Howe after them in a vague belief that Van Stabel would then pass to the south. Howe followed, and two days later, on the afternoon of May 31, the two admirals prepared for battle. There is some doubt whether the French had no choice but to fight. The tactics of evasion put a strain on Republican nerves. The officers craved action, the men were enthusiastic, all wanted glory; they loathed the British, their historic enemy, now the enemy of the Revolution; they were eager to fire their new guns, to smash the aristocrats who coldly planned the starvation of the French people.

The battle which followed, known to the British as the Glorious First of June, was a contest between experience and enthusiasm, since the physical forces were equal. Both fleets were poor in lighter craft; the French had twenty-six capital ships, the British twenty-five, though the French thought they had thirty. Naval warfare was then more technical than warfare on land, and French impulsiveness was less successful against Howe than against Coburg.

The British, after introductory broadsides, pierced the French line in six places. This meant that certain French ships were virtually surrounded, while others found temporarily little to shoot at. The struggle broke up into simultaneous dogfights with vessels of each side intermixed. Responsibility fell upon the individual captains, for signals could not be read in the smoke, nor voices heard in the uninterrupted and unorganized blasts of guns. The French captains, all new at their posts, were far outmatched by the British captains in initiative and resourcefulness. The crews were emotionally unstable and overwrought, passing from exaltation to panic, in contrast to the phlegmatic steadiness of their opponents. The French gunners lost their heads, fired with wild abandon, hardly took aim, wasted their ammunition. Of the twenty-six French captains, according to a by no means hostile critic, only eleven came creditably through the ordeal. They were chiefly the men trained in the old navy, rather than the civilians from the merchant marine.

Villaret's flagship, the *Mountain,* with Saint-André aboard, was attacked by five and six of the enemy at a time, including Howe's flagship the *Queen Charlotte.* Built in the last years before the Revolution and now engaged in its first battle, the *Mountain* put up a terrific resistance with its hundred and twenty guns. The British could not disable it, though three hundred of the crew and thirteen of the eighteen officers were killed or wounded. The captain, Basire, had both legs blown off. Saint-André received a slight bruise on the hand as he tried to hail the neighboring *Jacobin,* the act in which Basire had just fallen. There were cases of exceptional gallantry: an ensign intoned the "Carmagnole" while his leg was amputated, and two sailors repairing a mast shouted the "Marseillaise" as the boat rocked with broadsides and shot poured through the air like rain. Basire is recorded to have said: "Assure the Representative of the People that in dying I send best wishes for the Republic."

The firing gradually ceased on the afternoon of June 1. Both fleets were out of line and in confusion, with dismasted hulks from both sides floating helplessly to leeward. Villaret, it appears, ordered the dismasted French ships to be taken in tow, but failing to get his orders enforced abandoned them, more or less voluntarily, and left the field. Howe then stepped in and collected the booty. One of the dismasted French vessels, the *Vengeur du Peuple,* sank as the British approached it. The British were unable to rescue all its crew, some of whom were therefore drowned, crying "Vive la République." London newspapers reported that the *Vengeur* refused to surrender and went down fighting to the end. The Committee of Public Safety, finding this heroic narrative in the English papers and inclined to believe it because it came from the enemy, instructed Barère to glorify the *Vengeur* before the Convention. Thus arose a famous story in French patriotic annals, and one for which Barère has been called a liar.

JEANBON SAINT-ANDRÉ

The French fleet staggered into Brest on June 11. Prieur came aboard at five in the morning, with the distressing news that Van Stabel was still at sea. It seemed that in addition to the loss of the battle the whole purpose of the expedition might miscarry. So the two representatives, rallying from their disappointment, forbade the crews to leave the ships and prepared immediately for another voyage. Fortunately Van Stabel was sighted the very next day, and on June 13 the convoy filed unscathed into the roadstead, a hundred and sixteen merchant vessels bringing twenty-four million pounds of flour.

Saint-André always maintained that though the battle was lost the campaign was won, because the safety of the convoy had been its only purpose. Van Stabel reported having passed over the very spot on which the two fleets met on May 29. The strategy of drawing the British to the northwest of this spot thus proved wise. Moreover the British fleet, though it won the battle and the booty, was so shattered that Howe returned directly to Plymouth. Only the smaller squadron patrolling the French coast remained for the convoy to fear. That squadron was large enough to deal with Van Stabel's few warships. It was by pure chance that the convoy missed it. The French expedition was successful in removing the main British fleet, but even so without luck the convoy would not have landed. As for the British, their Glorious First of June was not all profit. Their fleet was under repair, and the six captured hulks brought almost nothing when sold for junk. The real prize was the twenty-four million pounds of flour, lodged safely now in France.

The Committee of Public Safety was not altogether pleased on hearing of the battle. In the original of its dispatch to Saint-André there is a significant erasure: a phrase congratulating him on his judgment is replaced by a word of congratulation on his courage. The Committee was not convinced that the engagement had been unavoidable, or instrumental to Van Stabel's safety. It clung to its notion that the use of red-hot shot would have destroyed the British fleet. Saint-André had consistently opposed this idea. But there was no open breach between Saint-André and the Committee. In public the Committee emphasized the advantages to be credited to the battle, Van Stabel's safe arrival, the exposure of bad officers, the training of personnel, the whipping up of hatred for the English. The battle, said Barère in the Convention, was but the first incident in a prolonged struggle against Carthage.

In Brest the first jubilation at the arrival of the convoy soon turned to bitterness and suspicion. The officers whom Saint-André had found wanting became his political enemies. The local population was aggrieved at the crippling of its beloved warships and the seizure of six of them by the English. Despite Howe's temporary embarrassment the British still had control of the sea, for which uninformed enthusiasts blamed Saint-André. Never able to please the extremists, Saint-André left for Paris on June 23 or 24, as he had done once before in January, fleeing a scene of ingratitude and denunciation. So the ablest man in Brest made his departure, which turned out this time to be lasting. Prieur stayed on, governing the unruly town as best he could.

On the Belgian frontier, at this same time, events unfolded toward their climax.

The months after Wattignies had seen no important shifts of position except in Alsace, from which the French entered German territory in December. Saint-Just made a rapid tour of the Army of the North at the end of January, surveying, as he had in Alsace, the state of discipline, drill, personnel and supply. Pichegru, at that time the favorite general of the Committee of Public Safety, was transferred from the Rhine to the North, where he replaced Jourdan as commander. Jourdan attended absently to his dry-goods shop in Limoges, lost in memories and anticipations, until in the middle of March the hoped for letter came, appointing him to lead the Army of the Moselle. Jourdan assumed his new duties on March 19.

The Committee of Public Safety, mapping out the campaign of 1794, planned to deliver the main blow in Belgium. Knowing that the Prussians in the Rhineland had no zest for the war, and feeling free to leave the Rhine army weak, Carnot directed northward the swelling streams of conscripts and munitions. Coburg still occupied not only most of Belgium but the French towns of Condé, Valenciennes and Le Quesnoy. Francis II, Holy Roman Emperor, King of Hungary and Bohemia, Archduke of Austria, held court in May on the territory of the Republic, at Valenciennes.

Carnot's strategy aimed at invading Belgium from three directions. The left wing of the Army of the North, under Pichegru, was to take Ypres and move in from the west. A mixed force, composed of the right wing of the North and the whole small Army of the Ardennes, was to operate along the river Sambre. Jourdan with the Army of the Moselle was to enter Belgium from the south, strike at Namur and Liége, and by overrunning eastern Belgium threaten Coburg's communications with Germany. Since Namur is on the Sambre where it joins the Meuse, Jourdan was in a position to cooperate closely with the mixed force in the French center.

On neither side were operations under the control of a single commander or a central general staff. The Allies continued to wrangle and suspect each other. The Committee of Public Safety still feared to make one military man too strong. To impose unity on the generals and diplomats of the coalition was the purpose of the emperor's visit to Belgium. Saint-Just was sent north by the Committee on April 29 for somewhat the same reason. Carnot continued to coordinate the French armies from Paris; but in the field it was Saint-Just, more than anyone else, who thought of the various generals as a unit.

The mission of the emperor, who was even younger than Saint-Just, failed completely. He had indeed an impossible task. His advisers were divided. The most influential favored concentration in Poland. A great plan for defeating the French was drawn up by Mack, the same Mack who eleven years later surrendered an entire army at Ulm, but whose reputation as a master strategist was still unshaken. He could not get his plan adopted; the Prussians would not cooperate, nor would the Austrian government accept their cooperation. Mack resigned on May 23, expressing his opinion that the reconquest of Belgium was hopeless. On the next day at a council of war the Austrian generals voted that further efforts in the Low Countries were useless. The new Prussian commander, Möllendorf, was known to belong to the peace party. The British implored action and offered money, but they had only a handful of troops on the Continent and were therefore little regarded. Coburg and the duke of York denounced and mistrusted each other. The duke accused the Austrians of leaving the small British force to French mercies, and of course no one believed that the duke, or the British envoys who urged others to fight, pursued any interests except those of England. In these circumstances the emperor returned to Vienna on June 13, leaving verbal instructions, as we have seen, which made provision for, without ordering, the evacuation of Belgium.

But the Allies, however divided, would not have succumbed to defeatism if the French had not proved unexpectedly powerful. Those historians, like Von Sybel, who attribute the French success of 1794 entirely to the faults of the Allies only vent their prejudices against the Revolution. The government of the Year Two could count on something besides the incompetence of its enemies.

Saint-Just, accompanied by Le Bas, stationed himself with the mixed central army on the Sambre. The army spent its time in pointless, or at least fruitless, crossings and recrossings of the river, for which Saint-Just was undoubtedly largely responsible, since after every repulse he insisted on an immediate counterattack. The deadlock on the Sambre was broken by a decision of the Committee on June 8. It was the day of the Feast of the Supreme Being, a day on which the Committee did little business. But Carnot was as usual at his office, where he signed an order instructing Jourdan to unite, under his own command, the main body of the Army of the Moselle with the force made up of the Ardennes and the right wing of the North. Thus was created the famous Army of the Sambre-Meuse, though it did not yet receive that name. It was to be nominally dependent on Pichegru, who received a general supervision over all the armies from the Meuse to the sea.

The English authority Phipps, a retired colonel who spent his life exploring these subjects, declares that the Army of the Sambre-Meuse came into being by chance, without foresight or intention. Colonel Phipps, however, wrote to teach a simple message, that the intelligence in the Revolution lay with the army men, and that the civilians were mere revolutionists and bunglers. There is strong reason to believe that the new army was conceived of by Saint-Just, whom Colonel Phipps particularly detested.

Saint-Just, while on the Sambre at the end of May, wrote to Jourdan almost daily. He demanded, in dispatches to the Committee, that Jourdan be ordered to integrate his movements with those of the central army. On May 31 Saint-Just was back in Paris, urgently summoned by Robespierre, who said that the factions again threatened to rise. Robespierre's reasons for wanting Saint-Just in Paris prove nothing about what Saint-Just did or said when he got there. On June 6 the Committee again sent Saint-

Just to the front, this time commissioned to all the armies from the sea to the Rhine. He left on June 6 or shortly after, joining Jourdan. On June 8 Carnot's order created the Army of the Sambre-Meuse. From the evidence it seems safe to imagine a conference in the green room, at which Saint-Just advised the concentration of authority, with himself as general representative on mission, Pichegru generalissimo, and Jourdan in command of all French forces in the center.

Jourdan's new army, 90,000 strong, again passed the Sambre and was again driven back. On June 18 it crossed again, the seventh time for some contingents, and the last. The siege of Charleroi, often interrupted, was resumed. On that day Ypres fell to Pichegru. From Richard, representative with the Army of the North, the Committee heard encouraging news: how the emperor declared his helplessness publicly, how he called upon his peoples for aid, how his peoples would not listen, how the enemy, torn by dissension, was amazed at the unity of the Republic.

Saint-Just exulted, supremely confident, sensing that the Republic was about to fall irresistibly on the old Europe. "Europe is decadent," he wrote to the Committee, "and it is we who are going to flourish!" Jourdan called upon Charleroi to surrender. The garrison, not knowing that Coburg was at last marching to relieve it, sent out an officer to discuss terms. He presented conditions in writing. Saint-Just was icy.

"What I want is not paper but the town."

"But if the garrison surrenders at discretion it will dishonor itself."

The answer combined aloofness with a sneer.

"We can neither honor you nor dishonor you, just as you have not the power to honor or dishonor the French Nation. There is nothing in common between you and us."

The baffled envoy returned to his superiors, who at once surrendered unconditionally. Having won his point, Saint-Just allowed terms to be made, by which the garrison received the courtesies of such occasions. His relenting did not express official policy. Carnot, at this same time, informed Richard that the Committee disapproved of the terms of surrender at Ypres. Some of the articles of capitulation, said Carnot, "show a certain esteem and condescension for enemies toward whom we must proclaim hatred and contempt, unless we wish the French soldier to turn soft and to take pity on the fate of hypocritical and bloodthirsty enemies of our liberty." The Committee regretted that some French generals treated captured officers with consideration. The incident shows, with glaring concreteness, how professional warfare changed into the modern warfare of national hatred.

Scarcely had Charleroi opened its gates when Coburg arrived with the main force of the Austrians—if Austrians they may be called, for the irrelevance of nationality was shown in the names of the generals: Quasdanowich, Alvinzi, Latour, Beaulieu, the princes of Orange and of Kaunitz, Zopf, Schmertzing and the archduke Karl. It appears that Coburg asked the British to join him, but that they preferred to remain in west Flanders. Coburg, having Pichegru to watch, could bring only 52,000 men against Jourdan, who produced a somewhat superior number against him. Firing began before dawn on June 26 near the village of Fleurus, and continued for sixteen hours until seven in the evening. By that time Coburg's divisions were in full retreat. They straggled northward, their second encampment being twenty miles from Fleurus, near Waterloo. The French waited several days before following, too broken themselves for immediate pursuit. Saint-Just seized a coach as soon as victory was apparent, and rode toward Paris during the night of June 26.

One feature of the battle, minor at the time, is of enough interest to the twentieth century to justify a slight digression. The Army of the Sambre-Meuse was the first in history to be served by an air corps. It was a small and primitive air corps to be sure. But the matter is of more than antiquarian importance, for it shows the eagerness of the Committee to apply the latest scientific discoveries to the art of war.

The brothers Montgolfier, paper manufacturers by trade, built the first successful balloon in 1783, by introducing heated air into a large bag made of tough paper. Hydrogen was substituted for air, and cloth for paper, within a few months. By 1785 several persons in Europe had reached altitudes of ten thousand feet, and in that year two hardy aeronauts crossed the Straits of Dover after an incredibly hazardous voyage. The great difficulty was that the new machines could be neither propelled nor steered. The problem of locomotion was attacked by many, among them Carnot, then an engineer in the old army.

Carnot presented his ideas in a memorial to the Academy of Sciences in 1784. Dismissing the various projects for oars, wings and sails, he proposed that balloons be equipped with paddle-wheels, an idea not wholly fantastic in view of the side-wheel steamer which came in later, and which in fact had already been demonstrated by a Frenchman, to no effect, in the Saône. Carnot suggested the newly invented steam engine as a source of power for air navigation in the future. He predicted that the steam engine would soon bring revolutionary changes, as it did. Meanwhile, in 1784, he asked whether the force of human muscle, mechanically amplified, might not turn the wheels to move an airship.

Ten years later Carnot was still interested in aviation. So were Prieur of the Côte-d'Or, who had also been an engineer in the old army, and the scientific men who worked with the Committee. There was much discussion of the uses of balloons in war. A private citizen submitted a plan for "bringing death and destruction from the air." The Committee appropriated several thousand livres for experiments, which went on in great mystery at Meudon, the proving ground of the Committee's secret weapons, where the tests were also made of the redhot shot that was to destroy the British fleet.

Prieur, in charge of matters of armament, concluded that the aeronautical experiments were successful, to the extent at least that balloons could be adopted for taking observations. The Committee created a small company of "aerostatiers" (balloons being called aerostats), headed by a captain and composed of twenty-eight men. The men were chosen from technicians of the kind then available, locksmiths, carpenters, masons, chemists' assistants. They were sent to Meudon for special training. In May 1794 the Committee dispatched a specially constructed balloon with the attendant force to the front, together with orders that they should be used. The orders were not superfluous, because some of the military men objected to employing so unfamiliar a contrivance.

At Fleurus, therefore, both armies saw an "aerostatic globe," a hundred feet in circumference, hovering five hundred feet above the ground, to which it was held captive by a long rope. Captain Coutelle, head of the "air force," remained aloft for nine hours during the battle. A number of generals went up for shorter periods. Soldiers on the ground moved the balloon according to signals by tugging on the rope, along which bulletins were sent down by the observers, who viewed operations through their telescopes.

Precisely what contribution this ancestor of modern aircraft made to the victory at Fleurus is unfortunately doubtful. The French troops were encouraged by the sight, which to them was a new proof of the enlightenment of the age. In the motley and superstitious ranks of the Austrians many were alarmed, fearing a new invention of Jacobin devils. From the chief engineer of the French army we hear that the balloon gave valuable information. The representative Guyton de Morveau, who was present, reported enthusiastically to the Committee and began to organize another company of aerostatiers on the following day. Military conservatives were of course not convinced. A young lieutenant-colonel named Soult, later one of Napoleon's marshals, looked on with disdain, if we may believe the recollections that he wrote in his old age. In the wisdom of years Soult thought the whole episode ridiculous, declared that no one at Fleurus paid any attention to the aerial proceedings, and affirmed, most improbably, that the officers in the balloon were too high up to see anything distinctly. "The sole causes of our victory," says the marshal, "were the valor of our troops, the wise arrangements of the commander during the battle, and the unshakable firmness of the other generals."

Soult's notion that victory in the Year Two was won entirely by martial virtue need not detain us, but it is probably true that the famous balloon contributed little in proportion to the effort expended. The best reason for believing so is that the enemy never imitated the new French weapon. Two years later the Austrians captured the balloon that served at Fleurus. They put it in a museum. In 1812 the Russians considered using balloons, not for observation, but to carry sharpshooters to pick off enemy officers. Nothing came of the idea. The fact is that balloons were so unwieldy, so cumbersome to transport in an army that marched mostly on foot, so difficult to store, inflate and attend to, that they were not worth the trouble they cost. When Bonaparte came to power, balloons were dropped from the French army. Aeronautics made no significant progress for a century after 1785. The old problem that Carnot had faced was not solved: how to steer or propel the floating bags.

The battle of Fleurus, whether or not influenced by the balloon, was not in itself a spectacular victory, for the losses were about equal. But it was enough to turn the disgust of the Austrians into positive dismay, and it opened Belgium to the Republic. Jourdan moved in from the south, Pichegru from the west. They joined forces in Brussels with 180,000 men early in July. By the next winter the Army of the Sambre-Meuse stood on the Rhine and the Army of the North by the frozen Zuider Zee. In 1795 the British army abandoned the Continent, and Prussia, Holland, Spain and Sardinia withdrew from the war. When a constitutional republic replaced the Revolutionary Government in 1795 the annexation of Belgium was held to be guaranteed by the constitution. Thus the Revolutionaries committed themselves to conquest, identified their rule with a new balance of power, and threw themselves into the hands of a soldier dictator with whom the rest of Europe could not live at peace.

These developments came about after the fall of the Committee of Public Safety. In the month between Fleurus and Thermidor the Committee explicitly and repeatedly disavowed intentions of conquest or annexation. This fact (and fact it is) has enabled some historians to free the Committee from responsibility for the aggression which helped to perpetuate the war. The fall of Robespierre appears to these historians as a great public calamity which destroyed the last hope of peace. The historians concerned are a powerful family in the lineage of learning—Buchez, Hamel, Mathiez. It need not be said that there have always been others of a contrary opinion.

Today, in another age of revolution, and in America, far from the agitation of French politics, it is hard to believe that Robespierrism could bring peace. In any case, after Fleurus, Robespierre had less influence in the Committee than ever, and the Committee was so divided that no one can say what its policy may have become had it remained in power. Nothing is proved by quotation of its anti-annexationist intentions. Intentions do not determine the course of events. Nor do they determine responsibility, which depends rather on consequences so far as they can reasonably be foreseen. French rule in Belgium was a consequence of the actions of the Committee, and was in fact both foreseen and intended. Whether this rule should take the form of annexation is not really the chief question.

A kind of minimum program was laid before the Committee on July 16 by Carnot. Its tenor was defensive; nothing was said of the liberation of foreign peoples, whom Carnot thought unripe for a revolution like that in France. But the frontiers of the Republic were to be carried to Antwerp and to Namur, and French garrisons were to be maintained in southwest Holland at Dutch expense. French influence was to dominate Holland and the Bank of Amsterdam, whose wealth, said Carnot, was the life blood of the coalition but in French hands would make possible the humiliation of England. As for Belgium, Carnot advised "that it be not joined to the territory of the Republic, but made to contribute; that we extract from it whatever we can in both specie and goods; that the people nevertheless be spared, and their ways and customs respected, but that the country be rendered helpless to aid enemy armies; that all fortifications be razed, roads broken up, canals and locks put out of service, horses and wagons taken away, and all crops and objects of consumption removed, except what is rigorously necessary for the inhabitants."

The Committee never acted upon these recommendations, for domestic politics in mid-July were reaching a crisis, but no new decision was needed to introduce spoliation, which spread everywhere with the triumphant armies. To Carnot's practical proposals was added the impulse of revolutionary zeal. Carnot himself, who in private conference took care not to ruin the Bank of Amsterdam, urged the generals and representatives on mission to attack the rich.

The French armies poured over the frontiers crying "War on the castles, peace to the cabins!" The Republican government, consciously and knowingly, meant to conquer by sowing class division. The Committee repeatedly ordered that the burden of spoliation be thrown wholly on the wealthy and the privileged. It instructed its generals to avoid antagonizing the common people, to forbid looting by individual soldiers, to maintain special discipline among the troops on foreign soil, and to respect the Catholic religion. There is no reason to doubt the sincerity of these orders, though we may well wonder how much they were enforced. The rulers of the Republic, for the most part, expected to treat the common man beyond the frontiers much as they treated the common man in France. They believed that an aristocrat was inferior to a republican, but not that a Belgian was incurably inferior to a Frenchman.

But the French occupied the invaded regions for a purpose, whose execution could hardly leave the people undisturbed. Coming in the wake of the Austrians, who supposedly had left nothing valuable behind them, French agents assembled huge stores of hard money, food, forage, clothing, metals, leathers, blankets, horses, cattle and other commodities. Books, paintings and other art objects were carried off. Thousands of loaded wagons rolled into France.

Not meaning to punish the common people, nor believing in robbery, the French authorities paid for such belongings in the same money which they used to pay Frenchmen—assignats. No compensation was paid to nobles, absentees, government bodies and churches from which wealth was taken. The forced circulation of French paper money in Belgium, and the occasional introduction of Maximum price scales, bound together the economic fortunes of the two countries. Sometimes the inhabitants received bills drawn on the Belgian government, to be redeemed, said Carnot, when that government should pass more fully under French control. Many ordinary people, having lost most of their usable property, had therefore no hope of recouping themselves except in a régime dominated by the Republic. The troubles of the common man were not lightened when hostages were taken among local notables, gatherings of more than three persons forbidden, or labor requisitioned to dismantle old fortifications. "I shall be careful," wrote a representative on mission to the Committee, "to exercise the right of seizure established in the interior of the Republic. I shall also take notes on persons in these countries who have distinguished themselves for hatred of the French Revolution, and I shall not fail to have them arrested and arraigned before our revolutionary courts." So the Terror, along with the economic dictatorship, spread in the wake of the armies.

Such was the state of affairs when, on July 27, 1794, Robespierre fell, and the Committee of Public Safety went to pieces.

Could the Committee, in continuing to rule, have abstained from controlling the resources, opinions and foreign policies of the Low Countries and the Rhineland? Would England and Austria have tolerated such control any more willingly than they tolerated annexation? It is not likely. The fall of Robespierre was no blow to the peace of Europe. We cannot distinguish between a defensive Republic before Thermidor and an aggressive Republic after. The shift from a spirit of defense to one of expansion came about gradually, fostered by the successes of the great Committee, which launched the epic but bloody challenge to Europe that lasted twenty years.

But the very success of the Committee undermined it. The retreat of the Allies strengthened the argument of those who thought the Terror could be dispensed with. Others, who had no intention of ending the Terror, felt it safe to bring their quarrels into the open as the military menace receded.

CHAPTER XV

The Fall

READERS will perhaps feel by this time that the end of the eighteenth century was not unlike the middle of the twentieth. The resemblance need not be labored. There was also a significant difference. The real supremacy of the Committee of Public Safety lasted little more than a hundred days. The brevity of this rule has not usually been thought very remarkable, for until recently, believing in a historic tendency toward the free society, we have considered repressive governments to be in the nature of things bound to fail. But there is nowadays a sad relevancy in the question: Why did the Committee of Public Safety, though a highly developed dictatorship, not become established as a permanent régime—permanent as political régimes go, at least in France?

The answer must take account of both general causes and particular events. The events leading to the fall of the Committee were extraordinarily particular, even trivial, a series of personal intrigues culminating in a coup d'état. Robespierre was the victim of a plot, and the Committee collapsed in a kind of palace revolution. This is the Thermidor of history. But probably if these events had not occurred others would soon have led to the same conclusion and another Revolutionary month have given its name to reaction. The general causes would still have made trifles momentous, producing a situation in which the revolutionary dictatorship, conceived in the name of humanity, was at the mercy of half a hundred men.

The position of the Decemvirs was not that of a modern Führer, Duce, or dictator of the proletariat. The Committee could not appeal to personal loyalties, for the Revolution was totally lacking in the fascist principle of leadership; Jacobins agreed on much, but they never agreed on personalities, not even (contrary to general belief) on the personality of Robespierre. A clear theory of dictatorship had been formulated by the Committee, but no member of that body, not even Saint-Just, considered dictatorship a permanent form of government, or desirable in itself. Most of the Committee (certainly Robespierre) honestly saw in the Convention the seat of national authority intermediate between themselves and the people. They did not consider themselves absolute in law, nor were they so in fact, for even after Ventôse they had difficulty in controlling subordinates. The Committee was not popular, having aroused as many grievances as it settled. Robespierrists wanted the dictatorship to last until democracy was secured, but most people considered its usefulness over when the Allies were defeated. The politically effective element was then chiefly the middle class, which had an interest in introducing liberal institutions.

It may be added that the Committee, despite the Grand Terror and the law of 22 Prairial, did not put to death enough of its enemies to establish its rule as a permanent régime. The aims of the Revolutionary Government could be achieved only by a degree of extermination which revolutionists more often talked about than practised. Brought up in the eighteenth century, their minds formed by a rhetorical education, they habitually used an exaggerated manner of speaking; but they were in reality, for the most part, still checked by humane and Christian scruples. The forty thousand who died in the Terror, one-sixth of one per cent of the population (the figure includes those who succumbed in the prisons or who were executed without trial) are perhaps outnumbered by the victims of terrorism in our own time.

In these circumstances the régime of the Committee would probably have soon terminated in any case. How it actually fell is a much less philosophical story.

The story is difficult to reconstruct, for all parties hid their operations in mystery, and the Thermidorians, as the revolutionists who overthrew Robespierre are called, either destroyed or disfigured the evidence for political reasons. An old process was repeated. Revolutionists had abandoned one sinking ship after another. After the Girondists fell, no one could safely admit any past connections with the Girondists; after Danton was executed, no one could openly say that he had befriended Danton. So, after Thermidor, men who had worked with Robespierre and agreed with him vociferously declared, to protect themselves, that they had always been his enemies, that they had secretly opposed his hypocritical projects, or that, in their patriotic innocence, they had been his dupes. Their account of men and events before Thermidor deserves no more belief than what Saint-Just said about Danton, or Jacobin orators about Louis XVI.

The Thermidorian story of the Hundred Days was a simple one: Robespierre, consumed by ambition, and aided by Couthon and Saint-Just, meant to use the purges of Ventôse to make himself a dictator, contrived the religion of the Supreme Being and the law of 22 Prairial to achieve this aim, and was overthrown by a band of patriots, including the others in the Committee of Public Safety, who rose up to defend liberty from a tyrant. This version, being understandable at a glance, received wide credence, and throwing a sinister light on Robespierre, it has often appealed to conservative writers, although there is no reason why the Thermidorians should be more attractive than Maximilien to persons of conservative disposition.

The contrary version, which originated with Robespierre's friends, is more in harmony with what we can know of what really happened. It holds that Robespierre with his supporters, finding that the purges of Ventôse did not purify the Republic, struggled as always to found a moral and democratic state, and that the persons whom he menaced, joined by certain members of the Committee, united against him, so that his fall brought the triumph of selfishness and corruption. Those who think that Robespierre's ideas were capable of realization regard Thermidor as an incalculable tragedy. Others, while considering him impractical as a statesman, think better of him than of the revolutionists who overthrew him, most of whom had no intention of moderating the Terror.

In all versions a few leading facts are plain. The purges of Ventôse brought no peace. Once again it appeared that elimination of dissenters added nothing to unity. The execution of Danton and Hébert removed the visible heads of the factions, but faction itself only became more elusive and dispersed. The Convention was alive with secret animosities, its members terrified by the fate that had struck Danton, those who belonged to the Committee of General Security laying up grievances against the greater committee, those who had been arbitrary or dishonest on missions in the provinces —Fouché, Tallien, Barras, Fréron—fearing investigation of their conduct.

It is clear also that hard feelings within the Committee of Public Safety were increasing. One man who had sat in its counsels was already dead. Collot bore the stigma of Hébertism, Lindet of Dantonism. Saint-Just and Carnot quarreled over army matters. Prieur of the Côte-d'Or, bringing a contractor to the green room one day in April, came upon these two in a raging argument, each talking at the top of his voice, both refusing to back down, Carnot calling Saint-Just and Robespierre absurd dictators. Prieur's companion, surprised and horrified, had to be pledged to silence. The Committee kept its internal hatreds a secret so long as danger existed on the frontiers.

It is likely that increasing specialization within the Committee weakened the old sense of cooperation. In the month of Prairial Carnot, Lindet and Prieur drafted almost nine-tenths of the orders issued in the Committee's name. They had become, respectively, ministers of war, supply and munitions. Barère, Collot and Billaud were active at the green table. They initiated few decrees, but signed many, and they conducted the correspondence. Saint-Just was in the north in Prairial except for a few days. Robespierre and Couthon were present, but doing little in the work of administration. Their signatures are the rarest of all, except Saint-Just's, in the documents of Prairial. As for original authorship, Robespierre wrote only fourteen, and Couthon only eight, of the 608 orders whose authorship can be ascertained. The time had come described by Barère in his memoirs, when he classified the members of the Committee into three groups: the "experts" Carnot, Lindet and Prieur; the "high-hands," Robespierre, Couthon and Saint-Just; and the true "revolutionaries," Billaud, Collot and himself. It would be only human for the experts to think Robespierre and Couthon something between meddlers and idlers, and for the high-hands to believe that the experts understood nothing of politics.

In this atmosphere of irritation two events happened almost simultaneously, the Feast of the Supreme Being on June 8 and the passage of the law of 22 Prairial on June 10. Both brought the disagreements more clearly into the open. In both the initiative was taken by Robespierre and Couthon. Saint-Just showed little interest in either. Though in Paris on June 6, he did not linger for the great celebration. There is evidence to show that he would never have made an issue of the worship of the Supreme Being, and some reason to believe that he disapproved of the law of 22 Prairial.

Robespierre, however, at the festival of June 8, exposed himself to charges of personal ambition, and some members of the Convention, muttering sarcasms and insults during the proceedings, exposed themselves to the anger of Robespierre, to whom nothing was more distasteful than mockery of virtue and religion. The new religious policy seemed dangerously reactionary to the radical anti-Catholics, the rabid Dechristianizers of the past few months. These men were strongly entrenched in the Committee of General Security, most of whose members, huffish toward the greater committee, welcomed an excuse to view its policies with repugnance.

Two days later, on 22 Prairial, Couthon introduced into the Convention, in the name of the Committee of Public Safety, a law reforming the Revolutionary Tribunal. The reform was of course in the revolutionary direction, and it marked the high-tide of the terrorist legislation. Like the worship of the Supreme Being it was conceived as a means of founding the Republic upon virtue.

What was the substance of Couthon's argument? That revolutionary courts were still handicapped by old fashioned ideas. That the function of these courts was to protect society, not the enemies of society. That legal justice should be identical with morality, and morality with the right views in politics. That the good intentions of a court were more valuable than intellectual discernment. That patriots had nothing to fear from patriot judges and jurors, and that non-patriots deserved no consideration; that legal forms were a chicanery invented by lawyers; and that written records and oral testimony, since they might be false, gave no reliable proof. He deplored, as a prejudice of the old régime, the principle that "evidence could not rightfully establish conviction without witnesses or written testimony." By the new law, therefore, trials were reduced to a mere appearance before the court.

Since the value of forms had for some time been at a discount, and the right of defense ineffective, the most novel part of the law was its list of crimes. Even here the novelty was not great, for the same principles had inspired the law of suspects. "Considered enemies of the people" were those who sought to reestablish monarchy, discredited the Convention, betrayed the Republic, communicated with the enemy, interfered with provisioning, sheltered conspirators, spoke ill of patriotism, corrupted officials, misled the people, gave out false news, outraged morality, depraved the public conscience, stole public property, abused public office, or worked against the liberty, unity and security of the state. For all these offenses the sole penalty was death.

After Thermidor the survivors, including Barère and the others of the Committee, professed, and often felt, a profound horror for the law of 22 Prairial. They affirmed that Robespierre and Couthon had concocted it between them, forcing it through the Convention without previous consultation with the Committee. It may be that the members of the Committee had not discussed it as fully as they wished. Most of them were perhaps surprised when Couthon introduced it. The law, however, did not go beyond their views. The Commission of Orange, set up by the Committee on May 10, embodied the same philosophy of justice. Barère and Billaud-Varenne defended the new act in the Convention. Robespierre had always supervised the Committee's police work. So he did now. He could not understand why his motives should be suspected. He was right in believing that the law applied, with some heightening of intensity, familiar principles and familiar methods to a familiar situation.

Providing grounds for the accusation of anybody, and reducing trials to physical presence of the accused in the courtroom, the new law greatly speeded the work of the Revolutionary Tribunal, which condemned more people to death in the seven weeks between 22 Prairial and 9 Thermidor than in the fourteen months preceding. The law was an omnibus on which all Revolutionary parties could ride. Each interest could add its victims to the total. No one interest, certainly not the ruling Committee and not Robespierre, was responsible for the whole holocaust. The prosecutor of the Revolutionary Tribunal, Fouquier-Tinville, was no friend of Robespierre's. His orders came most commonly from the lesser committee, only more occasionally from the greater. In a government fast losing its unity a lethal weapon existed, by which each party could make an end to its rivals, so that disagreement became more than ever an issue of life and death.

Death became a daily phantom. Robespierre, since the Admiral and Renault affairs in May, felt himself surrounded by potential assassins. So did others; it was Collot d'Herbois upon whom Admiral had really fired. Robespierre talked increasingly of his approaching end, of martyrdom, and of the future life. Couthon cannot have cared to live; he was now feeling in his arms the pains that had preceded the paralysis of his legs; he faced the prospect of living petrifaction. Saint-Just had macabre thoughts, which his supreme egotism turned into a challenge. "I despise the dust that forms me and speaks to you," he once said. "This dust you may persecute and kill, but I defy you to rob me of that independent life I have given myself in the ages and in the heavens."

The Convention, haunted also, had strong suspicions, not dispelled by the equivocations of Robespierre, Couthon and Barère, that the law of 22 Prairial was directed against itself. There were certainly a half-dozen deputies, including Fouché and Tallien, whom Robespierre meant to destroy. No one knew, or knows today, exactly who these half-dozen were; no one could then believe, nor can anyone believe today except the most faithful disciples of Mathiez, that these half-dozen would be the last. Every purge had been the "last"; Saint-Just, when indicting the Dantonists, had held forth visions of the serene world of confidence that was to follow.

Intrigue spread madly. Fouché whispered to panic-stricken colleagues that their names were on the list of the proscribed. Men ceased to spend the night at home. We hear that a conspiracy of nine deputies, as early as the end of May, was formed to assassinate Robespierre on the floor of the Convention. The information being post-Thermidorian cannot be readily accepted; after Thermidor it was politically convenient to boast of such patriotic resolutions. It seems, however, that Bourdon of the Oise, who had escaped the wreck of Dantonism but was one day publicly excoriated by Robespierre, resolved to kill him early in July.

The Committee of General Security, annoyed that it had not been consulted on the Prairial law, circulated the idea that the law was the private invention of Robespierre and his toady Couthon. To exhibit Robespierre as a dictator this same committee evolved a deep-laid scheme. Vadier opened the attack, not yet naming Robespierre, on June 15, when he reported on the affair of Catherine Théot, to the great amusement of the Convention.

Catherine Théot was a harmless demented old woman who preached a mysterious religion to a circle of devotees, including the doctrine that she would presently give birth to a divine being. Police spies had been placed in her sittings by the Committee of General Security. They endeavored to draw her into counter-revolutionary language. They wildly exaggerated the number of her initiates. The purpose was to conjure up a new menace of fanaticism; thus Robespierre's program of toleration for Catholics would be discredited; and he himself, perhaps, could be destroyed as an agent of the Foreign Plot. Through a certain Dom Gerle, who was a disciple and a kind of manager for the prophetess, and who had once had casual relations with Robespierre, Vadier and his confederates hoped to implicate the Incorruptible with this party of religious dreamers, expecting to prove, by forged documents or forced testimony, that Robespierre had applied to old Catherine to declare him the son of God. What his enemies said would thus be demonstrated: that in the worship of the Supreme Being Robespierre meant to deify himself.

To such absurd machinations was politics in the Republic now reduced. On such trifles did grave matters depend, not only the position of Robespierre but the standing of Catholics and all Christians, for Vadier, an extreme Voltairian, drew no fine distinctions between the ramblings of Catherine Théot and the theology of Holy Church. The Convention, accepting Vadier's report with enthusiasm, voted the arrest of the "conspirators" who met in the old woman's lodgings.

Robespierre raised objections in the Committee of Public Safety. On June 26 he tried vainly to get a new prosecutor in place of Fouquier-Tinville, who had opened proceedings in the Théot case. A terrific dispute occurred in the green room that night. Robespierre won; the ruling Committee prohibited the trial. Fouquier, on receiving his new orders, went to explain his predicament to the Committee of General Security, where he cried, "He, he, he is opposed!" by which all easily understood Robespierre.

In this clash of the two committees the superior body did not stand united, for Collot d'Herbois and Billaud-Varenne supported the Committee of General Security. Both had been fierce anticlericals for a long time. Both thought Robespierre a faint-heart and a laggard. Collot was alarmed at Robespierre's hostility to Fouché, his associate in the massacres at Lyons. He was fearful of Couthon, who had himself been at Lyons, disliked Collot's conduct there, and had the ear of Robespierre. Carnot would not support Robespierre because Robespierre always backed Saint-Just, with whom Carnot was now habitually on bad terms. Prieur took Carnot's side. Barère, his old love of non-committal courses reasserting itself, hovered uncertainly among the antagonists, explaining, mollifying, covering up, in a desperate attempt at reconciliation.

A few days later, probably on June 29, the day of Saint-Just's return from Fleurus, another fight broke out in the green room. Robespierre and Saint-Just quarreled violently with Billaud and Collot. The latter two branded Robespierre as a dictator; Robespierre shook with rage, and, accompanied by Saint-Just, left the room amid the taunts of the others. What the argument was about is not clear—either the Théot affair or the law of 22 Prairial. In any case, Robespierre thenceforward ceased to attend the meetings of the Committee. His ideas, in the last month before Thermidor, were kept before the others by Saint-Just and Couthon, who also took over the direction of the Police Bureau. The Committee twice tried to get rid of Couthon by sending him on mission, but Couthon refused to go.

The return of Saint-André at this time had no effect on the inner politics of the Committee, for he left almost at once for Toulon, to look after naval construction there. He had lately expressed to Prieur, back in Brest, a fear that the government was becoming too repressive, but it is not clear who he thought was responsible for the increase of Terror, and had he fully comprehended the situation, or believed the Committee to be on the verge of dissolution, he would perhaps have remained in Paris and supported the Robespierrists. The onetime Protestant minister had more in common with Robespierre than with Collot d'Herbois or Billaud-Varenne. It is even possible (but all this is guesswork) that the Committee, in Robespierre's absence, sent him away as they tried to send away Couthon, in order to weaken Robespierre.

The Incorruptible hurt his own case by absenting himself from the Committee. As usual he had no conception of how his conduct appeared to others; he could not see that, in sitting virtuously at home, or making self-righteous speeches at the Jacobin club, he reduced himself, in the eyes of men who continued to bear the burden of office, to the level of the agitators and free-lance orators against whom the Committee had always had to defend itself. He belied his old position. For a year he had claimed only to be, and had drawn his strength from being, the chief political spokesman of the Committee of Public Safety. He now made himself something more, a lone and lofty individual looking down upon the government. His refusal to cooperate probably inclined the neutrals in the Committee, Barère and Lindet, to side against him.

His influence was actually less in this last month than it had been in a long time. But it seemed more sinister because exercised behind the scenes. Those who knew of Saint-Just's nocturnal visits, at which affairs of the Police Bureau were undoubtedly discussed, naturally made the most unfavorable conjectures. A dictator certainly he was not, in the sense of wielding great personal power; he had no further part in the decisions of government, and though he had a friend in the president of the Revolutionary Tribunal, he was less involved than some of his enemies in the last convulsions of the Grand Terror. He saw the law of 22 Prairial applied in a way in which, if an absolute dictator, he would not have used it. To this development he and Couthon, by drafting the law in exceedingly vague terms, had directly contributed; but such vagueness in defining enemies of the people was no peculiarity of theirs.

Some hold that Robespierre wanted to moderate the Terror and was cut down by extremists for that reason. A number of the most informed contemporaries later expressed this opinion, Bonaparte, Cambacérès, Levasseur, even Barras, one of the Thermidorians. Certainly it was less a pleasure for Robespierre to use the guillotine than for some of his enemies. That Robespierre preferred in general a stable, peaceable and humane society cannot be doubted. That he thought himself any closer to it in July than in January there is not the slightest reason to believe. The factions, wrote his confidant Payan on July 10, at the height of the slaughter in Paris, "are profiting from our mildness and generosity. . . . But the time of indulgence will pass." The question, for Robespierre as for others, was not whether, but against whom, the Terror should be enforced. There was no agreement on who the "true conspirators," the "big rascals," the "real enemies of the people" were. Robespierre's idea of moderating the Terror was to apply it against the enemies of virtue, and so to halt those terrorists who applied it for other aims. In this respect, the situation in July was not essentially different from what it had been for the past year.

Conflict in the Committee became irreparable when the two factions took their quarrels outside its walls. The Robespierrists counted on the Jacobin club, where Robespierre won a great triumph by driving out Fouché, and on the Paris Commune, which since the reorganization of Ventôse was full of Robespierrist nominees. The anti-Robespierrists depended on the Committee of General Security and on the restless element in the Convention. Neither group had any significant popular following. The public had no knowledge of the intrigues, only a feeling that some crisis was approaching. The Robespierrist Commune had antagonized the working class in the city. The anti-Robespierrists were too notorious as persecutors of religion to be in popular favor. The common man had no reason to love Robespierre's opponents, and the more obscure or milder deputies in the Convention saw little to choose between Robespierre and Billaud-Varenne.

Barère strove to calm the wounded feelings of his colleagues. Saint-Just complained that his Ventôse policy was not carried out, that four of the six popular commissions authorized in the law of 23 Ventôse had never been set up. Barère persuaded the two committees, sitting jointly on July 22, to create these four commissions, whose function, as with the two already operating, was ostensibly to liberate patriots arrested as suspects, but actually (since only one-eightieth of the suspects examined by the two operating commissions were released) to prepare the cases of suspects for the Revolutionary Tribunal. The laws of Ventôse ordered that the property of condemned suspects be used to indemnify poor patriots. Some therefore see in the creation of the new commissions a concession to Robespierrist demands for reapportionment of property. The significance of the Ventôse program has already been discussed. Saint-Just, as we have seen, had apparently modified his views since Ventôse, believing now that not property, but farms, should be divided. The Robespierrists, when they fell, were not committed to a sweeping program of economic equalization. They were in fact less radical toward both property and religion than Collot, Billaud, or Fouché.

The creation of the new commissions offered a basis for compromise. Robespierre was invited to another joint session of the two committees on July 23, 5 Thermidor. He came, and though he showed little warmth, left his colleagues with the impression that an understanding had been reached. Saint-Just, who seemed more willing to bridge the gap, received an assignment to draw up a report to the Convention, explaining the new harmony within the two governing committees.

But Robespierre was not really won over by the overtures of 5 Thermidor. He had reason to be suspicious. Billaud, Collot and Vadier were not men to inspire trust. They represented the tail-end of Hébertism, being Dechristianizers and extremists, fundamentally opposed to what Robespierre stood for. But Robespierre would not limit or clarify his suspicions, would not distinguish among his opponents, would not see that Barère and Lindet, and probably Carnot and Prieur, not wanting to play the game of their most violent colleagues, might welcome a compromise with him. He chose, therefore, not to work within the Committee, where he might yet have prevailed, but to lay his case before the Convention, dissociate himself from the governing committees, and by that very dissociation to attack them. Telling no one, not even Saint-Just, who would have tried to dissuade him, he spent the next few days composing a long speech, which he delivered on 8 Thermidor.

This address, the last Robespierre ever made, was eloquent, profoundly sincere, predominantly truthful. It painted a black picture of the dissension and intrigue that honeycombed the state. It described the means by which its author was made to seem individually responsible for the worst features of the Terror. It predicted that if the Revolutionary Government should fail a military dictatorship would follow, and France be plunged into a century of political unrest. But the speech was tactically a gigantic blunder. If it expressed Maximilien's best qualities it unloosed all his worst; and it confirmed the most deadly fears of those who heard it.

Robespierre made his appeal supremely personal. Individualizing himself, he sounded like what the eighteenth century conceived a dictator to be. He gave the impression that no one was his friend, that no one could be trusted; that virtue, the people, the fatherland and the Convention, considered abstractly, were on his side, but that he obtained only calumny, persecution and martyrdom from the actual persons with whom he worked. He threatened right and left, indulgents and exaggerated terrorists, as in the past; but when asked point blank to name the men he accused, he evaded the question. The insinuations of Fouché and others thus seemed to be borne out; any man, for all he knew, might be on Robespierre's list. The members of the governing committees, moreover, whom Robespierre somewhat cryptically assaulted, were surprised to hear an outburst contrary to what they had expected. Having thought a compromise was in the making, they were now convinced that no compromise was possible. A few who knew themselves to be aimed at took the lead, and the docile and benumbed Convention, which at first felt a confused sympathy for the speaker, was stampeded against him.

The speech was referred to the two committees for consideration. Robespierre protested: "What! my speech sent to be examined by the members I accuse!" The protest only emphasized his antagonism to the committees. Failing to make good his remonstrances, on an issue vital to himself, he saw the support of the mass of the Convention, the relatively silent deputies known as the Plain, who had thus far given him their votes, dissolve beneath him.

It was not only the plots of his enemies, and not only his imprudence of the day, that caused this overturn of 8 Thermidor. A fatality in his own policies worked against him. He had always attacked indulgents and extremists together. Now indulgents and extremists joined against him. He had long associated virtue and terror. Now, pleading for political virtue, he could not allay the fears that were grounded in experience. The ghost of Danton stood between Robespierre and the Representatives of the People, a spectral memory that drove men weary of the Terror to combine with the most violent terrorists against him.

Saint-Just meanwhile pursued his own designs. He must have been present at the session of 8 Thermidor, yet he said nothing, so far as is known, during the onslaughts on his friend. He was apparently becoming a little impatient with Maximilien. He hoped for an understanding within the committees; since 5 Thermidor he had been preparing a report in the interests of compromise. Robespierre's speech seemed to him inept and ill-timed; and the fact that Robespierre, breaking a long intimacy, made so important a decision without asking his advice undoubtedly filled him with misgivings. He had two courses: to accept the new situation which Robespierre so awkwardly forced upon him, or to join with the others who found Robespierre impossible to work with. Whether the others would have him remained to be seen.

That evening Robespierre and Couthon went to the Jacobin club, to which Billaud and Collot also resorted, each pair determined to win that important citadel for the impending struggle. Robespierre read over the speech delivered in the Convention. The club rallied to his side. In a scene of almost unparalleled turbulence, with cries of "Down with the conspirators!" echoing in their ears, Billaud and Collot were driven out. Meanwhile Saint-Just installed himself at about eight in the evening at the Committee of Public Safety. Billaud and Collot came in at about eleven, extremely angry, and resolved to make an end to Robespierre the next day.

A joint meeting of the two committees was in progress. What happened was later recounted by Barère.

Saint-Just said as the two fugitives entered: "What's new at the Jacobins?"

"You ask me what is new?" cried Collot. "Are you the one not to know? You, with your collusion with the main author of our political quarrels, who only wants to lead us into civil war! You are a coward and a traitor. You are nothing but a box of apothegms, and you are spying on us in the Committee. I am convinced now by all I have heard that you are three rascals. But liberty will survive your horrible plots."

Elie Lacoste of the lesser committee added:

"It's a triumvirate of rogues, Robespierre, Couthon and Saint-Just conspiring against the country."

Barère claims to have said:

"Who are you then, insolent pygmies, that you want to divide the remains of our country between a cripple, a child and a scoundrel? I wouldn't give you a farmyard to govern!"

"I know you will perhaps have us assassinated this very night," Collot continued; "perhaps you will strike us with your plots tomorrow morning; but we are determined to die at our posts, and meanwhile we may be able to unmask you. Here in our very midst you are making plans against the committees. I am sure you have slanders against us in your pockets now. You are a domestic enemy, a conspirator."

Saint-Just at this point is supposed to have turned pale, babbled meaninglessly, and emptied his pockets of some papers, which no one would look at. Collot raged on:

"You are preparing a report, but from what I know of you, you are undoubtedly drawing up a decree of accusation against us. What do you hope for? What lasting success can you expect from such horrible treachery? You can take our lives, have us murdered, but you cannot delude the virtue of the people." Collot finally subsided, and Saint-Just, claiming to have sent away his manuscript to have a clean copy made, promised to bring it to the Committee the next morning before reading it in the Convention, and not to read it at all if the Committee disapproved.

Saint-Just stayed on until five in the morning, glared at by the others, who waited for his departure to arrange their coup d'état of the morrow. Probably he went to see Robespierre. A few last words with him, together with the menaces of the Committee, seem to have decided Saint-Just to support his friend, however erring he might think him. He finished his report in this sense in the morning hours, still keeping, however, as much as possible of that compromise which, on 5 Thermidor, the report had been designed to proclaim.

The morning of 9 Thermidor, July 27, was tense with the busy activity of sleepless men. Robespierre, Couthon and Saint-Just, for a triumvirate of conspirators, did surprisingly little in common. It was Robespierre's followers in the Commune who took such steps as were taken for a manifestation in his defense. Robespierre himself still looked to parliamentary methods to reverse the stand taken by the Convention on the day before. Couthon, apparently ignorant of developments during the night, appeared at the Committee at 10:00 a.m. and asked naïvely what the subject of discussion was. On being told that the Committee was acting to forestall the new conspirators, he warned against counter-revolution and wrangled with Carnot. The Committee sat waiting for Saint-Just. He did not come, but he sent a note at noon: like

Robespierre the day before, he was going to "open his heart" directly to the Convention. The two committees hurried off to hear him.

The most feverish activity that morning was among the deputies outside the committees—Fouché, Bourdon, Tallien, Barras, Fréron—making their last preparations, closing deals with the moderates, terrifying the timid, filling the ears of the credulous, gathering into one huge web all the scattered strands of anti-Robespierrist intrigue. It was agreed to prevent Saint-Just and Robespierre from speaking. Collot d'Herbois, since the past week president of the assembly, could be counted on to help.

The memorable session opened at the usual time, 11:00 a.m. For an hour members listened to the reading of correspondence, while the last hasty agreements were made in the corridors. At twelve Saint-Just prepared to speak, and the governing committees entered. Saint-Just read a few words; then Tallien interrupted on a point of order. The member, he said, like another member yesterday, spoke only for himself, isolating himself from the government—that is, the committees had not sanctioned the address. Billaud took over, discoursing volubly on his expulsion from the Jacobins, and accusing Robespierre of plots against the integrity of the Convention. The house warmly applauded.

An amazing thing happened. Saint-Just stood speechless under the verbal lashing, seemingly paralyzed, unequal to the crisis. Perhaps he was only suffering from fatigue. Perhaps some weakness in his enigmatic character, some softness revealed in his almost feminine face, suppressed until now in the rôle of athlete of the Republic, dissolved his will power at the supreme moment— had he not been seen to weep before the Jacobins of Strasbourg? Perhaps he was simply dumbfounded by the favor his enemies received. Or perplexed, unable to choose absolutely between the committees and Robespierre. For he had clung to his hope of conciliation. The speech so rudely stopped, which he still held in his hand, did indeed lay the blame for division in the government on Collot d'Herbois and Billaud-Varenne, but it did not recommend their arrest, it criticized Robespierre also, it offered proposals for constructive reorganization without vengefulness, it suggested means of escape from the endless circle of personalities and the endless repetition of purges. The young man now standing crushed in the tribune was about to express statesmanlike ideas, but the strength so often used to intimidate the Convention had unaccountably deserted him.

It was Robespierre who rushed forward to interrupt Billaud-Varenne.

"Down with the tyrant!" came the prearranged cry from all parts of the house. Robespierre's words were lost in the uproar. He could not get the recognition of the chair.

Tallien again spoke, and again Billaud. The house voted the arrest of certain Robespierrist leaders, including Hanriot, commander of the armed force of the Commune. Robespierre again tried to speak. "Down with the tyrant!" was all that could be heard. The cry went up for Barère. It was once said that Barère had two orations in his pocket, one for Robespierre, one against him, to be used as the course of events should dictate. The story at least shows how uncertain the outcome was felt to be. Barère made a speech, and submitted a bill, aimed against the military force of the Commune. Then old Vadier denounced Robespierre for indulgence toward Chabot and Desmoulins, and spoke darkly of a letter found in the mattress of Catherine Théot proclaiming Robespierre a kind of God. Vadier, becoming increasingly trivial, was stopped by Tallien.

"I demand the floor to bring back the discussion to the real point," said Tallien.

"I could bring it back," said Robespierre. They were among the few words he made intelligible in the hubbub. What he said or tried to say can never be known. "The blood of Danton chokes him!" someone is supposed to have shouted. More probably it was simply noise that deafened him. Others might better have been choked by the blood of Danton; Billaud-Varenne considered Robespierre a conspirator for having defended Danton so long, and said as much on that day to the Convention.

Finally an insignificant member moved Robespierre's arrest. It was carried. Augustin Robespierre demanded to share his brother's fate. His wish was granted. The attack turned against Couthon.

"Couthon," said Fréron, "is a tiger thirsting for the blood of the national representation. . . . He wanted to make of our corpses so many steps to mount the throne."

"Oh yes, I wanted to get a throne," answered Couthon wryly, looking at his withered legs. Fréron had let blood flow freely at Marseilles. Couthon's record at Lyons and in Puy-de-Dôme we know.

When Saint-Just's turn came Le Bas demanded to be included. In the end, therefore, five were arrested—the three triumvirs, never so much a triumvirate as in their common ruin, together with Le Bas and the younger Robespierre. They were made to descend to the bar of the house, and there listen to a moralizing harangue from Collot d'Herbois. The assembly echoed with assurances that liberty was saved. In reality no one knew what had happened or what had triumphed. The whole scene took place in not much more than an hour.

Agents of the Committee of General Security escorted the prisoners to five different prisons. But the jailers of Paris were controlled by the Commune. The keeper of the Luxembourg refused to receive Robespierre, who consequently was not incarcerated at all. The four others were quickly released. One by one during the evening they gathered at the city hall, Robespierre reluctantly, not trusting in an insurrection for which no thorough plans had been laid, still hoping to keep the law on his side, that law of 22 Prairial from which true patriots had nothing to fear. This recourse was taken from him when the Convention, about nine in the evening, placed the five expelled members and their adherents outside the law. As outlaws they had only to be seized and identified to be put to death. It was Saint-Just, a year before, who had first brought outlawry into political tactics, at that time against the Girondists.

The evening passed in a confused struggle between the Convention, acting through the committees, and the Commune, acting through an insurrectionary committee made up of Payan and others. Each worked to get control of the armed detachments of the forty-eight sections. Le Bas, from the city hall, tried to call out the cadets of the School of Mars; he failed, having never trained those youngsters as a personal following, and being outmaneuvered in any case by the committees. The sections responded variously and ambiguously to the conflicting calls. A year of government by the Committee of Public Safety had quieted their old revolutionary impulsiveness.

Even the working-class sections, which had given weight to previous uprisings of the Commune, showed little excitement. The Robespierrist municipality was not loved. Payan, the national agent since Ventôse, stood for puritanical police regulations, strict enforcement of the wage-maximum, suppressions of manifestations in the interest of labor. A number of pottery workers, at this very moment, were about to go to the Revolutionary Tribunal for having requested an increase of pay. Lately there had been trouble over "civic repasts," meals taken in the streets in a gay Parisian fashion, at which since the battle of Fleurus many toasts were drunk to peace. To express a desire for peace, because it implied a dislike for the Revolutionary dictatorship, was grounds for serious suspicion. Under the rule of such city fathers, the plain citizen tended to regard the break between Commune and Convention as a falling out between two factions of politicians.

Forces assembled before the city hall to defend the Robespierrists, but they were irresolute and listless, and as the night wore on they dwindled away into their homes. At 2:00 a.m. the newly raised forces of the Convention, in two columns, converged into the square, and almost without violence took possession of the building.

The eminent outlaws sat upstairs with the insurrectionary committee. Guardsmen broke suddenly into the room. Augustin Robespierre climbed out a window, but fell to the street almost dead. The helpless Couthon, trying to move, plunged down a staircase and injured himself in the head. Saint-Just, the strange inaction still upon him, yielded without resistance. Le Bas killed himself with a pistol, handing another to Robespierre, who shot himself in the jaw. Some say that Robespierre did not attempt suicide, but was wounded by a soldier named Méda who later boasted of shooting the tyrant. It is possible that Robespierre and Méda fired simultaneously as Méda burst into the room.

Saint-Just and Couthon were held until morning at the city hall. Robespierre was borne at once, unconscious, to the Convention, which refused to receive him, holding that "the body of a tyrant can bring nothing but pestilence," so that the stretcher-bearers finally deposited him in the antechamber of the Committee of Public Safety. He was laid on a table, his head resting on a box of samples of army bread. In an hour he opened his eyes, glanced wearily at the curious onlookers, and began to wipe away the blood that streamed from his mouth. Some of the spectators insulted him callously; some gave him pieces of paper, there being no linen, to staunch his wound. There is a curious story, probably not true, that Robespierre, reverting in these last half-conscious moments to habits formed in boyhood, and forgetting that Frenchmen were to be addressed only as citizens, murmured with the politeness that he had never lost, "Thank you, monsieur."

Couthon and Saint-Just reached the Tuileries about nine o'clock, Couthon being kept on a stretcher at the foot of the stairs leading up to the green room, Saint-Just, with his hands tied, allowed to ascend to where Robespierre lay. Saint-Just, we learn from an eyewitness, stared at his suffering colleague with sad and pensive expression. Then his old assertiveness returning, he nodded toward the Declaration of Rights hung on the wall and said ironically, "After all, I made that." A surgeon came in, instructed to prepare Robespierre for execution. He bandaged the shattered jaw and extracted two or three loose teeth. Robespierre gave no sign of pain. Presently the sufferer sat up on the table, pulled up his stockings, and staggered into a chair, asking for water and clean linen. Toward midday the three ex-members of the great Committee were taken from the scene of their year's labors— Couthon on his stretcher, Saint-Just handcuffed, Robespierre in an armchair, from which, by one report, he reached out to strike at one of the men who carried him.

Late that afternoon, after quick identification at the Revolutionary Tribunal, the death procession assembled. Saint-Just stood up in the first cart, his head held high, his neck bare, a carnation in his buttonhole, his eyes coolly surveying the crowds that lined the street. The old Saint-Just was restored who said, "I despise the dust that forms me and speaks to you." Behind him, less easily seen because unable to hold themselves up, came his two colleagues and Robespierre's brother. With them were some twenty others involved in the rebellion of the Commune. The watching throngs were joyful and lively, full of cruel quips and sneers, shouting death to conspirators and life to the Republic. It was a *décadi,* and many plain citizens were present, but one suspects that the front rows were full of habitués of the guillotine, who had seen with equal relish the king and queen, the Girondists, Hébert and Danton travel the same path.

Couthon died the first, under circumstances of particular ghastliness, for the executioner took fifteen minutes to force the twisted body on to the straight plank of the guillotine, during which the screams of the tortured man mingled with the frenzied howls of the audience. Saint-Just submitted without disturbance. Robespierre lay waiting for half an hour, until all but himself and one other were dispatched; then he was hurried up to the platform and strapped to the plank, but before his head was pushed through the little window the bandage was ripped from his wound, so that he too, like Couthon, left the world uttering a sharp cry of pain. The drums rolled, and the crowds roared; and that, though no one yet knew it, was the end of the bright hope for a democratic Republic.

Robespierre fell on July 27, 1794, exactly one year to a day after entering the Committee of Public Safety. His old colleagues, or the majority of them, thought they could go on better without him. Their expectations proved to be totally mistaken.

Most of those who joined in the assault upon Robespierre aimed also at the Committee. The dictatorship of the Committee was more a reality than the dictatorship of Robespierre, and it aroused an antagonism no less real. A great many of the representatives had always been restless under the domination of a handful of their equals. Billaud, Collot and the others, in accepting the alliance of the Talliens, the Bourdons, the Fouchés, denied the principles for which they had worked for the past year. They soon suffered the consequences of their folly.

The attack on the Committee began on the very day after Robespierre's death, when the Convention decreed that a quarter of the Committee must retire each month, so that no single group should henceforth long wield the public power. Six new members joined the old ones on July 31, to take the places of the four deceased and the two absent on mission. Chiefly moderates, they put Billaud and Collot in a helpless minority. Within a few weeks all significant authority was taken from the Committee, which was reduced now to equality with a dozen other committees of the Convention. A body called the Committee of Public Safety continued to exist for more than a year, but it was less than a shadow of its former self.

Billaud, Collot and Barère left the Committee on September 1, the first trio to go out under the new arrangement. They were already under attack, denounced violently in the Convention as accomplices of the late tyrant.

The charge was grotesque so far as immediate events of 9 Thermidor were concerned. Yet it had a sound foundation. To the very eve of the fatal day Barère had probably wanted to compromise with Robespierre, and both Billaud and Collot, in the early days of Thermidor, had at least been heard to utter conciliatory language. In any case, during most of the Year Two the Committee had been a unit, and its responsibility had been collective. The members had too long stood together not to fall together when once the breach was made. The three denounced in August succeeded at first in clearing themselves, by unloading upon Robespierre the odium acquired by the Committee; but the issue was soon reopened, and in the spring of 1795 the three were put on trial. All were condemned to deportation. Barère managed to evade the sentence, but Billaud and Collot were shipped off to Guiana, the "dry guillotine" as it came to be called.

The others of the once ruling Twelve were eliminated at different times. Saint-André, at Toulon, and Prieur of the Marne, still at Brest, ceased to be members of the Committee immediately after Robespierre's death, when the Convention forbade representatives on mission to belong. Lindet, the younger Prieur and Carnot retired by normal procedure on October 6, though Carnot, reappointed by special arrangement, remained four more months to direct the armies. These five all joined in the chorus of denunciation of Robespierre, but all of them, as time went on, found themselves compromised by their old association with the persons dead or disgraced, first Robespierre, Saint-Just and Couthon, then Billaud, Collot and Barère. The atmosphere of the Year Three was chilly and unwholesome for the men who ruled in the Year Two.

For Thermidor provoked an unexpected reaction.

In form, as it seemed at the moment to the victors, the overthrow of Robespierre resembled preceding steps in the Revolution. Once again patriots executed a band of conspirators; once again liberty was saved; once again the true Revolutionaries punished a deviation. The dead men were in their turn classified as monsters, and their sympathizers were ruthlessly hunted out. The Terror was not immediately disavowed; in September, to kill the hopes of conservatives, and to show that the policy of rigor was still in favor, the Convention ordered the remains of Marat transferred to the Pantheon. The "profound Marat" (so called by the same man who moved Robespierre's arrest) had been far more furious than Robespierre.

But in fact, to the consternation of extremists, 9 Thermidor fundamentally altered the Revolution. The extremists overthrew Robespierre by combining with moderates. They discredited Robespierre by blaming him for the violence of the Terror. Having made the law of 22 Prairial a main charge against the tyrant, they had to consent to its repeal. To preach terrorism after Thermidor was to expose oneself to suspicions of Robespierrism, suspicions which above all others had to be avoided. Terrorists of the Year Two identified the Terror with one man, that they might themselves, by appearing peaceable and humane, win the confidence of the moderates. Barère revealed what was going on, writing in self-defense when he was himself accused: "Is his grave not wide enough for us to empty into it all our hatreds?" This was precisely what happened. The living sought a new harmony by agreeing to denounce the dead. And Maximilien Robespierre, who in life could not have stopped the Terror, contributed to its end in his death, by becoming a memory to be execrated and vilified, his grave a dumping ground for others' hatreds.

The Jacobins, moreover, were this time on the losing side, having declared their faith in the late monster. Jacobins after Thermidor were distrusted by all parties. The provincial societies died out, and the Paris club was closed in November. The Jacobins had always claimed to be the true voice of public opinion. They were replaced now by public opinion of another kind, more vague and unorganized but on the whole more public, whose substance was a general relaxing of tension, a sigh of relief that the rule of virtue was over, a suspicion that not all those executed as conspirators in the past year were really such, a feeling at any rate that with victories abroad the repression at home, however useful once, was no longer needed. Moderates (a term always to be understood in a relative sense) found their counsels more readily listened to, and old firebrands and inquisitors slipped unobtrusively, when possible, into the moderate ranks. It was not always possible, as Billaud, Collot and Barère discovered, and as Carrier and Fouquier-Tinville learned also, being tried and guillotined for their actions during the Terror.

Revulsion against the Terror strengthened the original prejudice of the Revolution against strong central authority. The machinery built up by the great Committee was dismantled. The executive almost disappeared; the country was ruled by discussion which too often was only dispute; the old anarchy and confusion returned, not so dangerous this time with the foreigner far from the gates, but sufficiently upsetting since it lasted with only slight improvement for five years. The economic controls were relaxed; the Subsistence Commission withered away; businessmen received a free hand to make money, even by swindling the government in dishonest contracts. The Maximum was abolished; the assignats lost their purchasing power so that more had to be printed; the resulting inflation brought misery to the poor, uncertainty for all, and easy profits for a few. The Constitution, when finally produced in 1795, was born in a horror of dictators. It promised civil liberties and parliamentary government, but it failed to assure political order, economic stability or religious peace. Meanwhile the armies, acquiring a momentum of their own from the impulse given them in the Year Two, extended their conquests in the Rhineland and Italy, committing to continued warfare a state not sufficiently organized to sustain it. Thus, as Robespierre predicted, the collapse of the revolutionary dictatorship prepared the way for dictatorship by a soldier, who, being a man of political genius, for a time gave satisfaction to the troubled country.

What, then, did the Committee of Public Safety accomplish? The Committee was the first war cabinet recognizably like a war cabinet of the twentieth century. As such it was highly successful. It called out the total resources of the country, human and material, moral and scientific. It defended the Revolution, and probably saved it from undoing, by checking the internal anarchy which in 1793 laid France open to invasion by the monarchs of Europe.

And it launched the Revolutionary offensive against the old order beyond the French frontiers, preached unsuccessfully by Girondists in 1792.

The Committee was also the first dictatorship whose stated aim was the complete regeneration of society. In this aim it failed. It did not found that democratic republic or republic of virtue (the same thing in the political philosophy of the time) to which military successes, in the eyes of the Committee, were but a necessary and preliminary means. It did not succeed in making permanent any republic at all. The politics of the Committee, went far beyond French public opinion. The members of the Committee, and of the Mountain, were a residue of the original Revolutionists, a minority for whose ideas most Frenchmen were not prepared. Their being a minority was one reason for their resort to Terror. The Terror, in turn, though it protected the Revolution, injured the Republic which it was supposed to found. To the average Frenchman, for almost a hundred years, the Republic suggested violence and discord, repression of civil liberties, denial of parliamentary freedom, persecution of religion, government by politicians. These ideas, which made difficult the establishment of the Third Republic, contributed indirectly to its end. After the Terror France was more divided than ever. The political régime, whatever it might be at the moment, was always detested by considerable minorities, and therefore, though successful enough in times of prosperity or of glory, was in danger of overthrow by small determined groups in times of strain or humiliation. Seen in this light, the years 1799, 1815, 1848, 1870, 1940, have something in common.

This development was precisely the reverse of what the Committee of Public Safety intended. The great aim of the Committee was to create a nation, a community with a single faith, where men of all localities, all religions, all dialects, all degrees of education, all stations in society, all variety of private interests, should cooperate in supreme loyalty to a common country. Along this path the French in the eighteenth century were farther advanced than any other people except the British. But the Committee of Public Safety, knowing that democracy (as well as victory in the war) depended on the unity of the nation, carried national control to a point not reached before the twentieth century, and at which, by our standards, it ceased to be democratic. The average Frenchman of that time did not want a state religion, nor a heavily political education, nor a moral code laid down by the government, nor compulsory service in the army, nor dictation of prices and wages, nor requisitioning of his property, nor extinction of his local peculiarities by a distant national government in Paris. Some of these are familiar in democratic societies today; all are found in states now called totalitarian, much more effectively realized than in 1794, because of the technical progress that has occurred since then.

There was long a tendency, especially in the English-speaking world, to feel that the significant and lasting changes brought about by the French Revolution were accomplished between 1789 and 1791, and that in the later years, 1793 and 1794, the revolutionists "went too far," falling into wild spasms of distressing radicalism. Yet it was the "moderates" of 1789 who destroyed the institutions by which Frenchmen lived, and the "fanatics" of the Terror, especially the Committee of Public Safety, who triumphed over the ensuing chaos, creating what Bonaparte called the only serious government of the Revolutionary years. That the reforms projected in the early years, parliamentary rule, civil liberties, legal equality, capitalist economics, were more lasting is true; at least they lasted, with minor reverses, from 1815 to 1940. It is not so true that the ideas projected under the rule of the Committee of Public Safety were of inferior significance. Only in 1793 and 1794 was democracy, in the sense of universal suffrage and increased economic equality, part of the ideal of the men in power. Those years raised the most portentous of political questions: the relation between democracy in this sense and democracy in the other sense, the democracy of individual liberties and representative government. The same years exhibited, for the first time, the spectacle of a nation risen in mass, organized totally by its government to prosecute a total war, and stirred to its depths by organized leaders bent on a vast program of world-renewal.

These are things that the twentieth century can understand. The meaning of the French Revolution is not exhausted in the glories of nineteenth century liberalism; the Revolution remains, even with the overshadowing of that liberalism, the crossroads of the modern world, to which the democratic and the anti-democratic states of our time can both look back. Our satisfaction, an ironic one, must be in this: that the revolutionary methods now used to overthrow democratic society were once used to bring it into being, and that at that time it was not those methods that succeeded.

EPILOGUE

EIGHT of the once ruling Twelve were still alive at nightfall of 10 Thermidor. They were all young as age is computed among men in such positions; Lindet was fifty-one, but Prieur of the Côte-d'Or was only thirty-one, and the average (both mean and median) was almost exactly half-way between them. They had half their lives to finish, having already lived, as far as politics is concerned, as fully as men can expect to.

Their ways diverged widely after Thermidor. After scarcely knowing each other before entering the great Committee, and then knowing each other under the most revealing of circumstances, getting tired together after midnight, conferring, reporting, accusing, arguing in high tempers, making up with lowered voices, somehow, until the end, cooperating for the good as all understood it, a compact group keeping its secrets from outsiders—after this year of inescapable intimacy, mutual annoyance and common satisfactions, they resumed their individual lives, eight men who saw no more of each other, yet whose minds went back irresistibly to the same scenes, except indeed for Prieur of the Marne, who was never in Paris during the Year Two, and for Saint-André, whose recollections of the green room were much broken by absence. Eventually they became old men, gray survivors of the past, strangely detached from the extraordinary events about them, still rethinking their year of power, dwelling on alternatives and might-have-beens, nourishing resentments against factions long extinct, meeting for reminiscence with old companions, or opening the eyes of youth by anecdotes of a titanic age. And as they grew old and declined something else took on new life and strength, the memory of Robespierre, whom they had combined to strike down, and whose death, in blasting the vision of the Year Two, had brought their own relegation to the sidelines.

Only Collot d'Herbois did not live to be old. He and Billaud reached Cayenne in the summer of 1795. They suffered the usual rigors, as desperate characters to whom no indulgence could safely be granted, and were kept apart from each other, until both came down with fever. Raving and delirious, both haters of the church, they were cared for by the nuns who kept a hospital in the settlement. Collot soon expired while his old colleague lay deathly sick in the next bed. They had been away from France just a year.

Billaud recovered under the ministrations of the sisters, who grew rather fond of their dreadful patient and protected him from the pitilessness of the governor. In time the authorities became less strict. Always a Rousseauist, Billaud adjusted himself to the state of nature, took up farming, and settled down with a Negro slave girl, aptly named Virginie, who remained faithful to him for the rest of his life. He enjoyed a kind of peace, troubled only by political memories and occasional outbursts which the loving Virginie must have found incomprehensible. News came in 1800 that all political prisoners were pardoned by Bonaparte, but Billaud refused the opportunity to return. Years went by, years spent in tropical agriculture taught him by Virginie, years of rumination which led him to regret the death of Robespierre and Danton, years devoted to lamenting the failure of the "puritan Republic" as he called it, and to the writing of all but unintelligible memoirs, which show a mind progressively deranged by the contemplation of its own virtue. Billaud changed some of his opinions, but he never wavered in believing himself a man of exceptional goodness persecuted unjustly.

When Guiana, long shut off from Europe by British sea power, was returned in 1815 to Bourbon France, the aging exile, fearing a renewal of severe treatment, went with Virginie to the United States, which he did not find to his liking, so that in 1817 he settled in Haiti. The authorities of Haiti, which was then beginning its career as an independent colored republic, welcomed him warmly but with some alarm lest he embroil them with France. The president felt obliged to protest when Billaud, having scarcely arrived, stormed openly against the Bourbons and ex-Girondists who held sway in Paris. But Haiti had uses for so ardent a republican, an authentic old Jacobin now turned native. He became counsellor to the high court, advising the citizens on the mysteries of law, which after all he had once studied. He died in 1819, a white-headed man of sixty-three, with Virginie and Haiti left to mourn him, a dignitary in a republic not too far removed from nature.

Jeanbon Saint-André, a very different person, found a very different salvation. He was not known for partisan fury, and was not involved in the machinations of Thermidor. Surviving the surge of reaction against the Committee, he received new administrative assignments, and was presently sent on a mission to Algeria. The Turks took him captive and held him for three years. He returned to France in 1801. Bonaparte, seeing in him one of the ablest of the republicans, offered him employment.

Saint-André faced a question which not all old Jacobins answered in the same way—whether or not to take part in the authoritarian republic which Bonaparte set up in place of the liberal one. Much could be said on both sides, and honest men were of contrary opinions. Saint-André had not abandoned his Revolutionary principles, but he hated inefficiency and disorder, and he saw in Bonaparte a creature of the Revolution, whose enemies were the enemies of the Republic. He accepted the First Consul's offer. He became prefect of Mainz, a position of delicacy and importance, involving the government of a newly annexed German population on the strategic Rhine frontier.

The republic changed gradually into an empire, and Saint-André changed with it, or perhaps only reverted to a deeper character underlying his republican phase, for he had been no radical until the Revolution made him one, and might have been content before 1789 (when he was already forty, and of mature opinions) with a reorganization of the monarchy in the interests of legal equality, and a chance for Protestants to enjoy public careers—both of which Bonaparte gave. Saint-André accepted the new aristocracy that was presumably based on talent. He became a baron of the empire and officer of the Legion of Honor. He stood at receptions, this onetime orator at the Jacobin club, among marshals, dukes and counts, royalists, émigrés and high functionaries of the church. Yet observers noted that he dressed more simply than others, that he seemed to harbor a half-expressed disdain, that he neither regretted nor concealed having served on the Committee of Public Safety, that he let no one forget that when others present had been in hiding or in connivance with the enemy, when the country was reduced to revolutionary chaos and even the emperor was only an artillery captain, he had done his part to hold the government together.

Remnants of the Grand Army, retreating from Moscow, poured into Mainz in 1813. The hospitals filled up with sick and wounded. Cholera raged in the city. The prefect, making the rounds of the hospitals, caught the contagion and died. He had participated in the whole tremendous drama of his generation, but he was spared the dénouement of Waterloo.

Carnot also accepted Napoleon. He had reason to be disillusioned in the Republic. Thermidor he survived, and he continued to be active in politics, but he was victimized in a later coup d'état (Fructidor this time, of the Year Five), and although a Director, one of the five chiefs of state, he was almost deported to join Billaud in Guiana. He had his property confiscated, was deprived of his seat in the Institute, and saved himself only by fleeing to Switzerland, where the Republican government still relentlessly pursued him. He returned after Bonaparte seized power, and for a few months acted as minister of war. But despite his experiences Carnot remained firm in his old convictions. He surrendered his ministry and entered the Tribunate, the one body in the new government where public discussion was allowed. There he spoke out against some of Bonaparte's policies, which were to him a profound disappointment, departing as they did ever farther from the republican ideal. In 1807, when the Tribunate was abolished, he retired to private life, busying himself with mathematics, the theory of fortification, and his two children.

The empire rose to heights undreamed of, but the old organizer of victory remained aloof. Then the crash came, and Carnot flew to the emperor's support. The threat of 1793 was repeated; foreign armies were within the frontiers, bringing with them the Bourbons, worse enemies than Bonaparte in the eyes of unconverted Republicans. During the Hundred Days Carnot tried vainly to repeat the triumphs of the Committee of Public Safety. He served as minister of the interior, and accepted also, without enthusiasm, the title of count of the empire. He was one of the few not to lose his head when news came of Waterloo. But France, exhausted by a generation of struggle, laid down its arms.

Louis XVIII and his advisers had at first held out a program of clemency and oblivion. Even the regicides, those members of the Convention who had voted death to Louis XVI in 1793, had not at first been officially molested. But after the return from Elba, and the Hundred Days, and Waterloo, the restored government took the view that some elderly Jacobins were incorrigible. Regicides who had rallied to Napoleon after his return from Elba were ban-

ished in 1816. Over a hundred who had sat in the Convention thus
went into exile, among them Carnot, now sixty-three years old.

Alexander of Russia allowed him to settle in Warsaw, where,
however, he found the climate too severe. He moved on to Prussia,
wandering aimlessly, not yet a national hero, only an old man, a
mathematician, an unrepentant revolutionary in a world longing
for peace and stability. He relieved the tedium of exile in long
conversations with his son, a boy hardly twenty who plied him with
questions, took notes from his dictation, and eventually wrote
recollections wherein the father took on the lineaments of a giant.
Carnot's grandson became a president of France. He himself died
obscurely at Magdeburg in 1823.

Robert Lindet and the two Prieurs gradually slipped back into
the middle-class existence from which they had come. They lost
their revolutionary excitement, but not their revolutionary beliefs.
Seemingly commonplace, their later lives were in reality full of
meaning. There were thousands like them, daily engaged in ordinary business, reliable and solid citizens, preeminently bourgeois,
who however had once astounded the world, and still withheld
their sympathies from the government. That the Revolution, even
the Terror, had drawn the support of such men, and that the reaction, when it came, allowed them as a rule to reintegrate themselves
into society, illuminates the difference between that day and ours.

Lindet and Prieur of the Marne stayed on in public life for a
while after Thermidor, holding rather to the leftist side. Prieur,
involved in a neo-Jacobin uprising in 1795, went into hiding for
several years. Lindet was charged with complicity in Babeuf's
quasi-socialistic movement of 1796; he accepted the Fructidorian
faction that ruined Carnot, and acted as minister of finances in
1799. Neither Lindet nor Prieur of the Marne would recognize
Bonaparte's coup d'état of Brumaire. Both resumed the private
practice of law in Paris. Prieur drops from sight during Napoleon's
time, but Lindet is known to have made a fortune of 50,000 francs,
between the ages of fifty-seven and seventy-three, and to have
commented freely, in his correspondence, on the ostentation and
vainglory of the empire.

The last stand of Napoleon, making imminent the return of
Louis XVIII, stirred the two retired regicides in their quiescence.
Both were solicited by Jacobin friends to join with the emperor.

Lindet, an old man, refused; Prieur of the Marne, still hardly more than fifty, consented. Lindet consequently was untouched after 1815; he died peaceably in 1825, aged eighty-two, and was buried at Père Lachaise, the only one of the Twelve to have a grave in Paris. Prieur fled to Belgium, where a host of onetime members of the Convention were tolerated by the new king of the Netherlands, and where he dragged out eleven years of exile, dying in poverty at Brussels in 1827.

Prieur of the Côte-d'Or had little part in public affairs after Thermidor. After Brumaire he withdrew still further from the political stage. Like his friend Carnot, he went back to his interests in science. Restless from inactivity, a bachelor without family concerns, he finally made overtures to the imperial government, applying for a post as inspector in the educational system. Failing to obtain it, and still in his early forties, he went into business, setting up a wallpaper factory in Paris. He made a fair living, wrote a book on the "decomposition of light," and won a prize for the coloring matter that he used in his factory. In 1811 he was pensioned as a retired colonel, he who had once been minister of munitions. He stood by indifferent while the empire fell, and so remained in France under the restored monarchy, suffering only unofficial embarrassments, as when the Academy of Dijon, in a surge of royalist sentiment, dropped him and Carnot from its list of members. Carnot's son, returning to France after his father's death, sought him out, and the two discoursed at length on the great days of the Committee of Public Safety. Finally in 1832 Prieur died at Dijon. He was buried with the honors due a colonel of engineers, but the funeral was kept quiet, for the authorities feared a Republican demonstration. The Republic in 1832 was a revived and growing threat.

Meanwhile Barère lived on and on. Condemned to share the fate of Collot and Billaud, conducted with them through a jeering country to the very wharves from which they departed, saved by a trifling sequence of accidents ("the first time Barère failed to sail with the wind"), placed in confinement and managing to slip out of it, hunted and hidden until the political storm blew over, Barère gradually emerged again into open view and labored to make himself a new place in public life. There was no living man in France, and few dead ones, more closely associated in the public mind with the Terror. He was the Anacreon of the Guillotine, the spokesman of the Committee of Public Safety, the orator whose inflammatory Gascon eloquence had more than once reached the verge of hysteria. And being supple by nature, too realistic to cling to lost causes, too amiable to be a factional chief, too devoted to the Revolution not to assist the revolutionary group in power, he had the reputation of being a weathervane, a false friend, purely self-seeking.

In 1798 he sought to regain official favor by publishing an enormous book, *The Freedom of the Seas, or The English Government Unmasked.* It was a continuation of his diatribes in the Convention, and anticipated the main ideas of the Continental System. The successful revolutionary factions, thinking him presumptuous even to show his face, spurned the olive branch that he offered. He therefore welcomed the advent of Bonaparte. He hoped for high office, such as Carnot obtained, but he received only a few commissions to write propaganda. His attitude toward Napoleon fluctuated in the following years, as did that of many men of less pliable allegiance, but in the end, during the Hundred Days, he threw in his lot with the empire, and so was banished in 1816.

In Belgium Barère mixed with other exiles, especially for a time with Buonarotti and with Vadier, now in his dotage. A symbolism hangs over the reunion of these three. Vadier personified the eighteenth century. Born in 1736, he spoke the language of the "philosophers." For Vadier the Revolution meant the stamping out of Catholicism. He had schemed against Robespierre in the famous Théot case because he thought Robespierre too religious. Barère was the Revolution itself, the reflection of its successive phases, sensitive to all its enthusiasms, hopes and hatreds, changeable and volatile yet possessing a core of consistency, a belief in the rights of the individual and of the nation. Buonarotti was the Revolution of the future. Not much younger than Barère, active like him in 1793, though unimportant, Buonarotti understood by the Revolution the conflict between rich and poor. He had been a leader in Babeuf's "conspiracy of equals." He was a living link between the First Republic and the socialist writers of the 1830's, in whose circles he became a familiar figure.

The three expatriates talked mostly of the past. All now lamented Thermidor, for however they differed in what they thought the true Revolution was, they could all agree that Thermidor had perverted it. Buonarotti reproached the two others with having betrayed the cause by joining against Robespierre. Vadier and Barère, to justify themselves, expatiated on the purity of their intentions; they had felt it their duty, they said, to halt the mad progress of a dictator. Buonarotti thought that had Robespierre lived the Revolution would have reached its true consummation, a social reorganization in the interests of the working class. So the Robespierre legend grew, or rather two distinct legends, portraying a Robespierre whose irresponsible ambition had led to calamity, and a Robespierre who was an early friend of the proletariat, about to embark on economic revolution when he fell. Both portraits owed most of their vitality to the psychological needs of those who drew them.

Barère returned to France after the revolution of 1830. The new Citizen King enjoyed talking with the old man, trying to probe into the secret facts of the Revolution, and in particular the history of his father, the duke of Orléans, Philippe-Égalité. Once a year for many years the octogenarian regicide, whose circumstances were not very prosperous, received a thousand-franc note sent by the royal hand. The government also made payments to him as a confidential informer. It is not known against whom he informed; the Orléans monarchy, like most French régimes, had irreconcilable enemies to both right and left. He spent his last years at Tarbes, his birthplace at the foot of the Pyrenees, to which he had been a stranger since his youth. There he lived revered by some, regarded by all with awe, an affable old man with the manners of the old régime but with modern ideas, elected by radicals to sit in the council of the department, talking endlessly of the past, writing mountains of memoranda which, when published after his death as his memoirs, became a byword for self-extenuation and unreliability.

The industrial revolution spread rapidly through France in the 1830's. Poorly paid workingmen objected to a régime operated by the small top layer of the moneyed class. They believed that once, forty years before, a democratic republic had been on the very threshold of existence. Cheap reprints of speeches and writings of Robespierre circulated in the popular quarters. His Declaration of the Rights of Man was avidly read and eagerly discussed. The historians were at work: the laborious Buchez, a democratic mystic, was producing volumes (forty in all), in which the Incorruptible rose up as the Messiah and sacrificial being of the Revolution. In 1840 the first reasonably complete edition of the martyr's works appeared. With Robespierre as its symbol the Revolution was again stirring, preparing the eruption of 1848 and the Second Republic.

Barère had no deep understanding of the world of his old age. Yet he too, for all his hobnobbing with the Citizen King, still dreamed the dream of the Republic, an ideal state to be hoped for, the substance of everything good. The time being one in which progress was occurring, and believed to be universal, Barère felt an unbounded confidence in the future. The supposed cynic, the suave purveyor of words, shared in the vision.

"The Republic," he wrote in his closing years, "is the wish of elevated minds and free hearts. It is the utopia of ardent and energetic spirits nourished on the enlightenment of civilization and independence. It is the government of common sense, justice and economy. It is the inevitable tendency of the human race." He came too to revise his opinion of Robespierre, whom in the heat of political passion he had called a monster, and whose grave he had designated as the repository of political hatred. "He was a man of purity and integrity," he said on his deathbed, "a true and sincere republican."

Shortly after making this confession, at the age of eighty-six, in the year 1841, almost half a century after his days of eminence, the last member of the Committee of Public Safety, with his hopes set on the future, left the troubled and revolutionary world in which he had always lived.

NOTES AND REFERENCES

FOR a full list of the materials from which the history of the Committee of Public Safety can be reconstructed see the author's study in the *Journal of Modern History,* vol. XIII (1941): "Bibliographical article: Fifty years of the Committee of Public Safety." This article is easily accessible to students of the subject, and makes less necessary a detailed documentation here. All direct quotations in the preceding pages are translations from printed sources, chiefly Aulard's *Actes du comité de salut public avec la correspondance officielle des représentants en mission,* Aulard's *Société des Jacobins,* the *Réimpression de l'ancien Moniteur,* the *Archives parlementaires,* and the separate or collected works of members of the Committee. The interested reader may trace the author's steps through these compilations in many cases without difficulty, since to find an item in them it is usually enough to know its date, which is usually indicated in the text above. Apart from these source collections the main funds drawn upon are biographies and monographs described in the article referred to, and articles and occasional items in the special journals devoted to the Revolution. The illustrations are from A. Challamel and D. Lacroix, *La Révolution française: Album du centenaire* (Paris, 1889); they are woodengravings made by an unidentified nineteenth-century artist using eighteenth-century portraits as his models.

The following notes deal chiefly with novel statements of fact and with controversial interpretations.

In Chapter I the causes of the Revolution are passed over hurriedly. The matter is arguable, but too general to be supported by specific references. Barère is presented in a somewhat favorable and revisionist light; see Leo Gershoy, "The young Barère," in *Persecution and liberty: Essays in honor of George Lincoln Burr.* There is an alternative and less scandalous story of the origin of Couthon's illness in Mège, *Correspondance de Georges Couthon,* p. 14 n. 2; the better authenticated version, here adopted, is from Cabanès, *Le cabinet secret de l'histoire,* 3ᵉ série, pp. 225-80.

Chapter II draws upon the source collections named above, and on the police reports in Caron's *Paris pendant la Terreur.* Figures for the number of voters in the Paris sections (p. 27) are from Mellié, *Les sections de Paris,* p. 92. For the number of Jacobin clubs see L. Cardenal and H. Chobaut in *Annales historiques de la Révolution française,* III, pp. 450-55, IV, pp. 78-79, 163-64, VI, p. 407. The results of the vote on the constitution are given in Aulard, *Histoire politique de la Révolution française,* p. 309.

In Chapter III, p. 56, we reach the disputed question of the nature and purpose of the Terror. A brief statement of contending theories may be found in D. Greer, *The incidence of the Terror,* pp. 5*ff.*; see also, more generally, L. R. Gottschalk, "The French Revolution, conspiracy or circumstance?" in *Persecution and Liberty: Essays in honor of George Lincoln Burr,* pp. 445-72; A. Cochin, *La crise de l'histoire révolutionnaire;* C. Brinton, *A decade of revolution,* pp. 158*ff.* The question of Robespierre's attitude to the war is also controversial; the strongest case for his pacifism is presented by G. Michon, *Robespierre et la guerre révolutionnaire.* On the assignats and financial policy see S. E. Harris, *The assignats.* On Saint-Just see the biographies, especially E. N. Curtis's, and the review by G. Lefebvre, *Ann. hist. Rév. fr.,* XIII, pp. 553-59.

For Chapter IV add to the sources Charavay, *Correspondance générale de Carnot,* and to the authorities, Chuquet, *Hondschoote.* For new views on Carnot's strategic ideas (p. 91) see Warschauer, *Studien zur Entwicklung der Gedanken Lazare Carnots über Kriegführung,* which, however, stops just before Hondschoote. Historians differ over Bouchotte; the favorable judgment here adopted is that of Herlaut in *Ann. hist. Rév. fr.,* IV and XIV. That half the French troops were able to read may be inferred from E. Levasseur, *La population française,* II, p. 478. English and continental historians differ on whether the British government in 1793 planned to keep Dunkirk; that some British statesmen wished to keep it is clear from Auckland, *Correspondence,* III, p. 79.

On the so-called *conspiration de l'étranger,* in Chapter V, the great monographs of Mathiez furnish almost the only authority. Mathiez's statements of detail on this matter may be safely adopted, but his fear of putting the Revolution in an unfavorable light sometimes inhibited his conclusions. Mathiez is also the most reliable guide on the Dechristianization movement, on which his views may be accepted with less reservation. The article by J. M. Thompson, (p. 109) is in *Ann. hist. Rév. fr.,* x, pp. 454-60; his findings may be compared with those of the present author for the month of Prairial (See below). The emphasis on the law of 14 Frimaire is a new development in Revolutionary studies, though the idea is as old as de Tocqueville; see for example Lefebvre, Guyot and Sagnac, *La Révolution française,* pp. 222, 230. The figures on executions under the Terror, (p. 129), and all such figures throughout the book, are from Greer, *The incidence of the Terror.*

For Chapter VI see Mège, *Le Puy-de-Dôme en 1793 et le pro-consulat de Couthon*. Chapter VII is based largely on E. Herriot, *Lyon n'est plus*; see also Madelin, *Fouché*. Collot's letters to Paris (pp. 164*ff*.) are printed in *Papiers inédits trouvés chez Robespierre*, I, 311-34; see also *Recueil des actes du comité de salut public*, VIII, p. 668 and IX, p. 91; and Riffaterre, *Mouvement anti-jacobin à Lyon*, II, pp. 527*ff*. For the Temporary Commission (p. 167) see Herriot, *op. cit.*, III, pp. 95-129.

Chapter VIII draws heavily on Saint-Just's *Oeuvres* and E. N. Curtis's *Saint-Just, colleague of Robespierre*. A photostat of the recently discovered manuscript (p. 180) is printed, with comment, by Curtis, pp. 356-58. On Hérault-Séchelles consult Mathiez, *Etudes robespierristes*, E. Dard, *Hérault de Séchelles*, L. Gaudel in *Révolution française*, 1935, pp. 4-45. On the fugitives from Alsace, R. Reuss, *La grande fuite de décembre 1793 et la situation politique du Bas-Rhin de 1794 à 1799*, and M. Marion in *Revue historique*, 1923, vol. 142, pp. 210-228.

For Chapter IX the fundamental work is L. Lévy-Schneider *Jean-bon Saint-André*, a colossal monograph which is also the best study of the navy during the Revolution. P. Bliard's *Prieur de la Marne* is a diatribe against the Terror. For the situation in the west there are, among modern works, L. Dubreuil's *Histoire des insurrections de l'Ouest*, definitely pro-Jacobin, and E. Gabory's *L'Angleterre et la Vendée*, which gives a fair account of British plans for intervention. For news of the *noyades* in Paris see *Archives parlementaires*, LXXX, p. 290, and *Ann. hist. Rév. fr.*, I, p. 383; for the relations of Carrier and the Committee the *Recueil des actes du comité de salut public*, VII, pp. 86, 115, 286-89, 368; for the number drowned A. Velasque in *Revue historique de la Révolution française*, XIV, pp. 161-77.

On Chapter X: Mathiez, *La vie chère et le mouvement social sous la Terreur*; C. Richard, *Le comité de salut public et les fabrications de guerre*; F. Nussbaum, *Commercial policy in the French Revolution*; G. Lefebvre, "Le commerce extérieur de l'An II," *Révolution française*, LXXVIII, pp. 133*ff*.; G. Pouchet, *Les sciences pendant la Terreur*; P. Caron, *La commission des subsistances de l'An II : Procès-verbaux et actes*. On the number of wage-earning proletarians in Paris (p. 240) see Braesch in *Révolution française*, LXIII, p. 320.

Chapter XI develops the present author's views in the controversy over the nature of the Terror mentioned in the notes to Chapter III above. The interpretation of Robespierre may seem to some unduly sympathetic; on this matter everyone must decide for himself, reading Robespierre's speeches and reconstructing imaginatively the situation in which Robespierre acted. The easiest way to justify Robespierre is to represent the other Revolutionists in an unfavorable or disgraceful light. This was the method used by Robespierre himself. It was used also by Mathiez, but it is awkward for a French Republican, defending the Revolutionary tradition, to insist that most of the Revolutionists, including Danton, were of such dubious character as to deserve the fate to which Robespierre consigned them. The best justification of Robespierre, in the present author's opinion, is not to inveigh against all the Revolutionists except Robespierre and his closest associates, but to recognize that the Revolution itself was an ugly thing, making men not essentially bad conduct themselves in a deplorable manner. Specifically, on Danton, see G. Lefebvre, *Ann. hist. Rév. fr.,* IX, 385*ff.*, where Danton is partly rehabilitated from the campaign of hatred which Mathiez waged against him. On Desmoulins see H. Calvet's edition of *Le vieux Cordelier*; it is doubtful whether Desmoulins will ever recover from the attacks of Mathiez and his disciples; the type of liberal who once idealized Camille is disappearing from the twentieth century world. The dating of the dispatch to the representatives on mission (p. 270) follows Bégis, *Billaud-Varenne,* p. 40; Bégis saw the actual document in the Archives, and Aulard, in the *Recueil des actes,* is known to have made mistakes. The letter to the Revolutionary clubs (pp. 270-71) is attributed to November 1793 by Michon, *Correspondance de Robespierre,* p. 213, following Hamel, *Robespierre,* III, p. 211. Reasons for attributing it to late January are indicated in the text. The argument that the attempt to introduce democracy was a factor in prolonging the war (pp. 277*ff.*) would be distasteful to the French Republican writers, but would be commonplace to Sorel and others of more conservative view, and indeed seems incapable of refutation.

In Chapter XII the chief matter for dispute is the relation of Robespierre to the laws of Ventôse. The evidence is meager for Mathiez's identification of Robespierre with a program of redistributing property. Mathiez emphasized a remark written in Robespierre's *carnet* eight months before Ventôse, holding the bourgeoisie to be a menace to the Revolution, and a charge written by the Thermidorian Vilate, accusing the victims of 9 Thermidor of communistic intentions. The use of such evidence reveals the weakness of more relevant arguments. Lefebvre, *Questions agraires au temps de la Terreur,* p. 57, declares that without Saint-Just's *Institutions républicaines* we should never know that the Robespierrists differed from other *Montaguards.* Neither Lefebvre nor Mathiez, nor any of Mathiez's school, calls attention to Billaud's *Eléments du républicanisme*; and though

all argue that Robespierre, Saint-Just and Couthon did not constitute
a triumvirate, none makes much of the differences between Robespierre and Saint-Just, which are pointed out, however, by G. Walter,
Robespierre, II, pp. 276*ff*. That the fall of the Hebertists marked a
step toward reaction and the reassertion of authority is emphasized
by Lefebvre in Lefebvre, Guyot and Sagnac, *La Révolution française*,
p. 228. The letter now in the Library of Congress (p. 303) is analyzed
by Carl Becker in the *American Historical Review*, XXVII, pp. 24-46.

On the *grande Terreur*, in Chapter XIII, every historian has his
own opinion; no recent writer is as shocked by it as the writers of the
more peaceable nineteenth century. On the Police Bureau see A.
Ording, *Le bureau de police générale du comité de salut public*, one
of the most successful monographs in the Mathiez school; its conclusions are accepted by J. M. Thompson, *Robespierre*, II, p. 202. On
the new economic policy see the works cited for Chapter X. On the
working out of the laws of Ventôse see Lefebvre, *Questions agraires
au temps de la Terreur*, pp. 4-59. The metrical translations of Chénier
(p. 317) are from A. J. Bingham, *Marie-Joseph Chénier*, and are
printed here with Mr. Bingham's permission. On the *fête de l'Etre
Suprème* see principally Mathiez, *Contributions à l'histoire religieuse
de la Révolution française*.

For the international relations dealt with in Chapter XIV the
great authority is still A. Sorel, *L'Europe et la Révolution française*.
The spuriousness of the speech attributed to Saint-Just (p. 338)
was shown by Mathiez, *Annales révolutionnaires*, VIII, pp. 599-611;
a contemporary English reprint was found at Cornell University by
Geoffrey Bruun, *Ann. hist. Rév. fr.*, IV, pp. 275-77. On the Venetian
spy see Sorel, *op. cit.*, IV, pp. 70-71; but also Romanin, *Storia docu-
mentata di Venezia*, IX, pp. 227-28, 521-22, the authority which Sorel
cites, but which he somewhat misapplies. For naval operations see
Lévy-Schneider, *Jeanbon Saint-André*, and the briefer account in
Mahan, *Influence of sea power on the French Revolution and Empire*.
The campaign of Fleurus is harder to reconstruct than that of
Wattignies, because the fourth volume of Carnot *Correspondance* is
less satisfactory than the third; see Jomini *Guerres de la Révolution*,
chapter XXXI and Phipps, *Armies of the First French Republic*, vol.
II. On aerostation the most accessible information is in the encyclo-
pedias of the time.

The attempt is made in Chapter XV, on the causes of Robespierre's
fall, to state only what can be most generally agreed upon. For the
literature see the bibliographical article referred to above. The only
new contribution of fact in Chapter XV is the study of the authorship

of orders issued by the Committee in Prairial. The *Recueil des actes*
prints 762 such orders; of these the authorship of 608 can be stated
with some confidence; a member of the Committee is assumed to have
been the responsible author of an *arrêt* (1) when he was the sole
signer, or (2) when the editor's note states that the minute is wholly
or partly in his hand. Unfortunately the *Recueil* is neither complete
nor always accurate. The findings are therefore of only a tentative
value.

PRESUMPTIVE AUTHORSHIP OF ORDERS OF THE COMMITTEE
OF PUBLIC SAFETY, MAY 20-JUNE 18, 1794

SUBJECT	TOTAL	LINDET	PRIEUR	CARNOT	BARÈRE	SAINT-JUST	ROBESPIERRE	COUTHON	COLLOT	BILLAUD
Supply and transport	195	183	7	1	4					
Munitions	120	4	114	2						
Army and Navy	143	2	9	130	1	1				
Personnel and police	21	3		1	7	1	8	1		
Public opinion, welfare and propaganda	24		5	2	11		1	2	3	
Miscellaneous and administrative	105	15	22	41	11	2	5	5	4	
	608	207	157	177	34	4	14	8	7	0

The question of Robespierre's responsibility for the law of 22 Prairial
will always be controversial; responsibility is not a factual question,
and the relevant known facts are few. For the assertion that Saint-
Just may have disapproved the Prairial law see Curtis, *Saint-Just*,
pp. 246, 271; the whole matter of the relations of Saint-Just and
Robespierre at this time is debatable; the present author believes in a
partial estrangement. That the scene in the Convention on 9 Thermidor
lasted less than two hours is a novel fact stated, with evidence, by
Sainte-Claire Deville in *Revue des questions historiques,* April 1939,
pp. 69-70. The old story that it rained at midnight on 9 Thermidor
is probably not true (Mathiez, in *Ann. hist. Rév. fr.,* IV, p. 16);
hence the dissolution of the Robespierrist forces cannot be attributed

to this cause. The dialogue in the Committee room on the night of 8-9 Thermidor is from Barère, *Réponse à Lecointre,* reprinted in the *Révolution française,* XXXIV, pp. 157-8n.; that in the Convention on 9 Thermidor is from the *Moniteur* of 11 Thermidor.

For the epilogue see chiefly Kuscinski's *Dictionnaire des conventionnels* and relevant biographies. It is not positively known that Barère informed for the government of Louis-Philippe, but his name was recently found in a list of persons receiving money for such services: see *Ann. hist. Rév. fr.,* XII, p. 546.

Index

INDEX

Academy of Sciences, 355
Acadia, 165
Achard, 171
Admiral, 328
agriculture, 235-36, 240, 314
Aigueperse, 149
Alexander I, 392
Algeria, 390
Allier, 250
Allies, advance of 1793, 24; plans to
  partition France, 57; discord among,
  87-88, 336-39, 351
Alsace, 4, 57, 116, 177-99, 320, 350
Alvinzi, 354
Amar, 295
Ambert, 131, 134, 138, 140
America, see United States, convoy
Andelys, 249
Angers, 252
Antwerp, 358
armaments, see munitions
Arms Administration, 241
Army, before Revolution, 7-8; disor-
  ganized by Revolution, 23-24, 78 *ff.*,
  212; reorganized, 81 *ff.*, 96 *ff.*, 182-85,
  306; miscellaneous, 46, 74, 124, 339-
  40, 384
Army of Condé, 179
Army of the Alps, 103, 153, 251
Army of the Ardennes, 79, 97, 351, 352
Army of the Côtes de Cherbourg, 214
Army of the Eastern Pyrenees, 103, 251,
  341
Army of Italy, 245, 251, 341-42
Army of the Moselle, 78, 91, 104, 180 *ff.*,
  341, 350, 351, 352
Army of the North, 78, 80, 82, 91-105,
  183, 212, 245, 341, 350 *ff.*
Army of the Rhine, 79, 87, 91, 104,
  180 *ff.*, 341, 350
Army of the Sambre-Meuse, 352 *ff.*
Army of the West, 103
Arras, 6, 7, 307
Artois, count of, 24, 205
arts, 317-20
Arts Commission, 295
assignats, 61-62, 239, 284, 359

Athens, 19, 315
Augereau, 96
Aulard, 56-57, 193, 271-72
Austria, 5, 22, 57-58, 80, 87 *ff.*, 337 *ff.*,
  351 *ff.*
Austrian Netherlands, see Belgium
autarky, 227-30
Auvergne, 13, 118, 130-52
aviation, see balloons

Babeuf, 260-61, 392, 394
Baden, margrave of, 178
Baillif, 249
balloons, 82, 236, 354-56
Bank of Amsterdam, 358
Bank of Discount (*Caisse d'Escompte*),
  114
Barbary coast, 250
Barère, before Revolution, 8-9, 16, 18,
  20; election to C.P.S., 31; functions
  in C.P.S., 31, 109, 364; on June 2,
  32; on September 5, 45, 53; economic
  nationalism, 225, 228-30; on England,
  229, 239, 350, 394; on dictatorship,
  298; on Robespierre, 40, 333, 370-81,
  383, 395-96; laws of Ventôse, 286,
  313; arts and literature, 318 *ff.*; education, 321; *Vengeur*, 346; law of 22
  Prairial, 366; Thermidor, 369, 370-
  81; after Thermidor, 382-84, 393-96;
  character and personal details, 8-9,
  31, 108-9; miscellaneous, 38, 55, 71,
  91, 95, 100, 101, 106, 116, 118, 123,
  124, 156, 163, 200, 238, 243, 253, 278,
  282, 288, 292, 318, 333, 340
Barr, 191
Barras, 363; on Robespierre, 370, 376
Basel, 338
Basire, 346
Basques, 320
Bastille, 293-94
Batz, baron de, 114, 295
Baudot, 188-89, 191, 198-99, 256-57
Bavaria, 57
Bay of Biscay, 343
Beaulieu, 354